LOLLARDS AND PROTESTANTS IN THE DIOCESE OF YORK

1509–1558

BY

A. G. DICKENS

THE HAMBLEDON PRESS

The Hambledon Press 1982
35 Gloucester Avenue
London NW1 7AX

History Reprint 1

ISBN 0 907628 05 2 (Cased)
ISBN 0 907628 06 0 (Paper)

First published by the Oxford
University Press for the
University of Hull 1959

Dickens, A. G.
    Lollards and Protestants in the Diocese of York
    — 2nd ed. — (History series; no. 10)
    1. Catholic Church. *Diocese of York* — History
    2. Lollards
    I. Title
    274. 205   BX4901. 2

Printed and bound in Great Britain by
Robert Hartnoll Ltd Bodmin Cornwall

PREFACE TO THE SECOND EDITION

When in 1932 I started my research on Tudor Yorkshire, I had in mind something more than the obvious pleasures which one derives from participation in the long and powerful tradition of English local history. In addition I had two objectives. I wanted to study on all the social levels one particular crisis in our history: the English Reformation and its sequels. Even more basic was my desire to build up local and biographical studies into regional histories, which in turn would some day help to augment and reshape our national history. I sought to examine the nation's grass roots rather than its political and institutional pinnacles. Of course, I soon came to realise that the completion of so gigantic a task would lie far beyond the capabilities of any one historian, even were he granted a long lifetime. The source-materials lay not only in parish and county records, or in our remarkable episcopal archives, then hardly touched, but also in the huge central resources in the Public Record Office and the British Museum, essential for English society as well as for the organs of government. Again, beginning with the newly acquired Bodleian manuscript of the obscure priest Robert Parkyn, which Professor Powicke made over to me in 1932, I began to realise that the middle and lower orders of society had mental and even cultural lives, which included personal responses to religion, beginning with Lollardy and culminating in the predominantly working-class martyrs of the Marian persecution.

Parts of this present book were written, and some published in the form of articles, during the thirties and the years immediately after a five year interruption occasioned by the Second World War. I read huge quantities of topographical histories and local documents in print and in manuscript. Insofar as I derived any general inspiration at this early stage, it came not at all from philosophically-minded historians but from that fine work of Rachel Reid, *The King's Council in the North* (1921), distinguished through its social background as through its institutional research. Needless to add, I also took example from that fusion of central and local research in the work of the

Misses Dodds, *The Pilgrimage of Grace and the Exeter Conspiracy* (1915). Discreditably to myself, though in common with most English historians of that day, my labours owed nothing to the parallel views upon French regional history expressed by Lucien Febvre. Indeed, I knew almost nothing of the resultant periodical *Annales* until the time I had finished this present book, though by then I had received broad confirmation of my outlook from various contributors to the early numbers of *Past and Present*.

Another desirable note on *Lollards and Protestants* concerns its scope and its title. Anxious during the fifties to stress the survival of Lollardy in so many parts of England, I included the word in my title, a step which caused some readers to see the book as primarily concerned with that particular contribution to religious change. Nevertheless the book remains in essence a general history of early Protestantism in Yorkshire and Nottinghamshire. It does however seek to detect the Lollard strain not merely in the few pre-Lutherans at the beginning but in several Reformers of the succeeding decades.

Though it might be presumptuous to claim that this book started a 'new' tradition in the historiography of the English Reformation, it did help to encourage younger scholars to undertake local and regional researches in that field. The earlier of these, such as Margaret Bowker, Christopher Haigh, Peter Heath and Mervyn James, were by no means 'disciples', but independent thinkers who investigated different records and came up with their own answers. Indeed, the necessity of extensive regional studies could not be better illustrated than by a comparison between this present book and Dr. Haigh's admirable work *Reformation and Resistance in Tudor Lancashire* (1975). When such different developments occurred on either side of the Pennines, any facile generalisations concerning the 'Tudor North' would seem riskier than in the days of Rachel Reid. What numerous differences of emphasis shall we need to recognise, when the millennium arrives and when regional Tudor historians have fully covered this small yet infinitely varied and richly documented realm of England?

A. G. DICKENS
December 1981.

ADDITIONS AND CORRECTIONS

pp. 30-31.

Edward Freez, a painter by trade, must be identified with Edward Paynter, whose enforced profession and punishment at Jervaulx (*c.* 1526) is related in *L. & P.* v. 1203 and (by himself from prison, *c*.1532) in *ibid.*, App. 34. One can only marvel at the corruption to 'Bearsy' by the time the story reached Foxe.

p. 61, note 9.

For Sir Francis (Mauleverer) read Sir William.

p. 84.

For the suit against Abbot Hexham of Whitby in regard to the ship *Jesus* of Danzig, stolen by French pirates, see *L. & P.* iv (2), 2521 and *ibid.* iv (3), 5430. Cf. the Star Chamber documents printed by E. Peacock in *Y. A. J.* ii. 246-51.

p. 169.

The rising of 1569 also affected many parishes in Cleveland and Birdforth Wapentakes. Cf. H. B. McCall in *Y. A. J.* xviii. 83-4.

p. 200.

John Hoode, King's Chaplain, was presented to Stokesley in November 1540. See *L. & P.*, xvi. 305, no. 53.

p. 203, note 5.

Noting 'Commentaries' in the plural, I revert to my original belief that the comma should come after 'John', referring to a second commentary by Musculus, not to the christian name of Brentius.

pp. 214ff.

One of the most fanatical Protestants of mid-Tudor Yorkshire was Elizabeth, daughter and coheiress of Roger Aske of Aske. She married Sir Richard Bowes of Stretlam and became mother of Sir George Bowes, who in 1569-70 put down the Rising of the Northern Earls. Against strong family opposition she married her daughter Marjory to John Knox, whom they joined at Geneva in 1556, and upon whose spiritual guidance Margaret depended all her life. (*D. N. B.*, s.v. Bowes, Margaret).

pp. 214ff.

In addition to these Edwardian Protestants, Foxe (v. 705) tells the story of John Hume, servant to Mr. Lewnax (*sic*) of Wressle and his wife Margaret, who in 1547 had him arrested and sent up to the Archbishop of Canterbury for denying Transubstantiation and the Mass in vigorous terms. Foxe found no record of his punishment.

pp. 223-4.

Beverley had an earlier tradition of Lollardy. The Scottish proto-martyr (1528) Patrick Hamilton had been won over by John Andrew Duncan, son of the Laird of Airdree in Fife, who, captured and brought into Yorkshire after Flodden, lived at Beverley with his mother's kinsman Alexander Burnet, whose daughter he married. Burnet taught Duncan Lollardy and obviously belonged to a Lollard group, *c*. 1513. Having tried to rescue Hamilton from Cardinal Beaton in 1528, Duncan fled to Beverley, where he spent the rest of his life. The story, taken from family memoirs, is printed in *Biographia Britannica* (2 edn. 1793), v. 492-3. For the background see T. M. Lindsay in *Scottish Historical Review*, i (1904), pp. 260-73.

PREFACE

MY thanks are chiefly due to Canon J. S. Purvis, Archivist of the Diocese of York, whose unrivalled knowledge of the York archives and of the history behind them has been generously placed at my disposal over a period of twenty years.

Both by forceful precept and by inspiring, if inimitable, example, Dr. A. L. Rowse has long urged me to write books, as distinct from articles. To Professor C. W. Dugmore and to my colleagues Mr. F. W. Brooks, Professor E. B. Castle, Mr. E. Gillett, Dr. J. Atkinson, and Mr. Philip Larkin I owe useful help.

I have also received much courteous assistance from the staffs of the Public Record Office, the Bodleian Library, the British Museum, the Borthwick Institute, the Lincoln Diocesan Record Office, the Folger Library, Washington, D.C., the Library of the University of Hull, and the Reference Libraries of the cities of Hull and York.

Though the present work is concerned with new fields little touched by my earlier publications, I am indebted to the editors of the *Church Quarterly Review* and the *Yorkshire Archaeological Journal* for permission to use in chapters iv and v extended portions of two articles formerly contributed to those periodicals. Acknowledgements are also due to Miss J. Pope for some accurate typing of involved drafts, and to the learned proof-reader of the Oxford University Press for his expert guidance.

To my wife I owe the conditions which have made research and writing at all possible during the recent busy years.

The University
Hull
August 1958

CONTENTS

CHIEF ABBREVIATIONS

B.M.	British Museum.
D.K. Rep.	*Deputy Keeper's Report.*
D.N.B.	*Dictionary of National Biography.*
E.H.R.	*English Historical Review.*
Foxe	J. Foxe, *Acts and Monuments*, ed. Cattley.
L. & P.	*Letters and Papers of Henry VIII.*
M.R.D.Y.	A. G. Dickens, *The Marian Reaction in the Diocese of York* (St. Anthony's Hall Publications, nos. 11, 12).
P.R.O.	Public Record Office.
R.	York Diocesan Records at the Borthwick Institute, York.
Test. Ebor.	*Testamenta Eboracensia* (vol. iv, Surtees Soc. liii; vol. v, ibid. lxxix; vol. vi, ibid. cvi).
Valor Eccles.	*Valor Ecclesiasticus* (ed. J. Caley and J. Hunter, 6 vols.).
V.C.H.	*Victoria County History.*
Y.A.J.	*Yorkshire Archaeological Journal.*
Y.A.S. Rec. Ser.	Yorkshire Archaeological Society, Record Series.

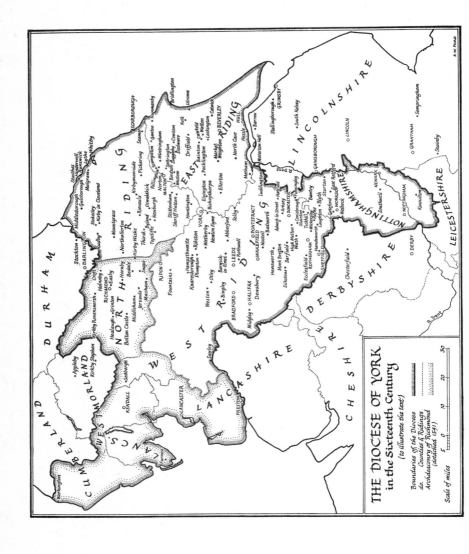

THE DIOCESE OF YORK
in the Sixteenth Century
(to illustrate the text)

Boundaries of the Diocese
do. Counties & Ridings
Archdeaconry of Richmond
(detached 1541)

Scale of miles

I

INTRODUCTION

IN a field of historical investigation which involves modern religious controversies, the vice of over-simplification readily asserts itself and the manifold delicate tones of reality are overlaid by the crude black and white of discordant abstractions. That such partisanship has often enfeebled both the selectivity and the generalizing of Reformation historians is now so widely agreed that its grosser excesses seem unlikely to be repeated. Here, nevertheless, has lain only one of the obstacles to sound progress. Working on too ambitious a scale, arbitrarily accepting as typical a few minute sections of the surviving evidence, bemused by the personalities of monarchs and statesmen, emphasizing those facts which happen to fit modern economic and social theories, historians have commonly ended by constructing patterns which bear little relation to the development of the English people as it can be revealed by patient research into personal, local, and regional history. So far as possible, the present writer wants to shun the well-worn themes of high policy and central government, of monarchs, parliaments, statesmen, and theologians. Instead he will take a large area of mid-Tudor England and try to observe, with as many concrete examples as possible, how the Reformation made its initial impacts upon a regional society.

To what extent the resultant picture will correspond with those of other regions can only be revealed by parallel researches elsewhere, yet meanwhile we shall at least have abandoned textbook dogmas in favour of real persons and documented ideas. One thing seems certain: that the area selected cannot be regarded as non-typical, simply because most of it lies north of Trent. It is far too big to be dismissed in terms of 'local history' or of 'county history'. When Henry VIII ascended the throne, the vast medieval diocese of York stood as yet undiminished, exceeding in area, though not in population, its gigantic neighbour of Lincoln. It stretched from the Soar valley in the heart of the Midlands to the Tees frontier with Durham, from the coasts of Cumberland to those of Holderness on the North Sea. It embraced all Yorkshire and Nottinghamshire, while its archdeaconry of Richmond protruded north-westward across the Pennines to embrace not merely Richmondshire, but the deaneries of Amounderness, Lonsdale, Kendal,

and Furness in Lancashire and Westmorland, together with that
of Copeland in Cumberland. In 1541 this immense but sparsely-
populated archdeaconry was cut off to form the northern half of the
new diocese of Chester, yet the event subtracts relatively little from
the theme of Protestantism. Though a few cases of heresy emanated
from Richmondshire and Kendal, the Richmond archdeaconry was for
obvious geographical and social reasons little touched by heretical
currents of thought. This book is therefore primarily concerned with
Yorkshire and Nottinghamshire, though it will avoid undue pedantry
over boundaries and will not shrink, for example, from mentioning
important events in Richmondshire even after the official severance.
Even in its reduced state, the diocese of York comprised a very considerable section of English society. The diocesan returns of 1603 give
it 214,470 communicants[1] and its total population must have exceeded
300,000, a round figure which can broadly be supported by reference to
other criteria and may in rough terms be regarded as constituting a
tenth of the nation.[2] The area remains in fact too large and varied to
invite easy generalization. Though even in the mid-Tudor years, feuds,
affrays, and murders continued to disfigure its social life,[3] much of it
cannot for a moment be regarded as belonging to the 'backward', 'im-
mobile', and 'reactionary' north of historical convention. The social
and economic facts give little support to such neat categories. If it
remained predominantly rural, so did every other English region of
comparable size. Its industries were in fact extremely diversified; several
of them existed upon a scale important by Tudor standards, and some
had entered upon a period of lively development. By the accession of
the second Tudor, weaving had almost completed its migration from
the old chartered municipalities of York and Beverley to the ample
parishes of the West Riding, where water-power was available for
fulling mills, domestic fuel could be cheaply bought, a few animals
pastured upon a nearby meadow,[4] and where regulation and inspection

---

[1] B.M. Harleian MS. 280, pp. 157–72. See the tables set out in B. Magee, *The
English Recusants*, p. 83. The diocese of Lincoln is given 242,550 communicants.

[2] Cf. the present writer in *T.A.J.* xxxvii. 32. In the Hearth Books of 1690, Yorkshire has nearly a tenth of the national total of houses.

[3] It is arguable that the state of public order in mid-Tudor Yorkshire was lower
than in most parts of England; the Yorkshire Star Chamber and Requests cases
provide some rich illustrations. Cf. also *infra*, pp. 87 seqq., and again J. Lister,
'The Life and Times of Dr. Haldesworth', in *Papers of the Halifax Antiquarian Soc.*,
1902–8, *passim*.

[4] These three points are made by the Mayor of York in 1561 (*York Civic Records*
(Y.A.S. Rec. Ser. cxii), vi. 17).

were reduced to a minimum.[1] The West Riding and Nottinghamshire coalfields had been exploited in many places throughout the Middle Ages;[2] by the end of our period they had begun a more rapid stage of development foreshadowing their future importance in the Industrial Revolution.[3] For centuries iron-mining and smelting had been even more widespread in Yorkshire.[4] The merits of Sheffield steel had been advertised by Chaucer himself, while between 1510 and 1552 documentary evidence shows water-driven grinding-wheels in at least ten places near Sheffield.[5] The lead-mines of Richmondshire provided York merchants of the reign of Henry VIII with what they called their 'principal commodity'.[6] Long treatises might likewise be compiled on the river fisheries of Trent and Ouse, the tanneries in many towns, the stone-quarries of the Pennines, the alabaster and gypsum industries of Nottinghamshire, the barge-traffic along the Humber and its tributaries, the fishing communities of the east coast, the port of Hull, long amongst the most flourishing and progressive in Europe. It is hard to see how internal trade could have been so negligible as some writers suggest. According to the Calendar of Charter Rolls, no less than 124 places in Yorkshire alone were granted a fair and a market during the later Middle Ages and the vast majority of these continued active in Tudor times.[7]

As for agriculture, the diocese could boast some of the richest as well as some of the barrenest soils of England. When Henry VIII visited Yorkshire in 1541, Bishop Tunstall 'took upon him about Scawsby Leazes [near Doncaster] to show his Majesty one of the greatest and richest valleys that ever he [Tunstall] found in all his travels through Europe'.[8] Again, Holderness had been the granary of the north centuries before Michael Drayton made the East Riding boast, 'Rich Holderness I have, excelling for her grain.' Shortage of cash, widely attested in the Tudor north, did not necessarily indicate paucity of stock and

[1] Cf. H. Heaton, *The Yorkshire Woollen and Worsted Industries*, pp. 51 seqq.
[2] *V.C.H. Yorks.* ii. 338–41; *V.C.H. Notts.* ii. 324–6.
[3] Cf. J. U. Nef, *The Rise of the British Coal Industry*, i. 57–60.
[4] *V.C.H. Yorks.* ii. 341–51 gives many references.
[5] M. Walton, *Sheffield*, p. 41.
[6] The expression is used by them at least twice: *York Mercers and Merchant Adventurers* (Surtees Soc. cxxix), p. 125; *York Civic Records* (Y.A.S. Rec. Ser. cvi), iii. 72. Cf. *V.C.H. Yorks.* ii. 351–4.
[7] Cf. the list in *Thoresby Soc.* xxxix, app. i. *Owen's Book of Fairs* (1770) has 98 for Yorkshire (ibid., app. ii).
[8] William Vavasour's relation in B.M. Lansdowne MS. 900, printed in J. J. Cartwright, *Chapters in Yorkshire History*, pp. 366 seqq.

chattels. The tenants of the Forest of Knaresborough are described by James I's surveyor as 'generally rich', with good soil and an abundance of sheep; their wills support his description, yet they very seldom mention or suggest the possession of coin.[1]

These diverse economic activities have not failed to leave some splendid memorials upon the face of the land. It would be hard to find any region of England boasting a more glorious range of minsters, parish churches, monasteries, and castles than the diocese of York. These alone would suffice to indicate that historians of the Reformation will not find themselves chiefly concerned with poor upland shepherds, or with those herdsmen of Fountains Abbey, who, just before the Dissolution, milked their kine on the lonely fells above Kirkby Malhamdale with their swords and bucklers at their side.[2] We are in fact confronted by a remarkably varied society, almost with a microcosm of Tudor England. In thinking of the Tudor north as a whole, it may well be felt that even its greatest historian, Dr. Rachel Reid, has sometimes generalized a trifle too boldly. 'The north' inevitably tends to become foreshortened when viewed from the recesses of London libraries and archive-repositories; it may easily seem invested with a homogeneity which it has never possessed, for the social and material differences between the primitive Borders and the well-developed agriculture and industry of south Yorkshire were then in all likelihood far greater than those between south Yorkshire and Essex.

Though this is no occasion for a prolonged excursus upon the cultural history of the diocese, it seems also important to avoid embarking upon our inquiry with over-rigid and stylized concepts concerning northern barbarism. While it is true that the remoter provinces of Tudor England produced few original and creative ideas, they were as far as possible from being hermetically sealed. We shall subsequently illustrate at length the great mobility of certain orders of provincial society and its connexion with the spread of Reformed doctrines. Yet the educated stay-at-home might also enjoy his contacts with the great world of ideas. Frequent mention will be made of Robert Parkyn, a conservative cleric who had seldom, if ever, left south Yorkshire, yet whose intellectual life happens to be exceptionally well recorded. He received large 'fardells' of books and other goods from his brother John, fellow of Trinity College, Cambridge: not merely books to supplement his considerable divinity library, but also such items as Harding's Chronicles

---

[1] *Knaresborough Wills* (Surtees Soc. civ), pp. xi, xxiii.
[2] *Select XVIth Century Cases in Tithe* (Y.A.S. Rec. Ser. cxiv), ed. J. S. Purvis, p. 164.

and copies of the current Acts of Parliament. These were brought to him by Kendal merchants on their way north. Going into the neighbouring town of Doncaster, he left his own letters with 'myn ost' John Shaw, who forwarded them by a rudimentary postal service to Cambridge.[1] Robert Parkyn also received local letters from his neighbouring colleagues and friends;[2] a few have survived to remind us of the trivial everyday correspondence of our Tudor ancestors which, to the immeasurable loss of social historians, has so largely perished. In far remoter places, some mid-Tudor priests possessed libraries of surprising scope and costliness.[3] Though in the thirties and forties the books of the parish clergy were for the most part no longer fashionable,[4] the intellectual climate thenceforth changed very rapidly. As I have shown elsewhere,[5] the history of south Yorkshire clerical writers and readers traverses the enormous gap between medieval mysticism and modern science during the short period between 1550 and 1580. Many parish priests lived lives not much dissimilar to those of yeomen; a few knew barely enough Latin to say mass, yet others with no greater incomes were assiduous students of the Fathers and the medieval exegetes. Apart from serving the chantry schools and endowed grammar schools, numerous priests dispensed elementary education to the youth of their parishes.[6] And though many villages lay remote from grammar schools, opportunity for secondary education remained far from negligible. For Yorkshire a careful census of old grammar schools has recently been compiled;[7] it shows the number of these institutions as much greater than would appear from earlier researches. During the first half of the sixteenth century there were about forty-six grammar schools in the county: extremely few of these suffered irrevocably through the Chantries Act, while no less than sixty-eight new schools appear for the first time between 1545 and 1603. Doubtless some of these schools were small, and others inefficient, yet considering that they served a total population not much in excess of 300,000—say a pertinent age-

---

[1] Cf. the present writer in *Cambridge Antiquarian Soc.* xliii. 23–24.

[2] *Hunter Archaeol. Soc. Trans.*, vol. vi, pt. 6, pp. 278 seqq.

[3] e.g. Edward Knipe of Cliburn, Westmorland (*Cumberland and Westmorland Antiq. Soc. Trans.* new ser. xliv. 151 seqq.), and John Vicars of Newton Kyme, near Tadcaster (*Catalogue of Manuscripts*, pp. 72–73, appended to T. D. Whitaker, *Ducatus Leodiensis*). [4] Cf. *infra*, p. 138.

[5] *Archiv. für Reformationsgeschichte*, Jahrgang 43 (1952), pp. 51 seqq.

[6] R. VI. A. 1, fos. 38 seqq.; cf. J. S. Purvis, *Tudor Parish Documents in the Diocese of York*, pp. 104 seqq.

[7] P. J. Wallis and W. E. Tate, *A Register of Old Yorks. Grammar Schools*, Univ. of Leeds Institute of Education, *Researches and Studies*, no. 13.

group of less than 20,000 boys—the spectacle appears anything but one of unlettered barbarism. And there were other ways of obtaining education. Roger Ascham, perhaps the greatest scholar of Renaissance England, first saw light in the remote Richmondshire village of Kirkby Wiske, being third son of the steward to Lord Scrope of Bolton: he was admirably trained in the household of Sir Anthony Wingfield, who happened to take an interest in the brilliant boy.[1] Another famous man of letters, Miles Coverdale, was more obscurely born in the city of York,[2] but like many others of his day reached the university by way of a religious order. Whatever textbooks may say concerning the rise of the cultured layman in the Tudor age, the clergy included a far higher proportion of literary and literate men than did any other major social group. As for the gentry, their educational attainments varied even more widely. If Sir Francis Bigod imported from Wolsey's household and from Oxford all the humanist graces, some of his neighbours and social equals wrote letters which it would be indulgent to describe as semi-literate.[3] Despite such variations, despite their feuds, moral irregularities, and unruly households, the gentry were becoming increasingly aware both of the value of education and of their own social and administrative obligations. In speaking thus of the gentry, we are discussing a numerically larger sector of northern society than is generally realized. The Herald's Visitation of 1584, supplemented by another of 1612, gives no less than 628 major pedigrees for Yorkshire.[4] As this class in general married early and had very numerous offspring, these families represent a total of many thousands of persons. Little attention has as yet been paid to the cultural history of the groups immediately below them. Though literacy of various levels was very widespread, few York citizens and an even smaller number of West Riding clothiers seem to have possessed serious books. Yet literate habits proved no indispensable basis for religious conviction or even for serious attention to complex doctrinal issues. We shall encounter a Yorkshire apprentice who could neither read nor write, but who

[1] Ascham's connexions with Yorkshire remained close throughout his life. Cf. in particular T. D. Whitaker, *Richmondshire*, i. 265 seqq.
[2] References in J. F. Mozley, *Coverdale and his Bibles*, p. 1.
[3] Cf. Matthew Boynton in *L. & P.* xii (1), 164, or John Barker in *York Civic Records* (Y.A.S. Rec. Ser. cx), v. 66–67.
[4] *Glover's Visitation of Yorks.*, ed. J. Foster. Many new families had attained the highly fluid ranks of the gentry during the reign of Elizabeth, and though this list has its omissions, one might think in terms of a somewhat smaller figure for the mid-Tudor period. Flower's Visitation of 1563–4 (Harleian Soc. xvi) has about 360 pedigrees for Yorkshire, but is manifestly very incomplete.

received instruction from distinguished Protestant teachers, crisply rejected Catholic doctrines in argument with Bishop Bonner, and ended by achieving a confident martyrdom.[1]

In the politico-religious field the northern Englishman has proved the peculiar victim of simplification. Even in learned accounts, society north of Trent appears uniformly backward-looking, feudal, and monastic in its allegiances, monopolized by stubborn religious conservatism and constantly tempted into treason and rebellion. Both local and regional writings purporting to describe the Reformation too often restrict themselves to the converse theme, that of Reaction, as if the north could boast no history of Protestantism before the seventeenth century. Having formerly helped to swell the output of research upon the Pilgrimage of Grace and the subsequent reactionary movements, I propose in the present essay to skirt this theme and to concentrate upon Lollardy, Protestantism, Edwardian Anglicanism, and other sorts of heretical and Reforming activities manifested in the diocese between the accession of Henry VIII and that of Elizabeth I. I shall avoid also the dissolution of monasteries and chantries, the institutional, economic, and material results of contemporary policy, except in so far as they affected the character and progress of the new doctrines. Significant in their own right, all these matters continue to demand research, yet at this juncture it can do no harm to reassert the primacy of intellectual and spiritual elements in the story of the Reformation. When we leave the sphere of central government and survey the broad fields of English society, the opportunity for this emphasis upon ideas does not diminish. In the diocese of York the materials for such an approach remain considerable, even if they have been little explored. However great their gaps and their unsolved problems, these sources will allow us to grasp the complex character of contemporary religion and to trace some of the channels through which the new opinions were flowing across this large and important sector of English society.

Before embarking upon this regional survey, it would seem desirable to take our bearings, though not to prejudge our findings, by a brief glance at the origins of Protestantism in English society as they are just beginning to emerge in modern scholarship. This theme has little in common with the old Tudor saga: Divorce, Reformation Parliament, Dissolutions, and Prayer Books. Whatever the long-term effects of such high policy, its creative part in the early development of Protestantism has in general been much exaggerated. Again, the ingredients of

---

[1] Cf. *infra*, p. 222.

early Protestantism proved already numerous in the reign of Henry VIII, yet among them Lutheranism may scarcely be regarded as predominant and Calvinism as yet remained almost negligible.[1] Whatever Gairdner—who knew little about ecclesiastical archives—may have thought, we may nowadays confidently ascribe a role of some importance on the popular level to the still vital force of Lollardy. This 'secret multitude of true professors', as Foxe dubs them, continued pertinacious in certain areas during and even beyond the first three decades of the century. In the London diocese, especially in Essex, Bishop Fitzjames prosecuted about 50 Lollards in 1510 and about as many again in 1518. Between 1527 and 1532 his successors Tunstall and Stokesley caused at least 218 heretics to abjure: Colchester shows 20 convicted persons, Steeple Bumpstead 40, and Birdbrook 44. A mixed heresy had now become apparent in the London diocese, yet while Lutheran doctrines emerge in a few cases, the basic and predominant element clearly remains Lollard. Another classic locality of the old English heresy was the Chilterns area, especially around Amersham and Buckingham, where about 45 cases were presented to Bishop Smyth of Lincoln in 1506-7. His successor Longland organized here in 1521 a major drive which resulted in 50 abjurations and 5 burnings. Longland continued active in later years, notably around 1530. This area connected through a number of scattered communities in the Thames Valley with others in Berkshire, Wiltshire, and the Cotswolds. At Newbury, six or seven score heretics are said by Foxe to have abjured together some time during the early years of the century. The final centre lay in south-west Kent, in the clothing towns of Tenterden, Cranbrook, and Benenden. In 1511 some 46 Kentish Lollards were denounced to Archbishop Warham, 5 being burned, the rest abjuring. Between these various groups some links obviously existed: Thomas Man, burned at Smithfield in 1518, had moved about instructing Lollard communities in East Anglia, the Chilterns, the Thames Valley, and Newbury. Late Lollardy appealed chiefly to working-class people, especially to cloth-workers, who were mobile, but worked in compact communities with an old and fiercely independent tradition deriving from medieval town-life. In his detailed lists, Foxe also mentions tailors, shoemakers, carpenters, wheelwrights, and other small tradesmen and artisans. Mainly in the London diocese, there appear a very few merchants, friars, secular priests, and professional men.

[1] The works of Calvin nevertheless occur on a list of prohibited books dated 1542 (Foxe, v, app. x).

What, by this time, were Lollards believing and teaching? Sensibly, if briefly, Foxe summarizes their heresies: 'In four principal points they stood against the Church of Rome: in pilgrimage, in adoration of saints, in reading of Scripture Books in English and in the carnal presence of Christ's body in the Sacrament.' These four points merely represent some of the commoner positions. The beliefs charged against any given Lollard do not necessarily include them and may include many others. In Morton's archiepiscopal register, a carpenter of the diocese of Bath and Wells admitted in 1491 to denying Transubstantiation, Baptism, the Confessional, obeisances to the cross, and, curiously, damnation for sin, 'for then Criste must nedis dampne his owne flessh and blode that he toke of the Virgin Mary'. The same register gives the abjurations of two priests in the diocese of Salisbury under the year 1499. They had disbelieved in Transubstantiation, and had thought 'that it is no nede to be shrevin to a prest or to any other mynestre of the Chirch, but that it is inowgh to be aknowyng to God and to be sory for the synne, being in wil to returne no more to the sinne'. In addition, they had held that images should not be worshipped or pilgrimages undertaken, 'that the Pope is antecrist', and 'that prestes and bysshoppes have no more auctorite thenne a nother laymann that folowith the teching and the good conversacioun of the Appostolles'. Finally, they had supposed 'that the curses and other sentences of the Chirch be of noone effect'.[1]

Amongst these varied positions, the denial of Transubstantiation was one which brought the severest and most frequent danger to the Lollards; it sprang from the late doctrine of Wyclif himself and from Wyclifite books like the *Wycket*, that favourite *vade mecum* of late Lollardy. The struggle with heresy continued to centre around the mass both in Henrician and Marian times; it tempted the heretics into crudely materialist denials and their orthodox persecutors into crudely materialist affirmations, distasteful alike to modern Catholics and Protestants. In the preoccupation of our York documents with this theme of Transubstantiation we shall witness only one small facet of an unimaginably complex and widespread European controversy, the full implications of which are seldom satisfactorily comprehended by modern historians. Readers tempted to suppose that the cases in episcopal registers or in the pages of Foxe involve a simple dichotomy of believer versus non-believer may find food for thought in the fact that Christopher Rasperger published in 1577 a book discussing no

[1] For these cases see C. Jenkins in *Tudor Studies presented to A. F. Pollard*, pp. 46-50.

less than two hundred interpretations which had been placed on the text, *This is my body*.[1]

Though so many cases of Lollardy are recorded during the first quarter of the sixteenth century, modern researchers are unlikely to approach any statistical estimate of the problem, for long experience had made the Lollards adepts in the art of concealment. Moreover, very few sought martyrdom; they come to light through their abjurations rather than through their sufferings. A little is known concerning their relations with Friar Barnes and with other early disseminators of Lutheran ideas and of Tyndale's New Testament. In one recorded confession, Essex Lollards are seen visiting Barnes in London with their old manuscript English Testaments and then being sold Tyndale's up-to-date publication by the enterprising friar. And though the Cambridge intellectuals who first took up Lutheran and Zwinglian doctrines owed little to Lollardy, their allies the 'Christian Brethren', who financed early Lutheran bookselling in England, apparently included men of Lollard affiliations. Even Little Bilney of Cambridge preached to East Anglian Lollard communities. During the 1530's there grew a merging tendency between the old and the new movements. Nevertheless, if the Lollard element gained stiffening from the Continent, it preserved many of its original characteristics throughout the reign of Henry VIII and even beyond.[2] Its social ethos and its doctrines had relatively little in common with moderate Lutheranism, the sacramental and justificatory tenets of which stood at variance with those of Lollardy.[3]

A continental movement much nearer to Lollardy was Anabaptism, which certainly infiltrated from the Netherlands during the thirties.

[1] *Ducentae verborum 'hoc est corpus meum' interpretationes* (Ingoldstadt, 1577).

[2] On the survival of Lollardy see E. G. Rupp, *Studies in the Making of the English Protestant Tradition*, ch. i; P. Hughes, *The Reformation in England*, i. 126 seqq.; T. M. Parker, *The English Reformation*, pp. 19 seqq.; C. Sturge, *Cuthbert Tunstal*, ch. xv; H. Maynard Smith, *Pre-Reformation England*, pp. 268 seqq.; M. Deanesley, *The Lollard Bible*, ch. xiv; W. H. Summers, *Lollards of the Chiltern Hills*. A valuable group of original documents on Lollardy is formed by the confessions of the Essex Lollards of 1528 (which include the Barnes episode), printed in Strype, *Eccles. Memorials* (1822), vol. i, pt. ii, pp. 50–62. For details on the more important heretics of the Lincoln diocese under Bishop Longland see G. E. Wharhirst in *Lincs. Archit. and Archaeol. Soc. Reports*, vol. i, pt. ii, pp. 30–38. Gairdner's *Lollardy and the Reformation* shows much less knowledge of ecclesiastical records than might be anticipated; it therefore underestimates the share of Lollardy in the English Reformation.

[3] Lollardy apotheosized the simple and practical Epistle of St. James; Lutheranism deprecated the latter, concentrating on Romans and the intellectual emphasis upon Justification by Faith. Cf. Rupp, op. cit., pp. 4–5.

The numerous 'Dutch' heretics burned or charged in England,[1] the denunciations of Anabaptism in proclamations and in sermons by conservative Protestants like Latimer,[2] may nevertheless encourage an overestimate of its effects in this country. The unwary might easily mistake Lollardy for Anabaptism. Between two such many-sided and amorphous attacks upon tradition, common doctrines necessarily existed, the most important being a denial of Transubstantiation.[3] There were, indeed, few orthodox religious and social traditions unsubjected at some stage or other to Anabaptist attack.[4] In examining 'Dutch' heretics in the diocese of York, we shall certainly need to approach them with an open mind and without the assumption that every 'Dutch' heretic was a recent immigrant who had learned his theology in Anabaptist circles abroad, and had imbibed nothing from his English environment.

The remaining ingredients of early popular Protestantism are too obvious to require detailed description. Concerning the wide dissemination and profound influence of Tyndale's New Testament there can be no doubt. It supplied a vital link between these varied movements, since it enormously facilitated vernacular Bible-study by laymen and women. What inspiration to heroism, what intellectual dangers were entailed by that exhilarating pursuit in an atmosphere of personal discovery and conviction, these are things our own age finds it increasingly hard to imagine. And not far from Tyndale stood Frith, whose violent attack upon Transubstantiation, published already in 1533,[5] soon obtained widespread acceptance in England and supplied fresh weapons to this important section of the old Lollard armoury. The great influence of publicists found acknowledgement in a number of proclamations by an alarmed government. Even the Pilgrims of Grace gave them a prominent place among their grievances: 'To have the heresies of Luther, Wyclif, Husse, Melangton, Elicampadus,[6] Burcerus,[7] Confessa Germanie, Apologia Melanctonis, the works of Tyndall, of Barnys, of Marshall,

---

[1] Cf., e.g., Wriothesley, *Chronicle of England* (Camden Soc., new ser. xi), i. 28 , 90 for the burnings in 1535 and 1538.

[2] Cf. R. W. Dixon, *History of the Church of England*, i. 301.

[3] Stowe, *Annals* (edn. 1615), p. 570, shows this of the Dutch Anabaptists, who asserted that the Sacrament of the Altar was 'but bread only'.

[4] But Canon Maynard Smith goes too far in saying (p. 280) that Anabaptists were 'indistinguishable from Lollards except in name'. For detailed classification of Anabaptist beliefs, see E. B. Bax, *The Anabaptists*, pp. 30 seqq. They will be seen to include points uncharacteristic of Lollardy.

[5] Cf. *infra*, p. 43.

[6] *Sic* for Œcolampadius.   [7] *Sic* for Bucerus.

Raskell, Saynt Germayne and other such heresy of Anabaptist destroyed.'[1] This list does not, however, suggest that its compilers had
any close knowledge of the continental works, and may well have been
based upon hearsay and upon the more elaborate lists of prohibited
foreign books such as that drawn up at the instigation of the bishops in
1529.[2] After the brief 'liberal' interval of the later thirties, the government continued to pay tribute to the great influence of books and
naturally enough came to see that the English-language publications
formed the key to the situation. In an entry for the year 1546 the
London diarist Wriothesley provides a characteristic list of the authors
then judged to exert lively influence, at least in the London area:

> The seventh daie of Julie was proclamation made in the cittie of London
> with a trompett and an harold-at-arms, with the serjeant-at-armes of the
> cittie and one of the clarkes of the Papers, for certaine Englishe bookes which
> contain pernitious and detestable errors and heresies to be brought in by the
> last daie of August next coming, the names be theise: the text of the New
> Testament of Tindales or Coverdales translation: the bookes of Frith, Tin-
> dalle, Wyckliffe, Joy, Roy, Basiley,[3] Barnes, Coverdale, Tourner,[4] and
> Tracye, which bookes after the bringinge unto the mayor or bishopp shal
> be brent, as further by the said proclamation doeth appeare.[5]

Apart from these personal and particular influences, the tide of anti-
clericalism enveloped devout and profane, Protestant and Catholic,
rich and poor alike. It was the common heritage of Europe in the age of
Erasmus, but it reached a new intensity in England with the Hunne
crisis of 1514–15 and again during the ministry of Wolsey, whose career
brought clerics themselves to the point of anti-clericalism.[6] In the north
it was not lacking, even at the height of the Pilgrimage of Grace.[7] In
the violent aversion of some provincial heretics to the confessional we
shall see but one of its many manifestations. Alongside it, there appears
what modern conservatives sometimes call the 'tavern-unbelief' of the

---

[1] M. H. and R. Dodds, *The Pilgrimage of Grace*, i. 346.
[2] Printed in full by Foxe, iv. 667–70.
[3] i.e. Theodore Basille, the pseudonym under which Thomas Becon published
several Protestant tracts in 1542–3. Cf. Pollard and Redgrave, *Short Title Catalogue*,
s.v. Becon, Thomas, and *B.M. Cat. of Printed Books*, s.v. Basille, Theodore.
[4] William Turner: cf. *infra*, p. 192.
[5] *Chronicle*, i. 168–9.
[6] Cf. for example the present writer's edition of *The Register or Chronicle of Butley
Priory, Suffolk*, p. 59.
[7] e.g. *L. & P.* xii (i), 687 (2): 'they (the commons) would never be well till they
had stricken off all the priests' heads, saying they would but deceive them'. Cf. for
other aspects R. R. Reid, *The King's Council in the North*, pp. 122–3.

age: the questioning attitude of the sceptical, materially-minded lay-man confronted by the more 'difficult' doctrinal demands of the Church. This factor did not produce martyrs, but it projected not a few people into the ecclesiastical courts on charges of heresy. Indeed, the line which divides it from positive Lollardy and Protestantism is not in-variably easy to draw. Some of the martyrs themselves evinced a straightforward intellectual inability to accept the miracle of Transub-stantiation. In the present writer's view, it is by no means fanciful, when reading certain pages of Foxe, to feel appreciably nearer to the age of Voltaire than elsewhere in our sixteenth-century literature. These elements must again be distinguished from the doctrine which thinkers so diverse as Frith and Thomas Starkey derived from Melancthon: that many hitherto accepted beliefs and observances are neither scriptu-ral nor necessary to salvation, but mere *adiaphora*, or things indifferent. During the thirties adiaphorism can have had few repercussions outside educated circles, but it was destined to become a pillar of Anglicanism and to be enshrined in nos. XX and XXXIV of the Thirty-nine Articles.[1] The earliest stages of English Protestantism could thus, unlike most of the later stages, become the subject of fascinating chapters in the pre-history of both religious toleration and Rationalism. Mid-Tudor disbelief thus consisted of numerous and most heterogeneous elements, between which the orthodox clergy themselves seldom troubled to make nice distinctions. For example, the great list of *mala dogmata* compiled by the convocation of 1536[2] deserves much more careful analysis than it has received. Some of the heresies here listed could have a straight-forward Lutheran origin; many more unquestionably derive from Lol-lardy; a few might come from either, while yet others might be either Anabaptist or Lollard. Here also are examples of the popular materialist scepticism, perhaps representing crude derivatives of Anabaptist or Lollard heresies. All these aspects of the repertoire we shall soon en-counter in the diocese of York.

Concerning the influence of the contemporary social and economic patterns which underlay these intellectual developments, there can be no exact judgements. Historians who reject economic totalitarianism are unlikely to accord them more than an auxiliary role, since, with many foreign examples in mind, it requires no great effort of imagina-tion to envisage the spread of Protestantism in a society and an economy

---

[1] W. G. Zeeveld, *Foundations of Tudor Policy*, ch. vi.
[2] Fully listed by R. W. Dixon, op. cit. i. 405 seqq.; for references cf. ibid., p. 409 n.

very differently organized from those of Tudor England. Nevertheless, certain favourable secular patterns undoubtedly accelerated the rise of the new opinions. The weaving community of Hadleigh in Suffolk seemed to Foxe 'in respect of scriptural knowledge rather a university of the learned than a town of cloth-making or labouring people'.[1] Cloth-workers were now especially exposed to foreign immigrant influence; it will also be observed how personal mobility inside their industry could bring the new opinions out of East Anglia into Yorkshire. In later years the fierce Protestantism of the former was to have its Yorkshire counterpart in the extensive parish of Halifax. Again, it is difficult to exaggerate the role of common lawyers in the development of anti-clericalism. During the fourteenth and fifteenth centuries they had occasionally betrayed their ambitions to bring all ecclesiastical juris-diction into the uncertain boundaries of the statutes of Praemunire. The judges figured prominently amongst those who attacked the church courts and clerical privilege in the crisis of 1515. Christopher St. German was an eminent theorist and Simon Fish a scurrilous pamph-leteer, yet in 1529–31 these two struck the harshest blows at the Church, and both were common lawyers. The numerous provincial gentry who went up to the Inns of Court thus moved instantly into a world of advanced ideas in the heart of the metropolis.[2] Even in the diocese of York we must be prepared to meet a few recorded examples of gentlemen who thus encountered the New Learning while in search of this secular instruction. Finally, we cannot doubt the connexions of the merchant-classes and the ports with both English and continental Reformers. In May 1530 Bishop Nix of Norwich denounced the preva-lence of heretical literature in English and added, 'the gentilmen and the commenty be not greatly infect; but marchants and suche that hath ther abyding not ferre from the see'. This pattern finds illustration with the London–Antwerp group of Protestant merchants and with the active circulation of Protestant literature in Bristol.[3] Likewise Roger Dichaunte, merchant of Newcastle, abjured before Bishop Tunstal the opinions that the mass 'crucifiethe Christe of newe', that 'man haith

---

[1] Foxe, vi. 676. This was the town where Bilney and later Dr. Rowland Taylor were so active. For a graphic account of early scripture-reading by working people at Chelmsford, see *Narratives of the Reformation* (Camden Soc. lxxvii), p. 349.

[2] Several sufferers for religion from the Inns of Court appear in Foxe. A classical example is that of James Bainham, son of Sir Alexander Bainham of Gloucestershire, who married the widow of Simon Fish and was finally burned for heresy in 1532 (Foxe, iv. 658, 697 seqq.). Other examples will appear *infra*.

[3] Cf. Rupp, op. cit., p. 7, citing More's account.

no fre will', that 'every christen man is a preste', that 'every preste myght and ought to be maryed', and that 'the lyfe of relygiose men lyvinge in their cloysters is but ypocrisye'.[1] The second of these beliefs presumably indicates continental influence. We might reasonably expect to find some traces of a similar process in Hull and York.

All these and other factors of the social and economic background did no more than facilitate the advance of ideas already strong, militant, and intrinsically attractive, yet their significance cannot be dismissed as negligible. The soil was all the more speedily and broadly irrigated, since these old and well-cut channels lay in the path of the rising flood.

The foregoing paragraphs represent merely a few clues and pointers derived from the sketchy sources already at our disposal. They are far from being a definite 'national picture' of early English Protestantism, since this picture has still to be built up by painstaking research into regional evidence. To one distinctive region we now turn.

[1] C. Sturge, *Cuthbert Tunstal*, p. 117, from Tunstal's Register, fo. 8.

II

POPULAR HERESY IN THE REIGN OF
HENRY VIII

1. 'Dutchmen' and Other Early Heretics

OUR inquiries at York begin with the archiepiscopal registers of Archbishops Bainbridge (1508–14), Wolsey (1514–30), and Lee (1531–44), which together yield an interesting selection of heresy cases mostly unnoticed by historians. That of Archbishop Bainbridge indicates that Lollardy was not unknown in the diocese during the first decade of Henry VIII. Yet even allowing for the elusive character of this phenomenon and for the probability of omissions from the register, there are no grounds for envisaging it as then widespread. Under Bainbridge the most sensational group of prosecutions passing under the title of heresy remain scarcely relevant to our present theme, since they concerned merely sortilege and the conjuration of spirits. A case running from September 1509 to June 1510 involved three priests and five laymen practising these ungodly arts at Bingley; they were apparently in court on charges of heresy because of their alleged use of consecrated bread to defend them against the malevolence of the spirits. It need scarcely be added that these people showed no signs of Lollard belief. They were finally absolved and did penance.[1]

In February 1511 a process *de excommunicato capiendo* was initiated against Thomas Cudworth of the parish of Silkstone, by certificate to the king. Unfortunately, we learn nothing of his doctrine beyond the facts that he was vehemently suspected of heretical pravity, had been cited to appear, but had declined to undergo purgation.[2] On the other hand, a clearly recorded case of Lollardy is that brought against Roger Gargrave of Wakefield.[3] The documents are numerous and lengthy: a commission of 8 March 1512 directed by the archbishop's vicar-general to William Melton, Chancellor of York, to inquire into the heresy of which Gargrave was vehemently suspected; articles of inquiry ministered by Melton to the accused; the latter's confession and abjuration (19 March and 1 April 1512); the penance finally awarded him.

---

[1] Reg. Bainbridge, fos. 68–73ᵛ.
[2] Ibid., fo. 74. A copy of the royal writ for his arrest follows.
[3] Ibid., fos. 75–76.

Amid this tautological and repetitive wilderness a few interesting facts emerge. In his abjuration Gargrave admits:

I helled and affirmed certaigne articles and erroneouse opinyons agaynst the blessed sacrament of the alter, our lordes owne body in forme of brede, in withdrawing due reverence frome the said holy sacrament and openly saying that if a calff were uppon the alter I wold rather worship that then the said holy sacrament, allegyng scripture for me in forme following; *tunc imponent super altare tuum vitulos.*[1] And further more showing and openly affirmyng that the date was past that God determyned hyme to be in forme of brede, contrarie to the faith of holy churche.

The purport of the text he had cited is that God desires not sacrifices except those which follow upon a contrite heart; it clearly lent itself to a Lollard interpretation. In the second of the articles it transpires that Gargrave said these things publicly before the parishioners of Wakefield and stated that the latter heresy had been transmitted to him 'by a certain priest of the county of Lincoln'.[2] It seems closely related to the argument we shall later find more clearly stated: that since Christ had once for all made the sacrifice of his natural body on the Cross, his corporal presence was no longer to be found in the consecrated elements of the mass. This may be presumed the point of Gargrave's somewhat eccentric phrase; in any case there can be no doubt that both his heresies constituted attacks upon Transubstantiation. The main theme of heresy in the diocese is thus foreshadowed from this stage.

The remainder of our first group of cases appears towards the end of Wolsey's register and early in that of Lee. Among them occur certain Dutch immigrants whose doctrines demand comparison with those of contemporary English heretics. The term 'Dutchman', translated in one instance *natione tutonicus,* was then a very wide one, but the names of most of our men suggest actual Netherlanders rather than Germans. Chronologically the first is a man referred to as 'Gilberte Johnson of the parishe of the Holie Trinitie in Conyngarth[3] within the citie of York, ducheman and carvar, layman'. He latinizes his signature: 'per me Ghilbertum Johannes', which still leaves the continental surname uncertain. His admissions take this form:

I the said Gilberte said and affirmed that I wold make my confession onlye to God omnipotente bot to no preist; also that nother Pope, Archbushope or

---

[1] Psalm li. 19 (Vulgate l. 21): 'then shall they offer bullocks upon thine altar'.
[2] fo. 75ᵛ, 'et dixisti publice hoc tibi relatum fuisse a quodam presbytero de comitatu Lincoln'.
[3] i.e. of Christ Church parish.

ordinary haith auctoritie to curse any man or woman; also . . . that prayers
and suffragies of the churche here in erthe colde not helpe nor do no succor to
ded folkes, and I said I did not beleve that suche suffragie(s) myght helpe
them that wer departed. Furthermore I . . . did saye and affirme that there is
no vertue in holie brede nor in holie water, bot that the holie brede is good
and vertuose for a man or woman that is hungrie, and the holie water for a
man or woman whan they are hotte, to cast opon them to cole them. Therwith also I . . . did bere no candle of candlemes daye, saying thies wordes,
'What vertue is ther by?' Also I . . . denyed to fast and to kepe abstinence,
opon vigillis and other tymes commanded to be fasted by holie churche, bott
onlie at myne owne pleasor. Also I the said Gilberte did saye and affirme that
preistes ar worse than Judas; whie, Judas sold Almyghtie God for xxxd, and
prestes will sell God for half a penny. Also I did denye to paye my offeringes
or tithes to any persone or curate, albeit I wolde have yeven oblacions of
offering dayes.[1]

Johnson's abjuration was read in the Consistory Court of York on
16 May 1528 before Brian Higden, Dean of York and vicar-general to
Wolsey.

The elaborate character of the penances awarded in these early cases
may reflect the growing concern of ecclesiastical authority in the face
of a rising tide of heresy elsewhere in the kingdom. Johnson's penance
was closely linked to the impending Rogation-week processions in the
city of York. On the Monday of that week he had to precede the cross
heading the procession from York Minster as far as St. Mary's Abbey,
and to carry a faggot on his left shoulder, a pair of beads in his right
hand, having his feet and head bare and clad only in his shirt. At certain
places on the route he must humbly undergo discipline at the hands of
the Dean of the Christianity of York. On arriving at the high altar of
St. Mary's he had to say kneeling various prescribed prayers, and remain there until the end of high mass, then return with the procession
to the Minster. On the Tuesday he must likewise go through the
suburbs of York in front of the procession to the Friars Preachers, and
there hear the sermon before returning. On the Saturday after Ascension Day he was ordered to enter the market on the Pavement in York,
similarly clad, and receive discipline from the same Dean at the four
corners of the market-place—no doubt an even less attractive assign-
ment. On the Sunday, Johnson must finally lead the procession, with
the usual conspicuous accoutrements, around his own parish church of
Holy Trinity in Coneygarth. And all this accomplished, he had finally
to reappear before the vicar-general on the Friday before Whitsun and

[1] Reg. Wolsey, fo. 131ᵛ.

'submit himself to the will of the said vicar general': the probable point of this interview being to ensure the due completion of the orders. Even at a time when penances were no infrequent spectacles, so prolonged a series—no doubt conducted in the face of a caustic throng—must have given pause to other potential offenders in the city.[1]

The next 'Dutchman' described himself as 'Lambert Sparrow ooderwise callyd Lambert Hooke, dowchman borne, now of the diocese and jurisdiction of Yorke' and he signed his abjuration 'Lambert Sparrow, other Hooke'. The document[2] is undated but situated between two others, respectively of 14 October and 25 November 1533. Sparrow admits a long list of heresies, about twenty in number, which I briefly summarize in the order they are given. Divers and sundry times within the parish of Worksop and before divers persons, he had affirmed that 'there ys no preste but God onelye'. He had also alleged that the sacrament of the altar is but bread and not Christ's body, unless received with faith and in the name of Christ; there is no temple of God, except man's body and soul; no priest can make one water holier than another; no bishop or priest can assoil any man of his sins; every man ought to be baptized in common water; any man may christen another; tithes and oblations are not due and ought not to be taken; there is no such thing as hallowed ground; no bishop or other man can make one place or one thing holier than another; no man is bound to keep the commandments of the Church, or those of bishops or priests, about fast-days or holy days; there are no souls in heaven till the day of doom; there is no purgatory; men should not go on pilgrimage to saints or holy places. He had also believed that no man being in sin can consecrate the body of God, or assoil another sinner; burial by a priest has no more value than burial by a layman; Saints Peter and Paul 'wer no prestes ne ministred enye sacramentes, but that they wer only teachers and preachers and bad every man goo home to thie (*sic*) house and take there of thye breade in remembrance of Christes bodye and take of thie drynke in remembrance of hys bloode, without anye halowed placys'; contract of matrimony is sufficient without solemnization in church; pardons and blessings of bishops have no value; a man should neither pray to saints, nor confess to any priest, but only to God. Sparrow's abjuration of this extensive catalogue of heresies ends with the promise 'ne that I woll hereaftre use, reede, teache, kepe, bye or sell any bookes, volumes or quears or any workes callyd Luther's or anye odre mannes bookes of hys hereticall secte or of any oodre, conteighneng heresye in

[1] Ibid., fo. 132.   [2] Reg. Lee, fos. 50–50ᵛ.

them or prohybyted by the lawes of holy churche, ne be conversannte or familier wyttingly with any person or persons suspecte or deffamyd of heresye', but detect such persons to their ordinary.

A more elaborately documented case demanding discussion alongside that of Sparrow occurred a year later. It begins with articles 'objected' by William Clyff, Archbishop Lee's vicar-general,[1] to Gyles Vanbellaer, 'douchman borne, now of the diocess of York'.[2] These are sixteen in number, nearly all identical with or closely similar to the heresies of Lambert Sparrow. They rehearse that Vanbellaer has 'taught, redd, defendid and holden in the parish of Workesopp' the following: there is no priest but God; no priest has power to consecrate 'the very body of Christ as he was here reynyng in yerth', or to take away man's sins; the apostles had no power to consecrate the body of Christ; the sacrament of the altar is only bread, unless received with faith and in Christ's name; God does not dwell in temples or churches made by man's hand, but in the faithful Christian; no man can make water any holier than God made it, therefore the holy water in church is no holier than the water in the river; every faithful Christian man can baptize another as well as a priest; tithes and oblations ought not to be taken; a bishop cannot make one ground holier than another; no man is bound to fast or keep bishops' or priests' commandments, or any holy days except Sunday; prayers made to saints are of no value; no man should go on pilgrimages; a man may be confessed of a layman as well as of a priest; there is no purgatory, but only heaven and hell. The case proceeds with an account of Vanbellaer's appearance in the Consistory Court[3] on Friday, 27 November 1534. Here he faced Dr. Clyff and a formidable assembly of dignitaries: Richard Langrige, S.T.D.,[4] Geoffrey Downes, S.T.D.,[5] George Palmes, LL.D.,[6] Stephen Thomson, M.D.,[7] Arthur

---

[1] William Clyff, LL.D., prebendary of St. Paul's, 1526; archdeacon of London, 1529; prebendary of York, 1532; precentor, 1534, and last treasurer, 1538–47 (D.N.B.).   [2] Reg. Lee, fos. 89ᵛ–90.

[3] On the reasons for attributing these cases to the Consistory Court, see *infra*, pp. 241–2.

[4] Archdeacon of Cleveland, 1534–47 (Le Neve, *Fasti Ecclesiae Anglicanae*, ed. T. D. Hardy, iii. 148).

[5] Prebendary of York and Southwell; chancellor of York, 1537–61 (ibid. iii. 165, 193, 442).

[6] Subsequently prebendary of York and archdeacon of the West Riding (ibid. iii. 134, 199, 223).

[7] Alias Thomason, physician to the sixth Earl of Northumberland, who rewarded his services by a 21-year lease of his lands and tenements in York city and suburbs (De Fonblanque, *Annals of the House of Percy*, i. 407, n. 2). His loyalty to the Crown in 1536 was, however, noted by Wilfrid Holme. Cf. *infra*, p. 118.

Cole, M.A., Richard Farley, B.C.L., together with various minor officials and proctors.[1] The articles being ministered to him, the accused
'respondebat quod vellet eosdem erronios opiniones abiurare, renun-
ciare et ad gremium ecclesie redire, et sponte et voluntarie abiuravit et
renunciavit eisdem sub eo qui sequitur tenore verborum'. There follows
the text of this abjuration[2] and it includes one point which appears
neither in the articles of accusation nor in the other heresy-cases: 'Also
I have kept, holden, taught and redd oon booke called the New Testament in the douch tonnge of fals and corrupt translacion, prohibite for
me to have to thinfection and evell example of good Christien people.'
There follow the usual contrite promises of obedience, including a repeti-
tion of Lambert Sparrow's undertaking to have nothing to do with
Luther's or any other man's heretical books. The abjuration concludes:
'In witnes wherof to this my present abiuration I have subscribed my
name and sette the signe of the crosse. Gelen Vanbellaer +.' Its reading
was duly followed by the absolution and imposition of penance.[3]

What are we to think of the influences behind these three interesting
immigrant-heretics? Sparrow and Vanbellaer clearly belong to the same
group; they both come from Worksop and admit closely similar lists
of errors. On the other hand, the heresies of Gilbert Johnson of York
do not bear a close resemblance of detail to those of Sparrow and Vanbellaer. At this stage of his inquiry the present writer constructed two
lengthy schedules, one of Anabaptist, the other of Lollard heresies.[4] He
then compared these with the above offences of the three Dutchmen,
expecting that their continental affinities would in some respects become manifest. Exactly the reverse was the outcome. Every one of the
numerous charges made against the three can be precisely paralleled in
the Lollard list. Two charges—rejection of Transubstantiation and
refusal of tithes—appear on both the Anabaptist and the Lollard lists.
On the other hand, not a single offence by any of the Dutchmen can be
classed as exclusively Anabaptist, while many characteristic doctrines
of that sect, such as adult rebaptism, property-communism, pacifism,
the sinful character of oaths, have no place with either Dutchmen or
English heretics. On further reflection, one should probably feel no
great surprise at this lack of Anabaptist background. Unless these

---

[1] This is the passage (fo. 90) which styles the accused *natione tutonicus*.
[2] Reg. Lee, fos. 90–90ᵛ.
[3] Ibid., fos. 90ᵛ–91.
[4] Cf. *supra*, p. 10, for some works of reference. Some typical Lollard cases also
occur in J. Gairdner, *Lollardy and the Reformation*, i, ch. i. My Anabaptist schedule is
based on the very full summaries in E. B. Bax, op. cit., pp. 30 seqq.

three men were either very recent immigrants, or else frequent visitors to their homeland, they are not very likely to have been adherents of the sect, which in the Netherlands was essentially a movement of the thirties. The documents merely state that they are Dutchmen by birth; they may for all we know have entered England many years before Anabaptism spread to the Netherlands.

What of the Zwinglian and Lutheran heresies, both of which affected the latter some years earlier? Four of these tenets—denial of Transubstantiation, of images, prayers to saints, and of Purgatory—were in fact prominent Zwinglian, as well as Lollard, positions. Yet the whole list cannot be dismissed as characteristically Zwinglian. As for Lutheranism, there seems every reason to doubt its direct influence, since its sacramental teaching was opposed to that of the Dutchmen, who also show no sign of its justificatory and predestinarian aspects. As for the singling out of Luther's name in the prohibition of heretical books, I take it to mean very little. We shall shortly find this precise phraseology in a case unconnected with Dutchmen; it apparently became a common form, at all events in the cases of heretics known to be literate. The York judges of 1533-4 may well have suspected the influence of imported books, but their mention of the German heresiarch cannot be taken to indicate that they had made a close comparative study of the respective influences of the chief continental heresies upon the accused.

What then are the probabilities concerning the doctrinal antecedents of the Dutchmen? While it remains possible that they came over predisposed, perhaps by contact with Zwinglian circles, perhaps merely through the diffused pietism of the *devotio moderna*, to accept new doctrines, the detail of their beliefs as admitted by them in 1528-35 shows every sign of native English Lollard inspiration. We do not need to assume that this process of assimilation occurred initially or chiefly at York or at Worksop. It is perfectly possible that the three chief Dutch heretics may also have lived, like so many of their compatriots, in London or East Anglia or Kent, where heresy of this type was more widespread. Their tenets compare fairly closely with those confessed by the Essex heretics of 1528.[1] Further social factors may have given them a somewhat deceptive prominence in the York records of heresy. Xenophobia is a phenomenon all too familiar to social historians of Tudor England; in the York diocese as elsewhere, the chances that a Dutch suspect would be reported to authority were no doubt materially higher than those of an Englishman holding similar beliefs. And in

---

[1] Cf. Strype, *Eccles. Memorials* (1822), vol. i, pt. ii, pp. 50-62.

York city a fierce exclusivism directed against all save York men is painfully obvious throughout the Tudor records.

One modifying factor in the case of Vanbellaer should nevertheless be given its place. This man had in his possession a 'Dutch' New Testament, yet this proves nothing concerning the sources of his doctrinal beliefs. It proves little more than the facts that he had not forgotten his native language and that, at a time when both Tyndale's version and 'Dutch' versions were smuggled in,[1] he took the latter, perhaps because he could read it more easily, perhaps because he thought it less likely to attract attention. The case for the predominance of English Lollard doctrinal influences is not weakened by this mention of a foreign Testament. Altogether the cases of the Dutchmen suggest the need for a critical reassessment of foreign influences upon Henrician heresy.

Despite its much later date, one further case may deserve mention alongside the foregoing. On 3 September 1540 a woman named 'Dionisia'[2] Johnson abjured heresies before Dr. Clyff, was absolved and ordered penance only in York Minster. It might therefore reasonably be conjectured that she lived in York[3] and—though no reference is made to any 'Dutch' connexion—that she was related to Gilbert Johnson, whose heresies had been revealed twelve years earlier.[4] Of her 'divers sclaunderous and erronious opinions and articles agaynste the trewe faithe of holy churche', only 'the principalle hereafter followethe; that is, I have erronyously and heretically holden and belevyde that the sacramente is not the blissyd body of Christ'. She was not charged with teaching or disseminating this belief and shows no sign of being educated. No mention of heretical books occurs and she affixed to her abjuration, not a signature but only the sign of the cross. Though, as will later appear, there were numerous heresy-cases in the diocese during the last years of Archbishop Lee, these do not appear in his register, but chiefly in an act book of his Court of Audience. In the actual registers of Wolsey and Lee,[5] I observe only three certainly English heretics. In the case of

---

[1] Conversely, Dutchmen were engaged in selling English New Testaments in England (ibid., vol. i, pt. ii, p. 65).

[2] Spelt 'Dionisie' in the English part of the document. Various forms of Denise are found as girls' names in England from the twelfth century onwards. 'Dionise' was borne by several members of the Markham family, 1574–1631 (*Oxford Dict. of Eng. Christian Names*, ed. E. G. Withycombe, s.v. Denise).

[3] Had she lived elsewhere she would almost certainly have been required to do penance also in her parish church.

[4] The dates make it quite possible that she was a daughter and born in this country.

[5] Reg. Lee, fo. 141ᵛ.

Stephen Kendal alias Sadler of Kendal in the archdeaconry of Richmond, there is recorded merely a commission to Drs. Clyff, Langrige, Kellet, and Dakyn to proceed against the accused in a cause of heresy, without specification of its nature. The document is dated at Cawood, 5 February 1536.[1]

Of far greater interest is the case of Robert Robynson of Hull, layman, which was transacted in July 1528, but has ramifications far beyond the pages of Wolsey's Register. Turning first, however, to the latter, we find Robynson abjuring these beliefs: 'that God bad no man fast'; 'that God maide never prayers', presumably meaning formal prayers; 'that if I wer at the poynte and article of deith, I wolde not confesse me at a preist, bott that I wold confesse my self to God'; 'that sancte Peter was never the pape of Rome'; 'that sancte Peter was never ordered preist'. Like Denise Johnson, the accused was apparently not fully literate. He concluded: 'in wittenes herof I make this crosse with myne owne hand', and again no mention of heretical books occurs. The case was treated seriously, Robynson being assigned prolonged and humiliating penances. On the Sunday after the feast of St. Mary Magdalen (26 July in 1528) he was to go before the procession in the Minster carrying on his left shoulder a pair of faggots and in his right hand a burning candle of wax, with bare feet and uncovered head, clad only in his shirt, and to offer his candle before 'the principal image', saying certain prayers on his knees. On the Sunday after the feast of St. Peter ad Vincula (2 August) he must precede the cross before the procession around the chapel of the Holy Trinity at Hull, and when he reached the choir, remain standing and sitting to the end of mass. The Sunday following, he was to go around Holy Trinity with a candle. Also on the next market-day he must enter the market-place at Hull, similarly clad, and receive discipline at the hands of the curate of Holy Trinity at the four corners of the market-place. Finally, the performance of the penance must be certified by letters from the curate to the vicar-general by the feast of St. Matthew (21 September).[2] Robynson's beliefs are all paralleled in unquestionably Lollard cases and though some of them are also Lutheran and Zwinglian, they would not in this combination suggest continental influences. Yet there follow complications of much interest. By a lucky chance we happen to know that Robynson was one of a group of Hull sailors or merchants who had actually seen Lutherans worshipping on the Continent. This unexpected addition to the picture derives from some visitation records of the diocese of

---

[1] Reg. Lee, fo. 105.   [2] Reg. Wolsey, fos. 132–132v.

Lincoln: it so happens that one of Robynson's shipmates came from the south bank of the Humber and that he also fell under suspicion on his return from the voyage. The record refers to events earlier in this same year 1528.

Henry Burnett came from the village of Barrow, Lincolnshire, almost opposite Hull, and his narrative to the Lincoln diocesan authorities was both clear and graphic. About Candlemas last (2 February) he and five Hull men passed overseas in a Dutch ship freighted with merchandise of Hull. He lists his companions as 'five of Hull: Roberte Clarcke, Roger Danyell, Nicholas Bayly and one William (*blank*) apprentice with M. Mycolow of Hull, and Robert Robynson of Hull'. They first landed 'in Holand in a town called Hamsterdam', spent six or seven weeks there, then took ship and went to Bremen, where they loaded a ship with wheat. At Bremen they tarried five weeks and found that 'the people did folowe Luter's warkes and no masses were said ther, but on the Sondaye the priest would revest hym self and goo to the aulter and procedid till nygh the sacryng tym, and then the prest and all that were in the church, olde and yonge, wolde syng after their mother tong, and ther was noo sakryng'. The Englishmen stayed here at Bremen from Easter (12 April) till the week before Whit Sunday (31 May). During that time they could not be shriven ('howselyd'), though according to Burnett they would have observed this rite, had it been possible. During this time they visited divers places of Friesland and through all the country there was no mass, 'but after Luter's opynyons was the people ordered, and thei had every Sondaye sermondes and preachinges, but this respondent nor noon of his company did understand them'. In the Whitsun week (31 May–6 June) they came back to Hull, where Burnett left his company and ferried the four miles across the Humber to his home in Barrow. There trouble soon developed. One gathers that he not only talked too much about these scandalous continental spectacles, but was also slack in his observances. Within four days of his return, he continues, he asked the vicar of Barrow 'to be confessid and howselyd', but the vicar refused to comply without the consent of the ordinary and sent him to Dr. John Prynn, a prebendary of Lincoln. The latter sent him on to the diocesan chancellor, Dr. Nicholas Bradbridge. Interrogated as to whether he or any of his company had visited 'that countrey to lerne Luter's warkes or opynyons', he said 'naye, and thei were not nygh Luter not by l. dutche mylys'. He understood no Latin, but could read English. He had never possessed a book of Luther's opinions, but his friend Roger Danyell 'had the gospelles in Englyshe, which the Dean of Yorke hath'. On the fish days when they were overseas, they had eaten flesh; after his return to Barrow Burnett had continued so doing for two days, but never since then, 'and he beleveth in Goddes lawis as a good Christen man shold do'. He had since these events been twice to Lincoln to speak with Dr. Prynn and to be shriven, but 'went home without any word', for the prebendary was not on those occasions in Lincoln. It says much for the vigilance of the clergy that such a man was so narrowly examined. Burnett nevertheless convinced the judges that he had done nothing very serious, since he escaped without punishment. The case concludes with his being finally ordered on pain of the greater excommunication 'that he shall never teache nor show to eny folkes such erronyous opynyons and dampnable abusions as he hath hard and seen in ffrice land and the countries ther abowt'.[1]

At least two of his friends from Hull fell into trouble in the diocese of York. Roger Danyell lost his copy of Tyndale's New Testament, which he may have bought on the Continent, and which fell into the hands of the Dean of York. This latter dignitary would receive the offensive volume by virtue of the other important office which he held, for at this date he was Brian Higden, who happened also to be vicar-general of the diocese. As such, he received the abjuration of Robert Robynson[2] and as such, no doubt, he investigated the conduct of Roger Danyell. Had the correctional act books of the archiepiscopal courts survived for this year 1528,[3] they would probably have furnished records of the case brought against Danyell, but adjudged of too little significance to be entered in the Register itself.

Of this group, the serious offender was Robert Robynson; he too leaves us with the knottier problems of interpretation. What should we suppose concerning the source of his heresies? They seemed in the York act book so convincingly Lollard in character and were unaccompanied by any charges involving contact with Lutherans or Lutheran books. Yet carefully examined, Burnett's story is not really inharmonious with the record of Robynson's trial at York. The probability remains strong that Burnett spoke the truth when he said that none of the party could understand the Lutheran sermons being preached in Bremen and in Friesland, and that none were capable of receiving the continental doctrines in Latin. The whole narrative surely weakens rather than strengthens any attempt to dub these men Lutherans: it

[1] E. Peacock, *Extracts from Lincoln Episcopal Visitations* in *Archaeologia*, xlviii. 257–8.
[2] Reg. Wolsey, fo. 132.   [3] Cf. *infra*, p. 241.

agrees broadly with the ostensible lack of Lutheran emphases found in the case of Robynson. It would be much easier to assume that this man, a trader or a sailor, had at some earlier date contracted English forms of heresy in London or in the south-east and that his mind was far from orthodox when he paid this visit to the Continent. In such a spirit the Lollards of Buckinghamshire listened in a secret gathering where Nicholas Field of London recounted what he had recently seen of Lutheran practices in Germany. 'He was beyond the sea in Almany, and there they used not so to fast nor to make such holy days'.[1] Such a hypothesis could easily be reconciled with a suspicion that Robynson and his companions may have felt much more curiosity about the Lutheran religion than Burnett pretended. Through Tyndale's Bible they had a link of sorts with the continental heresies, while this recent spectacle of a Lutheran commonwealth may well have tempted Robynson on his return to open his mouth more freely than he had hitherto dared. Whatever be the most accurate interpretation, we receive here a precious glimpse of the earliest stage of Protestantism in a sea-faring community which later developed a Protestant tradition destined to achieve great influence upon regional and national history. Until the reign of Edward VI the extant records tell us little more about the religious history of this interesting town. With unusual success, the men of Hull contrived to lead their own lives and keep their beliefs to themselves. They formed a lay community; unlike their trading rivals at York, they had few priests within their walls and no resident Council in the North constantly prying at close quarters into their daily lives.

The remaining early case in the York Registers comes also from east Yorkshire; doctrinally, it shows somewhat more distinct marks of continental influence and, unlike the foregoing series, it involved a priest. In 1531 Richard Browne had been instituted vicar of North Cave, a small village under the escarpment of the Wolds, but on the main road between Hull and the West Riding. In an abjuration made before Dr. Clyff on 20 August 1535 he confessed that he had been accused and detected before Clyff for having 'spoken, affirmed and declared divers erronyous opinions and articles agenst the true faeth of the holie church'. These were two in number.

First I have affirmed, saed, redd, taught and defendid in the parish of Northcave of the saed diocese that the sacrament of thalter did but present

[1] Foxe, iv. 584.

the bodie of Christe. Item, that yf a man were desposed and thought it convenient, (he) myght be confessid of a lay man.

Browne then made the usual profession:

I was brought before you, to them and every oon of them to make answere,
by whome I am nowe sufficiently and truely enformed that thies articles and
every oon of them be erronyous and hereticall and contrarie to the true
undrestonding and interpretacion of the holye scriptures and the holy
doctrine of the good and catholique doctors approved by our modre the
holy church and agenst the true faeth of Christ and the church and her
determination, sclaunderous and evill soundyng to all true and faethfull
Christen eares. Wherfore nowe I knowleg, confesse and beleve upon the true
catholique faeth in all poyntes, and do abiure . . . everie thies erronyous
opynyons and heresies premissed.[1]

He then swore on the Gospels to refrain from affirming any heresies
and, in the common form already observed in cases of literate heretics,
not to read, keep, or sell Luther's works, any other man's books of his
sect, or any other heretical books. After absolving Browne, Dr. Clyff
suspended him in writing from the vicarage of North Cave for two
months.[2]

Suggestions arose in later years purporting to connect Browne with
the nearby port of Hull and with the Continent. The popular but unlearned Irishman Thomas Gent of York, who published his *History of
Kingston-upon-Hull* in 1735, had evidently read the account of Browne's
case in the York Register. He had also heard that in 1522, thirteen
years earlier, the church of the Holy Trinity at Hull had been placed
under an interdict. He then ascribed the latter to some anti-Romish
sermon, connected this with the import of Tyndale's books from Antwerp, and in the same breath made Browne recant and do penance in
Hull.[3] The Hull historians Hadley (1788) and Tickell (1798) improved
on this already remarkable passage. The former sentenced Browne for
possessing heretical books; the latter made him preach a heretical sermon in Holy Trinity and even gave 'Town's Records' as his authority.[4]
Nearly a century later, J. G. Hall in his *History of South Cave* (1892)[5]
placed Holy Trinity under an interdict because of Browne's sermon!
Important and interesting as such connexions with Hull and the Continent would be, these attempts to establish them illustrate the imagina-

---

[1] Reg. Lee, fo. 99ᵛ.   [2] Ibid., fos. 99ᵛ–100.
[3] T. Gent, op. cit., pp. 18–19.
[4] I have searched Bench Books 1, 2, 3, 3A, which seem to contain no documents
remotely relating to this type of transaction.
[5] Hadley, pp. 71–72; Tickell, p. 160; Hall, p. 85.

tive Celtic qualities of Thomas Gent; on the part of other local historians they show a range of bad habits amongst which literary cannibalism is the least reprehensible. All the same, continental connexions, direct or indirect, seem possible enough in the Browne case. Attention should be directed to the phrase 'that the sacrament of thalter *did but present* the bodie of Christe'. The emphasis clearly lies upon 'present', meaning to represent, signify, symbolize; Browne had probably taken this Zwinglian heresy from Tyndale's *The Supper of the Lorde*, published two years earlier.[1]

In these early years orthodox local opinion envisaged heretics as people who went about cherishing forbidden books of one sort or another. This view finds illustration in a conversation between Thomas Ricard, gentleman, of Hatfield[2] and Lord Hussey in the latter's garden at Sleaford. This was reported when, after the Pilgrimage of Grace, Hussey's treasonable conduct came under review, but the talk seemingly took place in the summer of 1535. Hussey inquired of Ricard 'what newes and saynges he hard in his contre as in Yorkshire consernynge eryses'. Ricard replied that there 'wasse littill there, except in a fewe particoler persons who carried in there bosomes certan bokes'. He prayed that Hussey and other noblemen would put the king in 'remembrans for reformacion therof'. Hussey answered, 'that we cannot do without helpe of you and hit will never mend without we fight for hit'.[3] In the York family of Freez, which we are about to examine, books, Dutchmen, and heresy all figure prominently.

2. Heretics before the Northern Council

By 1539 the king's courts were enabled more effectively to initiate proceedings against heresy. The Act of the Six Articles now made denial of Transubstantiation or depraving of the sacrament punishable at once by burning of the person and confiscation of lands and goods. Persons teaching the necessity of communion in both kinds for lay people, or that auricular confession was unnecessary, became subject to confiscation for the first offence and death for the second. On the basis of this Act, secular courts could initiate proceedings for heresy and amongst those involved was the King's Council in the North. Its

---

[1] Cf. C. W. Dugmore, *The Mass and the English Reformers*, pp. 102–4.
[2] There were five Thomas Ricards in succession at Hatfield covering 1519–1612. Cf. *Glover's Visitation of Yorks.*, ed. J. Foster, p. 567.
[3] P.R.O., E. 36/119, p. 74; cf. *L. & P.* xii (1), 576.

President, Robert Holgate, Bishop of Llandaff and in 1545 Archbishop of York, will soon figure prominently in our survey as a holder of moderate Reforming opinions and by temperament a disliker of extremities. He was nevertheless a diligent servant of the State and in any case is unlikely to have experienced grave qualms of conscience in condemning convicted sacramentarian heretics, who were denounced in the strongest terms by Reformers of his stamp.[1] Though the minute books of the Northern Council have unfortunately perished, records happen to have survived of at least two heresy cases, involving in all four persons, which came before it at York under the Six Articles.

The unfortunate brothers Edward and Valentine Freez represent the second generation of a most interesting York family. Their father Frederick had in 1497 been entered in the Register of Freemen as a 'bokebynder and stacyoner'. He was obviously an immigrant from the Low Countries and his original name probably Vries or de Vries. In 1506 the Corporation granted him a ten-year lease in Coney Street, referring to him as 'a Dutchman and an alien enfranchised'. Though in 1510 he received mention as a 'buke prynter', no examples from his press are known. By 1515 he was living in the parish of St. Helen-on-the-Walls. Concerning his brother Gerard, who adopted the surname Wanseford and died in 1510, a good deal more is known. In York and elsewhere Gerard appears as a large-scale dealer in printed books and a publisher, for whom an edition of the *Expositio Hymnorum et Sequentiarum* was printed by Pierre Violette of Rouen in 1507. These brothers were familiar with Wynkyn de Worde and with other immigrant and continental members of their craft; the family had ample opportunities to develop contacts with Netherlandish Protestantism,[2] but how far it did so remains obscure.

The younger members of the family seem to have been touched by heretical influences before 1530. Concerning Edward Freez, the martyrologist John Foxe has preserved almost all our surviving information. Apprenticed to a painter in York, he became known to the abbot of a certain monastery, corrupted in Foxe's text to 'Bearsy Abbey'.[3] This abbot, seeing in him 'a boy of pregnant wit', bought him out of his

---

[1] Cf. the present writer's *Robert Holgate* (St. Anthony's Hall Publications, no. 8).

[2] On the first generation of the Freez family, cf. R. Davies, *A Memoir of the York Press*, pp. 7–15, and E. G. Duff, *The English Provincial Printers, Stationers and Bookbinders to 1557*, pp. 43–51.

[3] Bardsey is too remote to fit the story; Bardney could hardly become 'Bearsy'. Barmsey is a not uncommon form of Bermondsey and would suit better.

apprenticeship and made him a novice. Edward, not liking the monastic life, escaped to Colchester, married, and lived there like an honest man. After a considerable time, he was hired to paint certain cloths for the new inn in the market-place of Colchester and in the upper border of their cloths wrote certain sentences of scripture denoting him as a heretic.

Arrested in the inn yard, he was imprisoned in Fulham Palace along with other Essex Protestants and, alleges Foxe, fed with bread made partly of sawdust. His wife, while attempting to enter the palace to see him, was kicked by the porter and, being pregnant, died. Edward Freez was subsequently removed to the Lollards' Tower and manacled, so that his flesh 'grew higher than his irons' and his hair became matted together. When his brother Valentine sued to the king on his behalf, Edward was kept 'without meat' for three days before the hearing, and coming to court in a demented state, could say nothing but 'my Lord is a good man'. Having been sent back to 'Bearsy Abbey', he contrived ultimately to leave it, though he 'never came to his perfect mind to his dying day'.[1] Foxe dates these events as occurring in 1529–31 and indicates that some of the stories came from Valentine Freez himself.

Regarding the latter, we need no longer solely depend upon a narrative, which, though probably in the main true, may contain some embellishments and is presented in a partisan spirit. Foxe remains, however, the source for Valentine's initial offence. In 1533 Andrew Hewet, the martyr destined to suffer with Frith, was imprisoned in the house of the Bishop of London and cast into irons. 'Being there a good space, by means of a certain honest man, he had a file conveyed unto him, wherewith he filed off his irons.' Foxe then notes that 'the man that gave him this file was Valentine Freese, the painter's brother, who was afterwards, with his wife, burned in York'.[2] Soon after this adventure, Freez fell into the hands of Roland Lee, Bishop of Coventry and Lichfield and President of the Council in the Marches of Wales. In October or November 1534 Lee wrote to Cromwell,[3] probably from Ludlow, that he had received from the Dean of Westbury[4] a letter showing that 'Mr. Denys' had made suit to Cromwell 'for his servant'. By the king's favour and yours, continues Lee, I fear not the best of

---

[1] Foxe, iv. 694–5.
[2] Ibid. v. 16, n. 2.
[3] *L. & P.* vii. 1353. The letter is unsigned, but in the hand of Lee's clerk; it otherwise fits the position and character of Lee.
[4] i.e. dean of the College of Westbury-on-Trym, near Bristol.

them in administering judgement. When a man in my position is afraid of anybody, let him pipe and play, but occupy this office no longer. 'I intend not to let Frise go, but with solemnity in open court.' If I do not release him immediately, do not be displeased. 'His master has divers times used his words like a young gentleman of no experience.' The identification of this prisoner with the Protestant martyr finds support in the fact that the Dean of Westbury, who interested himself in the case, was none other than John Barlow, the servant of Anne Boleyn and brother of the famous Protestant bishop William Barlow. In this same year 1534, John Barlow told Cromwell that he was on the side of Reform.[1] It would thus seem that Freez, compelled to flee from London, yet understandably hesitating to reappear in York, had entered the service of a young 'Mr. Denys', perhaps in the Marches of Wales. There his reputation had caught up with him, or he had committed some new indiscretion. As for the pleas of Mr. Denys on his behalf, we know that Cromwell's papers of about this date once contained a supplication regarding Freez,[2] a fact which supports our identification. The actual document has unfortunately been lost and with it our best chance of obtaining further evidence on this stage of the future martyr's life. After this report by Lee, Freez vanishes again for about five years, only to reappear working in his native city. In 1539 'Valentine Freez cordyner', son of 'Frederick Freez stacyoner', was admitted a freeman of the city of York by patrimony, but opposite his name in the margin of the register is written 'Combustus erat apud Knavesmire propter heresem',[3] a sinister addition made not long after the initial entry. On 18 March 1540 Robert Holgate as President of the King's Council in the North sent Cromwell one of his routine reports on the work of that body. Since signing their letters, his Council had, he continues, received knowledge of two sacramentarians, Valentine Freys and his wife. Enclosing depositions (now lost), they requested a commission to inquire concerning heretics, according to the Statute of the Six Articles, for the city of York and other areas lying outside their present commission, which included only Yorkshire.[4] No doubt the York pair ultimately suffered, like so many contemporary extremists, under the 'Whip with Six Strings'. Neither the exact date of their deaths nor the

---

[1] The *D.N.B.* is confused on the Barlows. For John Barlow see Rupp, op. cit., pp. 64–65; he later became archdeacon of Westbury and Dean of Worcester. He was not, of course, a sacramentarian and may even have informed against Lambert.

[2] P.R.O., T.R. Misc. Book 139, fo. 102: 'Item a supplic. of Valentyne Frees.'

[3] *Freemen of York*, i (Surtees Soc. xcvi), p. 259.

[4] *L. & P.* xv. 362.

name of Valentine's wife and fellow sufferer have been discovered. Foxe merely informs us that they 'gave their lives at one stake in York for the testimony of Jesus Christ'.[1] Their non-appearance in our diocesan archives can thus be explained on the assumption that they were the victims of statutory and not of ecclesiastical law. Condemned by the Council in the North without trial in the church court, they passed through Micklegate Bar to the Knavesmire along that same *via dolorosa* traversed in later years by so many sufferers for an opposing faith.

In the last months of the reign the Northern Council had to deal with certain followers of the martyr John Lascells, himself linked with the diocese at least by origin and family background. On 16 July 1546 he was burned at Smithfield along with the Lincolnshire lady Anne Askew, an Essex priest John Hemley, and a tailor John Hadlam, all having been found guilty of denying Transubstantiation. Lascells himself came of 'a ryght worshipfull howse of Gatforde in Nottinghamshire ny Wursoppe',[2] various other branches of which lived in Yorkshire and Nottinghamshire.[3] He became a gentleman of Furnival's Inn[4] and one of the sewers of the King's Chamber.[5] His connexions with his county, though quite possibly maintained, fall from this point into obscurity, and his personal story thus becomes marginal to the history of the diocese of York. Anne Askew herself lived outside the borders of the diocese, but her father's and brother's homes lay not far distant from that of Lascells[6] and it seems likely enough that she may already have been known to him before she came to London early in 1546 and shared his profession of faith. Sir William Askew and his unfortunate daughter must indeed have attracted widespread attention throughout the east Midlands for some years previously, if only because Anne had been repudiated by her husband.[7]

The group headed by Lascells was one of those, seemingly very rare in the provinces but less so in London, within which gentle and prole-

---

[1] Foxe, iv. 695.
[2] *Narratives of the Reformation* (Camden Soc. lxxvii), p. 43. The family was of Gateford and Sturton.
[3] Cf. *Glover's Visitation of Yorks.*, ed. J. Foster, pp. 61, 185; Thoroton, *Antiquities of Notts.* iii. 116.
[4] *Greyfriar's Chronicle* (Camden Soc. liii), p. 51.
[5] Wriothesley, op. cit. i. 169; cf. Foxe, v. 550.
[6] Sir William lived at Stallingborough near Grimsby, but Anne's brother's house at South Kelsey was only twenty miles from the Lascells seat at Sturton.
[7] On Anne's biography see E. Trollope in *Assoc. Archit. Soc. Rep.* vi (1862), pp. 117 seqq.

tarian heretics associated on a left-wing basis. It might be conjectured that Lascells had formerly been somehow linked with his immediate neighbours the Worksop heretics,[1] but here positive proofs seem most unlikely to emerge. Whatever its provincial background, Lascells and not Anne Askew was the leading spirit of the group which Gardiner and Wriothesley took pains to destroy because of its close personal contact with the king. They also hoped that its fall might implicate their enemies, Queen Katherine Parr, the Duchess of Suffolk, and the Countesses of Sussex and Hertford.[2] In later years the Jesuit Parsons placed Lascells among 'the schollers and disciples of this yong mistresse, Anne Askew',[3] yet here he is directly contradicted by much more convincing evidence. John Bale, the first of Anne's martyrologists, received reports of the execution-scene from Dutch merchants actually present; he is concerned to glorify her memory, yet he specifically mentions Lascells as 'a gentleman which had been her instructor'.[4] Lascells had probably fallen foul of the conservatives as early as 1541, when he had given evidence against Katherine Howard. His Protestant views seem in 1546 exceptionally mature; the writings of the two martyrs, printed by Foxe, demonstrate his more solid intellectual attainments as compared with Anne's pertness and eloquence. His letter written in prison[5] was recognized by Parsons himself as one of the most persuasive documents in Foxe; the Jesuit devoted some interesting pages to its demolition and showed that Lascells's attack on Transubstantiation followed neither Luther, nor Zwingli, nor Calvin, but apparently derived from the extremist Carlstadt.[6] In short, here is no mere offshoot of English provincial Lollardy, but a London group having 'Dutch' sympathizers and some German theological inspiration.

The last phase of its story again touches the diocese of York. On 22 December 1546 the King's Council in the North reported to Henry VIII that at a session of the Six Articles it had convicted two sacramentaries, Richard Burdone and John Grove, 'who repaired hither immediately after the execution of Anne Askew, Lassels and others, and were present at the same'.[7] The story is thence expanded by some

[1] Cf. *supra*, p. 19.
[2] Trollope, op. cit., p. 126.
[3] *Narratives of the Reformation*, p. 310.
[4] *Select Works of John Bale* (Parker Soc. 1894), p. 243.
[5] Foxe, v. 551–2.
[6] R. Parsons, *Examen of I. Fox his Calendar Saints* (1604); a lengthy excerpt is in *Narratives of the Reformation*, pp. 307–11.
[7] *L. & P.* xxi (2), 596.

entries in the York House Book[1] referring to notable events in the mayoralty of William Holme, 1546-7. 'Also the same yere thare was two taillors that came frome London and dwelte within this Citie, whiche two taillours was accused and indictyd of herysy and heronyous oppynyons concernyng the blyssyd sacrament of the alter; and theruppon they were commytt to prison to the Shyrryffs Kydcote,[2] beyng condempnyd and also adjugyd to be brynt, and so remanyd the space of vj weks.' Their attitude before the Council in the North must have proved submissive, for this body proceeded to refer their case to the king, who only a month before his death vouchsafed them a conditional pardon. The Privy Council book under the date 27 December 1546 records a letter to the President and Council in the North signifying that the king's majesty had pardoned two sacramentaries by them convicted, 'but now (as they affirmed) penytent, soo that they shuld make recantacion openly and foresake their former opinions'.[3] The York House Book then neatly completes the story: 'And then they were broght unto the Chapytour howse of Yorke mynster uppon sonday the xvj day of January and then and there they dyd bothe recant ther sayngs and heronyos oppynyons before a great multetewde of people beyng there present at the declaracon of the worde of God, and that done they were comyttyd againe to the Shyrryffs Kydcote.' It may in fact have been some months before they were liberated.

With characteristic unction, the York civic authorities allowed it to be thought that these were London heretics come to mar the city's perfect orthodoxy. Yet the intrinsic improbability that London Protestants without northern connexions would flee for safety to conservative York scarcely needs to be stressed. Richard Burdon no doubt did return to York from London in 1546, but the fact remains that sometime during the same year one Richard Burdon, tailor, was made a freeman of the city, and in 1549-50 became one of the city chamberlains.[4] There seems in short every reason to envisage Burdon and Grove as no mere sojourners but men of local origin, who provide one more illustration of the Tudor craftsman's mobility and consequent importance as a disseminator of new doctrines.

[1] *York Civic Records* (Y.A.S. Rec. Ser. cviii), iv. 150.
[2] The sheriffs' jail on Ousebridge.
[3] *Acts of the Privy Council, 1542-47*, p. 562.
[4] *Freemen of York*, i (Surtees Soc. xcvi), pp. 266, 269. Burdon occurs commonly in contemporary records, Grove much less commonly, though a tailor William Groves appears in the House Book a couple of pages after the passage cited above (*York Civic Records*, iv. 150).

3. *Heresy Cases in the Court of Audience or Chancery*

The remaining evidence for heresy cases in the diocese during the later years of Henry VIII is chiefly based upon an act book of the Archbishop's Court of Audience covering the period 1536–43.[1] I propose now to attempt a chronological summary of these cases, calling in such additional evidence as may be gleaned from external sources. The information is in itself novel; it throws light not merely upon religious opinion, but upon social conditions and contemporary manifestations of Yorkshire character.

The first case of this series involved Thomas Prat of Thirsk, who, when we first read of him, had already been incarcerated in the archbishop's prisons *super crimine heresis*, and then released on bonds. Prat was assigned on 5 April 1539 to appear before the archbishop, his vicar-general, or his commissaries. On 17 April he underwent examination upon six articles in the vulgar tongue. To the first of these he admitted he had spoken the words: 'that God never bled all his blode, for if he had bled all his blode he cold not have risen ageyn from death to liffe.' If there were other charges, they are not set forth. Though Prat proceeded to submit to correction, his case was treated as something more than one of mere ignorance. Ordered to receive penance, he was found on 13 June to have been arrested by the secular power in consequence of a royal writ, and to be in the custody of the Sheriff of Yorkshire. He was back in the Archbishop's Court on 8 August; again on 12 September and on 3 October. On the last day the judge repeatedly interrogated him as to whether he would abjure his heresy, and Prat ended by reading in public a written abjuration and signing it with the sign of the cross. Taking an oath to do penance, he was absolved.[2] So far as my observation goes, his heresy may be judged eccentric and individual. The case illustrates the element of materialist scepticism concerning the miraculous elements of the Faith, a scepticism we shall see repeated by more conventional heretics and which played a more prominent role in popular unorthodoxy than we should deduce from Foxe.

The next man to face a charge of heresy in the York court was John Burne, a Northumbrian from Holburn ('Howborne') in Belford parish. On 22 July 1540 this sojourner in York was presented by Henry Joye, rector of All Saints, North Street, and by two constables of the parish. It appeared that on the previous day, the eve of St. Mary Magdalen,

---

[1] Temporary reference: R. VII. A.B. 2.
[2] Prat's case is in R. VII. A.B. 2, fos. 81ᵛ, 82, 86, 90, 91ᵛ.

Burne had spoken to Helen, wife of Robert Peres, in the churchyard of All Saints, and asked, 'What holyday is to morowe?' She answered, 'To morow is Mary Magdalen day', and Burne rejoined, 'Nay it is Mary hoore Day. There is no moo Maries but oon.' It so happened that parson Joye sitting in his study by the churchyard—the latter is still little more than a passage between the church and the houses—overheard this profane remark and reported it to authority. The accused was warned to come before the vicar-general the following Friday,[1] but though on that day a heading was prepared for the case, no entry follows.[2] Perhaps Burne had fled to his own county. His case may have arisen from a boorish indiscretion rather than from any profound antipathy toward the cult of the saints, but even so the court would not deliberately have discontinued it without an appearance, an apology, and a penance.

On the same day the York act book begins its record of one of our most important and protracted cases—that of William Senes[3] of Rotherham. The earlier stages of this man's career are nevertheless illustrated elsewhere, in particular by three documents in the Public Record Office, all emanating from the year 1537. The first of these is a memorandum possibly written by Senes himself to draw attention to his plight in prison;[4] the second an indictment brought against him for heresy,[5] and the third a letter from John Babington to Thomas Cromwell, pleading for Senes.[6] Supported by the *Valor Ecclesiasticus*, the *Yorkshire Chantry Surveys*, and other works of reference, these papers afford a most vivid picture of the clash between Reforming and conservative groups at Rotherham.

In 1535 William Senes was chaplain in charge of the song school of Jesus College, Rotherham, with a modest annual stipend of £6. 13s. 4d.[7] Defamed of heresy, he was arrested there on 4 August 1537, together with Thomas Frauncys and John Padley, and taken before George, fourth Earl of Shrewsbury. This nobleman, now about sixty-nine years of age, had scarcely another year to live.[8] He had supported the Divorce,

[1] Ibid., fos. 125ᵛ-126.   [2] Ibid., fo. 127.
[3] The spellings Sennes, Senoose, Symmez, Senvys all occur, but there can be no doubt in any of the references below that the same man is intended.
[4] *L. & P.* xii (2), 436.   [5] Ibid. 436 (2).   [6] Ibid. 925.
[7] *Valor Eccles.* v. 45; the indictment also describes him thus. As will appear, he was not in priest's orders.
[8] He was born in 1468 and died in July 1538. The place of these interviews is not stated, but may have been at Sheffield Castle or at the Manor, previously built by the earl some two miles distant, in the park. With its fine alabaster effigies, his tomb in Sheffield Cathedral is amongst the most remarkable of the period.

taken a leading role in the suppression of the Pilgrimage of Grace, and received many grants of monastic lands. In religion he was nevertheless a prominent conservative and his will, which he made a fortnight after the events about to be described, displays a highly traditional type of piety, including a provision that a thousand priests should receive sixpence each to say *placebo* and *dirige* for his soul.[1] The events which followed may have lost none of their pungency in the telling, yet they seem well in character.

When the unfortunate chaplain appeared, the earl greeted him in no cordial manner: 'Come near, thou heretic and kneel near, ha, thou heretic, thou has books here!' Senes meekly replied, 'Yea my Lord, the New Testament I have.' Shrewsbury then retorted, perhaps somewhat incoherently in his choler: 'The New Testament nought thou has', and repeated very often that the New Testament 'was nought', i.e. worthless, injurious. He added, again not very subtly, 'Thou art an heretic and but for shame I should thrust my dagger into thee.' After this one-sided exchange, Senes dare say no more and he was put in a dungeon for seven days.

His friend Frauncys having been similarly arrested and imprisoned for the same time, was then, by reason of friends, released. When in his turn John Padley came before the irascible earl, the latter charged him: 'Thou art a heretic and a Loulere.' Padley answered, 'Nay my Lord, it is not so', and when Shrewsbury inquired what he had learned, he said 'Humanity'. 'That is well,' replied the earl, 'what has thou spoken?' 'Nothing', said Padley, 'but that that shall become a Christian to speak', and he continued to the effect that he had only spoken upon the commandments of God, which were to 'love God above all things and my neighbour as myself'. Shrewsbury then accused him of speaking against the sacrament and referred to the bailiff of Rotherham, who, however, denied having heard him so speak. Finally, Padley was sent to prison for the same time as Senes and from the prison Shrewsbury sent the two to the Duke of Norfolk, then President of the King's Council in the North. The duke proceeded to deliver them to the bishop's officer and at the time of writing this memoir—perhaps several weeks later—they were still in the 'bishop's prison', presumably the archiepiscopal jail at York.

Having related these events, Senes or his apologist proceeds to give what he calls the causes of his trouble. It was due, he argued, to his loyalty to the king, in opposition to a disloyal group of local priests. He

[1] T. Hunter, *Hallamshire*, ed. A. Gatty, p. 74.

had always spoken against the rebels, but when the Lincolnshire rising began, a priest, Sir Thomas Holden alias Alexandere, remarked, 'God was in Lincolnshire, for those was good lads, for they would put down those heretics Cromwell, Cranmer and Latimer, . . . we dare not stir; but let them rob us of our money.' Opposing these traitorous words, the virtuous Senes had declared, rather platitudinously, that those who withstood the king were rebellious. At this point another priest, Mr. Drapper, had said he trusted in the Earl of Shrewsbury as a favourer of the commons, but Senes replied that the earl would not favour them, for he had always been true to the king. 'In that case,' retorted Drapper, 'the Earl himself was nought.' 'Why', said Senes, 'is all nought that doth hold with our king? Yonder is Mr. Markhame,[1] he hath put out the abbot of Roughforthe (Rufford) and his convent according to the King's commandment.' Unrepentant, Drapper had then said that Markham too was a heretic and further, that he, Drapper, might resist if the king tried to take away his chalice, which was for the service of God—an obvious reference to the rumour that the king intended to seize church plate.[2] At this point the two descended to abuse, Senes calling Drapper 'Sir John Lack-learning', and Drapper replying, even more tritely, 'Whoreson knave!'.

When Senes reported these exchanges to his superior Robert Nevill, the provost of Jesus College,[3] he was merely sent on to the bailiff of Rotherham. The latter either regarded Senes with disfavour or wanted to obviate further trouble with higher authority, for he merely asked the provost if he could not rule his own house. Nevill, obviously irritated by this repercussion, called Senes and threatened to expel him from the house if he complained again. So ends this narrative. I know little or nothing else about his friends Frauncys and Padley, but his two clerical enemies can be usefully identified. Thomas Holden was in 1535 cantarist of the chantry of St. Katherine in the parish church of Rotherham, with the clear stipend of only £4 per annum.[4] He continued to occupy a chantry there during the Chantry Surveys of 1546 and 1548, being in the latter year 46 years of age and still having no other living.[5] As for

---

[1] Presumably Sir John Markham of Cotham, M.P. for Nottinghamshire in the Reformation Parliament and active in the suppression of the monasteries. Cf. A. C. Wood, *Hist. of Nottinghamshire*, p. 129.

[2] Cf. Dodds, op. cit. i. 76–77.

[3] Robert Nevill, S.T.B., collated to the provostship in 1518; died, having held numerous other livings, 1550. *Test. Ebor.* iv. 112 n. gives details.

[4] *Valor Eccles.* v. 62.

[5] *Yorks. Chantry Surveys* (Surtees Soc. xci, xcii), pp. 205, 379.

'Mr. Drapper', he was none other than the chaplain teaching the grammar school in Jesus College,[1] and the fact that he was Senes's own colleague lends point to the taunt which the bailiff administered to their superior, the provost.

That these two were not the only informers against Senes may be gathered from the text of the indictment. This document states that on 8 June, 29 Henry VIII (1537), in the parish church of All Saints, Rotherham, William Senes had shown the chantry priest Thomas Holden some printed ballads against the prayers of the Church used in the hallowing of water, the blessing of bread and of bells, and touching Purgatory, which ballads, Holden commented, were not authorized by Parliament. In reply, Senes made a bold attack on authority, saying 'that such books as were sent down to the curates was made by heretics and none of them true'. Moreover, he continued, the soul after death went straight to either Heaven or Hell, and no prayer for it could avail. These we may recognize as all characteristic Lollard positions, but—as will shortly appear—Senes could boast some more modish influences.

The indictment proceeds to further similar offences, reported from a new quarter. William Ingram, parish clerk of Rotherham, was present in the church on Friday, 4 May, hearing mass. A priest, Thomas Pylley, had in fact said mass for the soul of Henry Carnbull, and finished by sprinkling water upon his tomb, 'as the custom is'. On witnessing this, Senes ridiculed the act, and when Ingram said he believed as his father had done, Senes replied in terms which suggest that a man of the Gospel might sometimes display a fanaticism even more revolting than that of his opponents. 'Thy father was a liar and is in Hell, and so is my father in Hell also; my father never knew Scripture and now it is come forth.' The ceremony which gave rise to this dispute revolved around the memory of a local celebrity of the last generation: Henry Carnbull, Archdeacon of York, who had in 1505 founded a chantry in the parish church to pray for the royal family, his patron Archbishop Rotherham, founder of Jesus College, and himself. Of this chantry Thomas Pylley is in fact recorded as priest both in 1535 and 1546.[2]

Further charges against Senes then arise from the indictment. On the Sunday before St. John the Baptist's Day, 10 June,[3] the parish clerk

[1] *Valor Eccles.* v. 45. His annual stipend was £10, much higher than that of Senes.
[2] Ibid. v. 45; *Yorks. Chantry Surveys,* p. 205; the latter gives a full account of this foundation.
[3] In 1537 the Sunday previous to 24 June was in fact 17 June.

Ingram had another conversation with the accused in the church, during which Senes asked, 'When didst thou see God?' Ingram replied that he did so every day at mass, in the priest's hands, to which Senes rejoined, 'Thou sawest but bread.' Then on 24 June he had told one Richard Wade, who along with Katharine Bretton was reading a Life of Christ in Rotherham church, that the Blessed Mary was not the mother of God,[1] that prayer to her could do no good, and that the sacrament of the altar was not the body of Christ, 'for God is here upon my hand, in my body, in this stulpe (pillar) and everywhere'. He had also used similar language to one Cutler of Rotherham on 6 July. His last point could be derived from Wyclif, but I cannot help suspecting it to represent the Lutheran doctrine of the ubiquity of Christ's glorified body. The case brought against Senes in Yorkshire did not run its full course. On the following 16 October John Babington, son of Sir Anthony Babington of Dethick and Kingston-upon-Soar,[2] wrote to Cromwell at the request of 'divers honest neighbours', to whom Senes was a kinsman. He transmitted a copy of a presentment of a Yorkshire jury against Senes, which the relatives had said was untrue, demanding indifferent judgement for him. Babington also sent 'a paper written on both sides of the leaf', which Senes had written to his friends, showing that in the time of the rebellion he was honest, and that the provost and the bailiff of Rotherham deserved punishment for the concealment of the seditious conversations reported to them by Senes.[3] By this paper Babington evidently means the memorandum we have already studied. His letter and enclosures had their effect: referring back to the indictment, we observe that it is headed in another hand 'A cirsiorare (sic) corpus cum causa out of the King's Bench'. This means that, in accordance with a practice which had become increasingly common since the early fifteenth century, a writ of *certiorari* had been issued together with a *habeas corpus cum causa*, in order to withdraw the body and record of the accused from an inferior court into the King's Bench.[4]

Another letter from Babington to Cromwell written from Kingston,

[1] Some heretics maintained that Christ did not take flesh of the Virgin, sometimes supporting their view by crude analogies. Cf. *infra*, p. 75.

[2] Sir Anthony was borough M.P. for Nottingham (A. C. Wood, loc. cit.) and John Babington was among Cromwell's many close adherents. For some illustrative particulars of these relationships, see, e.g., *L. & P.* xii (2), 1061.

[3] Ibid. 925.

[4] On this practice and on the attempts of 1601 and 1624 to check it by statutes, see Holdsworth, *Hist. of Eng. Law*, ix. 109–10.

Nottinghamshire, on 21 August 1538 carries the tale a stage farther. He writes of the suit of William 'Senewes' the bearer, who is associated with Robert Nevill the provost and two others, all priests in the College of Rotherham. At present Senes has his living by music in the said church, but being no priest can get no promotion there. He thinks he might employ his time better, and pay off the debts which, 'by the wrongful procurement of that country', he lately incurred to save his life. To this end Senes desires Cromwell to tender his suit to the said provost (a delightful euphemism!) for the vacant farm of Laxton, 'near me here in Nottinghamshire', and appropriated to the college, that he may have it under the college's seal for forty years.[1] The reference is to the rectory of Laxton, which the college was in 1535 farming for £23 per annum.[2] The present writer is unaware as to the success or otherwise of this enterprising essay in coercion through Cromwell, who was soon to be accused by his enemies as a maintainer of heretics. So far as the State papers are concerned, we should now have reached the end of the story of the music master of Rotherham College. Returning, however, to the act book of the York Court of Audience, we discover a further and almost equally interesting chapter of his biography. It might very reasonably be surmised that he had become one of those marked down by the conservatives for further observation and for prosecution when circumstances should again permit. It seems significant that his troubles recommenced in Yorkshire immediately upon the execution of his protector Thomas Cromwell.

In the York act book his case begins without the usual heading and seems to refer to some unrecorded earlier proceedings at York. We are first told that on 10 September 1540 in a certain low parlour under the chapel in the archbishop's palace[3] before the vicar-general, William Senes 'confessed and said that Sir Thomas Holgat[4] and William Yngram asked him forgevenes for that they had deposed agenst him before that time'. This suggests that the two accusers had thought it wise to placate Senes with a view to avoiding possible counter-charges of treason against themselves. Senes now continued with a reference to new charges made since his return.

He saith John Grene, Herry Smith and Richard Sewall were present *in domo dicti* Senes in Rotheram, anone aftre that Senes came from London. The

---

[1] *L. & P.* xiii (2), 149.   [2] *Valor Eccles.* v. 44.
[3] 'In quadam bassa parlura subtus capellam infra palacium domini Archiepiscopi Ebor'.' (fo. 129).
[4] An obvious error for Holden.

said Senes denyed that he said to Richard Sewall that as the ale poole [pole] signifieth that there is ale to sell and yet no ale in the poole, so, Firth (*sic*) said in his booke, is the sacrament of thalter. The said Richard Sewall there present said before the said Senes then and there that the said Senes spake the same wordes to him as is abovesaid.

This interesting reference to the work of John Frith, who had suffered burning in 1533 at Smithfield for his denial of Transubstantiation and Purgatory,[1] was followed up by other evidence purporting to show that Senes had been a zealous student of heretical books. Examined on oath under articles at a later session, he denied writing certain notes on the sacrament of the altar, but admitted writing others 'out of odre bokes, but he saith that he did never affirme them ne beleve them'. Reference was then made to a paper book in the accused's hand; in reply he professed to believe not what he had written there, but to believe merely 'as the catholique Church teacheth and beleveth'. Still further writings —the nature of all these can only be surmised—he claimed merely to have copied 'out of the notes of the Bible sett forth by Thomas Mathew and imprinted by the Kinge's licence'. The commissary, Dr. Palmes,[2] had by now called in two assistants, the chancellor, Dr. Geoffrey Downes,[3] and Dr. Cuthbert Marshall;[4] he was dealing with a serious case of heresy. On 23 November Senes again faced his accusers *in loco consistoriali* and the judge read the attestations of certain witnesses who had been examined on some previous occasion. Senes thereupon claimed 'that he was discharged of this by the last Earl of Essex (i.e. Thomas Cromwell, executed the previous July) and by the Kynges Counsell, and also allegid that he hadde the Kynges pardon by the generall Act of Parliament'. This sentence fills part of the gap between our two chief sources. It seems clear that the Rotherham schoolmaster, having been brought up to London under the *certiorari* writ, had in due course succeeded in reaching the more sympathetic atmosphere of the Privy Council under Thomas Cromwell. Once discharged thence, no one had seemingly ventured to touch him until his protector died and the Six Articles persecution began.

Even now, the York commissioners showed no desire to go to

[1] Senes had obviously read *A boke made by Johan Fryth* (1533), which contains this simile of the ale-pole. Cf. C. W. Dugmore, op. cit., p. 99.
[2] Cf. *supra*, p. 20.   [3] Cf. *supra*, p. 20.
[4] Prebendary of Husthwaite, 1526–50; archdeacon of Nottingham, 1528; wrote preface to King Henry's Primer, 1535; questioned in 1541 by the Privy Council regarding his part in the Pilgrimage of Grace; died Jan. 1550 (C. H. and T. Cooper, *Athenae Cantabrigienses*, i. 97; Dodds, op. cit. i. 382, 385; ii. 256).

extremes, while Senes, no doubt reflecting on the dangers presented by the recent change of political climate, prudently decided to undergo the forms of submission. The court now assigned him a day for the abjuration of his heresy *si voluerit*. This day was 26 November 1540, when Senes at long last admitted the truth of the articles of accusation and of the witnesses' evidence, submitted himself to correction and offered to renounce his opinions and heresies. 'And for the opinion conteyned in his abjuracion, he confessith it and offerith hym self to abjure it as concernes the sacrament of the altare.' He then read the formal act of abjuration from a schedule, which he signed with his full names and with the sign of the cross, taking oath on the gospels. The judge absolved him from excommunication and appointed a day for enjoining his penance. The next pertinent entry occurs, however, on 17 December, when Senes was found to have performed the penance at the Minster and was ordered to repeat it in his parish church of Rotherham. In due course he returned to report orally on this, but was sent back again to get an actual certificate from the curate of Rotherham: so, having fulfilled this last requirement on 21 January 1541,[1] he vanishes. Certainly if his unrecorded experiences with the Privy Council had been half as irksome as those with the ecclesiastical court of York, William Senes would thereafter think twice before becoming involved in heresies. Behind these tedious forms, so often tantalizing in their avoidance of specific fact, we may sense in Rotherham an example of a serious but unheroic Protestant group.

Almost equally detailed is the contemporary case of James Hardcastell, a butcher of Barwick-in-Elmet. It is a morass of conflicting evidence and represents, not merely the story of an anticlerical individual, but also that of a parish quarrel, perhaps not untypical of the many which must have sprung from the religious tensions of these years. As with the case of Senes, the subsidiary detail leaves quite a vivid impression of the great controversy as it was waged upon these lowly levels of society. Thomas Mettringham, formerly curate of Barwick,[2] testified on 24 September 1540 that he had 'herd James Hardcastell say that there was no thing in the church that cold do him good, and he wold beleve in none of them, and even anone aftre, Hardcastell said that he belevid in the blissed sacrament of thaltare and said that he said the foresaid wordes to prove what such a dronken preist wold say'. This had happened the last 8 October in John Carter's house at Barwick,

---

[1] The Senes case is on fos. 129, 148^v, 149, 154, 154^v, 156^v.
[2] And probably an ex-Whitefriar of York. Cf. *D.K. Rep.* viii, app. ii, p. 51.

in the presence of Miles Walker, chaplain there, and three other witnesses. Mettringham had also 'herd oon Benyson of the same parish, which had his wief to be buried, say that James Hardcastell sayd that it was agenst the Kinge's articles to have *Dirige* said for a dede body, for it could not prevaile'. Hardcastell, he continued, was 'named and suspected in the parish of Barwicke a man of yll opinions'. On 3 July last, Mettringham had heard Hardcastell say in the house of one Gilson at Barwick, 'I wold that Cromwell had reigned longer, that he myght have punysshed you priestes, for yf he had continued, than I wold have trusted that a lay man shuld have said Masse as well as a priest.'

Two lay witnesses having failed to substantiate these charges, William Lounde, cantarist at Howden but a native of Barwick and acquainted with Hardcastell for twenty-six years, deposed that he had heard Mettringham, then curate of Barwick, rebuke James Hardcastell, saying that 'such wordes wold putt him to payne'. Lounde had asked Hardcastell 'whie he wold have had [Cromwell] to a reigned longer?' Hardcastell pertly replied, 'To have punisshed you priestes.' The case was continued on 1 October, when Miles Walker, chaplain to Sir Thomas Johnson, knight,[1] testified that

about Whitesonday last past he was present in oon John Carter housse in Barwicke in Elmett, where also were present William Ellys of Kiddall, Robert Rawson, Sir Thomas Mettringham, then curat of Barwicke, and James Hardcastell and oder mooe. This deponent [Walker] and William Ellys satt at the table, and Sir Thomas Mettringham and James Hardcastell satt by the chymney side, and he saith that he and William Ellys hard Sir Thomas Mettringham and James Hardcastell at woordes and herd Sir Thomas say unto James Hardcastell, 'Yf thow use this, thow wylt be brente', at whiche wordes this deponent asked Sir Thomas Mettringham what the matter was, and Sir Thomas Mettringham said that James Hardcastell sayd that there was no thing in the church that could do him good. And then this deponent said to James, 'No James, the blessid sacrament is in the church. How say ye by it?'

James avoided this rather crude clerical trap by replying, 'I take it and beleve in yt as a trew Christen man ought to doo.' At this stage of the case, Thomas Jackson of Barwick, labourer, produced the utterly devastating statement that 'on Sonday last was a forth night, Sir Thomas Mettringham wold have gevin this deponent xl s. to have said as he wold have had him to asaide'. The court seems

---

[1] Apparently of Linley, near Otley. Cf. *Harleian Soc.* xvi. 78, but I have no genealogy of the family in my collections.

blithely to have ignored this grave charge of bribing a witness and turned to hear the evidence of Robert Rawson, a butcher aged sixty-seven, who had known Hardcastell for twenty years. This witness related the notorious incident at Carter's house, saying that Mettringham and Hardcastell 'were at hiegh wordes' and that he remembered hearing the latter say 'that yf he Sir Thomas were in the church he wold sett nothing, nother by him Sir Thomas, ne by any thing that was in the church, for it wold do him no good, except the sacrament of thaulter'. The chaplain Miles Walker, recalled to the witness-stand, testified that 'it haith byn said in Barwyke in this last yere that James Hardcastell haith byn very busye in raling of prestes and ymages in the church'.[1] Thomas Evers, servant of Sir Thomas Johnson, knight, prefaced his account of the meeting at Carter's by saying that Mettringham and Hardcastell were 'communyng aboute mendyng of the church of Barwick', when Hardcastell said 'that there was no thing in the church that wold doo him good but God above, and with that worde Sir Myles Walker, priest, there present, asked James Hardcastell yf he did not believe in the blessid sacrament of thaulter, and the same James said, "Yes mary, that doo I believe in it", and with that did of [off] his cap, and said that he said thoes wordes to prove what a dronken priest wold say therto'. Walker's intervention had obviously caused Hardcastell to do some quick thinking and to pretend that he had merely been baiting a priest.

On 8 October another lay witness was brought in, but could depose nothing on the articles. Whether or not Mettringham had tried to corrupt a witness, his charges seem not to have lacked substance. At all events, on 13 November Hardcastell saw the danger of his position and made a confession to the effect that he had said 'that there was no thing in the church that cold do him good but only the blessed sacrament of thaulter, and he saith he spake thies wordes when he was over seen with drinke, and he saith he never belevyd so, ne doth, but doth beleve in all the seven sacramentes of the church and is sorry for that he said and submitteth him self to penance'. As other cases indicate, this was the safest line to take in the face of a pertinacious accusation by a knot of priests in the church court. It probably deceived nobody, but the court could be relied upon to avoid extreme punishments when the accused humbled himself. In this case, Hardcastell made formal abjuration and was ordered 'una dies fustigationis circa ecclesiam de

---

[1] The original MS. has the phrase after the word busye, 'aboute of yll opinyons and suspected of them all', but this phrase was subsequently struck out.

Barwick', with the usual order to certify. Though on the appointed day
he failed to provide the certificate, no further entry concerns his case.[1]
'A day of scourging' around the church was much less painful than the
words might suggest: other cases make it clear that the victim passed
only once round the church at the head of the procession. The vigour of
the flagellant doubtless varied with local sentiments and personalities,
but as anticlerical groups arose in the parishes, such ceremonies can
have added little to the popularity of the clergy.

An incomplete entry on 5 August 1541 concerned Guy Clitheroe,
rector of Finningley, and what the court scathingly called 'his negligence and lacke of wit and lerning in putting an host not consecrat in
the brest of the ymage on Ester day last'.[2] He claimed that the host
had never been 'worshyped', and in all likelihood he was innocent of
any heterodox intent. On 27 January 1542 Ralph Wynne of Masham
faced a heresy-accusation for saying 'that he haithe served God longe
and he wyll do nothinge for hyme, and therfore he wyll serve the
Devell and se whether he wyll do any thing for him'. The accused
explained away these sentiments by relating that 'ther was certen
deare kyllede in his mastere's parke, wherof he ys kepar, and he coulde
not know by whome, and then he sayde he wolde have knowledge
therof gladlye; whether it were by God or the Devell, he carede not
whether'. After some postponement, he was assigned two days for
floggings around the parish church,[3] though the ostensible evidence
suggests no more than common profanity.

Much more interesting than these last two trivial cases is that
against Richard Flynte, parish clerk of Topcliffe, who admitted failure to
make confession for 'tow yeres before Easter last was, a twelfmonneth
before the date hereof'. He was examined on 12 December 1542 by
Dr. Clyff in the presence of Robert Davell, LL.D., and others, and
answered 'that he was not confessid by the said tyme, sainge the cause
movinge him to the same was that there was a sainge in the countrie
that a man might lefte up his harte and confesse himself to God All-
mightie and neded not to be confessed at a prieste. Further examyned
of whome he herd the same saing, he saieth that as he shall make

[1] For the Hardcastell case, see R. VII. A.B. 2, fos. 130, 130ᵛ, 131, 131ᵛ, 133ᵛ, 134,
134ᵛ, 135, 136, 147ᵛ.
[2] The judge interdicted him from ministration until he had obtained grace of the
archbishop and ordered him to make public declaration of his fault the following
Sunday in the pulpit. He was assigned a coadjutor during his interdiction (ibid.,
fos. 185ᵛ–186).
[3] Ibid., fos. 213, 215, 234.

aunswer to God, he knoweth not, nor yet in what place.' A second entry indicates that Flynte admitted the truth of the charges,[1] but no record of his punishment survives. The interest of the case lies, of course, in the saying allegedly current in the region, that a man might lift up his heart and confess himself to God without the mediation of a priest. If this belief were in fact widely prevalent in north Yorkshire in 1542, a new perspective would be added to the early history of Protestantism, or rather of Lollard survival, in northern England.

A subsequent heresy case in this same act book illustrates the mobility of labour so characteristic of the Tudor age and its inevitable concomitant: the spread of East Anglian heresies to the more conservative regions of England. William Bull, a twenty-two-year-old shearman, had been born in Dewsbury, but apprenticed for six years at Waldingfield in West Suffolk; he then worked for 'a certeyn space' as a journeyman at Waldingfield, Ipswich, and Hadleigh—these last two places soon to be especially notorious as nurseries of Protestantism. Fresh from this *locus classicus* of heresy, he then 'came owte of the South countrey to visite and see his father and mother', accompanied by William Nicholson and Matthew Brill, 'his brother sheremen'. On 26 February 1543 he found himself giving these biographical details to the Archbishop's Court. He was followed by a Dewsbury husbandman, Thomas Barkstone, who had known Bull since his childhood and who now testified that he had heard him say before various other witnesses last St. Stephen's Day at night in his house 'that the fonte is but a stinkinge terne and he had rather be christened in the rynnynge river than in the saide terne,[2] standinge stynckinge by halffe a yeare, for when God made the warldde he halowed both water and lande'. The witness 'badde him holde his peace for shame', but, unabashed, Bull went on

that he hadde rather be confessed at a leyman than at a preste, oneles the preste coulde shew him suche wordes as he wolde axe him in the Epistle and Gospell, sainge that he wolde not shewe his offences to the preste, as yf he had japed[3] a fayre weman, or such lyke offence, for the preste wolde be as redye within two or thre dayes aftre to use hir as he; recitynge then two of the first articles of our Crede, sainge that [if] he belevyd stedfastlye in God, callinge to God with a sory harte for his offences, God wolde forgive him, sainge the preste his confessor ys a knave.

At the same time and place, Barkstone had also heard Bull say 'that

[1] R. VII. A.B. 2, fos. 280–280ᵛ.
[2] Cf. the *mala dogmata* of 1536 in Dixon, op. cit. i. 406.   [3] Seduced.

the anunctement [last unction] ys but a sybertie sawce, and that he wolde have no suche sibertie sawce mynistred unto him at his death' and 'that he belevid in God, Father Almightie, maker of heven and earth and Jesu Christe his onely Sonne our Lorde, by whome he trustyd to be saved, yf he had no suche sybertie sawce[1] at his death'. Also lodging at Barkstone's was one Dalariver, 'whiche was sometyme servante in the Abbay of Pountefreyte', and this man 'reasoned with William Bull and marvelid and blissed him, that he wolde saye as he then said'. He had indeed provided a fine example of Yorkshire working-class radicalism.

Another shearman from Dewsbury, Nicholas Walker, proceeded to corroborate Barkstone's account in detail: after the remarks on confession to a priest, he described Bull as 'recitynge then ii of the firste articles of our Crede, sainge that [if] he belevyd stedfastlye in God, callinge to God with a sory harte for his offences, God wolde forgive him, sainge the preste his confessor ys a knave'. The evidence above summarized covers fos. 297ᵛ, 298, and 298ᵛ, of the act book, but fos. 299 to 305ᵛ are left blank, perhaps for the entry of the subsequent stages, though the gap is of unprecedented length for this book. The implication that the remainder of the case must ultimately have been entered elsewhere is in fact borne out: turning to another act book headed *Curia Cancellarie* and covering the years 1544–7,[2] we find the case of William Bull *nuper de Dewisburye super heresem*, noted under the date 18 January 1544.[3] Here nothing of substance follows, but on the subsequent 14 March the young man emerged 'from the prisons' of the Archbishop of York. It would be of interest to know exactly how long he had spent in this unhealthy place, for the dates make possible a stay of several months. Whatever the answer, his attitude now paid tribute to the efficiency of the repressive machinery, since he confessed his erroneous opinions, humbly submitted himself and abjured his heresy. The judges thereupon gave order that betwixt this present Friday and the fourth Sunday in Lent he must say seven psalms and the Litany daily; on the fourth Sunday he must be ready in York Minster at the time of the procession and there like a penitent person go before it with

---

[1] 'Sibber sauce' was later metaphorically used by Tudor protestant controversialists to represent the supposedly false garnishings of the Romanist cause. For examples from Olde, Stubbes, and Cartwright see *New Eng. Dict.*, s.v. The *mala dogmata* of 1536 include the saying that holy water was better for sauce than other water, because it was mixed with salt (Dixon, loc. cit.).

[2] R. VII. A.B. 21.

[3] Ibid., fo. 3.

a faggot on his shoulder. On the fifth Sunday he must repeat the performance in the church of Dewsbury.[1]

The remainder of the cases in the Audience act book are scrappily and incompletely entered. It would appear that in 1543 the court was still in combat against heretics opposing the Confessional. On 13 April 1543, the recorded omissions of William Malome of Hampsthwaite[2] included this, while a note[3] upon the examination of Robert Lackenby by Dr. Clyff involves the same offence, and rather more. According to this last fragmentary record, Lackenby said 'that he was a salter and now he is a tawbryter[4] and that he was borne in the towne of Seton besides Hartillpoole'. Furthermore he admitted 'that he was not shriven this v yeres last paste, the cause whie was, he saieth, bicause that he thought that yt was not profitable for his soule. And also he saieth that he did not resave the blissed Sacrament of the aulter this v yeres laste paste, bicause he belevid that yt was not the verie Bodie of Christe, but onelie breade.' After the names of those present at the examination, the entry suddenly ends. It is followed on fo. 320 by a note on John Watson, born in Stockton and now a parishioner of St. Michael's, York. He testified that he was shriven last Lent by the vicar of Bishopthorpe and the previous Lent by the parson of St. Michael's; he admitted that he did not receive the sacrament of the altar last Easter. Again with a mere list of names, the note abruptly terminates. To this picture the act book of 1544–7 adds singularly little, apart from the conclusion of William Bull's case above noted. Amid its 250 large folios, chiefly occupied by cases arising from sexual offences, I note only the story of John Swailes of Selby, who came up on the last day of May 1545 on a charge of failure to receive the sacrament at Easter. He defended himself by saying that this omission did not spring from contempt, but from the fact that he was then travelling without money and for shame dare not ask a strange priest to administer the sacrament to him. We recall here the common theme of anticlerical satires—that priests sold the benefits of the mass—and we wonder whether this was said with offensive intent. On his return to Selby, Swailes's own priest dare not offer it, and so to the present date he had not received. The judges, plainly suspicious, examined him concerning his sacramental beliefs, but he gave the right answers and penitently submitted himself for his negligence. The penances awarded are so exceptionally prolonged and elaborate as to suggest that something more than mere negligence was

---

[1] R. VII. A.B. 21, fo. 11.   [2] R. VII. A.B. 2, fos. 317–317ᵛ.
[3] Ibid., fo. 318.   [4] ? Tow-heckler. I have not met it elsewhere.

still presumed by the court.[1] Performance was duly certified on 12 June 1545.[2]

If it be assumed that these two act books provide year by year a fair sample of offences presented for archiepiscopal correction,[3] it would follow that a relatively notable incidence of prosecutions during the years 1539–43 was succeeded by three years of quiescence. However likely this picture, a more detailed knowledge of the operation and interrelation of the various courts and their records is required before it may be regarded as fully confirmed. A more certain feature of these act books lies in the fact that not one of their heresy cases enjoyed the distinction of a record in the Registers of Archbishops Lee and Holgate. Whatever the reasons which underlay it, the fact should give pause to those in danger of assessing the heresy-jurisdiction of the English Church by reference to episcopal registers alone. Had no act books survived in the diocese for this mid-Tudor period, a most distorted image both of heresy and of its repression would have remained. Consequently, dioceses which have been less fortunate should certainly not claim to possess accurate knowledge of this important phase of their history.

What in general may be said as to the origins and character of popular heresy during the two decades which preceded the death of Henry VIII? They begin with several elaborately documented cases, which, both by their content and their continuity from others early in the century, must be pronounced wholly or almost wholly Lollard. From 1537 a further and larger series presents features more complex. These later offenders were chiefly sacramentarians, though in addition a tendency to refuse auricular confession also attained importance. These two features could in themselves be Lutheran or Zwinglian, as well as Lollard. Nevertheless, the atmosphere of these cases remains Lollard and, given the certain fact that Lollardy had locally survived into the thirties, we are compelled to regard it as still the predominant ingredient of a now admittedly 'mixed' popular heresy. How much evidence at this point does in fact suggest the influence of the continental Reformers and their English disciples like Tyndale and Frith? Significantly but not surprisingly, it occurs in the two educated men: the parish priest Richard Browne and the schoolmaster William Senes. The phraseology of the former on the eucharist suggests Zwinglian influences. As for Senes, he presents an admirable specimen of the composite heresy. While the Earl of Shrewsbury was probably speaking with

[1] R. VII. A.B. 21, fos. 39ᵛ–40.   [2] Ibid., fo. 43.
[3] On the problem of 'coverage' by surviving act books, see *infra*, pp. 241–2.

no great precision when he called the friend of Senes a 'loulere', Senes himself did actually exhibit several specifically Lollard emphases. On the other hand, he had read Frith and may have held the Lutheran doctrine of Consubstantiation. Yet with these exceptions, the demonstrable role of the new continental movements remains upon these lower levels of society a very modest one. Things were otherwise in the more elevated regions which we are now about to visit.

III

SIR FRANCIS BIGOD AND HIS CIRCLE

I. *The Inheritance*

FOR a few days in January 1537 the rebel Sir Francis Bigod[1] stood at the centre of the historical stage. In the summer, still some months before his thirtieth birthday, he paid for his adventure by dying the ugly death of a traitor. Historians have concentrated unduly upon this melodramatic climax, neglecting the more significant and almost equally sensational episodes of Bigod's earlier life and thought. That he trod the scaffold as a sequel to the reactionary Pilgrimage of Grace might justifiably be taken as one of history's freaks, since his true place is among the advanced Protestant thinkers and agents of the English Reformation. In this fact must lie the chief theme of any biographical essay, yet by no feat could it be isolated from several other themes: the financial misfortunes of a great landed family; the problems of monasticism and neo-feudalism in the Tudor north; the vagaries of a passionate temperament and a radical, inquiring mind. If from time to time we now embark on matters peripheral to the Reformation-theme, we thereby experience a rare and salutary corrective, since, all too often, historians treat the early Reformers as if they lived in a world of religious conflict remote from workaday experience. A student of Tudor religion and society becomes only too aware of the harsh unrealities which spring from this process of abstraction, but sometimes his materials furnish no means of escape. All too often the selective writing of Foxe or the terse legal formulae of ecclesiastical act books must involve him in falsities of emphasis. In the case of Sir Francis Bigod the situation seems appreciably happier. Though some unsolved problems remain, he must rank among the best-documented Englishmen of his status and period. Innumerable papers yield particulars of his family and personal life, while his own letters to Thomas Cromwell prove unusually self-revealing in a still somewhat inarticulate age. His story makes us healthily aware of the indeterminate frontiers of Reformation-history; we find here that interlocking of complex spiritual and secular matters so characteristic of sixteenth-century

---

[1] The spellings are numerous: Bygod, Bigot, Bygott, even Bygate. I use Bigod, since it is the form affected by Sir Francis in his personal signature.

society. For once, granted a minimum of skill and insight, we can come near to writing about life itself.

Loyalty towards a family tradition played so large a part in the outlook of Sir Francis that we are compelled to begin with a brief glance at the history of the Bigods of Settrington.[1] At the time of his birth they represented far more than a mere average sample of the Yorkshire gentry. Descended from two of the great baronial lines of medieval England, they had come to enjoy estates almost befitting a family of the peerage. The house may be thought to have taken its effective origins in 1302, when Roger Bygod, the last of the old Earls of Norfolk, granted his brother Sir John the manor and advowson of Settrington. From Sir John's eldest son sprang the Bigods of Stockton; from a younger son the line of Settrington, its lands initially by no means commensurate with its high lineage. A century later its fortunes were enormously enhanced by marriage. At some time before 1410 the great-grandson and namesake of the original Sir John married Constance, daughter of the seventh and penultimate Peter de Mauley. Readers familiar with the personalities of the early thirteenth century will recall the origins of this other remarkable line.[2] The first Peter, Poitevin adventurer and evil counsellor of King John, was later credited by Hemingburgh with the murder of Prince Arthur. On the other hand, he died on crusade after giving benefactions to Meaux Abbey, building Mulgrave Castle near Whitby, and acquiring a formidable array of manors in various parts of Yorkshire.[3] In 1415 the long succession of Peters came to an end, leaving the lady Constance Bigod as coheiress of her deceased brother; on her eventual death in 1451 her share of the Mauley lands went to her son Sir Ralph Bigod. They included not merely Mulgrave Castle with the neighbouring manors of Hinderwell and Seaton, but a more considerable group of lands down in the East Riding near Settrington itself, together with a few scattered properties in Lincolnshire and the West Riding. By this coup the modestly endowed descendants of the Earls of Norfolk were immediately placed among the most substantial landed families in Yorkshire. Yet, as so often in this tragic age, eminence and personal misfortune came hand-in-hand. Sir Ralph had enjoyed his mother's lands for scarcely ten years when he was killed, along with his young heir Sir John, on the bloody

[1] A full account of the earlier generations and the less-known branches of the family by C. Moor is in *T.A.J.* xxxii. 172 seqq.

[2] For a brief account of the successive barons see J. W. Clay, *Extinct and Dormant Peerages of the Northern Counties of England*, pp. 132–4.

[3] *D.N.B.*, s.v. Mauley.

field of Towton. His grandson, another Sir Ralph, succeeded at the age
of four and lived a relatively long and prosperous life, long enough
indeed to see the double tragedy of his infancy re-echoed in another.
From 1483 onwards we know much of the biography of this grandfather of our present subject Sir Francis: holding numerous offices under
both Richard III and Henry VII, he stood among the most eminent
Yorkshiremen of his day.[1] His example came above all others before the
eyes of relatives giving counsel to the young Sir Francis.[2]

In the sphere of private life Sir Ralph's activities were no less notable.
He married three times, and besides five legitimate children, probably
by his first wife Margaret Constable,[3] had two acknowledged bastards,
Arthur and John Bigod, whom by his will he ordered to be bound
prentices in London.[4] Of his heir Sir John, the father of Sir Francis,
relatively little is known. About 1491 this young man married Joan,
daughter of Sir James Strangeways of Whorlton. They resided at the
manor of Seaton in Hinderwell parish, a house which seems from time
to time to have been used by younger sons or by the heir during his
father's lifetime.[5] There Francis and his brother Ralph were both born,
the former on 4 October 1507.[6] They can have known little of their
father, since he was killed, together with their uncle Ralph, in the
Scottish War—perhaps at Flodden itself, where Sir John's own uncle
Sir Marmaduke Constable was a commander. This catastrophe left
little Francis heir to his grandfather Sir Ralph, whose will, dated
22 January 1515, was proved on the following 7 April. As so often with
wills, it has no occasion to mention the heir to the testator's lands,
though it leaves Ralph, the younger grandson, £5 per annum for life.
On 21 June Sir Ralph's Inquisition post mortem was taken at York[7] and,
seen together with a subsidiary inquisition of 7 August 1529,[8] it gives
a detailed account of the ample estates to which Francis, aged seven in
1515, became heir.[9] The lands descending from Roger, Earl of Norfolk,

[1] Cf. for details *T.A.J.* xxxii. 195–8.   [2] *Infra*, p. 60.
[3] One of the seven daughters of Sir Robt. Constable of Flamborough; his third
wife Agnes, daughter of Constable of Dromonby, became second wife of Sir Ralph
Eure, who had licence to marry her 18 Jan. 1516.
[4] *Test. Ebor.* v. 56.
[5] Seaton was one of the former Mauley manors (*V.C.H. Yorks., North Riding*, ii.
369–70).
[6] Cf. the Inquisition of 23 Sept. 1529, cited *infra*. After the execution of Sir
Francis, his brother Ralph obviously lived there. Cf. the details of his will cited in
T.A.J. xxxii. 200.
[7] P.R.O., E. 150/1227, no. 11.   [8] P.R.O., C. 142/50, no. 72.
[9] To these sources must be added the accounts made after the attainder of Sir
Francis (E. 315/288, fos. 31 seqq.) mentioned *infra*. These list the following: Settring-

were Settrington manor and advowson, together with messuages and lands at Norton and Sutton near Malton, in Malton itself, in Rillington nearby, and at Weston near Otley. Those from the Mauleys consisted, besides Mulgrave and Seaton in the north, of the manors of Birdsall, Bainton, Hunmanby, Lockington, Duggleby, Westow, Wheatley, Ewerby (Lincs.), and Healaugh in Swaledale.[1] We can scarcely doubt that from his early days Mulgrave Castle with its romantic situation and its strange legends of the giant Wade and his wife Bell must have made a profound impression upon the young heir. A few years later Leland wrote that 'it stondith on apon a craggy hille: and on ech side of it is an hille far higher then that whereon the castelle stondith on. The north hille on the toppe of it hath certen stones communely called Wadde's Grave, whom the people there say to have bene a gigant and owner of Mougreve.'[2] While, however, we hear much of Bigod in his later years at Mulgrave and at Whitby nearby, the chief family seat was thirty miles to the south, at Settrington in that charming and still unspoiled countryside between the north-western corner of the Wolds and the winding course of the Derwent. Amongst the Augmentations Books at the Public Record Office[3] are preserved accounts of the Bigod estates as they stood shortly after the attainder of Sir Francis, and these afford a striking picture of the economic realities behind the impressive but somewhat misleading list of the family lands. In round figures, out of a gross annual income of about £385, no less than £354 came from only five manors: Settrington (£139); Bainton (£40); Birdsall (£35); Healaugh ('Swadall', £49); and Mulgrave (£90). No one of the other ten properties listed brought in more than £8. The general impression arising from this rent roll is one of a 'traditional' landlordism making little effort to exploit either the tenants or the mineral resources of the land.[4] The acres and the income derived predominantly from the East Riding, from the triangle between Lockington in the south, Westow in

ton, Birdsall, Bainton, Hunmanby, Healaugh ('Swadall'), Mulgrave, Westow, Norton, New Malton and Grimston, Duggleby, Rillington, Sutton, Wheatley, Weston, Ewerby.
[1] On this manor in Grinton parish see *V.C.H. Yorks., North Riding*, i. 241.
[2] *Leland's Itinerary in England*, ed. L. T. Smith, i. 59. For some other references to the Wade myth see *V.C.H. Yorks., North Riding*, ii. 390.
[3] P.R.O., E. 315/288, fos. 31 seqq. This general account is followed (fo. 75) by a more detailed account of Settrington.
[4] By far the greater part of the receipts is in fixed rents from the free and customary tenants. A nil entry occurs opposite the slate quarry at Westow (fo. 37ᵛ); from the fishing at Runswick and Staithes (fo. 36ᵛ) 112s. was forthcoming; the mill at Settrington (fo. 31ᵛ) yielded £6. 13s. 4d.; otherwise the income from mills, sale of timber, and other non-rental sources was very small.

the west, and Hunmanby in the east. Significantly enough, Sir Francis was to raise a rebellion in this area, while, on the other hand, his territorial influence was negligible in the immediate vicinities of the two objectives he tried but failed to capture: Hull and Scarborough.

Towards this ultimate catastrophe Bigod was drawn by many chains of circumstance reaching back through the years. One of them began when, on 9 May 1515, his wardship was granted to Cardinal Wolsey.[1] Many men thought him fortunate when he subsequently entered the prelate's household, since it afforded training and opportunities seldom to be found outside the court of a prince. Its total numbers probably approached a thousand persons[2] and, in Strype's words, it resembled a university 'for those many accomplished men in all kinds of knowledge and good learning that were his domestics'.[3] 'O domum illam augustam', exclaimed Erasmus, 'ac felicem! O vere splendidum cardinalem, qui tales viros habet in consiliis, cujus mensa talibus luminibus cingitur.' Though it inevitably contained many churchmen, its emphasis lay on service to the State rather than to the Church: Sampson, Pace, and Tunstall all achieved ambassadorial rank, the first despite his oft-repeated preference for academic study.[4] In short, young Bigod entered not merely the 'nursery for the court', but the training-school for the higher officialdom of later years. While here, he must have made the acquaintance of Thomas Cromwell, who became during the later years of his tutelage a key-figure in the suite of the cardinal. Judging from his letters of subsequent years, one would suppose their early relationship to have been intimate. The easy ascendancy which Cromwell came to exercise upon Bigod had a quality beyond the control of a powerful minister over a subordinate. It was reciprocated on the side of the young man by a naïve frankness equally difficult to explain save on the basis of a long-standing friendship. And if it might seem excessive to ascribe to Cromwell a genius for friendship, he certainly possessed a wonderful capacity for gaining, and for keeping, the personal confidence of all sorts and conditions of men.

To Cromwell we cannot reasonably ascribe Bigod's early progress toward Protestantism, for there were far more distinctively Protestant influences at work not far from Wolsey's entourage and their extension to the young man during his formative years can scarcely be doubted. The ward of the cardinal did not spend all his time in the London

[1] *L. & P.* ii. 432, 1360, 1868.   [2] A. F. Pollard, *Wolsey*, pp. 326–7.
[3] *Ecclesiastical Memorials* (edn. 1822), vol. i, pt. i, p. 194.
[4] W. G. Zeefeld, *Foundations of Tudor Policy*, pp. 19 seqq.

household, but is known to have been sent to study in the University of Oxford. The present writer has failed to establish the precise dates of this period; the few heirs to great estates who received such advantages did not normally take degrees, and Bigod proved no exception.[1] He may well have been attached to Cardinal College soon after its foundation in 1525; even if not officially a member, he can scarcely have omitted to form close connexions with his guardian's great foundation during its first two or three years. It was then speedily achieving notoriety as a focus of the new religious opinions, for Clark, Cox, Frith, and Taverner were transferred thither in 1526 from Cambridge, where they had been nurtured at the White Horse Tavern, the cradle of English Lutheranism.[2] At this early date these young men were probably not deeply imbued with the new faith,[3] but they were soon carried forward by that 'busy Lutheran' Thomas Garret (alias Gerard, or Garrarde), the known facts of whose life place him amongst the earliest and most effective Lutheran propagandists in England. His relevance to our theme does not lie merely in the possibility of his Oxford connexion with Bigod, but in the certain fact that before many years had passed he had become Bigod's personal chaplain and chief agent in his Reforming activities in Yorkshire. Here, it would seem, we have the seminal mind which created the first circle of Oxford Lutherans and, either then or soon afterwards, placed Francis Bigod himself on the side of the Reformation. Garret's early career was spent in eager study in both the universities. Matriculating at Corpus Christi in August 1517, he took his Oxford B.A. the following year and his M.A. in 1524.[4] At some stage of his Oxford career he was resident at Cardinal College, but in the middle twenties he worked mainly in Cambridge, where he proceeded B.D. and ultimately D.D. He is mentioned by Erasmus as a bookseller in December 1525; at this date he was doubtless already selling books with a distinct theological bias, though, like other early Reformers, he would combine financial profit with idealism. The following year he became curate for his friend Forman, rector of All Hallows, Honey Lane, but, according to Foxe, he also visited Oxford to sell Biblical commentaries and Tyndale's translation of the New Testament.[5] Subsequently he passed through Reading and sold the prior

---

[1] Wood, *Athenae Oxonienses*, ed. Bliss, i, c. 101.
[2] References in Zeeveld, op. cit., pp. 26–29.
[3] Cf. Dr. London's letters printed in Foxe, v, app. vi.
[4] References, where not otherwise given, will be found in *D.N.B.*, s.v. Gerard, Thomas, where the Spanish chronicle is given unjustifiable prominence.
[5] Foxe, v. 421.

sixty books, yet by this time he was being hunted by ecclesiastical authority. His narrow escapes in Oxford and his final capture were afterwards movingly related to Foxe by one of his many undergraduate friends at Cardinal College, Anthony Dalaber, who there furnished him with one of his disguises. Garret postponed martyrdom for many years by a recantation before the Bishops of London, Lincoln, and Bath and Wells. The charges were numerous and place him amongst the most advanced Lutherans. He had distributed heretical books in Oxford and Cambridge, maintained salvation by faith alone, denounced pardons, ecclesiastical laws, bishops, fast-days, and saint-worship. He had also asserted a dogma which in later years appealed strongly to his patron Bigod: that every man may preach the word of God, and that no law to the contrary can be made.[1] The substantial truth of Foxe's account finds ample confirmation in two long letters, now in the Public Records. They were written on 24 and 26 February 1528 by Dr. London, Warden of New College, Oxford, to the Bishop of Lincoln;[2] they describe in amusing detail the recent activities of Garret among the young men of Cardinal College and include a most impressive bibliography of Lutheran and other Protestant works recommended to them by the enterprising colporteur. Characteristically enough, Dr. London dismissed Garret as a mere interloper from Cambridge: 'Wold Godd my Lorde is Grace (Wolsey) hadd never be motyonyd to call hym nor any other Cambridge man unto hys most towardly colledge.' Surrounded by powerful enemies, Garret should have counted himself fortunate to gain Wolsey's pardon and patronage. His subsequent and proved connexions with Bigod will shortly attract our attention. While their personal contact in the Cardinal College circle does not come into the field of documented fact, it may be regarded as something beyond a mere interesting possibility.

The residence of Bigod at Oxford gave him more than a contact with the first English Lutherans. It formed part of an education far more thorough than that attained by the vast majority of contemporary landed proprietors. He emerged with a scholarly grasp of Latin, strong legal and theological interests, and above all a mastery of lucid and forceful English. This latter characteristic will scarcely suggest itself with sufficient emphasis except to readers familiar with the fumbling incoherencies which emanated from the average semi-educated gentry and middle classes in the reign of Henry VIII. Apart from the contro-

[1] Ibid. v. 428.
[2] L. & P. iv (2), 3962, 3968; both are fully printed in Foxe, v, app. vi.

versial writings soon to be examined, Bigod is said by Bale, who had
good sources of information,[1] to have translated certain Latin tractates
into the English tongue.[2] Whether, like so many of his compeers, he
also studied at the Inns of Court, is unknown to the present writer.
The contemporary records of admission to this 'third university' of the
realm remain incomplete and cannot be used by way of disproof. A
period of systematic legal study constituted the normal higher education for a man in his position; in Bigod's case it would help to account
for some of his most pronounced intellectual traits.

That the years in Wolsey's household and at Oxford caused Bigod to
diverge mentally from his native background will become all too clear:
this divergence and disharmony should be numbered among the basic
ingredients of his personal tragedy. The light in which his people at
home in Yorkshire viewed his service with the cardinal is exemplified
in a letter of June 1527 by William Constable the elder, 'To my right
worshipful nephew, Francis Bygod, esquire and servant unto my Lord
Cardinal's grace.' Constable rejoices to see his young relative in my
Lord's favour, as appears by his learning and diligent service. He
proceeds, however, to show that something more tangible than intellectual and social rewards lay at the end of the road. Uppermost in the
uncle's mind were not merely offices and emoluments under the Crown,
but also fees, fat stewardships, and power on the councils of the northern
noble households, as yet unbroken and unsubjugated by the heavy
hand of the king. As a result of your learning and the cardinal's favour,
writes Constable, 'I doubt not but ye may attain unto all such foreign
offices as your grandsire (and) your father had afore you, and mo too.'[3]
He wishes that Bigod had by patent of the Lord Percy the stewardships of both the Percy lands and those of the Earl of Cumberland
within the East Riding; Constable also proposes to get for them both
from Sir Edward Nevile a joint patent for the stewardships of Great
Driffield, of the Graystoke lands in the East Riding, of Scampston from
Lord Latimer, of Sledmere and other lands.[4]

This revealing letter seems to presage the opening of Bigod's public
career, for it is probable that he left Wolsey's service soon afterwards

---

[1] *Infra*, p. 106.

[2] J. Bale, *Index Britanniae Scriptorum*, ed. R. L. Poole, p. 72.

[3] *Inter alia* Sir Ralph had been commissioner of the peace in the East and North
Ridings; commissioner of array in Kent and the East Riding; collector of the sub-
sidy in the North Riding; knight of the body and master of the King's Ordnance to
Richard III; and constable of Sheriff Hutton to Henry VII (*Y.A.J.* xxxii. 196).

[4] *L. & P.* iv. 3146.

and rapidly became caught up in this insidious web of Yorkshire affinities. In early Tudor England the struggle for place, power, and money seems as unremitting as that amongst the Elizabethans. In the north the prizes still lay, however, among the tottering ruins of the feudal and monastic systems; as yet they were to be found elsewhere than among the false glamour and the awful disenchantments of the royal court.

At the end of 1528 or early in the following year Francis married Katharine, daughter of the first Lord Conyers of Hornby. Wolsey's register at York has a dispensation granted on 4 November 1528 to Francis Bigod *armiger* and Katharine Conyers *generosa*, allowing them to marry, although related in the third and fourth degrees of consanguinity.[1] This relationship with his wife's family seems to have lain— though here the pedigrees are not conspicuously accurate or complete —on the side of the young heir's mother, the house of Strangeways.[2] On 23 September 1529 an Inquisition for proof of age was held at York Castle, where it was shown that Francis was born at 'Seton How' on 4 October 1507 and was therefore now of full age.[3] He had livery of his grandfather's lands by patent of 21 December 1529[4] and was soon afterwards knighted. In 1532 his name appears on the Commission of the Peace for the East Riding.[5] To complete this fair prospect, his marriage proved immediately fruitful; his daughter Dorothy appears already in Tonge's Visitation dated 1530.[6] Shortly afterwards came a son Ralph, for whom, in the manner of the time, an advantageous match was planned in infancy. In October 1534 Sir Francis made an indenture with Lord Latimer agreeing on a marriage between Ralph, then aged three, and Latimer's daughter Margaret.[7] The two Bigod manors in Swaledale, worth £50 per annum, were given into the hands of Mr. Parr[8] and other feoffees, Latimer to draw £25 of this income and Bigod's mother and Lady Eure[9] the other £25. When Ralph reached the age of twenty-one, these manors were to pass to him and his wife. The

[1] Reg. Wolsey, fo. 132ᵛ.

[2] The first Lord Conyers and Sir James Strangeways were both grandsons of William Neville, Lord Fauconberg (*Glover's Visitation of Torks.*, ed. J. Foster, pp. 71, 202–3).

[3] P.R.O., C. 142/50, no. 115.   [4] *L. & P.* iv. 6135 (21).

[5] *L. & P.* v. 838 (30); 1694 (ii).   [6] *Surtees Soc.* xli. 67.

[7] Or between any other son and heir of Bigod and any other daughter of Latimer, or any other woman nominated by him, so long as it was without disparagement to the Bigods.

[8] Probably Sir William Parr, later Marquis of Northampton, Latimer's brother-in-law.

[9] 'Lady Malyvery and lady Ewer.' His mother's second marriage had been to Sir Francis Mauleverer. Lady Eure was the third wife of Sir Ralph (*supra*, p. 55, n. 3).

feoffees also received an estate of £10 a year to the use of Sir Francis for life, but with remainder to Ralph. After the deaths of Sir Francis, his wife, mother, and Lady Eure, all the rest of his manors should go also to Ralph, leaving Sir Francis free to will properties only to the value of £10 a year. For this marriage and the accompanying covenants, Latimer paid Bigod 700 marks.[1] These already involved provisions were soon further complicated by other transactions which will demand notice. Meanwhile Latimer undoubtedly handed over the 700 marks and even this large sum seems to have made little impression on the debts which by that time crowded upon the unfortunate knight of Settrington. The match itself was nevertheless as good as he could have reasonably hoped to arrange.

John Nevill, third Baron Latimer, was descended from a brother of Richard, Earl of Salisbury; by inheritance and grant from the Crown he held very extensive lands in Yorkshire and Worcestershire.[2] He lived chiefly at Snape near Bedale, where his magnificent castle, now partly in ruin and partly reconstructed in the last century, powerfully evokes the last age of northern feudalism.[3] It appears likely that he or members of his household became well disposed to the New Learning. His connexions and those of his brother with the Bigods are far from the only clues pointing in this direction. Two or three years earlier he had married Katharine Parr, a young lady highly educated along humanistic lines and subsequently, as Queen of England, endangered by her associations with Protestants.[4] A third clue is encountered in a letter of Robert Plumpton, professing simultaneously his zeal for Tyndale and the English Bible and his anxiety to enter the household of Lord Latimer.[5] Nevill's will[6] is admittedly conventional in its religious provisions, but this proves little, since it was written at the height of the Six Articles persecution by a man who had been in grave danger for his own complicity in the Pilgrimage of Grace,[7] and who had every reason

[1] This and the later transactions are summarized in 'The shorter abstract of the bargaines and covenantes made betwene the lorde Latymer and Sir Fraunces Bygod' in P.R.O., S.P. 1/86, fos. 126–8. On this document cf. *infra*, p. 68.

[2] *D.N.B.*, s.v. Neville, John.

[3] *V.C.H. Yorks., North Riding*, i. 348–50, describes it. Cf. Whitaker, *Richmondshire*, ii. 90.

[4] She showed lively sympathy with Coverdale, Udall, and other Reformers; Foxe (v. 553 seqq.) tells the story of Gardiner's dangerous attack upon her: it may lose nothing for his telling, but is unlikely to be a mere fabrication.

[5] *The Plumpton Correspondence* (Camden Soc. iv), pp. 231–2. On Robert Plumpton cf. *infra*, pp. 131 seqq.

[6] *Test. Ebor.* vi. 159 seqq., dated 12 Sept. 1542 and proved 22 May 1543.

[7] Cf. Dodds, op. cit. ii. 184–6.

for avoiding further trouble with the Crown. With equal reason, he was bound to repudiate the proposed match upon the attainder of Sir Francis Bigod.[1]

Lord Latimer was a neighbour in Richmondshire of the Conyers family, and it seems likely that Bigod, who later complained that he inherited no suitable house, spent a good deal of his early married life with his father-in-law at Hornby Castle, the picturesque Tudor courtyard of which survived until recent years.[2] An interesting glimpse of this phase is afforded by Edward Leghton, one of Cromwell's agents, who toured the north in 1533 in order to press various claims of the Crown, the finances of which had now come under business management as shrewd and forceful as that of Henry VII himself. On 7 May Leghton wrote from York recounting calls paid two days earlier on Lord Scrope of Bolton at St. Agatha's Abbey, and on Lord Conyers at Hornby. He had found the latter unable to speak with him, being in bed with the gout. He transmitted the king's letter by a servant and Conyers then sent out to him 'a young gentleman named Bigot, who was in the cardinal's service'. The dispute concerned the patronage of the parsonage of Rudby, which the Crown claimed had been impropriated to the late Cardinal's College in Oxford, now fallen into the king's hands. On behalf of his father-in-law Bigod argued that such impropriation had never been lawfully made and that 'if tried by law it would be found so'. Notwithstanding any grant made by him, Conyers considered himself still patron of the living and argued moreover that he owed no such money to the college as the king now ordered him to pay.[3] In view of the attacks upon impropriations soon to be made by Sir Francis, he must have found such a family negotiation highly congenial.

At this stage the documents introduce some darker aspects of the Bigod inheritance, for in the summer of 1533 occurs the first of a series of letters alluding to the financial straits of the young heir. Sir Francis himself wrote later that his troubles sprang from the impoverished and indebted condition of the estates at the time of his entry. Though we can draw no very detailed picture of the family finances, his statements accord not only with the known facts but with a common contemporary pattern. The inheritance of broad acres did not necessarily mean the acquisition of disposable wealth. The very heavy payments made

[1] Cf. infra, p. 68.
[2] Cf. Whitaker, Richmondshire, ii. 44; J. E. Morris, The North Riding, p. 192.
[3] L. & P. vi. 453.

by an heir to the Crown for the livery of his lands might alone embarrass him for some years. For example, Bigod's own friend Lord Latimer had livery on 17 March 1531, but in April 1534 he was still asking Cromwell to excuse him from expensive attendances in Parliament, since he had neither paid the king all that was due for livery of his lands nor yet disbursed all the sums laid down in the wills of his father and mother-in-law.[1] Moreover, the bidders who competed so keenly to receive wardships from the Crown did so for reasons the very reverse of philanthropic;[2] by granting long leases and other privileges in return for appropriate considerations, and by trading in the marriages of wards, they not only recouped at the expense of their charges but strove to make a handsome profit. It should be frankly recognized that this exploitation arose in large part from the rapacity of the Crown, which, whatever conventional historians may say, was by no means the unequivocal friend of the gentry, and was fortunate to find in the monastic lands a timely means of recompensing many of this justly aggrieved class. The extent to which Wolsey's agents impaired the Bigod estates remains obscure. So too does the impact of his grandfather's debts upon the position of Sir Francis, though it is clear that in 1515 some of the estates were already heavily mortgaged.[3] Nevertheless, these three factors are all likely to have been operative and without assuming, as did Froude,[4] that Sir Francis was a spendthrift, we can easily account for his difficulties along other lines. How far did he increase his burdens by architectural extravagance? Should his complaint that he failed to inherit an adequate house be interpreted as an excuse for building while still in debt?

Sir Ralph and Sir Francis are recorded as building a chapel in their manor-house of Healaugh Park.[5] Considerable evidences of mid-Tudor or Elizabethan reconstruction are visible at Mulgrave,[6] but these could easily date from the long occupation of the castle by Bigod's widow Katharine and by their heirs the Radcliffes. At York Sir Francis allowed the family residence and almshouse to fall into ruin.[7] At Settrington the large Georgian manor-house has obliterated all traces of its predecessors, though at the church nearby the conjunction of Bigod and Conyers

[1] *L. & P.* vii. 438.
[2] On competition for wardships and other relevant topics see H. E. Bell, *An Introduction to the History and Records of the Court of Wards and Liveries*, ch. vi.
[3] Cf. the complicated transactions alluded to in Sir Ralph's will (*Test. Ebor.* v. 56).
[4] *Hist. of England*, iii. 8.
[5] *V.C.H. Yorks., North Riding*, i. 244.
[6] Details in ibid. ii. 391–3.   [7] *Infra*, p. 79.

arms on the wall of the south aisle may conceivably indicate an extensive reconstruction at the expense of Sir Francis.[1] The same suggestive
apposition of Bigod and Conyers shields occurs on the Perpendicular
tower of Wintringham church.[2] Nevertheless, had Bigod been a great
builder, we should probably know much more about his activities than
this. On the other hand, he spent much time in London and in travelling on public and private business. He seems to have maintained a
fairly numerous and sometimes unruly household; he certainly supported various Reforming divines as his chaplains. As already observed,
he does not appear to have been among the few Yorkshire gentry who
at this date were rationalizing their estate-management; his accounts
make it hard to believe that he was extracting the maximum yield
from his numerous manors. The most obviously self-inflicted part of his
burden arose from an exaggerated concern for his heirs and for the
prestige of his house. For years this sense of duty forbade him to
purchase peace of mind by the obvious method: an outright sale of land
to pay off the load of debts.

With these general factors in mind, we may rapidly review the relevant correspondence. On 3 August 1534 the London financier Ralph
Latham writes to Thomas Cromwell and acknowledges the minister's
letter desiring him to 'forbear Mr. Bygott till Martinmas'. But whereas
Bigod had told Cromwell his day of payment was at Lammas, the
money was actually due at Midsummer last. 'Such poor men as I',
Latham continues, 'must occupy their money, for we have no other
land to live upon.' This protest made, he nevertheless agrees to follow
Cromwell's pleasure and give Bigod more time.[3] On 31 January 1535
Sir Francis himself asks Cromwell's help to pay his debts. Lord Latimer
would release him of so much land as must be sold to discharge
them,

yet for all that, sith my abidyng with my wife and childern, my harte
doith even blede in my belye to parte with any of it for ever from my
saide childern; besides the great obloquy shall therof go in my cuntre,
and even so Godes worde and his trewght, wiche for my parte is sum-
thyng plantid and sette owte, shulde then be slanderowsly reportid of, so

[1] J. E. Morris, *The East Riding*, p. 303. I take the Conyers arms on trust from earlier
writers, but failed to descry them on a recent visit.
[2] Ibid., p. 354. Here the family of Eure, also related to the Bigods, is also represented: the conjuncture of the three might well suggest a date in the sixteenth
century. Nevertheless these shields have been subject to alterations in even more
recent times; they do not necessarily date the structure around them.
[3] *L. & P.* vi. 935.

grosse and weake is the jugemente of many, and rather then I shall be
thoccation of this, I myche soner desier to be owte of this worlde, *verita-
tem loquor in Christo et non mentior.*

He then begs Cromwell to procure the king's compassion to lend him
£1,200, for which he would give in pledge a lordship worth £140 a year
and pay £100 annually into the king's Treasury at St. Mary's, York. To
reward Cromwell for his pains in this matter, Bigod offers him land of
£20 a year to him and his heirs for forty years. 'Thus may yower
maistership', he adds rather inappropriately, 'at the Lorde's blessed
hande gett you immortall rewarde, and of all my fryndes and my selfe
perpetuall servise and prayer.' He does not presume to ask these
favours from the king for his own sake or services, but rather on
account of the service of his father, 'wiche with his brother boith to
gethers shedde ther bloude and lost ther lifes for his [i.e. the king's]
sake in his servise agenste the Scottes, I then beyng a yonglyng'. He is
more bold to ask, since it is known to all his country that he came 'so
barely' to his land, 'havyng no thyng, nather good howse nor any thyng
therto belongyng', and thus having 'greate occasions to be in debte'.
If Cromwell consents, people will imagine he has laid down much
money for Bigod and is content to recover it, out of mere benevolence,
over a long period. Serjeant Chamley,[1] who knows of a previous deal
proposed by Bigod, can show Cromwell the covenant of marriage of
Bigod's son, whereby the state of the family lands may be seen. Meanwhile the writer is at Cambridge and dare not come to London 'so
fearde I am for maister Gressam and maister Lodge'. If he were out of
debt, he would meddle no more with the world, but occupy himself
with what he has more knowledge of, and more delight in. He ends in
the neat Italic hand, to which he invariably changes when breaking
into Latin: 'Interim valebis in christo honorande vir. Ex edibus meis
Januarii ultimo, Franciscus Bigodus tibi deditissimus.'[2] The reference to
his creditors obviously includes that famous lender of money to the
aristocracy, Richard Gresham, who himself rose to a knighthood two
years later.[3]

By 20 May the debtor's pleas had become even more abject. He was

---

[1] Roger Cholmley, serjeant-at-law; later Recorder, M.P. for London, knighted
1537, and Chief Justice of the King's Bench 1552 (*D.N.B.*). He was of the Whitby
family and, like Robert Aske, no doubt did much business for fellow Yorkshiremen
in London. Cf. *Glover's Visitation of Yorks.*, ed. J. Foster, pp. 219–20 and *infra*, p. 67.

[2] P.R.O., S.P. 1/89, p. 110. The summary in *L. & P.* viii. 135 misses several
interesting points.

[3] *D.N.B.* s.v. Gresham, Richard.

then actually in London, but explained to Cromwell that he was writing instead of calling personally, because he had not yet such money as he owed Cromwell. He was never so ashamed of anything, and unless Cromwell would wink at his 'lewdness' he would count himself utterly cast away. Since his wife had not purveyed him the money she had expected to bring, he himself was riding home post-haste to procure it, and Cromwell should certainly have it soon after Pentecost, when Bigod would receive his rents. He concludes by reminding Cromwell of the text 'Si peccaverit in te frater tuus septies in die . . . .'[1] The succeeding months brought no financial mitigation. On 7 January 1536 Bigod, writing from Whitby, begged Cromwell to 'stay maister Gressam that he take no prossesse agaynste me this terme or [ere] I cume my selfe, and likewise maister Richard Lodge dwellyng at Sancte Anthonies, to whome this berer shal convey yower letter of requeste if it so please yow'. At his coming he trusted to content all of them justly before Cromwell.[2]

While his chief debts were doubtless owing to these city financiers, there are at least three references to Bigod's loans from Cromwell himself, money-lending being among the secretary's long-established pursuits. Amongst the latter's remembrances, one of the debt-lists includes 'Sir Francis Bygod, 50 l.'[3] That the young knight also owed money to the abbot of Whitby will also become apparent.

In his last letter upon this theme, written on 3 July 1536, only a few weeks before the Pilgrimage of Grace, he refers Cromwell to his agent 'Chamley' and to 'maister Recorder' for particulars of his affairs. Court proceedings—possibly those earlier threatened by Gresham and Lodge —had clearly been initiated; the debtor was by now resigned to selling land and desperate to achieve a settlement. The creditors, sure of their prey, negotiated with maddening deliberation. 'My fryndes, nay rather my foes, have dreven me from poste to piller, pretendyn a diligence to conclude with me even whiles yesterday at after none and then playnely tolde me it coulde not now this terme, where as I have all redy syngned [sic] articles to have agreid.' What they wanted, he continued, was to get his land. Nothing grieved him more than the suggestion that his misfortunes sprang from his new-fangled religious beliefs. He had in fact been told: 'Men thynketh ye cowlde never do better; ye can not thrife bycawse ye keape theis new opynyons.' Nothing could be less

---

[1] P.R.O., S.P. 1/92, p. 193; cf. *L. & P.* viii. 735.
[2] P.R.O., S.P. 1/101, p. 39.
[3] *L. & P.* x. 871; cf. ibid. xi. 503.

true. Much of the matter came only upon his 'bare enteryng' to his land. Admitting that Cromwell had done more for him than any other man, he addresses to the minister another emotional plea for further help, even if this amounted to no more than a comforting letter.[1] Whether any substantial advances toward a settlement were achieved between this effusion and the outbreak of the Pilgrimage remains doubtful. Such unparticularized sales of land may relate in part to the further agreements made by Bigod and Lord Latimer after the marriage-contract. In the account left by Latimer these new 'bargains, sales and leases' are assigned no specific dates, though they must all have taken place between October 1534 and the end of 1536. Latimer began by purchasing part of Settrington manor to the annual value of £40 at a price of £600, of which he had paid off only £400 by the time of Bigod's fall early in 1537. Next, Bigod leased the residue of Settrington manor to Latimer for twelve years at £80 a year. Of this same land, Bigod then actually sold £20 worth, annual value, to Sir William Sidney and subsequently another £13 worth to the same buyer. Sidney proceeded to resell both these parcels to Latimer, who had already been leasing them. On the attainder of Sir Francis, Latimer thus found himself with an enormous stake in the forfeited Bigod estates. Fearful of losing his rights, he reported the whole complicated story to the king, estimating his total payments for the marriage and the lands at £1,610. 3s. 4d.[2] This account he accompanied by a petition[3] pointing out that, since he could not 'have the effect of the said mariage according to the said covenantes', he was entitled to the Swaledale manors. Latimer then acknowledged that he owed the king the unpaid residue of the £600 which he had been paying Bigod for the Settrington lands, a passage which dates the composition of this group of documents after the attainder of Bigod in 1537 and not in the year 1534, where they were placed by the editor of the Letters and Papers of Henry VIII.[4] The further dealings of Latimer with the Crown lie outside our subject, but the foregoing relations between the two Yorkshire families afford a vivid picture of the complex structures of debt and land-investment characteristic of their class in Tudor times.

The letter of July 1536 might have inaugurated a happier period had the rebellion not supervened. Bigod had been chastened to a less obsti-

[1] P.R.O., S.P. 1/105, p. 9; cf. L. & P. xi. 23.
[2] P.R.O., S.P. 1/86, fo. 127. The figure includes £83. 10s. of miscellaneous debts owed by Bigod to Latimer.
[3] Ibid., fo. 128.   [4] L. & P. vii. 1341.

nate mood and was adopting a more realistic attitude toward his creditors. The emotionalism and the desperation remain; they suggest a sensitive, highly strung, and overwrought mind; indeed, his reaction to these financial problems prepares us for some strange behaviour, should a greater crisis envelop our subject. On the other hand, it would be fatally easy to overestimate the effect of these problems upon Bigod's activities both before and during the Pilgrimage. If his financial vulnerability and Cromwell's patronage gave him a strong incentive to labour for Cromwell's Reforming policy, one may nevertheless find clear indications of the sincerity of his religious views. With all his faults, Bigod cannot be numbered among the mere hirelings of Protestant policy. Again, he did not plunge into the Pilgrimage of Grace with a view to the creation of a new régime which would cancel his debts. So far from hastening to ride the whirlwind, he made vigorous attempts to avoid its clutches and only after many vicissitudes did he allow himself to be drawn to its centre. As usual, the crude economic explanation fails to cover the facts. While at this stage of the story we have not yet touched upon the more complex aspects of his mind, the reader will not have failed to note that with the problem of debts and land many other notions are inextricably intertwined: not merely family affection and ancestral loyalty, but credit in the county and the very prestige of the Reformation movement upon the dubious soil of the north.

2. The Reformer

During the years 1534–6 Sir Francis appeared among the most conspicuous agents of the English Reformation. The surviving State papers preserve much information about his activities; we know far more about the last three years of his life than about the other twenty-seven. His work as a Reformer falls under two chief heads: the statement of theory and the administration of Cromwellian policy toward the northern bishops, clergy, and monasteries. His actual relations with the monasteries seem so personal and complex as to demand separate treatment, but the problems of monastic reform will be found from the outset to occupy a prominent place in his thinking. That he was no blind tool of Cromwell, but a convinced and independent doctrinaire, can scarcely be doubted by any attentive reader of his book *A Treatise concernyng Impropriations of Benefices*. This revealing and readable little work has occasionally been mentioned by modern historians. On the other hand, they show no signs of having read it, perhaps because of its extreme rarity,[1] perhaps because its title may have suggested dull and technical problems little related to the melodramatic fate of its author. Than this latter notion, nothing could be less true. It is a duodecimo volume of 47 printed pages published by Thomas Godfray, but not dated. Its publication must be placed at some date between the birth of the Princess Elizabeth in September 1533 and the disgrace of Anne Boleyn early in May 1536, since it pays tribute to both these ladies. The year 1535 has rightly been taken by bibliographers as most probable.[2] The book thus stands among the earlier apologetic works of the Cromwellian circle and its author cannot be dismissed as a disciple of the more distinguished members like Starkey and Morison.[3] A fulsome address to Henry VIII occupies the early pages. Encouraged by the king's 'incomparable gyfte of gentelnesse and humanyte', the writer has overcome his shame 'so to attempte rudely, folysshly, and rather presumptuouslye to trouble and disquyet such an imperiall maiesty with this my rude and barbarouse writynge, in the hynderaunce of youre godly and spirituall studies, with whiche your highnesse taketh such intolerable payne'.[4] We are bound to praise and glorify God for sending us so Christian a king, 'by whose great and inestymable dilygente labour, charge, studye and payne we be delyvered from the harde, sharpe, and xM tymes more than judiciall captivytie of that babylonycall man of Rome, to the swete and softe servyce, ye, rather lyberty of the gospel'.[5] By way of thanksgiving, the author, 'accordinge to the small talent of lerninge' that the Lord has lent him, seeks to put his Grace 'in remembrance of the intollerable pestilence of impropriations of benefices to relygyouse persones (as they wyll be called)'. This is a thing 'playnly repugnant to the most holy and blessed decrees and ordynaunces of allmighty God, and highly to the extollinge, supportinge, and mayntenance of the usurped power of the bysshop of Rome'.[6] It is impossible to detect all the frauds of the papists, and the writer will limit himself to one subject: 'the craftye iuggelynge, clean convey-

---

[1] I have used the B.M. copy, the only one listed in the *Short Title Catalogue*. There is another, however, in the Library of Lambeth Palace, bound up with other tracts; these seem the only two extant.

[2] Its mention of the Royal Supremacy does not help much, since Henry had been demanding its acknowledgement since 1531. 'This most noble empyre of England' (A. iii) would suggest 1533 or later, but the Dissolution of 1536 does not cast its shadow upon Bigod's treatment of the monasteries.

[3] The printed works of these men appeared 1535–9; Bigod could, however, have read Edward Fox's *De vera differentia* (1534). He is much more likely to have been influenced by earlier writers like Simon Fish; cf. *infra*, p. 73.

[4] A. ii[v].   [5] A. iii.   [6] A. iiii.

aunce and lewde legerdemayn used amongest some men (ye knowe whome I meane) concernynge the impropriatyons of benefices'.[1] Truth will now prevail. God has ordained his congregation 'one specyall kynde of ministers' to publish his word. St. Paul said, 'The Lorde hath not sent me to baptyse but rather to preache.'[2]

These expressions strikingly foreshadow the Puritan phraseology and temperament; the author is also clearly concerned to impress laymen, and his many texts are first given in Latin, but then immediately translated. This emphasis on preaching now develops into the cardinal argument. The labourer, continues Bigod, is worthy of his hire and they which minister in the Temple must have their finding by the Temple. The preacher in particular must be 'honestly found'.[3] The godly provision of tithe by virtuous men was intended to give the parson opportunity to study, to apply himself, and to minister the true word of God, yet 'my maisters impropriated or improper maisters' have undone all this. Bigod thus apostrophizes them: 'Have nat you (I saye) by the glykynge and gleynyng, snatchynge and scratchinge, tatchynge and patchynge, scrapinge and rakynge togyther of almost all the fatte benefyces within this realme and impropriatynge them unto your selves, distroyed this most godlye and holy provisyon. . . . For howe can the people have any faith in God withoute preachinge?'[4] And how should the people have any preachers when the impropriators have robbed the ministers of their living? If the people have no faith, how can they have charity? If they have no charity, why marvel 'if they ronne hedlonge and be caryed from one vyce to another, from one mischefe to another'? Who else but impropriators must take the blame? 'Do we nat say such an abbot is parsone here, such a priour is parsone here? Yea, suche a prioresse is parsone here? How saye ye? Thinke ye that men be foles? Thynke ye that they ben asses? Thinke ye that they ben stockes and stones, blockes and bones? . . . Is nat this abomination? Is this tollerable?'[5] It affords no excuse if a monk be appointed to the impropriated benefice, because the balance of that benefice ought not in any case to go into the coffers of a monastery, but be expended in hospitality. No man ought to be given a benefice merely in return for prayers; Christ himself denounced the scribes and Pharisees for living idle lives on the plea that they were praying for the people. Only he who ministers, teaches, and preaches should have a living, and no one else, 'albeit he mumble up never so many matenses, David psalters,

---

[1] B. i^v.   [2] B. ii^v–B. iii.   [3] B. iii^v–B. iiii.   [4] B. vii^v–B. viii.
[5] B. viii^v.

trentals, diryges, and suche lyke longe prayers.'[1] The writer goes on to attack the pluralists who set in each of their livings 'a Syr John lacke laten, that can scarce rede his porteus, orels a ravenynge wolfe as canne do nothynge but devoure the sely shepe with his false doctryne, and sucke their substaunce from them'.[2] Some pluralists have even been known to ride past a parish without knowing that its benefice belongs to them, but the same men will nevertheless ride a hundred miles to venerate an image. Until the king puts a stop to these abuses, all will not be well 'in this church of Christ in England, whereof his grace is the supreme head'.[3]

The objection was sometimes raised that, without impropriations, monasteries would have to live in poverty. Surely, argues Bigod, this would be merely in accordance with monastic professions. In actual fact, many houses would still possess great properties, more than Benedict, Bernard, Dominic, or Francis ever enjoyed.[4] And what would it matter 'if all these inprofytable sectes, and stronge sturdye route of idle paunches were a lytell poorer, to thende that the trew relygion of Christ might thereby somethynge be sette up and avaunsed, and suffycient company of the ministers of Goddes true worde provyded for in all partes'.[5] In lively manner, Bigod then embarks upon his favourite theme:

I praye you, what an idle sorte be founde and brought up in Abbeyes, that never wyll laboure whyles they ben there; nor yet whan they come thence to other mens servyce, in so moche that there goth a comen proverbe; That he which hath ones ben in an abbey wyll ever more after be slouthefull; for the whiche cause they ben called of many men, Abbey loutes or lubbers. And some saye that many of our holye fathers spende nat a lytell upon my cosyn Jane, Elsabeth and Marget [sic] (ye knowe what I meane) insomuche that even they which be most Popysshe of all, and knowe none other god almost than the gret drafsacke of Rome, can not deny this to be trew. Which popysshe persons nat withstandynge wyll nat ones open their lyppes to sue for a reformation to the kinge our most sovraine lorde. And the cause why, as is noysed, and as good synifycations ben therof given, is for that some such abbot or priour will nat styck to gyve an hundreth poundes at a clappe to such a champyon to speke in his favour in tyme of nede.[6]

Despite this crafty bribery, the monks continue to live all too sumptuously. Bigod here tells the story of an unnamed blind abbot 'which

---

[1] C. v–C. v[v].   [2] C. vi–C. vi[v].

[3] This story is repeated c. 1546 in the *Supplication of the Poor Commons* (Early Eng. Text Soc. extra ser. xiii. 78).

[4] C. vii.   [5] C. viii.   [6] C. ix[v].

never wolde set him downe at dyner but he wold fyrst undo the poynte before his bely, and let it oute a certayne length, and to such tyme he had fylled his paukener to the poynt, he wolde never cesse, as blinde as he was'.[1] Only God can remove the efficient cause of all this—the spirit of the Devil—but as for the material cause, 'their infinyte sommes of ryches, of golde and of sylver, may soone be removed, if it plese our most redouted prince, with his most honourable counsell'.

In both matter and manner these passages bear a close resemblance to the more famous tract of Simon Fish,[2] which had appeared some five years earlier, but of the two Bigod is much the less crude and the more constructive. He does not, for example, envisage a complete dissolution of the monasteries: in his book, as in his conduct towards his monastic neighbours, he calls for reform, not for abolition. 'Take from them their improper impropriations with other superfluytes and within a while peradventure they may be good men. And if nat that, I am sure that outwardly they shal nat be a quarter part so yll as they be now.'[3] Let us not argue, he continues, that our fathers allowed impropriations. Did they do right or wrong? Were there not as great fools in the past as there are now? Urging his opponents, if any drop of grace be in them, to hear these arguments, or else to take up their pens and answer his charges, Bigod ends by commending the problem of impropriations to the king and his council.[4]

The most striking characteristic of this book is not its invitation to the king to strip the monasteries of their surplus wealth: others beside Sir Francis were even then pursuing this line more ruthlessly than he. Likewise, there seems nothing extraordinary in the propagandist attempt to depict the monasteries as hotbeds of vice and strongholds of papalism. More interesting than either of these features are the puritanical grievances, proposals, and temperament of the author. Even in the brief quotations supplied above, the reader will not fail to detect some remarkably prophetic emphases. Rather than in his own tentative and equivocal age, Sir Francis would have found a multitude of fellow spirits in Jacobean England, where the 'ministers of God's true word' were fiercely and vociferously defending the 'liberty of the Gospel' against impropriators, pluralists, and hankerers for the 'ten thousand times more than judicial captivity of that Babylonical Man

[1] D^v.
[2] Cf., e.g., Fish in *Early English Text Soc.* extra ser. xiii. 14: 'set these sturdie lobies', &c.
[3] D. ii.   [4] D. iv^v.

of Rome'. Despite his optimism concerning the royal intentions, despite his flattery of the king, Bigod remained one of those whose thinking had already passed far beyond that of Henry VIII. His stress upon the pulpit and the liberty of the Gospel has a fundamentally anti-Erastian purport which he was soon to develop further. The partial expropriation of the monks and the education of the people by a new race of spiritual clergy, endowed handsomely from the recovered spoils: these were not after all to prove the achievements of the State Church of Henry VIII. It would be easy, and in some measure justifiable, to dismiss Sir Francis as an aggressive crank. He was nevertheless also an idealist and a man of the future, born half a century before his time.

One final aspect of his attack upon appropriations should not escape notice, since it possesses a regional significance. It should cause no wonder that a Yorkshire layman staged this attack, since in that shire the worst evils of the system stood revealed. At the time it had about 622 parish churches, of which no less than 392, or 63 per cent., were appropriated; more important, in over 100 of these no proper vicarage had been ordained and the churches were served merely by curates hired at cheap rates and dismissible at will. Of some 17 churches appropriated to Guisborough, at least ten or eleven lacked vicars.[1] To Bigod, the local abbeys must indeed have seemed to batten voraciously upon the parochial endowments of his countrymen.

Having examined the argument of Bigod's only surviving book, we must now return to the State papers and witness his practical Reforming activities during the crucial years 1534–6. By the summer of 1534 he is glimpsed at work among an energetic group of Reformers anxious to wage more effective propaganda in support of the Royal Supremacy. In a letter of 17 August the well-known London printer and lawyer John Rastell urged upon Cromwell a plan whereby the justices should give a charge at Sessions, denouncing the papal claims. With two or three 'wise men'—of whom Francis Bigod was one and could explain to Cromwell their intentions—Rastell and his friends would promote this plan, if supported by the Council; they thought it should in fact be put forth by authority of Parliament itself.[2] This letter, coming from an able Protestant extremist,[3] testifies to the repute which Bigod's zeal and knowledge had gained him in London Reforming circles. Con-

---

[1] A. Hamilton Thompson, *The English Clergy*, pp. 115–16.
[2] *L. & P.* vii. 1071. Cf. ibid. 1072, which also mentions Bigod's activities as an intermediary.
[3] Rastell was in 1536 arrested for his extremist views, which included the total denunciation of tithes, and died in prison (*D.N.B.*).

THE REFORMER 75

versely it helps to explain the young knight's failure to achieve harmony with his neighbours at home in Yorkshire, where there were few Protestant gentry and where slow-moving peers and squires were understandably scandalized by the irreverent teachings attributed to extremist Reformers. The point is illustrated in the course of an unsuccessful plea for mercy directed to Cromwell after the Pilgrimage of Grace by Lord Hussey. Here the supplicant related a conversation of midsummer 1534 with Lord Darcy and Sir Robert Constable, also destined to suffer for their connexions with the revolt. 'As we satt at the borde, yt happenede that we spake of Sir Frauncis Bygott and his priste in his sermone, (? which) lykenede our ladie to a poding when the meate was ought, with many wordes mo. And then my lorde Darcy said thatt he was a noughty priste; let him go, for in good faith I will non heretyke, and so said I, and lykewise Sir Robert Constable, for we will die Cristen men....'[1] Bigod's preaching chaplains will soon engage our notice, yet to which of them the present reference applies and with what accuracy we do not know. The heresy itself, presumably of Manichean origin, had been widespread during the Middle Ages and was ascribed both to Lollards and Anabaptists: it constituted a denial that our Lord took flesh of the Virgin, since he possessed a celestial body. In 1535 no less than twenty-five heretics are alleged to have admitted it under examination at St. Paul's; Anabaptists were charged with it in 1575.[2] The most celebrated offender with this doctrine was Joan Bocher, the Kentish woman, who maintained it with some acuteness against the 'orthodox' Protestant Roger Hutchinson, and was ultimately burned in May 1550.[3]

In January 1535 Bigod was appointed one of the commissioners for Yorkshire and York City, charged with the task of compiling the *Valor Ecclesiasticus*,[4] that great survey of ecclesiastical incomes upon which the Crown was to base its taxation of the Church. On the following 8 June Bigod delivered to Archbishop Lee not only the king's instructions for setting forth the Royal Supremacy, but also a letter from Cromwell blaming Lee for previous negligence in that task.[5] The next day Cuthbert Tunstall, Bishop of Durham, acknowledged receipt of

[1] P.R.O., S.P. 1/118, fos. 123–123ᵛ; cf. *L. & P.* xii (1), 899.
[2] References in R. A. Knox, *Enthusiasm*, pp. 125–6.
[3] *The Works of Roger Hutchinson* (Parker Soc. 1842), pp. ii–iii, 145 seqq. A variant appears in the *mala dogmata* of 1536; comparing our Lady with 'a bag of saffren or pepper when the spice was out' (R. W. Dixon, op. cit. i. 407).
[4] *L. & P.* viii. 149, 463.
[5] We know this from Lee's letter of defence written on 14 June (*L. & P.* viii. 869).

similar instructions, brought to him by Bigod.[1] The latter's duties, as
the bishops no doubt guessed, exceeded those of a mere messenger.
Two days later he sent Cromwell a report, written at Settrington, to
the effect that Lee and Tunstall had received the orders with great
humility, and that the latter had sent out his chaplains 'to execute the
effectes of theym in all godly haiste; he hym selfe turned to maike pre-
ceptes and sende theym to everye ecclesiasticall person within his
diocese'. The writer then goes on to describe his own plans for observ-
ing the preaching of the Supremacy at York. Here, to judge from the
Treatise and other letters, he must have felt in his element and enjoyed
every moment of his duties. He proposed to be there on Midsummer
Day and on St. Peter's Day (29 June), the most solemn festival of
the year at York. If Archbishop Lee preached sincerely in support of
the king's title, he would do much good, since all the dignitaries of the
Church must needs attend. Should he on the contrary prove negligent,
Bigod's chaplain, to whose qualities Dr. Crome, Master Latimer, and
Master Barnes could testify, would be ready to say the Word of God
truly, and to extol the king's prerogative and renunciation of the
Bishop of Rome. Bigod had procured for this chaplain licences from the
Archbishop of Canterbury and from the king himself, yet undertook
not to have him preach at York without Cromwell's consent.

The writer proceeds to pay further tribute to his own zeal. He had
made an abstract of the Statute of Supremacy, 'wiche I thynke to nale
on a table in my parishe churche and delyver all theym that can reade
a copye of it, to instructe ther famylie therwith at home and then on
the holy [day] they shall marke my chaplen's declaration of the same
myche more easely': an intriguing sidelight on literacy in the remote
Yorkshire village of Settrington in 1535.[2]

The appeal to the authority of three subsequently notorious Reformers is a significant feature of this letter. As for the chaplain, he was no
doubt Thomas Garret, whose early activities we have witnessed and
whom we shall presently encounter serving as Bigod's chaplain a month
later at Jervaulx.

When in London, Bigod seems also to have acted as an intermediary
between Reforming groups in the provinces and his patron Cromwell.
William Shipman and two others wrote from Bristol on 8 August 1535

---

[1] *L. & P.* viii. 849.
[2] P.R.O., S.P. 1/93, pp. 50–51; cf. *L. & P.* viii. 854. There seems in fact to have
been a grammar school at Settrington, though its history at this period remains
very obscure. Cf. P. J. Wallis and W. E. Tate, *A Register of Old Yorks. Grammar
Schools*, p. 31.

concerning a commission they had received to inquire into the activities of seditious preachers there. Sending a report to Cromwell by Latimer, now Bishop-elect of Worcester, they request instructions on the correction of offenders, 'adversaries to God's word', and have asked 'our loving friend Sir Francis Bigod' to keep reminding Cromwell of the matter, since 'he was a doer for us at London in the same behalf'.[1]

The interest of Sir Francis in preachers and preaching has already presented itself to our attention and will do so again in other contexts. That it became no less than an obsession appears in the strangest of all his letters to Cromwell, an undated one which may be placed around 27 April 1536. He expected, he writes, to have waited on the minister that morning, but has delayed in order to hear certain sermons in London, and will attend on Cromwell 'agaynst supper' to report on them. He is now informed, however, that Cromwell is to ride shortly with the king to Dover, so that in fact he may miss seeing him before he goes home to Yorkshire. As Parliament is dissolved, he will have no occasion to return to London for many days. He most humbly beseeches Cromwell to draw the king's attention to his services 'as well in his parlement as also in my cuntre in settyng forwarde Gode's Worde, havyng ther preachers of my owne coste, and rode all over the cuntre with theym'. This was but his duty, done for no mere lucre, yet he is loth to go home and there be mocked rather than rewarded for his diligence; such is the nature of his countrymen. Most of all will the Archbishop of York discourage him on perceiving that he is merely 'rejected' by the king and Cromwell. At this point Bigod makes what must then have seemed a most extraordinary request for a married man and a knight, a request which in itself shows the genuineness of his religious zeal. 'Spetially afore any thyng helpe me to be a preiste, that I may preache the Worde of God, or eles dispense with me, that, beyng no preiste, I may do it.' Here is all he will ever require from the king and Cromwell and he will never afterwards ask for anything all his life, 'for it shal please me bettre than all the riches in London'.[2] So far from being a mere royalist and anti-clerical, Sir Francis had become a fanatical Protestant-clerical zealot, exposing without hesitation his secret ambitions to the hard-boiled politician whose personal lack of spiritual enthusiasm he must surely have realized. At the same time, the letter shows the informal and intimate character of their relationship; it forms one of many hints that the granite-faced

[1] L. & P. ix. 189.
[2] P.R.O., S.P. 1/103, p. 86; cf. the inadequate summary in L. & P. x. 742.

administrator depicted alike by Holbein and by the historical textbook may not have been the whole Thomas Cromwell of actual history. We naturally, but most unfortunately, lack Cromwell's replies to Bigod. The latter may often have expected and received no more than an oral reply from the busy minister, since, when in London, he was amongst Cromwell's more frequent visitors. Faced by these one-sided surviving records, it would be easy, yet inaccurate, to conjure up a relationship between a hysterical client and an unscrupulous patron. Cromwell after all preserved Bigod from his creditors, lent him money and gave very considerable scope to his Reforming zeal. Though he did not instantly gratify his every plea, it must be conceded that the pleas were insistent and extensive, even by the indelicate standards of that period. If Cromwell exploited Bigod's indebtedness and religious zeal for political ends, he can scarcely be blamed in view of the fierce resistances in the north and its lack of convinced Reformers and Erastians within the higher social orders. So far as the long-term personal interests of Sir Francis were concerned, they might have been better served, not by a more obliging patron but by a harsher one, who from the first would have forced him to sell part of his lands, settle his debts and make realistic terms with the world.

Not the least interesting feature of this letter is Bigod's reference to his services in Parliament and the connexion between his London visit and the parliamentary session of February to April 1536. Though he appears in no extant lists of members,[1] it seems probable that he actually sat in the final session of the Reformation Parliament. In any case, he must certainly have been lobbying in parliamentary circles for the Cromwellian cause; by education, convictions, and social standing, few of Cromwell's friends can have been so well qualified for the task.

The mordant criticisms of monastic practice contained in the *Treatise concernyng Impropriations* have their counterpart in those curious letters which depict Bigod's actual relations with the Yorkshire monasteries both before and during the Pilgrimage of Grace. Sir Francis and his wife belonged to the rather select body of descendants regarded as 'founders' of religious houses. During their northern visitations of 1536, Cromwell's unlovable emissaries Legh and Layton reported[2] that

---

[1] One would not, of course, expect to find him in the original list dating from 1529 (*L. & P.* iv (3), 6043 (2)). Our knowledge of the representation of the Yorkshire boroughs is incomplete at this period.

[2] *L. & P.* x. 364, p. 139. The *Valor Eccles.* gives its gross income as only £12. 2s. 8d.

Sir Francis Bigod and George Salvain were founders of the little Grandi-montine priory of Grosmont, the former presumably through his descent from the third Peter de Mauley, one of its actual founders.[1] The Lady Katharine Bigod, along with her sisters, likewise figures as foundress of another minor house: the small Benedictine nunnery of Langley in Leicestershire.[2] The family was also linked with a small hospital or almshouse near Layerthorpe Postern, York, concerning which almost nothing is known, except for Leland's note made shortly after the fall of Sir Francis. 'Ther was a place of the Bigotes hard withyn Laithorp gate, and by it an hospital of the Bigotes fundation. Syr Francis Bigot let booth the hospital and his house al to ruine.'[3]

The episodes significant to our biography do not, however, derive from his connexions, honorific or otherwise, with all those unimportant institutions. They arise in relation to the great Yorkshire houses of Jervaulx, Mountgrace, Whitby, Guisborough and Watton.

The story of George Lazenby, the unfortunate monk of Jervaulx, has brought undeserved obloquy on Bigod from writers who expected a Tudor justice to have behaved as if he belonged to a modern liberal democracy. Sir Francis visited Jervaulx to preach the Royal Supremacy, but not to smell out treason. While he was there, Lazenby pertinaciously denounced the Supremacy before a large gathering and, rightly or wrongly, displayed his determination to become a martyr. Even had Bigod quixotically decided to risk his own neck by an attempt to conceal this action, he could not possibly have accomplished the feat. The particulars are given in a group of documents dating from July 1535. On the 12th of that month Bigod reported to Cromwell that he had visited Jervaulx, when his chaplain, 'this berer, maister Garrarde . . . preached ther the trew Worde of God in the presence of the abbot and all his brethren'. This took place on Sunday afternoon, 11 July. As the preacher was declaring the authority of every bishop and priest to remit sin, one of the monks, dan George Laysinbye, interrupting him openly *coram multis*, said that the Bishop of Rome had the first and most authority in all the world above all other bishops. The preacher having discreetly and peaceably concluded his sermon, Bigod commanded the monk to be brought before the abbot, himself and all the audience and demanded the cause of his 'folishenes'. Lazenby's answer was 'deliberately spoken' and repeated his treasonable view; he

---

[1] Cf. *V.C.H. Yorks.* iii. 193.
[2] *L. & P.* x. 364, p. 138.
[3] *Leland's Itinerary in England*, ed. L. T. Smith, i. 55; cf. *V.C.H. Yorks.* iii. 352.

moreover signed articles submitted to him, showing that he continued to uphold the Roman jurisdiction. Bigod then caused the constable of Middleham Castle to take him into custody till the king's pleasure should be known. The abbot and his brethren showed themselves agreeable to this step, behaving like 'faithfull men to the prynce'. The abbot in fact required Bigod to submit the same articles to all the brethren in order to avoid suspicion clinging to the house, and all replied 'as became trew subiectes'.[1] This letter is accompanied by a clear statement of Lazenby's denunciation of the Royal Supremacy, signed not only by Adam, abbot of Jervaulx, Bigod, Garret, and two other witnesses, but also by Lazenby himself.[2] However little one may admire the Henrican legislation, one could find no more manifest and admitted example of treason. Short of a complete abjuration by Lazenby or some extraordinary act of clemency by the king himself, nothing could now have saved him from the dire consequences.

From Middleham Castle on 13 July Bigod related that the monk was emboldened by another man in his treason; after a long examination Bigod concluded that his beliefs derived rather from 'one of the Mownte Grace' than from his own learning.[3] A week later Bigod reported a further examination of Lazenby, 'who I assure yew handled hym selfe in defeyndyng yonder same ydole and bloudsupper of Rome so boldly and stiflye as I never in all my days saw the like'. He was, however, unlearned and now sought to blind the simple folks and establish his treason by revelations, as he called them. One of these Bigod sends to Cromwell in Lazenby's own hand. The monk had told him of divers others, especially one of Our Lady of Mountgrace; how he was there in her chapel and she, appearing to him, said, 'George, George, be of good chere, for I may yit not spare the', with, adds the informant, 'siche owther madnesse'. Lazenby had finally told Bigod he was sure the Spirit of God was within him and that he was glad to die in so good a quarrel as to defend the dignity of the Church, of which the Pope alone was the true Head by God's law. Lazenby had now confessed that some of the monks of Mountgrace were of his counsel and Bigod himself had spoken to one of these suspected Carthusian monks. Nevertheless, the prior of Mountgrace had asked him not to vex his brethren, since he himself was already in consultation with

[1] P.R.O., S.P. 1/94, p. 24; cf. *L. & P.* viii. 1025.
[2] P.R.O., S.P. 1/94, p. 25. These are presumably the actual 'articles' drawn up on the day of the offence, 11 July, in Bigod's own hand.
[3] P.R.O., S.P. 1/94, p. 42; cf. *L. & P.* viii. 1033.

Cromwell about them. Bigod proceeds to cast suspicion not only upon these Carthusians, who were in due course induced to submit under extreme pressure, but also upon a Northumberland gentleman Anthony Heron, who had lately been at the Mount and had asked leave of the prior to convey two of the traitorous monks into Scotland.[1] We must recall in connexion with these reports that several men of note went to the block for mere failure to divulge treason. When Bigod says in this letter 'I dare not conceale it from yow', he was repeating the chief lesson which Henry VIII wanted to teach the gentry.[2]

George Lazenby's own note concerning further visions seems to a modern eye to display a pathetically superstitious and subnormal intelligence, as well as an orthography original even by Tudor standards.[3] Yet it is fair to add that men of better education were then apt to greet any remarkable dream or nightmare as a vision. Moreover, Lazenby was destined to become the only genuine martyr for religion among the Yorkshire monks, for we may scarcely place in this class the few religious men who merely happened to become compromised by rebellion. If the Yorkshire Carthusians ultimately failed to rival the magnificent gesture of their London brethren, they nevertheless managed to imbue an unlearned Cistercian with something of their spirit,[4] and he, whatever his incidental delusions, gladly died for a simple principle which he thoroughly understood. George Lazenby was condemned at the York assizes in August 1535 and executed.[5]

According to later Catholic martyrologists, another Jervaulx monk, Thomas Mudde, obtained the head of his executed colleague, and through favour and friendship escaped with it to Scotland. Returning to work as a schoolmaster at Knaresborough in Mary's reign, he ultimately died in 1583 as a Catholic prisoner in the North Block House at Hull.[6] Mudde's prolonged adventures were but one outcome of the Lazenby affair. Even in 1540, the King's Council in the North reprieved a priest, John Whaplod, as his offence in making 'the abominable rhyme

[1] P.R.O., S.P. 1/94, p. 115; L. & P. viii. 1069 (ii).
[2] One who learned the lesson well and taught it to his son was Sir John Gostwick, another servant of Wolsey who rose to prominence as an assistant of Cromwell. Cf. *Bedfordshire Historical Record Soc.* xxxvi. 40, 45.
[3] P.R.O., S.P. 1/94, p. 116.
[4] The mystical tradition of Prior John Norton and Richard Methley seems to have been preserved by the monk Robert Fletcher, who was on the Mountgrace pension list at the Dissolution (cf. Lincoln Cathedral Library MS. A.6.8, fo. 77).
[5] Serjeant Christopher Jenney reports his condemnation on 6 Aug. and says he will be shortly executed (*L. & P.* ix. 37).
[6] H. Foley, *Records of the English Province S.J.* iii. 239 from Fr. Grene's MS. 'F'.

for the death of the monk of Jervaulx' was thought to be covered by the pardon issued after the Pilgrimage of Grace.[1]

Shortly after his participation in this matter, Sir Francis joined in the campaign to convince Lazenby's teachers at Mountgrace of their error. Archbishop Lee tells Cromwell on 8 August 1535 that Bigod has confirmed the now submissive attitude of the prior and has been requested by the latter to procure a visit to Mountgrace by Dr. Horde, another Carthusian prior who could be relied on to 'allure' the 'simple brethren'.[2] Meanwhile Anthony Heron, the Northumbrian who had offered to spirit away the recalcitrant monks, was indicted for treason at Topcliffe and, reported the Earl of Northumberland, proved a 'simple' person, denied his former opinions and confessed himself a notable offender.[3] Early in January 1536 Heron lay in York Castle, together with a monk and a priest also charged with opposing the Royal Supremacy. There they received a visit from Sir Francis Bigod, whose report to Cromwell shows his essentially merciful character.

On arriving in York he had sent his servant with a charitable gift to the prisoners in the castle, and these three prisoners made urgent request to speak with him. Entering their evil-smelling quarters, he found the monk and the priest sitting there in strong fetters. Both begged him to intercede with Cromwell. The former—he was probably a monk of Roche named John Robinson[4]—denied any traitorous words against the king or in favour of the Pope, claiming to be laid there through the accusation of one man, his enemy. He protested that he would no more regard the Pope than one of the prisoners tied there with him. The priest merely pleaded that his offence had arisen through ignorance 'and also before the statute' of Supremacy. They both besought the king's compassion with weeping eyes. As for Anthony Heron, he was walking outside in the yard and Bigod talked longer with him 'by cawse of the aire'. He protested that he had been deceived and blind, thanking God and the king for his correction. When he had finished speaking, Bigod very characteristically 'openyd unto them all siche places of Scripture' as he could, 'for ther better establishmente in ther allegiance'. He now proceeds to ask Cromwell's instructions, assuring him that the prisoners are 'in extreame myserie' and 'the priste like to perishe for sustentation, I assure yower maistership *bona*

[1] *L. & P.* xv. 428.   [2] *L. & P.* ix. 49.
[3] *L. & P.* x. 77.
[4] Legh and Layton noted in Feb. 1536 that one of the Roche monks of this name was suspected of treason and imprisoned at York (*L. & P.* x. 364, p. 138).

fide.[1] In the event, Robinson survived to enjoy his pension, and Cromwell perhaps intervened to save the others also, since among his memoranda under February 1536 there is a note: 'the effect of Sir Francis Bigott's letters touching the priest and Heron'.[2] We must hope so, having received this vivid glimpse of York Castle jail, long before the erection of the neat and commodious Georgian buildings which survive today.

The curious and complicated story of the dealings of Sir Francis with Whitby Abbey has a more elaborate documentation, though it leaves many questions unanswered. His visits to Mulgrave must have familiarized him with the affairs of this house, at least from the time he married and settled in the north. Moreover, at some date unknown the Earl of Northumberland leased him for life the stewardship of the Liberty of Whitby Strand,[3] an appointment which significantly enhanced his interests and powers in this part of Yorkshire.

The long series of letters illustrating the struggle between Bigod and John Hexham, abbot of Whitby, begins in August 1535, when the latter complained to Cromwell that on St. Hilda's Day (25 August, the patronal festival of the abbey) Sir Francis, assisted by James Conyers, bailiff of the abbey, and others, made great 'fayssinge' and quarrelling with Gregory Conyers and other 'servants' of the house as they walked through Whitby Fair. They then lay in wait for Gregory at his return by night and, but for the intervention of other gentlemen, murder would have been committed.[4] The dispute obviously did not begin with this affray, since the letter alludes to Cromwell's previous demand that a 'general concord' should be made between Bigod and the abbey's tenants: it also states that Bigod and his followers had been indicted for a great riot against the convent, and refers to a promise made by him at the York assizes, to be 'in good agreement' with Gregory Conyers and the servants of the abbey. Sir Francis himself presumably referred to these earlier quarrels when in January 1536 he wrote that the abbot had once set his hand and convent seal to a false bill of complaint against himself.[5]

We should fall into extreme simplicity if we accepted the abbot's complaints as gospel truth. Whitby, set on its high crag overlooking the ocean, was an ill-governed community and, not long before this date, its servants had been in the Star Chamber on account of their

[1] P.R.O., S.P. 1/101, p. 38; cf. *L. & P.* x. 49.
[2] *L. & P.* x. 254, p. 93.
[3] *L. & P.* xii (1), 271.
[4] *L. & P.* ix. 216.
[5] *L. & P.* x. 49.

amusing but ruffianly faction-fights with the fishermen down below in the town.[1] One of their exploits began with a civil invitation to come up and receive half a barrel of beer; then, as the gullible mariners climbed the still familiar 'church stairs' to the abbey, the servants dashed their hopes with a shower of great stones. Before the contest closed, many men were severely hurt on both sides. In 1528 Abbot Hexham himself was accused in the same court of nefarious collaboration with two French pirates. According to the plaintiffs, these latter had seized a Danzig vessel in the Humber and sold her to the abbot, Gregory Conyers and others, who bought her well knowing the facts and then refused to restore her to the rightful owners.[2] The sinister role played by the Conyers family of Whitby in and around the abbey has many contemporary parallels throughout England; it is striking merely because complicated by an internal family quarrel. As it appears in their respective wills,[3] James Conyers was the uncle of Gregory. At the time of the latter's death in 1540, the two were sharing the office of bailiff of the Whitby liberties, Gregory having procured for his younger sons the reversion of this office, after the deaths of himself and his uncle.[4] Another interesting aspect of the struggle at Whitby lies in the fact that Gregory Conyers was an adherent of the Eures or Evers, an important landed family entertaining not only a strong interest in Whitby Abbey, but a pronounced rivalry with their relatives the Bigods, which culminated, as will appear, in a sensational case of murder. When in April 1537 the Duke of Norfolk related to the king the active part played by Gregory Conyers in Bigod's downfall, he referred to Conyers as 'not only a wise man, but somewhat learned and in great trust with young Sir Ralph Evers, his master'.[5] It seems highly unlikely that this relationship had just begun. On the other hand, Conyers was clearly a forceful and independent character playing for his own interests: his will shows him to have been a man of old-established family and substantial property;[6] his role would be unduly minimized, were he to be dismissed as a mere tool of the Eure interest.

Not long after Bigod's affray with Gregory Conyers, a number of

---

[1] For details of this amusingly recorded affair see Dodds, op. cit. i. 41–42. The case is undated and should presumably be placed around 1530.

[2] *T.A.J.* ii. 246–51 gives details. As so often, we lack the other side of the case.

[3] That of Gregory Conyers, proved 18 Dec. 1540 in *Test. Ebor.* vi. 108–12; that of James Conyers, proved 1 Sept. 1542, in ibid., pp. 148–50.

[4] Ibid., p. 109.

[5] *L. & P.* xii (1), 870.

[6] He mentions in his will his dwelling-house in Whitby, 'the whiche my auncytors hath hade tyme owte for mynde in occupacon'.

THE REFORMER

the monks confederated to replace Abbot Hexham by one of their own
number, William Newton, a kinsman and hitherto a confidant of the
abbot. Bigod naturally favoured this plan, but before it came to fruition,
Hexham changed his mind about resignation and, supported by the
faction under Gregory Conyers, sought Cromwell's support for the
retention of his office.[1] This happened in January 1536. Needless to add,
Cromwell also received violent epistolary reactions from Bigod, who
proceeded to denounce both Gregory Conyers for issuing letters in the
abbot's name and the abbot himself for his general duplicity. While
Hexham's official acts were governed by 'bondage' to Conyers, he was
privately confessing to young Newton that he heartily desired to see
him abbot. The hostile monks were watching their abbot like 'crowes
abowte a carion' and would no longer permit him to converse privately
with Newton. 'Is this man meete to be an abbott, that for feare of siche
parsonnes wil shame hym selfe, dampne his consciens rather then dis-
please theym?' Sir Francis begs Cromwell to send for them all to London and thrash out the matter face to face. Meanwhile 'the monckes
cracke that they shal wel stay yower maistership', but Bigod had no
fear that Cromwell would 'be corrupte with meade, for if I suspecte
any siche thyng I wolde not lett so to do, and likewise wil do, rather
then I shulde take shame at any of ther handes, as ye shal know farther
by this berer if it please yow here hym speake'.[2] The purport of this
interesting passage seems clear enough. Bigod is hoping his patron will
reject the bribes of the Conyers faction, but at the same time he tactfully suggests the possibility of a counter-bribe from himself rather
than see his opponents win. A letter of Dr. Legh written on 3 February
confirms his allegation that the abbot had at first offered to resign
and then changed his mind.[3]

This postal feud between the rival correspondents of the all-powerful
minister continued on its course, illustrating inadvertently the growing
power of Cromwellian central government over the affairs of this remote corner of England. On 18 April the abbot revealed another significant complication: that Bigod owed him money. If he would be peaceful
and repay it, as he had promised Mr. Serjeant 'Gene'[4] before Cromwell

[1] *L. & P.* x. 47, 48. [2] P.R.O., S.P. 1/101, pp. 38–39; *L. & P.* x. 49.
[3] *L. & P.* x. 238.
[4] Christopher Jenney, King's serjeant-at-law, had various connexions with
northern administration and was of the Commission of the Peace for both the
North and the East Ridings (*L. & P.* x. 777 (10 and 14)). As one of Cromwell's
informers, he reported on the alleged treason of Dr. Haldesworth in 1535. Cf. J.
Lister in *Papers of the Halifax Antiquarian Soc.* (1902, unpaginated).

himself, the abbot would not press the law against him. As for Gregory
Conyers, continues Abbot Hexham, he was a just and true gentleman,
and had never been at variance with the abbot, as Sir Francis had
reported.[1] A further letter of 19 June shows that Bigod had induced
Cromwell to support his own claim to the under-stewardship of the
abbey. The abbot now offered to submit to this only if it were the
king's pleasure, and if Bigod would refrain from using the position to
revenge himself. Were he to occupy it and his confederate James
Conyers the bailiwick, their combined malice would bring the house
into continual trouble. As for James Conyers, concludes the abbot, he
is a very uncharitable and angry man, and so aged that he is almost
past reason.[2] The trouble thus simmered on to the eve of the Pilgrimage
of Grace; not only did Hexham and Gregory Conyers manage to survive Sir Francis,[3] but as, we shall observe, the latter pursued him with
bitter malice to the death.

At this remove, moralizing verdicts are perhaps best left unattempted
on feuds like those between Bigod and Conyers. On both sides a grave
lack of forbearance is apparent, the conflict being primarily one of
temperament and self-interest rather than one involving rival religious
and political ideologies. For what it is worth, the will of Conyers indicates highly conservative religious views and, while seeking the support of Thomas Cromwell, he may possibly have entertained a cordial
dislike of the Reforming policy espoused alike by Cromwell and Bigod.
Nevertheless, though a man of some education and ability, he can
scarcely be regarded as other than a merciless and insatiable opportu-
nist. By the spring of 1538 the abbot and monks were all saying so in
unmistakable terms and attempting to shake off his malign influence
by bribes, lawsuits, and the usual frenzied letters to Cromwell.[4] His
struggle with Bigod was a struggle for the control of an inharmonious
and unsatisfactory religious house between two hot-blooded and push-
ing laymen; the one a tactless and violent Reformer whose moral status
was weakened by a debt to the house; the other in all likelihood a very
ambitious climber without any deeply felt principles beyond his own
enrichment. Whatever the accuracy of this verdict, the story serves at

---

[1] L. & P. x. 679.

[2] L. & P. x. 1167.

[3] Hexham did finally resign in 1537 and was succeeded in the following year by
Henry Davell, who surrendered the abbey 14 Dec. 1539 (V.C.H. Yorks. iii. 104–5).

[4] For their efforts see L. & P. xiii (1), 722, 769, 933; T.A.S. Rec. Ser. lxx. 147.
For a letter of Gregory Conyers to Cromwell on the same matter see L. & P.
xiii (2), 109.

least to remind us that the problem of the monasteries was far from being limited to the problems concerning the monastic life.

The foregoing episodes by no means exhaust the story of Sir Francis Bigod's relations with the Yorkshire monks. During the Pilgrimage of Grace he maintained a very active interest in their affairs and in particular tried to execute a private reformation of Watton Priory. This fantastic story may, however, be postponed until we are able to examine his share in the great rising.

Amongst the more unquestionably beneficent works of Henry VIII and Thomas Cromwell was the virtual destruction of Sanctuary by the Acts of 1534, 1536, and 1540.[1] Beloved by modern sentimentalists as 'green spots in the wilderness where the feeble and the persecuted could find refuge',[2] they had in fact become the permanent lairs of hundreds of the most dangerous criminals in the realm and a constant incitement to the appalling social disease which it is the glory of the Tudors to have cured. Long before this period, secular lords had been forced to relinquish these franchises; the Church alone was left to over-play its hand by defending its sanctuaries in the face of the most obvious precepts of morality and justice. In the south, it is true, they were 'small and scattered islets in the sea of the King's law'. In the north and the west they occupied hundreds of square miles, aggravating the problem of law and order precisely in those areas where many other causes made it exceptionally difficult to solve. Chief amongst these jurisdictions was the County Palatine of Durham, with its six large outlying dependencies in Northumberland and Yorkshire. Little less striking were the great liberties of the Archbishop of York in Beverley, Ripon, and Hexhamshire. Needless to say, the sanctuaries had many local defenders and the grievances of the Pilgrims of Grace contained a sweeping demand for their restoration.[3] As for Sir Francis Bigod, his story does not fail to produce a classic example of the abuse of sanctuary and a characteristic personal response to the situation.

On 4 March 1536 certain servants of Sir Francis during his absence murdered a servant of Sir Ralph Eure the younger. This latter family, seated at Malton and other places in the north, were amongst the most important neighbours of the Bigods. As already observed, Sir Ralph Eure's grandfather had married the widow of the grandfather of

[1] The best general account, giving numerous references to other authorities, is that by I. D. Thornley in *Tudor Studies presented to A. F. Pollard*, pp. 182 seqq.
[2] Hallam, quoted by Thornley, op. cit., p. 207.
[3] Dodds, op. cit. i. 355.

Sir Francis, yet things had not always gone smoothly between the two neighbouring households. In 1499–1500 there had been serious trouble between their adherents, culminating in an affray and a Star Chamber case.[1] Thirty years later the rivalry, though normally under control, can still be observed. We have in fact already noted the two interests contending for control of Whitby Abbey, and Gregory Conyers, the bitter enemy of Bigod, figuring as a 'servant' of Sir Ralph Eure. And on Bigod's fall, Eure, who had staunchly held Scarborough Castle through the period of rebellion, immediately petitioned the Crown for part of the Bigod lands, including Settrington itself.[2] Nevertheless, the evidence indicates that neither of the knights bore personal responsibility for the murder of March 1536.

The chief surviving evidence about the deed comes from Cromwell's papers and is a graphic deposition by Richard Forde, servant to Sir Francis, who was examined on 25 March 1536. Forde testified that on the previous 4 March he attended Ralph Bigod, the knight's brother, on a journey from Mulgrave Castle, where they had dined with the bailiff, to Pickering, sixteen miles away. There they 'bated' their horses and then rode on to Settrington, eight miles farther, arriving at the house of Sir Francis at seven in the evening. While they were at supper, someone brought word that Percival Worme, John Bygod,[3] Christopher Williamson, William Corneforth, Nicholas Harryson, William Dobson, Simon Arundell, Edward Fleccher, Wylfryde Fulthorpe, and George [blank] had ridden to Malton, two miles off, to murder a certain Davy Seignory, servant to Mr. Ewers. On hearing this, Ralph Bigod ordered their own horses in order to prevent the act, but before they came to Richard Reysyng's house, where the murder was done, they met Percival Worme and his company, who informed them that they had done it.[4] Richard Rasing was head of a family of small gentry at Malton[5] and presumably an adherent of the chief local family, the Eures.

The next stage of the story appears in a State paper copied out in the handwriting of Sir Francis himself and included but misplaced in the *Letters and Papers of Henry VIII*.[6] It is an order from Cromwell dated 20 July (obviously 1536, not 1534) to an unnamed person: it may

---

[1] *T.A.S. Rec. Ser.* xli. 13–15.   [2] *L. & P.* xii (1), 402.

[3] Gentle families often had kinsmen—no doubt often illegitimate sons or the offspring of such—in a menial or semi-menial capacity. Old Sir Ralph had, as observed, a bastard named John Bigod.

[4] *L. & P.* x. 553.

[5] *Glover's Visitation of Yorks.*, ed. J. Foster, p. 181.

[6] *L. & P.* vii. 990.

indeed have been widely distributed to sheriffs and justices. It orders the recipient to arrest Percival Worme, William Corneforthe, John Bygott, and William Dobson as guilty of a murder in the county of York. These men, being indicted for the same, fled to Scotland, but have since returned to the bishopric of Durham, where they ride about at their pleasure. Francis Bigod's own letter of 25 September recounts that he and many others were bound by the Sheriff of Yorkshire to attend at York Castle on the Tuesday before Michaelmas Day to know the king's commands. On their arrival, the commissioners—presumably commissioners appointed to investigate this murder and claim to sanctuary—told them that for divers considerations they could not proceed with the case that day, and ordered them to return on 10 October. Bigod, while undertaking to attend and advance the king's causes, now asked Cromwell to order the sheriff before that date to deliver again to their sanctuary in Durham all such sanctuarymen as were lately his servants. He would not intercede in their favour, because they were 'at this detestable act' and because the Lord abhors a man of blood. Nevertheless, 'Rafe Ewere', by the help of Serjeant Jennye, had given untrue information to the Lord Chancellor and had so 'obtained his letters to the Bishop of Durham'—one assumes letters ordering the bishop to deliver the murderers to the sheriff. Bigod enclosed a copy of this order and two 'testimonials' disproving Eure's suggestions to the chancellor. The bishop, the Earl of Westmorland, and the prior and convent of Durham had all made testimonials to the effect that the informations laid against these sanctuarymen were all untrue. Sir Francis acknowledges they committed the murder: the nature of these other alleged misrepresentations he unfortunately fails to explain. He does, however, request outright that, according to the grants made to the church of Durham, the criminals may be restored to sanctuary. Moreover, he gives a merely political reason for this concession: that Cromwell would thereby gain 'the hartes and prayer of all the Northe, spetially in the Bishopriche of Duresme: *adeo sunt suo dicati Cuthberto*'.[1] Before the matter could be further debated, the Pilgrimage of Grace had broken out. Its fate was to settle the fate of the sanctuaries.

As usual, Sir Francis had occupied an individual position. As a client of Cromwell he was admittedly in no position to play the part of the enraged northern magnate, defending his guilty servants and upholding the sanctuaries on their merits. On the other hand, he showed little understanding and sympathy for the vast and uncompromising plans

[1] P.R.O., S.P. 1/106, p. 220; L. & P. xi. 503.

of Henry and Cromwell to sweep away those feudal and ecclesiastical barriers which blocked the extension of the royal law to all men. With a political acumen which proved its short-term justification during the Pilgrimage, he stressed the local popularity of the Palatine immunities. A Protestant and an agent of Royal Supremacy, he nevertheless showed himself a regionalist as much as a centralizer; he continued to think in terms of humouring northern prejudice and particularism. This episode of the murderous sanctuarymen may provide one of the keys to his strange behaviour four months later.

3. *The Eccentric Pilgrim*

At the outbreak of the Yorkshire Pilgrimage of Grace early in October 1536, the reactions of Sir Francis were precisely those one would anticipate from a Protestant and a Cromwellian. He resolutely attempted to extricate himself, and but for the unruly autumnal moods of the North Sea he would have succeeded. He set out from Mulgrave for London by sea, but his ship was driven northward and he was compelled to land at Hartlepool. There he spent the night at the house of a former mayor of the town. Warned that the commons of Durham were coming to take him, he fled back to his boat and 'keeping now to the waters and now to the woods' he returned to Mulgrave. Thereabouts he was finally captured by the commons and carried along with them to York.[1] While there is good reason to suppose that the majority of the rebels were more concerned with their material grievances than with religious and political causes, the general unpopularity of Cromwell and the Reforming party cannot be questioned. Bigod's active sympathies with this party were widely known, and at this stage he feared their direct hostility even more than the chances that they would involve him in treason against the king. Indeed, he subsequently wrote that 'the commons at the fyrst begynyng had me in great suspect [*sic*] and jelowsye because of my lernyng and much conversacion with suche a lewde oon [*sic*] as they jugged wer enemyes both to Crist churche, the faithe therof & the common wealth, by meanes wherof I was not oonly in great slaunder & obloquye, but also in great dannger of my liffe when we wer fyrst att Ponntefrett'.[2] On the other hand, we must not closely equate the psychology of the Pilgrimage of Grace with that normally underlying modern rebellions. It was based upon the social

---

[1] *L. & P.* xii (1), 578.
[2] P.R.O., S.P. 1/114, p. 202; cf. *L. & P.* xii (1), 145.

structure of the north. By threats or blackmail the commons forced
many of the gentry to take their oath and then—strangely enough to
modern eyes—proceeded to accept their leadership. For short periods
this neo-feudal habit of mind could easily rise superior to the economic
tensions between gentry and commons: Sir Francis on his way to York
and Pontefract, half hostage, half commander of the Buckrose contingent, occupied a position similar to that of many others. The time
was not far distant when, despite his Protestant views, he would be
leading several hundred east Yorkshiremen in an independent rebellion.

Not long after his capture, Bigod embarked upon a fatal course
of thinking: he began to see the Pilgrimage of Grace as creating opportunities for his personal Reforming zeal. In particular, the lure of the
monasteries continued to draw him just as powerfully, now that
Thomas Cromwell's remote control had been cut off. About Martinmas
(11 November) he was already intervening in the affairs of Guisborough,
one of the few Yorkshire houses retaining great economic and social
importance throughout an extensive region.[1] In the previous February
Cromwell's agents Legh and Layton had induced James Cockerell its
prior to resign his house to them.[2] Bigod now raised the neighbouring
countryside in order to bring Cockerell back to Guisborough and reform the house. He also wrote to the Earl of Westmorland saying that
the new prior had not been put in by the laws of God and by custom,
but by the extort power of Cromwell. This being so, the commons
judged him no prior and, his accounts having been lawfully taken, they
intended to expel him and choose a new prior by virtue of the whole
community and the assent of all the religious men of the chapter.[3] This
account of Bigod's actions was given later by Cockerell; if it be accurate,
it shows that he was already committing himself to a dangerous
defiance of his former patron and already posing as the mouthpiece of
opinion among the common people. The leaders of the Pilgrimage did
not in fact accept his action at Guisborough and dispatched Sir John
Bulmer, steward of the house, to reinstate Robert Silvester, the new
prior.[4]

Bigod himself did not attend the Pilgrims' Council at York on
21–25 November and in fact never entered the inner ring of the leaders.

[1] An interesting reminiscence concerning the position of Guisborough will be
found in the *Description of Cleveland* later addressed to Sir Thomas Chaloner and
printed in *The Topographer and Genealogist*, ii. 406–7.
[2] *L. & P.* x. 271, 288; cf. also 927. He was subsequently charged with embezzlement (*L. & P.* xi. 1438).
[3] *L. & P.* xii (1), 1087, p. 499.   [4] *L. & P.* xi. 1135 (2).

Soon afterwards, however, Robert Aske sent him as a captain to Scarborough, where his rival Sir Ralph Eure continued as constable to defy the rebels throughout the rising. Here Bigod found as another captain John Hallam of Calkhill,[1] who actually gave him news concerning the discussions at York.[2] That this yeoman, soon to be involved as Bigod's chief accomplice, was a strong and forthright character cannot be doubted. He was 'so cruel and fierce a man amongst his neighbours', alleged another rebel, 'that no man durst disobey him'. The evidence nevertheless clearly shows that Bigod became the dominant spirit in the relationship which developed between them; their rising is distinctly mis-labelled by the customary phrase 'Hallam and Bigod'.

The visit to Scarborough must have been brief, since by 2–4 December Bigod was down at Pontefract attending the major Council which compiled the most important synthesis of the rebel demands. Like several other gentlemen, he there wrote a memorandum on Church and State. Though much more lengthy, elaborate and learned than the rest, this work apparently failed to influence the collective thinking of the leaders. Though the manuscript is no longer extant, we do not entirely lack knowledge of its thesis, since Bigod was characteristically prepared to read it to appreciative listeners, some of whom were later called upon to describe it. The most useful account occurs in John Hallam's testimony. When, early in January 1537, Bigod had sown doubts in Hallam's mind about the validity of the royal pardon,[3] he urged that 'the King's office was to have no cure of souls'. He then, says Hallam, produced and read a book made by himself, showing what authority belonged to the Pope, what to a bishop, and what to a king, saying that the head of the Church of England might be a spiritual man, as the Archbishop of Canterbury or such, but in no wise the king, 'for he should with the sword defend all spiritual men in their right'.[4] This represents an interesting but far from inconsistent development of his view since writing the *Treatise concernynge impropriations*. If in the latter he had written hopefully of the Royal Supremacy, he had already been an ecclesiast in the sense that the puritans were to be ecclesiasts; that

[1] Now Cawkeld, some two miles west of Watton Priory. 'Cawkelde' also occurs in 1537 (*L. & P.* xii (1), 201, p. 91).
[2] *L. & P.* xii (1), 533, p. 247.
[3] Cf. *infra*, p. 96.
[4] *L. & P.* xii (1), 201, p. 92. Cf. also the abridgement of Hallam's evidence in *L. & P.* xii (1), 370, p. 168. Hallam here says that Bigod argued that the king ought not to have cure of souls, 'showing a book of his own making on the power of Pope, bishop, and King'.

he should soon have begun to realize the dangers implicit in Henry's title and designs can afford no surprise. He thus turned away from the prospect of the Royal Supremacy, not, of course, back to Rome, but forward to the idea of a national church under the rule of reformed ecclesiastics and with the king merely as its secular protector.

We learn a little more about this second 'book' from certain depositions concerning Prior James Cockerell of Guisborough. According to these notes, Bigod himself gave evidence to the effect that he had declared that the king held his sword immediately of God, whereas Cockerell had maintained that 'the king has his sword by permission and delivery of the church into his hands and not otherwise'. According to another deponent, Cockerell 'commended the book made by Bygod of the said reasons and arguments of the king's authority, saying no man could mend [i.e. improve] it and he durst die in the quarrel with Bygod'. When the author promised him a copy, the prior said he would make as much thereof as of a piece of St. Augustine's works. Was this irony or *naïveté*? Cockerell is also on record as confessing that he saw 'Bygod's book against the title of Supreme Head, the Statute of Suppression and the taking away of the liberties of the Church'.[1]

The book may have gone somewhat farther than these particulars would suggest. Bigod is said to have confessed that he showed Hallam his book of notes of the defaults of the said pardon, and 'how for heresy both the king and the Bishop of Rome might be deprived lawfully; and of the king's authority'.[2] If Bigod cannot be proved to have supported in his treatise the legality of deprivation, as applied to heretical kings and popes, he was doing so very soon afterwards.

From these particulars we discern more of the common ground which Bigod had discovered between his own views and those of the conservative leaders of the Pilgrimage. He had now become as much an ecclesiast, as little an Erastian, as they; he desired as much to defend the Church from State control, even though he had a totally different conception of its organization, its doctrine, and its spiritual life. Again, it becomes clear that, however strongly he had once urged the seizure of impropriated livings from the monasteries, he still wished to reform and not to dissolve the latter. In the light of contemporary conditions this intermediate programme must surely claim some respect; but for the chronic financial problems of the Crown, the divisions among the ecclesiastics and their quarrels with the laity, some such programme might have become the basis of a just and moderate reform. These pathetic scraps

[1] *L. & P.* xii (1), 1087, p. 499.　　　　[2] Ibid., p. 495.

of information concerning a fundamental and speculative essay help us
to realize why Bigod left a reputation for 'wisdom' as well as for mere
learning. He was one of the few subjects of Henry VIII who thought for
himself on the problems of Church and State; had his final treatise been
preserved, it might have possessed a European interest as a precursor
of the Huguenot treatises of the subsequent generation.

When, about 9 December 1536, the Pilgrims were induced to dis-
perse by the king's pardon and the false pledges of the Duke of Norfolk,
Bigod returned to Mulgrave. On Christmas Eve he was rejoined by his
servant John Smyth, whose evidence throws a little light on the days
between the two rebellions. Smyth was a Lancashire man from Win-
stanley. At the time of the attempted flight by sea, Bigod had sent him
home with orders to rejoin him subsequently in London. On his belated
reappearance at Mulgrave, Bigod took him by the hand and asked him
what he had been doing 'in the busy time'. Smyth answered that he
had been with Lord Derby, and Bigod then remarked that he had seen
in Aske's purse a letter from the Earl of Derby, who, according to
Aske, 'would be with us in time of need'. Smyth then reported a conversation between himself and the earl, yet this contact appears to have
been a fortuitous one, and not initiated on Bigod's instructions. Smyth's
evidence also contains the point that they spent a quiet Christmas at
Mulgrave, whither there was no resort of gentlemen except for Mr.
Nevill, Lord Latimer's brother, who, together with his wife, came
visiting the Bigods.[1]

The outcome shows that during this interval Bigod did some furious
thinking. He had good reason. Estranged from Cromwell, yet distrusted
by the northern gentry, he must have foreseen a further worsening of
his position as soon as royal power should be re-established north of
Trent. Moreover, his keen and legalist mind detected flaws in the royal
pardon and developed a profound suspicion as to the king's intentions.

We next meet with Sir Francis on 9 January 1537, when he was riding
from Mulgrave to York, ostensibly 'for a matter between the Treasury
and the old prior of Guisborough'. On this journey he visited his friend
the prior of Malton, according to whom he criticized the pardon, saying
that it would enrage the Scots, who were there called 'our old ancient
enemies'. As we shall observe, he probably gave vent to more significant
criticisms which the prior could not, or would not, recall in this subsequent testimony. The prior on this occasion showed a copy of the
Pilgrims' Articles to Bigod, who gave the prior's servants two groats

[1] L. & P. xii (1), 578, p. 267.

to copy the Articles and send on the copy after him.[1] Leaving Malton for Settrington, where he expected to meet his brother, he continued on 10 January to John Hallam's house near Watton. Late in the day the two went over to the priory on foot, and, before he settled down to more dangerous business, Sir Francis indulged in a last dabble in the affairs of a monastery. As it happened, he was by no means the first layman to intervene in the affairs of Watton, for Hallam himself had done so during the Pilgrimage, though motivated less by reforming zeal than by his enmity for the prior, Robert Holgate, Master of Sempringham.[2] This distinguished Gilbertine and Cambridge scholar had, like Bigod himself, achieved notoriety as a friend of Thomas Cromwell. At the outset of the Pilgrimage he had wisely achieved what Bigod in vain attempted: a complete withdrawal from the area, though the story in Aske's confession that he left a large concourse of his monks and nuns without means is completely disproved by the evidence of numerous witnesses, including Bigod himself.[3] Hallam was 'greatly incensed against [Holgate] for putting him beside a farmhold' and, at the head of an armed band, had threatened to spoil Watton if the monks did not elect a new prior. They had then elected the prior of Ellerton, though they 'wanted him to bear the name only for fear of the commons'.[4] Finding matters still at this attractive stage, perhaps feeling it necessary to flatter and encourage Hallam, Bigod resolved to set the seal of his personal approval on those actions. Having reached the priory, he 'kindled' Hallam to move the brethren to a new election and drafted a document of nomination, which survives in his hand among the State papers.[5] It implicitly attacks Cromwell by asserting that his nominee Holgate had 'taken upon himself' to be prior and Master of Sempringham. It continues to the effect that Holgate has now been expelled by the commons, who will not suffer the house to receive its rents until they have a new prior; therefore the brethren have elected A.B.C. prior and have set the convent seal to this instrument. Bigod did not insert the name of the prior of Ellerton, and the draft was merely left in charge of 'one Wade dwelling by', so that if a new insurrection should occur, it could be immediately completed and sealed with the convent seal, subscribed by a notary, and shown to the commons to prevent the spoliation of the house.[6] By thus openly representing the commons both

---

[1] *L. & P.* xii (1), 534.
[2] See the present writer's *Robert Holgate* (St. Anthony's Hall Publications, no. 8).
[3] Cf. ibid., pp. 7–8.   [4] *L. & P.* xii (1), 201, pp. 99–100.
[5] Ibid. xii (1), 65.   [6] Ibid. xii (1), 201, p. 100.

at Guisborough and at Watton, Bigod was in effect already defying Cromwell and running enormous risks. By this evening at Watton he was planning to go much farther still along the path of defiance.

When Sir Francis and Hallam had supped at the priory, there took place not only the reading from the former's memorandum on Church and State, but also a discussion of the royal pardon and of plans for the renewal of rebellion. That the initiative came from Bigod there can be no doubt, for here we can follow not merely Hallam's testimony,[1] but also that of the sub-prior of Watton and two of the senior monks. These accounts confirm and amplify the arguments which Bigod based upon the text of the royal pardon. Producing a parchment copy from his purse, he urged that it was invalid, since it did not run in the king's name, but began 'as another man's tale', with the words 'Albeit the King's Highness'.[2] He therefore thought it Cromwell's deed, Cromwell being higher in favour than ever before. And whereas it rehearsed that the king had charge of his subjects both body and soul, he should have no cure of Bigod's soul. And if he, Bigod, were sheriff, he durst be bold, notwithstanding this pardon, to arrest any man, together with his lands or goods.[3] Again, it was dated two days after it had been read publicly at Scawsby Leys.[4] These were searching criticisms. And lest the reader be tempted to follow previous historians by supposing they represented merely the legal pedantry of Sir Francis, it must at once be urged that they were precisely the arguments which did appeal to contemporary audiences, including, as will shortly appear, an audience of peasants and yeomen.

Having thus attacked the pardon, Bigod left the sub-prior and the two monks sitting by the fire, took Hallam by the hand, led him to a bay window and talked with him for an hour.[5] Hallam himself subsequently summarized the strategic plan put before him in this secret conversation. Bigod said that he, along with the most part of the country around him, thought it best that Hull and Scarborough should be taken, 'for the country to resort to till Parliament time'. Should the Duke of Norfolk return to the north parts, the country should 'hold him forth', together with any others coming from the south, till the time of Parliament, for, thought Bigod, Norfolk 'would do this country no good for the purposes that they rose for in the beginning'. If he came, the

---

[1] L. & P. xii (1), 201, pp. 91–92.
[2] Ibid., p. 99.   [3] Ibid., pp. 101–2.
[4] The full texts of the pardons are printed and commented on by the present writer in *T.A.J.* xxxiii. 397 seqq.
[5] L. & P. xii (1), 201, p. 99.

country should capture him around Newburgh or Byland, and make him swear that 'they should have their intent that they rose for'.[1] Hallam's account does not exhaust Bigod's strategic plan, which was initiated in the definite expectation of a simultaneous rising by the commons of Richmondshire and Durham, supported by the Percy interest. Not only did he receive news of this design, but sent messengers northward to establish the link;[2] one of these went with a letter to the people of Swaledale, many of whom were Bigod's own tenants, but this man was captured and the letter forwarded to the Duke of Norfolk.[3]

On Saturday, 13 January, Bigod sent a servant to Hallam asking him to come over to Settrington the following day. On arrival, the yeoman found him in consultation with Ralph Fenton of Ganton and one of the friars of St. Robert's of Knaresborough, a community very active in propaganda throughout the earlier rising. Bigod gave his confederates news of fresh disturbances in Durham and the West Country, which he had received from one of Lord Latimer's servants. Hallam and Fenton then said, 'If it be so, we can see no remedy, but we must up again too.'[4] No doubt much of the detail was discussed on this occasion, but it was on the Monday that Bigod sent Hallam his final instructions by letter. The plan was to be set in motion the next day: Hallam to surprise Hull, Bigod to seize Scarborough, both to meet at Beverley on the Wednesday.[5] Bigod's whole scheme seems to the present writer the most interesting politico-military concept evolved by a Tudor rebel. It seized upon the crucial importance of Hull in a Yorkshire rebellion— a theory amply justified by experience a century later in the Civil War. It involved the seizure of *villes de sûreté*, soon to become a crucial factor in continental rebellion. Hallam, as befitted a yeoman, saw the struggle in terms of country against towns and commons against gentry.[6] Bigod, as a leader whose personal influence began and ended in the countryside, had no alternative but to link his strategy to these sentiments, unpalatable as he may personally have found them. One doubts whether he could have foreseen the vital need of a would-be Protestant magnate: influence in the towns. His plan certainly involved

---

[1] Ibid., p. 92. [2] References in Dodds, op. cit. ii. 66.
[3] *L. & P.* xii (1), 139, 217.
[4] Ibid. 201, p. 92. [5] Ibid., p. 99.
[6] 'It was rumoured', he said, 'that the king would fortify Hull and Scarborough; whereby the gentlemen might resort thither, make the towns stronger and the country weaker, and so subdue the commons that the country should be in like case as Lincolnshire was.' (Ibid., p. 91.)

more than an East Riding rebellion; it meant using the space and depth of the north. The utterly sterile process of the first rebellion—an inconclusive parley and unenforcable promises on the banks of the Don—this is rejected. Instead, the royal commander with his small force should this time be lured in north Yorkshire, outflanked, captured, and used as a hostage, perhaps as an accomplice, or at least as a genuine intermediary with the government. Bigod's brilliant strategic ideas contrast with his abysmal misjudgement of the social and psychological background in the north itself: this background proved entirely inadequate to his plan and he himself had neither the time nor the resources to improve it. The other northern gentry had not thought as fast as Bigod. Many trusted the king, while most conservatives must have realized the immensity of the abyss which separated Bigod's ideals from their own, and so have distrusted any movement initiated by him. The rising farther north came to nothing and Sir Thomas Percy muffed his last chance. Moreover, Bigod moved before he had established even the minimum network of contacts with the Yorkshire gentry. His utterances clearly show that he was casting the commons for a harder part in the drama than they could alone sustain. Even two subordinate commanders with real prestige and resolution might have gained the first objectives without undue difficulty. In short, an abstract military concept failed for lack of human materials. An organizer of popular rebellion cannot make the assumptions that are possible to a general in command of standing, disciplined forces.

When, by means of beacons and messages in the Buckrose area, Sir Francis organized on 16 January a muster of some hundreds of men, the gentry gave him the cold shoulder with a singular unanimity. Not only did Aske and Sir Robert Constable reject his plans and strive to arrest the spread of the rising; even Sir John Bulmer, his own uncle, refused to participate.[1] Only one gentleman is in fact recorded as presenting himself. This was George Lumley of Thwing, son and heir of Lord Lumley, who set out towards Settrington with a hazy notion as to the purpose of the muster.[2] His subsequent evidence[3] provides an extremely graphic account of Bigod's ideas and leadership during that critical day, when the fate of the rising was virtually decided. On his way from Thwing along the northern escarpment of the Wolds, Lumley 'mett

[1] Cf. Dodds, op. cit. ii. 76.
[2] This muster is said elsewhere (L. & P. xii (1), 730 (2)) to have been called to 'Borough': I presume this indicates the neighbourhood of Burrow House in Cowlam parish. In January this road from Thwing to Settrington would be preferable to the lower and more direct one.
[3] Printed in full in E. Milner, *Records of the Lumleys*, pp. 32–48.

certain men which brought him to a howe, where there were assembled upon a xxx or xl persons . . . and than cam Sir Frances Bygod with a c. or more of horses thether'. Refusing to speak privately with Lumley, the knight 'gate hym to the toppe of a hillocke' and made a remarkable speech, which not only impressed itself vividly upon the unfortunate Lumley, but aroused the assembly to great ardour. Realizing how completely his own class had failed him, Bigod threw himself in with the commons and began by telling them how the gentry had deceived them. Durham and Cleveland, he continued, were already in arms. On the other hand, the Duke of Norfolk was coming with 20,000 men to take Hull, Scarborough, and the ports, 'which shalbe our destruction onlesse we prevente hym therin and take them before'. He and Hallam had agreed to meet at Beverley that night and go forward to Hull. The commons should now command Mr. Lumley to capture Scarborough, Bigod himself having written a letter to the bailiffs there, demanding their assistance.[1] Another letter was to be sent to the Countess of Northumberland, so that she could summon Sir Thomas Percy to come forward with all his power, and 'he the said Bygod wold with the helpe the commons putt hym in possession of all suche lands as were my lord's of Northumberland's'.[2] Then producing a copy of the pardon, he said: 'It is no more but as if I wolde saye unto you, the king's grace will geve you a pardon, and badde you go to the Chauncerye & fatche it. And yet the same is no pardon. Also here ye are called rebells, by the which ye shall knowledge yourself to have doon ageinst the king, which is contrarie to your othe.'

We must, it seems, avoid thinking of the commons as all bucolic half-wits incapable of appreciating these issues. At this point one of them gave vent to a homely yet brilliant metaphor: 'the king hath sent us the fawcet and kepeth the spigot hymself'. Another cried, 'As for the pardon, it makes no matier whether [we] had any or not, for [we] never offended the king nor his lawes.'

Again, continued Bigod, the king had fixed no definite time and place for the Parliament. 'And also here is that the king shulde have cure bothe of your body & soule, which is playne false, for it is ageinst the gospell of Christ, and that will I justifie even to my deth. And therefore, if ye will take my parte in this and defende it, I will not faille you so

---

[1] The original no longer survives, but it was printed by Speed and reprinted in Dodds, op. cit. ii. 98.

[2] On the important role of the Percy interest and the loss to the king of the Percy lands cf. R. R. Reid, *The King's Council in the North*, p. 133. The Percies continued popular with the commons in Jan. 1537. Cf. Dodds, op. cit. ii. 80.

long as I live, to thuttermoste of my power.' He leaves us with rather
more than a hint that, having despaired of the conservative gentry, he
saw in the commons the real hope for the spread of Reforming doctrines
in the north. And that his mind still worked on the theme of ecclesiastical reform is proved by another passage of the speech, as recalled by
Lumley. 'Bygod in his said declaracion made to the people, said that the
fatt prestes' benefices of the South, that were not resident upon the
same, and money of the suppressed Abbeys, shulde finde the poore
souldiors that were not able to beare their owne charges.' As he rode
off, the commons were heard exclaiming, 'Blessed was the daye that
Sir Frances Bygod, Rauf Fenton, John Halom & the frier of Saint
Robert's mett together, for and if they had not sett their hedds together, this matier had never ben bulted out.'[1] Concerning Bigod's
clerical associates at this stage, our information is imprecise. Lumley
noticed 'one tall man that went like a preste in company with hym,
which was a greate feyrer of that busynes, and said if they went not
forwarde, all was lost that they had doon before, for all was falsehod that
was wrought ageinst theym'. This may well have been the friar of
Knaresborough, who, though an ally in rebellion, is not known to have
shared Bigod's religious views. Alternatively, it may have been one of
Bigod's chaplains, John Pickering of Pickering Lythe, who was subsequently arrested, condemned, and pardoned his share in the rising.[2]
We know little about the earlier career of this latter cleric, except that
he had lived at Coverdale in Richmondshire and at Tocketts near
Guisborough.[3] As a chaplain of Bigod, he must certainly be numbered
with the early Protestants of Yorkshire. The rest of the story has been
adequately told by others and throws relatively little further light upon
the mind and opinions of Sir Francis.

Hallam, appropriately clad in 'a privy coat of fence made with many
folds of linen cloth rosined, and a privy skull of his head', set off with
a small body of men to surprise Hull. Betrayed to the mayor by his own
confidants, he was met and recognized by a contingent under the
command of two stout aldermen, Elland and Knowles, also appropriately armed, and extremely anxious to retrieve their own and their

[1] Ralph Fenton of Ganton later led the commons at Scarborough and was
subsequently hanged at York. St. Robert's was the Trinitarian friary at Knaresborough.
[2] Cf. L. & P. xii (1), 1199 (2), 1207 (8), 1227 (9), 1239; xii (2), 12, 191 (34), 192.
He should not be confused with his namesake, prior of the York Dominicans, who
was executed for complicity with Bigod and Hallam.
[3] Ibid. 191 (34).

town's reputation with the king. After some romantic sword-play near
the Beverley Gate, Hallam fell captive.[1] At Scarborough Lumley
behaved much more ignominiously. Bigod was right in regarding
Scarborough as a secondary proposition and, for lack of alternatives,
accepted Lumley as the figurehead of the enterprise, giving orders also
directly to the commons under him. Nevertheless, Lumley's luke-
warmness sufficed to destroy the chances of an otherwise simple task.
He began by dismissing most of the men of Pickering, who had
assembled to meet him. Though receiving full support from the townsmen of Scarborough, he failed to enter the castle, which in the absence
of Sir Ralph Eure lay virtually unguarded.[2] Lumley could scarcely have
done more to thwart the plan had he been an active royalist, yet this
fact did not avail to save his life on the day of reckoning.

Meanwhile, having failed in the attempt to surprise Hull, Sir Francis
resolved, courageously but unwisely, to attack it in force. Holding a
muster early on 18 January at Bainton, he sent messengers to Hull
demanding the release of Hallam. He also appealed vainly for Sir
Robert Constable's support. In the afternoon he pressed on into
Beverley, driving the elder Sir Ralph Ellerker from the centre of the
town. He then sent a setter to his cousin Sir Oswald Wilstrope in the
name of the commons, upbraiding him for his loss of zeal and announc-
ing their intention of withdrawing to their friends in Richmondshire,
whence they would write to the king and Norfolk explaining the cause
of their 'assemblie'.[3] Writing also to the Dean and Chapter of York, he
indicated that he would advance upon York itself, but this does not
quite necessarily indicate that his mind had already become confused,[4]
since the two intentions were by no means inconsistent. Nevertheless,
the end came with a suddenness attributable only to a general collapse
of the rebels' morale in the face of the discouraging reports late in the
day concerning the counter-musters brought against them. Without
waiting for reinforcements, Ellerker counter-attacked before dawn,
drove the rebels from Beverley, and captured sixty-two prisoners. The
spoils included Bigod's private papers, even his work on Church and
State. The unlucky Reformer at once became a hunted fugitive, his
last days of liberty a rich subject for some historical novelist. Rejected
by his disillusioned neighbours of the East Riding,[5] he rode overnight

[1] Dodds, op. cit. ii. 63 seqq. gives a full account.
[2] On Lumley's mission see ibid. ii. 69 seqq.
[3] P.R.O., S.P. 1/114, pp. 198–200, has three copies of this incriminating letter.
[4] As argued by Dodds, op. cit. ii. 74.
[5] L. & P. xii (1), 533, gives details of his movements.

to Mulgrave, where Serjeant Middlewood was already seizing his goods. According to Bigod's own story, for which he claimed several witnesses, the inevitable Gregory Conyers arrived to assist in the task, saying to the Lady Katharine, 'Madame, and here are twain come for the commons', before proceeding to take, in the name of the latter, what Middlewood had left.[1] Meanwhile Sir Francis lurked in hiding near his castle. On Sunday, 21 January, Middlewood, Conyers, and even Bigod's former guest William Nevill, searched for him. Conyers ended by pursuing his enemy so closely that he took two of his horses 'and his sleeveless coat he ware on him, and drave him to flee on foot into the woods'.[2] The fugitive must have been fit and hardy, for even in this extremity he managed to elude everyone for almost three weeks and to cover a large distance across country. Acting on information from Sir Thomas Curwen, the Duke of Norfolk, now back at York, sent a party under Sir John Lamplough to search for Bigod in Cumberland. On Saturday, 10 February, they captured him 'in a chappell'[3] somewhere in that county.

The north remained very restive at this time and it was thought risky to bring the captive back through Westmorland. He was thus imprisoned in Carlisle Castle, whither the duke himself soon repaired. On 20 February Norfolk writes from Carlisle to Cromwell, 'I caused this berer to tary here alnyght to thentent he shold have with hym the confession of Bigod, with whom I have commyned at great leasure, and can geyte no more of hym than is conteigned in this his confession wich ye shall receyve herewith, nor think I shall have no more of hym, not withestondyng I shall strayctelie examine hym from tyme to tyme for thobteignyng of more of hym.' Norfolk proceeds to oppose Cromwell's view that Bigod should suffer execution in London, 'for in the contrarye it is not knowen what the rude people woll gaythre and note theryn, peradventure that we dar not to put hym to execution here'.[4] This suggestion of popular sympathy is confirmed by Wilfrid Holme,[5] who gives the rescue of Bigod as one of the objectives of the new revolt by the commons of Cumberland.

No complete text of Bigod's depositions appears to have survived, but much of their substance may be learned from a mutilated paper in Wriothesley's hand[6] and from a long letter of confession written to

[1] *L. & P.* xii (1), 532, 533.   [2] Ibid. 870; cf. ibid. 234, 810.
[3] Wilfrid Holme, *The Fall and Evill Success of Rebellion* (cf. *infra*, p. 114), H. iii.
[4] P.R.O., S.P. 1/116, fo. 88.   [5] Loc. cit.
[6] *L. & P.* xii (1), 532.

Cromwell.[1] This latter fascinating document is also somewhat mutilated, but it is throughout in Bigod's own hand, written with the knowledge of impending doom, but as firmly and clearly as in earlier days. Both documents are undated, but should presumably be placed late in February or early in March 1537. They make it clear that very little was extracted from Bigod concerning other suspects. Not surprisingly, he accused his arch-enemy Gregory Conyers of seizing his goods in the name of the commons. He also remarked that the Dean and Canons of York had purchased and kept in their houses great stocks of new harness since the first rising, but admitted he did not know the purposes of these preparations. His lack of accord with the conservative clerical leaders may easily, however, be deduced, since he also mentions their attempt to accuse Cromwell of heresy.[2] Regarding his own rebellious actions, he makes no attempt at palliation or concealment, probably expecting nothing but capital punishment and realizing the uselessness of any plea for mercy. By far the most interesting passage of these two documents is the concluding paragraph of the letter to Cromwell, which testifies most eloquently to his family affections and to his undaunted sympathy with the Protestant cause. He had called to witness his brother Ralph and Thomas Wentworth, but, he continues, 'I truste in yower gentilnesse ye wil not beare ather of theym any displesuere for riportyng to me what was said among the commones.' If Cromwell should summon them to London without publicizing his reasons, it would

cawse the cuntre thynke, and theym also to be afraid, that I had acusid theym as [? traitors or] counsellers in this noughtye matter of Halome's and myne, of wiche, so helpe me the blessid bodye of God wiche yesterday I resavid, they[3] are any more giltie, or yit of councell, or know of it more then the childe yit unborn (so far as I suppose or know);[4] and my mowther haveyng no mo childern but us twayne wolde be too ful of sorow. Therefore, good my lorde, if ye sende for theym, putte theym owte of this dowte, that it is not for my matter.

The last sentences of this pathetic letter have a greater interest in relation to our present theme.

I beseche yower good lordeship whether I live or dye to be good lord [to] maister Jherom, who in few wordes, boith for preachyng and [blank] haith few

---

[1] P.R.O., S.P. 1/116, fos. 163–64ᵛ; cf. L. & P. xii (1), 533.
[2] He also mentions prophecies by William Todd, prior of Malton, but Todd himself admitted this conversation and apparently escaped punishment.
[3] After this word he wrote 'ne none here resitid' and then struck out these words.
[4] The words in brackets were later interpolated between the lines.

fellowes, and a vere honeste man. In like case for Gode's sake helpe Cervyng-
ton, who in my cuntre dar not cum by cawse he is trew favorer of Gode's
worde. He is a proper gentilman and honeste and can do good service at a
table among owther qualities. Charitie byndith me to wisshe theym well.
And thus the lorde of all Lordes preserve yower Lord[ship]. Francis Bigod
prisoner.[1]

The first of these men must be William Jerome, the well-known
Protestant martyr. A monk of Christ Church, Canterbury, he was
educated at both universities, taking his B.D. at Oxford in 1530. His
presentation to the vicarage of Stepney on 2 June 1537 followed closely
upon Bigod's recommendation from prison. He remained associated
with Bigod's other former chaplain Garret and with the onetime friar
Barnes. After a sermon giving great offence at Paul's Cross, Jerome
was attainted of heresy by Parliament and burned along with Garret
and Barnes at Smithfield on 30 July 1540, the day after the execution of
their patron Cromwell.[2] In a religious sense, this execution of his two
principal chaplains represents the true culmination of Bigod's career.
As for Cervington, Bigod's letter does not actually state that he was
a preacher or even in holy orders, but no doubt he belonged to the
class of young family chaplains who were not above acting the part of
the gentleman's gentleman. He was presumably a poor member of the
Wiltshire family of that name:[3] he later became an associate of John
Bale and repaid his debt by transmitting to the latter the details about
Bigod preserved in the manuscript we now call *Index Britanniae Scriptorum*.[4]

Meanwhile on 13 March Bigod 'was browte owte of the Northe to
the tower thorrow Smythfelde and in at Newgat, rydynge soo thorrow
Chepesyde and soo to the tower, and Sir Raffe Elderker ledynge hym
by the hond with that he was bounde with alle'.[5] The trial of the principal offenders took place in Westminster Hall on 16 May. In addition
to the group-charges, Bigod and Lumley were naturally involved in
others concerning the second rebellion: in particular with assembling
500 persons[6] to levy war against the king. Sir Christopher Hailes,

---

[1] P.R.O., S.P. 1/116, fo. 164ᵛ.

[2] Foxe, v. 429–38, gives much detail. On Jerome see also C. H. and T. Cooper,
Athenae Cantabrigienses, i. 76, and their references: also Venn, *Alumni Cantabrigienses*,
s.v. Jerome.

[3] R. C. Hoare, *Hist. of Modern Wilts.* iii. v. 27.   [4] ed. R. L. Poole, p. 72.

[5] *Greyfriars Chron.* (Camden Soc. liii), p. 40. He was in the Tower for seemingly
less than three months, but the government was overcharged for his maintenance
(*L. & P.* xii (2), 181, printed in full, *Archaeologia*, xviii. 244).

[6] Holme (H. iiᵛ) says they mustered 'nygh twentie score'.

Master of the Rolls, appeared as prosecutor.[1] The defendants pleaded not guilty, but—a foregone conclusion—were condemned.[2] On 2 June there were 'drawne from the Tower of London to Tyborne Sir Thomas Percy, Sir Frances Byggot, George Lumley . . . William Woodde prior of Byrlyngtone, Adame Sedbarre abbot of Jarvys, and there ware hongyd, heddyd and qwarterd, save Sir Thomas Percy, for he was but heddyd and was burryd at the Crose Freeres, and the qwarters of alle the resydew was burryd at the Gray Freeres in the clowster on the north syde in the pa[ve]me[n]t.'[3]

It is impossible to doubt that Sir Francis died as he had lived, a man of the Protestant New Learning. Naturally enough, many of his contemporaries supposed he had simply been seduced to the cause of religious reaction. Wilfrid Holme, writing almost contemporaneously in Yorkshire, makes the lady *Anglia* say,

I have more inquisition
Of a latter commotion which greatly doth me greeve
Doone by Sir Frauncis Bigot which maketh my heart fremeske,[4]
For he was reconed one of the veritie perculent,[5]
And what a shame was it contrarie to flameske,[6]
And to forsake the truth such wrongfull things petent.

Holme replies to her:

According to the proverb and it please your grace, quod I,
The Dog is reversed unto his vomit againe,
And the Sowe cleane washed in hir puddle wil she lye.[7]

To the chronicler Edward Hall, Bigod was 'a man no doubt that loved God, and feared his prynce, wyth a right obedient and loving fear: but now being deceyved und provoked ther unto by false rebellyous persones, it was his fortune to tast of the ende which apperteigneth to rebelles: such are men whom God leaveth them to them selfes, and when they wyl enterpryse the doyng of that thinge whiche Goddes most holy word utterly forbiddeth'.[8]

A few people took a more discerning view. They apparently included Hugh Latimer, now Bishop of Worcester. A letter written from Mulgrave by the Lady Katharine Bigod shortly after her husband's death

---

[1] *L. & P.* xii (1), 1199, 3(ii).   [2] Ibid. 1227 (13).
[3] *Greyfriars Chron.*, p. 41.   [4] Cf. *New Eng. Dict.*, 'fremish', to waver.
[5] Perhaps in the sense of straining, sifting, and purifying the truth. I have not encountered the form elsewhere.
[6] Perhaps to 'flame out' in rebellion.   [7] H. ii.
[8] *The Triumphant Reigne of Kyng Henry the VIII*, ed. C. Whibley, ii. 278.

thanks him for his intercession with the king for her feoffment and begs him to continue his efforts for her and her children.[1] John Bale, the arch-Protestant, preserved the favourable tradition, having received it from Bigod's chaplain or protégé Cervington. To Bale, Sir Francis was no renegade, but 'homo natalium splendore nobilis ac doctus et evangelicae veritatis amator'.[2]

4. Bigod and His Times

The modern historians of the Pilgrimage of Grace began by discerning something of the puritanical strain in Bigod.[3] They ended, however, by writing that 'So Sir Francis concluded, enigmatical to the last. He was about to die for the old religion, and his last written words are a commendation of the new.'[4] A closer and more specialized survey would seem to dispense with this last verdict. We are left with complexity, yet with no insoluble enigma. We cannot say that Bigod died for the old religion, unless we persist in the popular fallacy that the Pilgrimage was simply a religious revolt, and that everybody whose death resulted from it must automatically have died for the old religion. In Bigod's case nothing could be less true. From first to last his expressed views on religion were consistently Protestant. His position and his acceptance by several of the leading Reformers has become sufficiently manifest. He was certainly not a sacramentarian extremist: his last remark on receiving the 'Body of God' reinforces this obvious point. Men like Garret and Jerome, from whom he derived so much, may be described as left-wing Lutherans,[5] but were not under Anabaptist or Lollard influences. Barnes, the fellow-martyr of Bigod's chaplains, took part in the persecution of John Lambert and other sacramentarians,[6] while Latimer himself held similar views concerning such extremists. Bigod's religion was one of affirmation, not of denial. His emphasis lay upon the 'painful and industrious minister', delivering the word of God according to the Scriptures. He himself is the evangelist *manqué*, the assiduous Bible-student, the married knight who pleaded for a dis-

[1] *L. & P.* xii (2), 194. He was successful and she continued in possession of part of the Bigod lands until her death in 1567. Cf. *T.A.J.* xxxii. 199.
[2] *Scriptorum Illustrium maioris Brytannie . . . Catalogus*, pt. ii, p. 103.
[3] Dodds, op. cit. i. 44.
[4] Ibid. ii. 199.
[5] It was Cranmer who spoke of Garret as a 'forward and busy Lutheran'; cf. *D.N.B.*, s.v. Gerard.
[6] *D.N.B.*, s.v. Barnes.

pensation either to receive priest's orders, 'that I may preache the Worde of God', or else that 'beyng no preiste, I may do it'.[1]

A layman anxious to vie with learned clerks, he scorns in private letters to quote the Bible in any save the Vulgate text, yet we may scarcely doubt his sympathy with the cause of public edification through the vernacular Scriptures. The pulpit and the Bible remained the centres of his religion. He attacked monastic impropriations not out of hatred for monasteries but in order that 'a suffycient company of the ministers of Godde's true worde' should be 'provyded for in all partes'. He even toured the north with his own team of preaching chaplains.

Outside the sphere of religion proper, his views became to some extent fluid and showed development. As his *Treatise of Impropriations* shows, he initially welcomed the Royal Supremacy and hoped it would usher in an age of rational church-government and active evangelism. Already under considerable obligations to Cromwell, he at first found self-interest and religious convictions uniting to make him an enthusiastic trumpeter of the Royal Supremacy in the north. The precise moment at which he began to abandon this naïve acceptance remains obscure, for whatever misgivings assailed him, he had no opportunity to express them before the outbreak of the Pilgrimage of Grace. Nevertheless, he was doing so in no uncertain manner by November 1536, and he may well have begun to entertain these critical doubts several months earlier. Why and how did his ideas on church-government undergo this crucial development? To this question the records yield some substantial clues, but no complete and precise answer. Quite apart from personal and secular matters, the ecclesiastical policy of the Crown had by now shown some disquieting characteristics. It had failed to produce any positive programme of reform along Bigod's line. The king had not, for example, abolished or modified appropriations; he had merely started dissolving monasteries without using the proceeds to endow a teaching clergy. A church supervised by Thomas Cromwell, its politician vicar-general, a church with its endowments increasingly controlled by a conservative and secularist gentry: this was not even the foundation of Sir Francis Bigod's ideal church. Moreover, the theoretical extension of the Royal Supremacy into spheres regarded by him as spiritual offended his deepest convictions. He was quick to notice every hint of this extension, as in the royal pardon, which provided him with such heavy ammunition in the north. However sound a Protestant, he shuddered as profoundly as any Catholic

[1] *Supra*, p. 77.

when he saw the king claim to have 'the chief charge of you under God, both of youre sowles and bodies'.[1] In his last memorandum on Church and State, Bigod proceeded to strike a blow against this far-reaching Erastianism, condemning the headship of any except a spiritual man, and designating for the king the merely external role of the Church's protector. This may be accepted as a rational development of his original view rather than as a mere volte-face: the objective remains unchanged, but the royal instrument, having shown itself dangerously different from that anticipated, is relegated to another function.

So much one can argue for the cohesion and integrity of Bigod's views on religion and church-government. At the same time, it becomes brutally evident that his relations with both churchmen and politicians were also affected by personal and secular factors, by motives less statesmanlike, less far-seeing, less spiritual, less altruistic, and less consistent. In particular, his many contacts with the Yorkshire monasteries had produced a deceptive amalgam of reform and self-interest. On the one hand, with or without Cromwell's backing, this young man still in his twenties traversed the shire, regulating monastic affairs like a lay bishop; on the other hand, he pursued the material interests and rivalries, which he and other gentry entertained within the monastic world, whether as paid stewards, debtors, or tenants. On the best of such occasions, it remains difficult to see Sir Francis as the impersonal instrument of the Divine purpose.

If we turn to the more purely political side of his career, we are again confronted with a major dichotomy. Prior to the rebellion, he had become a leading agent of the Crown north of Trent, in particular a confidant of Thomas Cromwell, one of the greatest exponents of administrative centralization in English history. At the same time, he stood among the territorial magnates of Yorkshire, embroiled in local feuds and affinities, bound to work with men who had every reason to hate Cromwell, extremely sensitive to opinion in his 'own country', anxious to preserve even the sordid but time-honoured sanctuaries in deference to local opinion. Above all, he held office from the Percies and, even when figuring as representative of the common people, publicly announced his intention of restoring the Percy lands recently acquired by the Crown. While diametrically opposed to the religious conservatism so prominent in the Pilgrimage, he was far from lacking sympathy with its political conservatism. Having so strong an interest in the monasteries and the nobility of the north, how could Sir Francis

[1] The pardon of 9 Dec. 1536, printed in *T.A.J.* xxxiii. 406; cf. *supra*, p. 99.

give the unquestioning loyalty demanded by the Crown? Here is no mere rhetorical question, since a little more imagination and generosity on the part of Cromwell might perhaps have kept him within the fold. Bigod did not receive sufficient incentive to loyal service. It has already been urged that one cannot reasonably dismiss him as the desperate debtor, at first tied to Cromwell, his protector against creditors, then hastening to embrace rebellion as the road of escape from impending bankruptcy. All the same, his letters show how profoundly under-rewarded he came to feel. He had struggled long and hard to preserve the family territories intact, yet to little avail, since just prior to the Pilgrimage he was being forced into sales of land. His sense of personal obligation to Cromwell and to the Crown had presumably now reached a low ebb. Even though at first he strove to evade its clutches, the Pilgrimage caught him in a highly unsettled mood, and before long he is found condemning, along with the other rebels, the excessive power attained by Cromwell. Seen as a personal response to a personal prob-lem, this change represents a natural enough reaction against a patron whose nod had long been arbiter of his destiny and who had neverthe-less continued to disappoint his high expectations, both financial and spiritual. His story thus evinces that mixture of idealistic and selfish motives so frequently recognizable in the heroes of history; the mixture which can seldom be analysed with much precision or confidence, because its true nature lies largely hidden from the hero himself. Such a man's idealism cannot without crudity be labelled as mere self-decep-tion or as the gross rationalization of selfish motives: even a rapid perusal of Bigod's letters reveals this to be an underestimate. At the same time, during the last three years of his life, he was never in a position to reflect coolly and impersonally upon the religious and political problems of his day. Having a humanist training and a gift for literary analysis, he was also called upon by birth and territorial posi-tion to play an active and a very difficult part in the tragi-comedy of the Henrician Reformation.

These broad considerations by no means exhaust the problems sur-rounding Bigod's participation in revolt. Behind the factors already enumerated, there lay a powerful individualism and a temperamental configuration far from uncommon among the English gentry from that day to this. Not without reason might we assimilate him to a familiar type of educated country gentleman: somewhat of a crank; opinionated, testy, pedantic, intelligent, but intellectually angular; enjoying to the full those nice distinctions of view which set him apart from his neighbours. Bigod was independent to the point of eccentricity. Moreover, he may well be envisaged as the thwarted man of talent, his urge to leadership hitherto repressed by his slow-moving neighbours, by his assertive rivals and creditors, by his all-powerful, parvenu friend Thomas Cromwell. That a young man of this type ended by snatching at the leadership of popular discontent and by believing himself clever enough to redirect it, need cause us little surprise. Beyond this point, more difficult questions present themselves. In deciding to renew the revolt, how far had he thought out the next task: that of canalizing its energies into his own purposes? How, precisely, did a Reformer propose to make an instrument of the forces behind the Pilgrimage of Grace? Again, the records provide only a few scattered clues; Bigod is unlikely, for example, to have unbosomed himself with complete candour in that speech to the assembled commons reported by Lumley. One would suppose him indeed to have done a good deal of thinking beyond what was worth revealing to Hallam. Those who view his problem in terms of converting a 'Catholic' into a 'Protestant' movement do violence to the facts. The revolt occurred, after all, in the fourth, not the ninth decade of the sixteenth century. Parties and programmes remained amorphous; material discontents could be directed into innumerable courses; few of the participants thought with the clarity of Aske or Bigod; the leader with social prestige and a glib tongue might gain a considerable following for a variety of causes. Despite his advanced beliefs and Cromwellian connexions, Sir Francis actually held some important opinions in common with mass-opinion in the north. His anti-papalism can have lost him little support, since even the clerical leaders were mostly lukewarm on this score. Bigod came to think the king a heretic worthy of deposition. He protested against the 'extort power' of Cromwell and against the Act of Succession. He wanted to preserve the Percy inheritance, the monasteries, the sanctuaries; he could make sweeping promises to attract the cupidity of the commons. He wished strictly to limit the Royal Supremacy. In the north the demand for ecclesiastical reform was very far from being limited to Bigod.[1] Was it not Lord Darcy himself who had roundly declared that 'there is no manner of State within this Realm that hath more need of reformation ne to be put under good government than the spiritual men'? In matters of high policy, the common man all too readily followed his natural superiors; no doubt a popular basis for Bigod's cherished plans of reform might with great patience have been constructed. Even the

[1] For examples see R. R. Reid, *The King's Council in the North*, pp. 122–3.

gentry lacked firm principles in this sphere; many who joined the first rising were within a very few years buttressing their fortunes with monastic lands. Bigod probably imagined that scriptural education and a teaching clergy would, as time passed, commend themselves on sheer merit to government and people alike. It is unlikely that he foresaw the functions and importance of the towns in the coming history of English Protestantism. Possibly he imagined himself in years to come as the chief broker of royal influence in the north—as the godly magnate who would interpret a chastened monarchy to its northern subjects and shape the course of a gradually emergent Reformation to the needs of the common people. Yet if he ever indulged in this last dream, he was seriously underestimating the nature and purposes of Tudor kingship.

In the early stages of this study, the present writer was inclined to couple the lurid phraseology of certain of the letters with the rashness ultimately shown by Sir Francis, and thus to credit him with a low degree of emotional maturity and a marked tendency to hysteria. A re-examination in the light of the whole story and of contemporary manners seems, however, to leave this hypothesis with less weight. Despite their veneer of formality, Tudor gentlemen were more addicted than their modern counterparts to exhibiting violent emotions and to emitting lurid verbal expressions: if Sir Francis must be dubbed hysterical, so must a high proportion of his documented contemporaries and of Shakespeare's characters. And so far as concerns his behaviour before and during his rebellion, reasons have already been given to show that his plans and leadership, though marked by great psychological and social miscalculations, were in themselves logical and in some details brilliant. His approach and conduct proved anything but those of a crazed fanatic. His whole attack upon political and strategic problems was more penetrating and prophetic than that of the other leaders. Former critics have too often dismissed Bigod as the unbalanced gambler who brought disaster upon the 'legitimate' northern leadership. With more force it might be argued that disaster overtook Aske, Darcy, Constable, and their movement because they were political simpletons who failed to follow the reasoning of a shrewder and less trustful judge of Henry and Cromwell. In supposing that the monarchy would, or could, allow the first rising to go unpunished and meekly accept its demands, the conservative leaders embraced a profound fallacy. If the government had not been presented with an excuse for retribution by Bigod's failure, it would, as soon as the vigilance of the north were withdrawn, have found some other excuse. Almost alone among the northern gentry, Bigod realized that the rebels had dropped their guard too soon. He saw through the mockery of the Doncaster pardon; he saw the necessity of remustering the north and of renewing armed pressure on the government before it became too late. He saw that a rebellion must rely upon the sanction of force, or else fail. In modern terms, Bigod was the only exponent of that *Realpolitik* which the situation of the rebels demanded. Like many politicians of this stamp, he lacked not logic, but 'instinct', the power to assess and allow for the reactions of more commonplace and susceptible minds. Unfortunately for his chances, if a man with Bigod's past were to achieve any significant personal influence in the north, he needed this 'instinct': he needed tact, patience, and power to compromise. Viewing his whole career, one could scarcely claim these as his predominant virtues.

This is not the place for an elaborate general verdict upon the Pilgrimage of Grace and its leaders, yet before leaving the story of Sir Francis Bigod we are concerned to establish a clear distinction between a sympathetic account and a favourable verdict in the light of history. The present writer is attempting to give Sir Francis the former and yet withhold the latter, since he feels no historical regrets over the triumph of Henry VIII. Tudor conciliar government was surely the 'right' solution to the problem of the north, the one outcome which could initiate the subsequent great contribution of this region to the English State and nation. The opposition showed itself hopelessly complex, fissiparous, retrogressive, lacking in administrative and judicial ideas. Its victory over Tudor kingship could not have given birth to a stable régime; indeed, it must soon have plunged Englishmen into a hideous morass of civil war and suffering similar to that which was about to engulf the luckless peoples of continental Europe. One may feel extremely little spontaneous enthusiasm for the authoritarian views of Hobbes, yet looking at the impending continental abyss and at English society as it existed in the fifteenth and earlier sixteenth centuries, the figure of Leviathan becomes almost attractive. It is hard both for modern liberals and for modern Catholics to conceive of the harsh psychological climate under which the Tudors undertook their task of building a nation-state. Their subjects were not nineteenth- or twentieth-century democrats in fancy dress: too many of them had still to be educated or conditioned into the elementary forms of social conduct and the observance of law. If the Tudors were not like the Stuarts, neither was the Tudor opposition like the Stuart opposition. The spectacle we have just witnessed—that of a Protestant individualist upholding the Percies and reviving a reactionary rising by a direct appeal to the peasantry—is but one of a long series of grotesque situations suggesting that the success of the northern revolt, whatever the high aspirations of some of its leaders, could only have thrown our nation back into the serpent coils of bastard feudalism, or, if it be preferred, forward into the era of pseudo-religious wars, since the old evil and the new were soon to merge and create a long winter for the common people of Europe. What type of autocracy would at last have emerged from such an atrocious episode in England we fortunately cannot say, but once again the continental analogies look uninviting.

Viewed against this broad background of history, the career of Sir Francis Bigod appears as a tragedy unredeemed by consequential developments. Despite intellectual gifts and courage of no mean order, despite some sincere ideals by no means wholly unattuned to the future of England, he suffered a traitor's death before he was thirty and yet failed to strike an effective blow for the cause nearest his heart. His death, misunderstood by those outside his immediate circle, served in fact to nullify the intentions of his life. That poor, simple-witted monk, George Lazenby of Jervaulx, did far better for an opposing creed. Seen, however, from another angle, the story becomes a tragedy of somewhat more classical and satisfying shape. Though Bigod cannot be claimed as the proto-martyr of English puritanism, he may yet be taken as its forerunner, since he embraced an evangelical theocracy remote alike from royalism and papalism. He came before his time and was born into the wrong setting. Whatever the later victories won by this Third Force, it commended itself to singularly few of the subjects of Henry VIII. So, rejected by both sides, Francis Bigod went down

> Between the pass and fell incensèd points
> Of mighty opposites.

For all that, minds of not dissimilar temper and far greater resources were already at work on the Continent. Some months before Bigod went to Smithfield, Calvin had published his *Institutes* and had come on his first mission to Geneva. Whatever Milton may have claimed a century later, there were at least some brands of religion which God did not reveal first to his Englishmen.

IV

SOME OTHER GENTRY

1. *Wilfrid Holme of Huntington*

WILFRID HOLME's politico-religious poem *The Fall and Evill Success of Rebellion* was written in 1537, but not printed until 1572–3, when Binneman produced two quarto editions,[1] now bibliographical rarities of the first order. The work used to be dismissed as a minor source for the Pilgrimage of Grace, but out of a total of 269 stanzas, only about 51 are in fact concerned with the events of the great rising.[2] The bulk of the remainder, while ostensibly dealing with the rebels' demands and the king's replies, broadens out into an elaborate essay upon the political and theological principles at stake during this supreme crisis of the English Reformation. Its value lies in the sphere of ideas and opinions, one to which English local historians, in their excessive concern with land and other material things, have hitherto contributed all too little. And it seems likely that the work was considered worth publishing in 1572, not so much as factual history, but as anti-treason propaganda in a year when very recent memories of another great northern rebellion were being freshened by the execution of the seventh Earl of Northumberland. The known facts concerning the author's life and background do not go far to account for his opinions. For what they are worth, the Tudor pedigrees show no less than ten generations of Holmes at Huntington, near York, before Wilfrid.[3] His immediate ancestors held 'landis and rentes in the citie of York and suburbis',[4] yet there is no evidence that they played a notable part in civic affairs. John, the grandfather of our author, describes himself as 'of Huntington, gentilman' in his will dated 20 December 1490.[5] He had married Isabel, daughter of William Snawsell,

---

[1] A copy of the 1573 edition is in the British Museum; the Huntington Library at San Marino, California, has copies of both editions. Cf. Pollard and Redgrave, *Short Title Catalogue*, nos. 13602–3.

[2] Of these, 20 are devoted to the actual events of the main rebellion, 6 to its fall, and 25 to the rebellion of Bigod and Hallam.

[3] *Glover's Visitation of Yorks.*, ed. J. Foster, p. 224; *Harleian Soc.* xvi. 162–3. The present writer gives fuller details of the family in *T.A.J.* xxxix. 119 seqq.

[4] John Holme mentions these in his will; Wilfrid himself had messuages there (*Yorks. Fines*, i. Y.A.S. Rec. Ser. ii. 80).

[5] *Test. Ebor.* iv 62–63.

goldsmith and alderman of York, and of Bilton. Their son, Thomas
Holme, succeeded to the estate in 1491, married Margaret, daughter
and heiress of Sir Thomas Bolton of Huby,[1] made a settlement of the
manor on the marriage of his heir Wilfrid with Elizabeth Constable in
1511,[2] and died early in 1520.[3] Elizabeth is identified as the daughter of
Philip Constable of Skirton,[4] third son of Sir Robert Constable[5] of
Flamborough and younger brother of the famed 'little' Sir Marmaduke,
who fought alongside his 'seemly sons' at Flodden.[6] If these details,
combined from various pedigrees, are correct, Wilfrid's wife was hence
a cousin of that major 'hero' of the Pilgrimage of Grace, Sir Robert
Constable, who expiated his treason by hanging from the Beverley
Gate at Hull, 'so trimmed with chains', wrote the Duke of Norfolk,
'that I think his bones will hang there this hundred years'.[7] Altogether,
it is easy to see why Wilfrid Holme regarded himself as of old and well-
connected county stock, 'in Huntington in Yorkshire commorant
patrimonial'. Though a fierce Protestant, he was anything but a parvenu
of the new age.

If he intended to publish his work, he had little time to seek a printer,
for he died within a year of its composition. An inquisition on the death
of Wilfrid Holme Esquire, held in the castle of York on 24 July 1538,
found that he had died in the previous June, and that his son and heir
Seth was aged eight years and nine months. Sir Marmaduke Constable
and Seth Snawsell his kinsman were then holding lands in Haxby and
Huntington belonging to him.[8] As for the manor of Huntington, it
descended from Seth Holme in 1588 to his heir, another Seth, and
finally in 1607 left the family by sale.[9]

These aridities of family history signally fail to illuminate the most
remarkable aspect of Wilfrid Holme's poem: its advanced Protestant
anti-clericalism, which runs completely outside the predominantly conservative tradition of the Yorkshire gentry and seems to stem from such

---

[1] Margaret apparently died about the same time as her husband, her will being
proved 18 July 1520 (*Harleian Soc.* xcv. 230).
[2] *V.C.H.* loc. cit. cites Chancery Inq. p.m. ser. 2, lx. 5; ccxix. 81.
[3] Thomas Holme's will was proved 10 May 1520 (*Wills in the York Registry, 1514–
1553*; Y.A.S. Rec. Ser. xi. 223).
[4] *Harleian Soc.* xvi. 163; J. Hunter, *Chorus Vatum* in Brit. Mus. Add. MSS. 24487–92,
s.v. Holme.
[5] Cf. *Harleian Soc.* xvi. 65, 163; one of these pedigrees calls him the second son; the
other shows a Robert who died *sans issu* as the second. Cf. also J. Foster, op. cit.,
p. 197.
[6] Cf. Dodds, op. cit. i. 46.   [7] *State Papers of Henry VIII*, v. 91.
[8] J. Hunter, *Chorus Vatum*, loc. cit.   [9] *V.C.H.* loc. cit. gives references.

works as Tyndale's *Practice of Prelates* (1530), Simon Fish's *Supplication for Beggars* (1529), and the various tracts of the London extremists. The author in fact displays himself as a fiercer anti-clerical than Sir Francis Bigod, whose final lapse into rebellion he chronicles with such bitterness. One cannot avoid suspecting that Holme may have spent some considerable time in London and that, were the records of the Inns of Court complete for the early years of the century, his name might well be found among them. Other members of the family are said to have studied the law[1] and, it need hardly be added, such a legal education was then the normal equipment for a young man of Holme's status. There seems no reason to connect him with the early Protestants of the city of York, a group outside his social and doctrinal orbit.

In the common form of contemporary poets, Holme describes himself as unlearned. Nevertheless, his literary knowledge must have exceeded that of the average country gentleman in the reign of Henry VIII. He shows an easy acquaintance with classical and English history, cites no less than 250 scriptural texts in his margins, is well abreast of contemporary religious polemics. As usual with our minor Tudor writers, it proves difficult to judge how far his numerous references to patristic and medieval authors may represent any first-hand or prolonged acquaintance with their texts. So far as his English style and versification are concerned, they derive from the obvious favourites of the early century and from Lydgate in particular. He may well have studied Skelton, possibly the early work of John Bale, and with both those rebellious spirits he shows a temperamental affinity. Like that of most versifiers between Chaucer and Surrey, his scansion is of an extremely rough-and-ready character. Another characteristic which he displays in marked though not unique degree is a vocabulary full of latinized neologisms, to modern taste bombastic and frequently ludicrous. Like the religious mind, the literary language is entering upon a phase of chronic experimentation; its gothic structure is overloaded by a plethora of Renaissance motives which it cannot assimilate.

From this point, our subject will best be clarified if we attempt a summary of *The Fall and Evill Success of Rebellion*, quoting a few lines where it seems most appropriate.

Holme's own verses are prefixed by five quatrains over the signature R.S., the owner of which I have failed to identify. In the trite Sternhold-and-Hopkins metre by then so fashionable, these lines impress the moral to be drawn in 1572:

[1] A note in *Surtees Soc.*, liii. 62, states that John Holme is called *apprenticius legis*.

> As haultie Holme in loftie stile
> Hath paint their doings trim:
> Oh rebels rue your wretched case,
> And warning take by him.

The poem itself, written in eight-lined stanzas,[1] takes the medieval form of a dream-allegory, one recently revived by Skelton[2] and still destined to a long life in English literature. The poet meets a dolorous princess, in this case *Anglia*, who orders him to tell stories of the fate of sedition. In the common form of medieval poets, Holme professes his own insufficiency, 'as a gemme without glosse unpublished to shine', but inevitably he is prevailed upon to begin. Having first evidenced the horrors of rebellion from an array of Biblical and Roman examples, he rapidly traverses English medieval history. Impervious, like most Tudor writers, to the charms of Magna Carta, he is

> . . . ashamed to pronounce to publish and declare
> The Baronage commotion, against John the King

and here he may well appear a disciple of John Bale, who, interpreting earlier history in the light of current controversy, had recently in his plays depicted King John as the victim of an aggressive Papacy. Meanwhile, having reached the rebellions under Henry VII, Holme is bidden by Anglia to recount the 'late commotion', otherwise the Pilgrimage of Grace.

He begins by describing the wild rumours which preceded the rising: that parish churches were to be dissolved; fasting, prayer, and good works forbidden, church fees raised, delicate meats reserved for men of estate.[3] The main events of the Lincolnshire and Yorkshire revolts are then briefly rehearsed. These three stanzas will serve as an example of Holme's jejune narrative style:

> Then Hul made a brag but anone it was yeelded,
> Then Yorkshire in general, it was nigh collected
> Yorke received them for there they abode, and builded
> Til the Countreis adjacent with the rumour wer infected

---

[1] The vast majority of the lines range between eleven and fourteen syllables and most have a well-marked caesura.

[2] In his *Treatise upon a Goodly Garland or Chaplet of Laurel*, conceived in 1523 when the poet was staying at Sheriff Hutton. A northern Elizabethan example is Richard Robinson's *Rewarde of Wickedness* (1574), written under the patronage of the Talbots at Sheffield.

[3] Civ–C. ii. Cf. for a list of such rumours drawn from other sources, Dodds, op. cit. i. 76–77.

And as I suppose they had letters directed,
Whereby was raised all Richmondshire and Tindale,
The borders of Lancashire began to be suspected,
Bishoprike rose cleare, with Sedbare, Dent and Kendale.

Sir Henrie Savil,[1] Sir Marmaduke Constable,
Sir Brian Hastings, Sir John Nevil,[2] the King they assisted,
Master Evers at Scarburgh to them was agreeable,
With all his companions, and would faine have resisted.
The Maire of Yorke[3] wold, but the commons he mistrusted,
William Maunsel also, and Knolles of Hull[4] cleere,
With the Archdeacon of Duresme of the same part consisted,
And flee from the Riotors did Leonard Bequet[5] Esquire.

Doctor Stephens, phisitian to Therle of Northumberland[6]
And Ratclif[7] had done wel, if Yorke had bene contented,
The Parson of Castlegate[8] was of the same covinant,
And the Bishop of Duresme of the same part consented:
I know but another which ought to be presented,
But which after spoyler to the commons did resorte:
Yet Sir Thomas Curwen earnestly invented,
With Sir Thomas Wharton to stay their counterporte.[9]

Anglia 'with an ardent fury' thereupon asks Holme what caused some of the gentlemen to join the rising: he denounces their folly, saying that some were compelled by the commons, but more 'seduced with the Papistes devise'. He then embarks upon the major task of the work: a discussion of the rebels' articles and the king's replies, which had been printed before the end of 1536. Significantly enough, the bulk of this discussion is devoted to Holme's own views, which often move

[1] The parts played by most of these loyalists may be followed by reference to the indexes of vols. xi and xii of the *L. & P.* and of Dodds, op. cit.
[2] On Sir John Neville of Chevet, who in 1541 was himself executed for failing to reveal a fresh Yorkshire plot, see *T.A.J.* xxxiv. 384 seqq.
[3] Cf. Dodds, op. cit., index, s.v. Harrington, William.
[4] William Knolles, alderman of Hull, originally surrendered the town to the rebels, but took a leading part in the suppression of Hallam's rising. Cf. Dodds, op. cit. i. 164; ii. 65.
[5] Leonard Beckwith, later knighted, of Selby. See in addition to the above authorities, the account of his career in W. W. Morrell, *History and Antiq. of Selby*, pp. 134–6.
[6] Stephen Thomason, M.D. Cf. *supra*, p. 20.
[7] On the capture of Roger Ratcliff by the rebels, see *L. & P.* xi. 1042.
[8] F. Drake, *Eboracum*, p. 285, gives Robert Ashbie as rector at this time. I have not noted any details of his role during the rising.
[9] C. ii–C. iii.

well to the left of the king's position. Under the article 'Of Fayth', he attacks 'our Prelates', the 'blinde Balaams' who believe in salvation by works.[1] No less than twelve stanzas are devoted to the thesis that the Church is not, as imagined by the rebels, 'the lapidous sinagoge proscript and relegate, The great citie I suppose of the whore of Babilon',[2] but the mystical body of Christ and the congregation of all the faithful. He thence continues with a lengthy diatribe against monasticism ('religion') and the use of images:

> But nowe Religion is a vile abomination,
> For Peter's name was Cephos which is a very stone,
> And we are living stones, by Peter's declaration,
> And Christ is the head Capitall, and other head is none,
> But they have this reversed and lefte this Church alone,
> And have gotten a newe God, even Daniel's desolation,
> And have set up Cragges coopert with houses many one,
> To cloke their deedes libidinous and incest fornication.

> They mumble with their lippes, with rich Copes, and Kels,
> And chaunting with their chastes like Owles in a frost,
> They duck and they sence, and they trumpe up their Bels
> And sprynkle water fast, but the red Cowe is lost,
> Candles are illuminate and set on every post,
> Before a gorgious Idol freshe figured and gylt,
> And though it maye be suffered, yet thereby hath ben lost
> Many a Christian man, and many a soule spylt.[3]

However exaggerated his views, it is important to realize that by 1530 a great number of intelligent Englishmen had come to see religious houses in the darkest possible colours; no puritan of later days could have written in terms more austere, no Legh or Layton with a sharper nose for sexual frailties, no Lutheran with a harsher distrust in the efficacy of good works for salvation:

> For dame Nice and dame Wanton, they set in the quire,
> Cheeping, like a Gosling, and looking on Sir John,
> They had rather than five pence to have him elsewhere,
> If one aske how I knowe it, I will ground on this stone,
> They are fat, and fayre of flesh bloud and bone,
> And have not receyved the spirit of veritie,
> And seing they be carnall, I maye judge them every one,
> To be fraile and incontinent with fleshly lubricitie,

[1] D. ii.ᵛ.   [2] D. iii.   [3] E. i–E. iᵛ.

None entreth to religion with any true devotion,
For the most part be infantes, and put in by coaction,
And none of freewill, except for promotion,
Or else for dispaire to do satisfaction,
And some for very slouth to do no worldly action,
Professing obedience, povertie and chastitie,
To which three essentialls they make their contraction,
And to many trifles moe the which is but vanitie.

And so for their povertie, ther is neither Knight nor Lord,
Earle, Marquess nor Duke like them in abundaunce:
And as for their obedience, al men can recorde,
They are high Rebellious against true allegiance,
Having both their King and their God at defiance:
And as for their chastitie the visitours knoweth wel,
For Sodome and Gomor had never such ordinance,
Their polution and wayes, I ashame for to tell.

Nowe beleeving in workes is dispaire and carnalitie,
Their vowes are like Jewes vowes, therefore they be vacuate.
For here is Christ, or ther is Christ, and hope not in him only
Is lyke to the devils faith from hope cleerely seperate:
Therefore they may marrie and leave their fond estate,
Because they were ignorant and make revocation,
For smal availeth baptysm though they be regenerate,
Where after they dispaire in Christes justification.[1]

So far as may be judged, Holme's detestation of the monasteries seems wholly sincere, there being no reason to suppose he was planning to benefit from their dissolution. Others expressing similar views stood in a far more vulnerable position. John Uvedale, from 1525 to 1550 secretary of the Council in the North, exemplifies the interested critic. Early in 1538 this important official tells Cromwell from York that he is persuaded the holy Word of God will in brief time hunt all manner of religious persons (as they have been called) out of their monasteries, cowls, and cloisters. When this happens, he continues without pausing for breath, will Cromwell obtain for him the farm of the house, demesnes, and parsonage of Marrick nunnery?[2] In such a case we witness naïve self-deception rather than conscious hypocrisy, since Cromwell's associates did not need to approach him in terms of pseudo-religious cant. In 1540 John Uvedale was also urging Cromwell to ensure that every bishop should set up two or three Bibles in his cathedral 'as

[1] E. ii–E. ii^v.   [2] L. & P. xiii (1), 49.

seemly and as ornately as they can deck them, with seats and forms for men of all ages to read and study in them'.[1] There can be no doubt as to his convinced Protestantism. Nevertheless, it will become apparent at a later stage of this inquiry that in many minds the Reformers speedily became invested with an air of gross hypocrisy. A vested interest was created at a very high price to the movement.

Oblivious to these impending dangers, Wilfrid Holme continues to celebrate the victory of the layman under his godly monarch. A discursive passage of some thirty-five stanzas[2] praises the king for abolishing mortuary dues and other clerical privileges, denies that the clergy are a 'spiritual' estate above other estates, denounces clerical attire, demands personal virtue and simplicity of the clergy, and boldly asserts their right to marry. Holme also denies any scriptural justification for auricular confession and justifies, by various texts, punishment for sin by the temporal authority. He exemplifies the rising bourgeois outlook by applauding the life of the layman, who works hard to support his household: we are not meant literally to take no thought for meat and drink. The clergy suffer further denunciation for misapplying the text in Matthew xxviii:

> And I am with you, sayd he, unto the worlds ende,
> That is, with us, say the prelates, for his church can not erre:
> That is not so, say I, marry God defend,
> For of all creatures there is no men werre [worse].

To support these attacks he recalls the familiar scandalous themes from papal history, including the story of Pope Joan, and concludes:

> For when Christ said, I am with you unto the worlds end,
> That was with you, and with such elect to faith prosperous,
> My grace by instinction wil I ever send.[3]

Holme's next section deals very forcefully with the Royal Supremacy. His argument runs along Erastian lines foreshadowed by both imperialist and royalist thinkers of the Middle Ages, but now increasingly being translated into facts. His Lutheran emphasis on the insufficiency of works is now followed by an equally Lutheran, if also Henrician, insistence on the principle *cujus regio, ejus religio.*

> Christes Kingdom was not heere, then who shuld have the power
> But the owners of the soiles to keepe truth legal
> Be he Marques or Duke, Prince, King or Emperor?[4]

For the clergy it is left to follow Christ in his humility, 'not in the

[1] Ibid. xv. 648.   [2] E. ii^v–F. iii.   [3] F. ii^v–F. iii.   [4] F. iii.

power of his glorification'. Some will say that the Apostles were not obedient to princes, but to them he puts the following example, 'by way of argument':

> If the Kings grace shuld send by his minde benevolent,
> Twelve discrete persons to the regions of Asia,
> To the Turks lands or Sophies to preach Christ omnipotent
> And to Prester Johns, and the great Canis of Catha,

then these missionaries might not have great regard for the laws and beliefs of the heathen potentates, yet might mix them with Christ's laws in order to gain converts the more easily. Once, however, the oriental rulers themselves were converted, the missionaries would certainly not seek to divest them of their temporal powers, but rather urge them to exercise such powers to enforce God's law.[1] In fact, St. Paul was 'all things to all men' and careful to accept as much of the old law as possible:

> To the Romaines he saith, let every soule submit
> Him selfe to the aucthoritie of the higher powers.

Again, the Bible shows how the Kings of Israel gave commands to the priesthood; and if the 'greedy Griffons and vile todes terrestrial' (i.e. the clerical party) 'beleeve expositors more than the truthe canonicall', let them look in Hamo, in Gregory's and Augustine's Epistles (references given), in the *de Regimine Principum* of Aquinas, and in other favourite commentators.[2] Against all these arguments for the subjection of clerical power and privilege, the decisions of Roman General Councils cannot militate. At this stage the author also adduces the customary examples purporting to show that Rome was never universally accepted as unquestioned Head of the Church itself.[3]

Next in order, a short section headed 'Of Holidayes' denounces saints' days on the grounds that we are forbidden to give spiritual honour to any creature except God himself. A similar section condemns the doctrine of Purgatory as detracting from the efficacy of Christ's sacrifice. After this prolonged doctrinal excursus, Holme returns to dispose of the fifth article of the rebels, who had demanded the punishment of seven allegedly heretical bishops. This he compares with a story in Isidore: how Philip of Macedon had demanded that the Athenians should hand over ten wise men to him, and how Demosthenes had told the Athenians the parable of the wolves, which induced the shepherds to hand over their dogs as the price of peace.[4] Thence we reach one of

---

[1] F. iii^v.   [2] F. iiii^v.   [3] G. i.   [4] G. iii.

the most remarkable passages of the poem. It shows Holme standing with the men of the New Learning, who ridiculed the old scholastic textbooks, the hair-splitting of metaphysicians, and who gleefully announced the dawn of a new age, when the old cobwebs of super-stition were fast being blown away. If we would understand why the Reformation happened in England, we must grasp this curiously exultant mood—for it may be called a mood of discovery rather than a philosophy—which seized the dominant groups in England around the time our author was writing. It is the mood of the *Epistolae Obscuro-rum Virorum*, but in England it was never better expressed than in the following stanzas. One may doubt whether Holme knew much about the books and the terminology which he ridicules: they are neverthe-less chosen with skill to suggest *démodé* obscurantism, idolatrous fraud, and ungodly pseudo-science.

> Thus our wolves irat these Duns doctors rixant,
> If they had obtayned, would have followed this fable,
> Devouring the elect all Chrystes lawes mitigant,
> Depriving the truth, to rumpe every sillable
> By craftie silogysmes and reasons variable,
> With counterfet gloses, and sense tropologicall,[1]
> Craftily sophisticate with reasons appliable,
> Making them to appeare to seeme anagogicall.[2]

> Thus would they have ruffled & rashed in their relatives,
> Searching night and day *manipulus curatorum*,[3]
> With the exornatory of Curates[4] and many inventives,
> As *Dormi secure*[5] and *Gesta Romanorum*,
> With the annal usage of *Ceremones parati*,[6]
> And the negotious search of *Sermones discipuli*,[7]
> And many mo than these besides their decrees,
> With constitutions and decretals, with suche suttle lyes.

---

[1] Metaphysical, figurative; a secondary sense or interpretation of Scripture, applied to conduct or morals.

[2] Mystical, with a hidden spiritual sense.

[3] *B.M. Cat.*, s.v. Curates, shows editions at Venice 1543–4 and 1566. MS. or earlier printed editions occur in English clerical wills.

[4] *Exornatorium* (or *Exoneratorium*) *Curatorum* (W. de Worde, ?1520; H. Pepwell, ?1530).

[5] *Sermones dominicales . . . alio nomine dormi secure . . . eoque absque magno studio faciliter possint incorporari et populo praedicari . . .* appeared in innumerable editions 1475–1530 (*B.M. Cat.*, s.v. Sermones).

[6] Properly *Sermones Parati de tempore et de sanctis*; for editions see ibid., s.v. Paratus.

[7] *Sermones discipuli* (i.e. the Dominican, Joannes Herolt) *de tempore per circulum anni*. A dozen editions appeared *c.* 1475–1590. The book included a section on the Miracles of the Virgin (ibid., s.v. Herolt).

Albertus de Secretis[1] with *Phisionoma Scoti*,[2]
With much Arte Magike, as Negromancie,
Some would studie Orminancie,[3] and some Piromancie,[4]
Some Idromancie,[5] some Geomancie,[6]
Some Pedomancie,[7] and some Ciromancie,[8]
Some Palmistrie, with the science Mathematice,
Lacking Christes musike and his geometrie,
With all his astrologie, and all his arsmetrice.

And also with their Metaphisiks, and arts supersticious
Over many to rehearse with their Philosophie,
Would have hindred Gods word to good men meticulous,
But thanks be to Chryst, and the high deitie,
Their purpose is defeted with all their vapiditie,
To the honoųr of god and our most christened Monarchie,
Our prince imperiall and flowre of Nobilitie,
Which the prelates named an unjust Heresiarchie.

Now therefore let all men which have inspiration
Looke for a sickle, for the harvest dothe approche,
Let them sing alleluia and make iubilation,
For the winter is past, and the sommer doth incroche,
To the Romane Antichrist and all his friends reproche:
Yea the Figtree is greene,[9] both faire and pulchritude,
My selfe of the small buddes a Sallet did incroche,
And me thought it was pleasant, right sweet and dulcitude.

For (thanked be God) sainct Francis cowle is spied,[10]
And sainct Brides head,[11] with sainct Hellyns quicking tree,

---

[1] The supposititious work *De Secretis Mulierum*, of which at least ten printed editions appeared 1478–1538 (*B.M. Cat.*, s.v. Albertus Magnus).
[2] The *Liber Phisionomie* of Michael Scott, transformed by legend into a magician; there had been many printed editions, some bound with the *De Secretis* (*D.N.B.*, s.v. Scott, Michael; *B.M. Cat.*, s.v. Scott, Sir Michael; Hain, *Repertorium Bibliographicum*, nos. 14542 seqq.).
[3] Perhaps a corruption related to 'hermetic', i.e. dealing with occult science, especially with alchemy.
[4] Divination by fire.
[5] Hydromancy, divination by water, or the pretended appearance of spirits therein.
[6] Divination by lines and figures, formed by throwing earth on some surface, later by jotting down on paper dots at random.
[7] Apparently divination by the foot.   [8] Chiromancy, palmistry.
[9] Cf. Mark xiii. 28–30; Luke xxi. 29–32.
[10] Alongside the subsequent passage cf. *L. & P.* xiii, xiv, indices, s.v. 'Images and Relics'.
[11] St. Bridget's head, removed from Down at the Reformation, was ultimately

Their girdles invented, and their faire hayres died,
With their chaulke oled for the milke of our Lady.[1]
Sainct Sithe[2] and Trenians fast,[3] with works of idolatrie
As sainct Nicholas chair and sainct Anthonies bell,
With S. Katherins Knots, and S. Anne of Buckstones wel.[4]

And S. Wilfred Boorne[5] of Ripon to kepe cattel from pain,
And his needle which sinners can not passe the eye,[6]
With S. John & S. Peters grease for to conserve the braine,
And S. Thomas hoode of Pomfret[7] for migreme and the rie,[8]
And S. Cuthberts standerd of Duresme to make their foes to flye,[9]
And S. Benets bolte, and S. Swithens bell,[10]
And Sainct Patrickes staffe and Sainct Williams head pardy,
And Sainct Cornelis horne,[11] with a thousand mo to tell.[12]

This passage on false relics has an obvious parallel in the contemporary
Fantasie of Idolatrie, later reprinted by Foxe.[13]
The sixth article of the rebels had complained concerning the king's
lowborn ministers. Holme in reply rightly points to the recent character of most nobility and gentry in England:

presented by Rudolph II to the Jesuits at Lisbon (Baring-Gould, *Legends of the Saints*,
ii. 22).
[1] At Walsingham: 'instead of the milk of our Lady a piece of chalk or ceruse'
(*L. & P.* xiv (i), 402, p. 156; cf. ibid. xiii (2), 101).
[2] St. Osyth, venerated at her monastery at Chich, Essex.
[3] On a St. Trinian's fast undertaken in 1537-8 by a Yorkshirewoman to injure the
king and the Duke of Norfolk, see *T.A.J.* xxxiv. 381.
[4] Sir William Basset sealed up the wells at Buxton and sent St. Anne's image to
Cromwell in Aug. 1538 (*L. & P.* xiii (2), 244, 256).
[5] Sic for bone. On the history of the bones and skull of St. Wilfrid see *Memorials of
Ripon*, iii (Surtees Soc. lxxxi), p. xx.
[6] A narrow passage in the crypt of Ripon, supposed to admit only the chaste.
This superstition was put down in 1568 (J. S. Purvis, *Tudor Parish Documents in the
Diocese of York*, p. 164).
[7] The hat of Thomas of Lancaster preserved in the chapel of Pontefract (G. Fox,
Hist. of Pontefract, p. 290).
[8] Rye-asthma; hay-fever.
[9] Most notably at the Battles of the Standard (1138) and Neville's Cross
(1346).
[10] The relics of St. Swithin were kept at Winchester, where he had been bishop.
In 1539 it was reported that 'St. Swithun and other reliques whereabout abuse of
hypocrisy was, are laid safe and not burnt' (*L. & P.* xiv (1), 402, p. 156).
[11] Pope Cornelius is depicted with a horn; I am ignorant as to where it was preserved.
[12] G. iii–G. iiii.
[13] Foxe, v. 404-9; he attributes it to one of the pamphleteers employed by Cromwell.

> And further let them looke upon their owne gentlenesse,
> Their estates, their bloud, and their long annositie,
> And few of them shal find their own worldly noblenesse
> Five degrees constant without mutabilitie.[1]

And it is not without significance that a writer of ancient birth can go
on to accept Fortune's Wheel, which turns

> ... an Earle to a gentleman of small habilitie,
> And a squire to a duke, thus is hir mutation.

At this point our author becomes conscious that he has wandered much
from his main theme and with a rare touch of humour makes Anglia
intervene:

> Then *Anglia* the Empresse inclusive
> Sayde, *Holme*, thy long processe and thy prolixitie,
> Hath last so long from our matter fugitive,
> That almost am I cast into a liturgie,
> And drowned in a dumpe with a tremous extasie,
> Therefore I beseech thee in this thing contentious,
> To shewe what the commons dyd after this replye,
> For the truth greatly to know I am desirous.[2]

She then asks Holme to describe the 'latter commotion' by Sir Francis
Bigod, formerly reckoned 'one of the veritie perculent'. Accordingly
with unmitigated scorn he tells the story of Bigod and Hallam, followed by the executions of the leaders of both revolts.[3]

> And divers hang on Gallowes in irons well parate,
> And many of their adherentes in sundrie countreyes seere,
> As fugitives and vagabonds they are cleerely fugate.
> Ah, ah (quod Anglia) thou makest me to smile,
> But I pray thee why showest thou not Lincolnshire rebellion?
> Nor yet of Norfolke why doest thou not compile?

But the poet has an alibi; he pleads that these 'shires are very far distant
from my habitacion' and that others should undertake the task.[4]

The final section of *The Fall and Evill Success of Rebellion* has puzzled
those students of the Pilgrimage of Grace who happened to lack acquaintance with its medieval background. It is entitled 'Of the Mouldwarp' and deals with the Merlin prophecies which derived from Geoffrey
of Monmouth and which, as the State papers also clearly show, were

---

[1] G. iiii[v].   [2] H. i.
[3] H. ii[v]–H. iiii. Cf. *supra*, p. 105.   [4] H. iiii–H. iiii[v].

widely current in the rebellious areas.[1] Holme gives no clear explanation of the prophecies, since he can assume his readers to be already
familiar with them. The 'Mouldwarp' prophecy, to which he principally
refers, is more properly called the 'Prophecy of the Six Kings to follow
King John'. Deriving ultimately from the *Book of Merlin*, it appears in
manuscripts of various dates, English, Latin, and French.[2] It acquired
real political importance when it was used by the Percy–Glendower
faction against Henry IV:

> . . . Sometimes he angers me
> With telling me of the moldwarp and the ant
> Of the dreamer Merlin and his prophecies
> . . . And such a deal of skimble-skamble stuff
> As puts me from my faith.[3]

The essential feature of the Galfridian type of prophecy is that it
represents historical figures by animals, and the political story by wars
and adventures between them. The 'Prophecy of the Six Kings' begins
accordingly with the Lamb of Winchester (usually understood to
represent Henry III) whose heart is holy, but whose reign is troubled
by insurrections. At his death his heir shall be in a strange land; this
heir is the Dragon (Edward I, on Crusade at his accession) who shall
terrify Wales from north to south and conquer many countries. He
will be thought the best knight in the world, and die on the borders of
another land. To the Dragon shall succeed a Goat (Edward II) whose
reign will bring hunger, death, and loss of land to the realm. After the
Goat shall follow a Lion (Edward III; in some versions typified by a
Boar), who after early troubles shall make his people meek, pass through
four lands in conquest, and wear three crowns before he dies. After
him shall come an Ass (Richard II) with leaden feet, a steel head, a
brass heart, and an iron skin, who for a time shall relinquish government to an Eagle, after whose death it shall revert to the Ass. Finally
a Mouldwarp, or Mole (Henry IV), shall become ruler of the land. His
hide shall be as rough as a goat's skin and he shall be cursed of God for
his misdeeds. A Dragon shall raise war against him and be joined by a
Wolf and then by a Lion from Ireland. These shall drive the Mouldwarp
from the country, leaving him only an isle in the sea, where after great

---

[1] Cf. on this theme Rupert Taylor, *The Political Prophecy in England* (Columbia
Univ. Press, 1911), and on its transmission to the Tudor period, H. L. D. Ward,
Cat. of Romances in the Dept. of MSS. in the Brit. Mus. (1883).
[2] Cf. Taylor, op. cit., pp. 48 seqq.
[3] Shakespeare, *Henry IV*, Pt. 1, Act III, sc. i.

trouble he shall die by drowning. England shall be divided into three parts by the conquerors and the heirs of England shall lose their inheritance.[1]

During several risings, variants of this farrago were skilfully manipulated by the astute, and credulously accepted by the simple. Before, during, and after the Pilgrimage of Grace, Yorkshiremen found it more than tempting to make Henry VIII the Mouldwarp in place of Henry IV, and otherwise to elaborate the story in consonance with the facts of their time. It need scarcely be observed that the strong Percy interest involved in the Pilgrimage[2] added much to the significance of the traditional allegories.

What has Wilfrid Holme to say about these prophecies and their role in the rebellion? However radical his condemnation of medieval learning, he is far from dismissing the Galfridian prophecy as moonshine. He merely argues that it cannot refer to the reign of Henry VIII. He points out that Henry III has always been accepted as the first of the six kings and that hence Henry VIII must be the twelfth, 'except ye skippe at pleasure'. Moreover, his present Grace in no way resembles the prophesied character of the Mouldwarp-king:

> The prophesie of the Mouldwarpe declareth he shal be
> A Caitife, a Cowarde, with a helderly skin:
> But is he a Caitife, when playnely we may see
> His protrature and vigor a very Herculine?
> And is he a cowarde the truthe to define,
> When in Fraunce and in Scotlande his noble chivalrie,
> And in many places mo so gloriously doth shine,
>
> That he is accounted a Gemme in activitie?[3]

After further compliments to the king, Holme cites examples of prophecies which can have a double meaning and gives, as a local example, the curious lines current during the Pilgrimage:

> Foorth shall come a worme, an Aske with one eye,
> He shall be the chiefe of that meinye,
> He shall gather of chivalrie a full faire flocke,
> Half capon and halfe cocke,

[1] Taylor, loc. cit.; the most important text is printed as an appendix to Hall's edition of Laurence Minot's *Poems* (1887).

[2] R. R. Reid, *The King's Council in the North*, p. 133, rightly remarks that 'nearly all the leaders were the fee'd servants of the Percies or one of the abbeys if not of both'.

[3] I. iv.

> The chicken shall the capon slay,
> And after that shall be no May.[1]

This is Galfridian in type, though obviously not in detail. More distinctly deriving from the original source is the prophecy next discussed by Holme: that after Cadwallader's death 'the Britons shuld never more in Britaine raigne', until Merlin's prophecies were fulfilled and Merlin's body translated back from Rome to Britain. The falsity of this prediction he regards as proved by the fact that Henry VII

> . . . Cadwallader's bloud renued
> And the King's Grace [i.e. Henry VIII] maketh Britons by number plural.[2]

Then, after a suggestion that the Mouldwarp could possibly have been Edward IV,[3] Holme produces a purple passage skilfully identifying Henry VIII with a whole range of prophetic types:

> This is the Britishe Lion by Sibilla prophesied
> This is the Egle surmounting, which Festome hathe notified,
> This is the King anoynted, which S. Thomas specified,
> This is the three folde Bul which Silvester magnified,
> This is the King which S. Edward in words glorified,
> Which shuld win Jerusalem with all the holy land,
> And many realms mo, with the crosse of the Christ crucified,
> By his abundant fortitude without dint of hand.[4]

> Is not his grace a Lion and accompt his audacitie,
> And a prodigious Egle high volant in things divine,
> And anointed with faith by the spirite of veritie,
> And of faith, hope and charitie, a fierce Bul in trine:
> He hath obtained Christes crosse as they did vaticine,
> With the heavenly Jerusalem above Ezechias,
> Repairing the true temple in vertuous wayes to shine,
> Maumetrie destroying as the vertuous Josias.

> Ye[a] this is he which hath made al the Romain bels to ring
> Without pul of hand, their false tongs papistical,
> Having oil in his lampe he is a maiden King,
> Though they take it otherwise by their senses carnal,

---

[1] I. iii. [2] I. ii\\ʳ.

[3] On the ground that he 'soweth his seed fatherlesse in a strange land'. Phrases of this type occur in other senses and relating to other kings in the earlier texts of the prophecy.

[4] For other mid-sixteenth-century recollections of these prophecies in B.M. Sloane MS. 2578, see H. L. D. Ward, op. cit., pp. 333–4; likewise on the 'maiden king', mentioned below.

And in the true vale of Josephat the scripture canonical,
There is no doubt but his grace is sepelite.
For doubtlesse all the English prophesies autentical,
Concerning these matters by the King is whole condite.[1]

The development of such counter-prophecy in favour of the king is
not peculiar to Holme, but is found in other royal apologists, notably
at the end of Sir Richard Morison's *An Exhortation to styrre all Englyshe-
men to the Defence of theyr countreye* (1539). Here the writer pointedly tells
us that his prophecy is 'not lately commen out of Wales', but derived
from the book of Esdras,[2] with its vision of the Lion [Henry VIII]
overcoming the Eagle [the Pope].

Se ye not, to what honour God calleth our nation? May not we reioyce that
God hath chosen our Kyng, to worke so noble a feate? God sayth, a Lion
shall teare this tirante's auctorite in peces. . . . Let this yelling Egle approche
towarde us, let her come with all her byrdes about her, let a traytour cary
her standard: doth not God say, her wynges shall be cut, her kyngedome
waxe feble, the Lyon waxe stronge, and save the residue of Goddes people,
filling them full of ioye and comfort, even while the worlde endureth.[3]

Wilfrid Holme was indeed close in sentiment, if not in manner, to the
gifted group of humanists then employed by the king and Cromwell to
defend their cause. From this point, his poem moves swiftly to its close. A
stanza of thunderous alliterations condemns the rebels, Anglia ascends in
a cloud ('Adew, Holme, quod shee'), and the poet, having been accorded
an apocalyptic vision of the angelic host, ends with a patriotic prayer:

Beseeching his prohennitie for the Kings magnificence,
That he may have long life, Gods word to fortifie,
And to send us of his body heire male for our defence,
All true espirites *Anglice* for to reioyce and magnifie.
Thus concluding by correction of the Kings maiestie,
And his Counsel honorable, with all those perfidious,
That with firm trust and hope beleveth Christ to iustifie
By his deed and his promise to make us all righteous.

The xiiii day of July componed and compiled,
In the xxix yere of the raigne of the viii Henry royall,
By Wilfride Holme unlearned, simply combined,
As a Pigme to writing with Hercules for triall,

[1] I. iii–I iiiᵛ. I am not clear whether this metaphorical fulfilment of the old prophecies is Holme's original idea; it seems almost too clever for him!
[2] 2 Esdras xi.
[3] *An Exhortation*, D. viiᵛ–viii, cited by W. G. Zeeveld, *Foundations of Tudor Policy*,
pp. 232–3.

In Huntington in Yorkshire commorant patrimonial,
Pretending and intending with Gods grace, to endever
My selfe to worship the Lord sempiternall,
Whereby I may be just to my God and Prince for ever.[1]

The foregoing summary should serve to indicate that Wilfrid Holme has been among the more unjustly neglected figures of Yorkshire history, and this largely because we have not yet learned to look at literature—and in particular at verse—with an historical eye. Like so much else in the Tudor age, Holme's poem is deceptively archaic in form, yet often modern in spirit. If its verses sometimes look back to the age of Lydgate, its sentiments form a model exposition of Reformation Erastianism, together with no slight anticipation of the puritan outlook. And that Holme's own influence proved so limited is partly due to the historical inconsistency of those two latter viewpoints. Holme wrote too early to be effective. Had he survived into the last reactionary years of Henry VIII, his devotion to the king might well have been shaken by the stern repression imposed upon people little more advanced in religion than himself.

Among the most striking attributes of our poem is its early date; parallel views were in fact being widely expressed in the reign of Edward VI, but to find them in the heart of Yorkshire ten years earlier underlines the complexity of our provincial life during the crisis of the Reformation. Holme merely provides one more example of the falsities entailed by modern simplifications of the Tudor north. *The Fall and Evill Success of Rebellion* seems more than worthy of study against the background of the critical fourth decade of the century. On the other hand, it cannot be claimed as an epoch-making book of the Reformation. Written to glorify Henry VIII as the liberating and gospel-spreading agent of God, it inevitably placed itself in a false position and consequently attained publication only in time to serve as a minor propaganda-piece in the creation of Gloriana.

2. *Robert and Isabel Plumpton*

Our second example of a gentleman of the New Learning in the diocese belonged to a family celebrated in later times for its steady adherence to the Roman faith and for its collection of family letters:[2]

---

[1] I. iiii.
[2] *The Plumpton Correspondence* (Camden Soc. iv). The letters were transcribed by Sir Edward Plumpton (1581–c. 1655).

the Plumptons of Plumpton near Knaresborough and of Waterton near Gainsborough. No very lengthy or elaborate biography of Robert Plumpton could now be written. He was born at Waterton in January 1516, heir to his father William and inheritor of an already ancient family tradition. His mother Isabel or Elizabeth Babthorpe came of another family which subsequently achieved great prominence among the Elizabethan recusants of Yorkshire. The correspondence presently to be discussed shows Robert in residence at the Inner Temple in the mid-thirties. On 2 September 1538 he married Anne, daughter of John Norton of Norton Conyers: yet another Catholic family in later years and one destined to notoriety for its part in the Rising of the Northern Earls. Plumpton died, aged only thirty-one but leaving a son and three daughters, about Christmas 1546, and was buried at Luddington in the Isle of Axholme, the parish church of Waterton.[1] Judged merely by the family tree, no less likely candidate for a place in Protestant history could be imagined, yet two of his letters in the family collection not only establish his Protestant opinions but also throw a revealing shaft of light into the mind of one who had found a lively certainty in the Gospels.

Neither of his letters is dated, though they may be placed approximately in 1536. They were both written from the Inner Temple with the express object of converting his mother to the new doctrines; fervent letters which it would be all too easy to criticize by reference to anachronistic standards. Only a reader lacking the historical imagination to envisage the force and freshness of conversion upon a young man during the dawn of the Reformation will dismiss Robert Plumpton as a prig.

His first letter begins upon the perennial theme of the student writing home. He thanks his mother for the money, but gloomily remarks that Christmas has cost as much as she sent, 'wherefore I am afraid I shall not have money to serve mee to Easter'. He then recalls how he has asked his parents to move Lady Gascoin to write to her brother Lord Latimer and ask that Robert should not 'bee only his servant, but of his household and attending unto him; for els he wold do as other lords do, [that] knowes not half their servants'.[2] By the bearer he sends his mother 'a godly New Testament'. If the prologue be too small, she

---

[1] *Dugdale's Visitation of Yorkshire*, ed. J. W. Clay, pt. viii, p. 394; cf. *Plumpton Correspondence*, p. cxxviii. At the time of writing the Protestant letters cited below, he probably spent most of his vacations at his father's chief house at Plumpton. Later on, his father was writing to him from Plumpton, though he mentions affairs at Waterton (ibid., p. 235).

[2] On Latimer and his probable inclinations to the new doctrines, cf. *supra*, p. 62.

can use his father's Bible, which has it printed in large letters. 'Yf it will please you to read the introducement', he continues, 'ye shall see marvelous things hyd in it. And as for the understanding of it, dout not; for God wil give knowledge to whom he will give knowledg of the Scriptures, as soon to a shepperd as to a priest, yf he ask knowledg of God faithfully.' The force of this last sentiment is the greater in that it comes from a gentleman born. The letter concludes, 'Wherfor, pray to God and desire Jesus Christ to pray for you and with you. No more to you at this tyme, but God fill you with al spiritual knowledge, to the glory of God, the helth of your soule, and the profit of your poor neighbour. Written at the Temple, the 12 day of ianuary. By your sonn, Robert Plumpton.'[1]

The 'introducement' by which the young enthusiast set such store was quite certainly the famous preface 'W.T. unto the Reader', which Tyndale attached to the 1534 and subsequent editions[2] of his New Testament. It was the only separately printed New Testament in English then available and, to clinch the fact, Plumpton made close use both of this preface and of the prologues attached by Tyndale to the various books of the Testament. This feature appears in another letter, shortly to be examined. At this date the whole work was highly suspect and inflammable, for, not content with denouncing 'the popyshe doctours of dunces darcke learninge', Tyndale went on to condemn confession to a priest as 'but mannes invencion' and to argue that it was all the same whether priests were called 'elders' or not.[3] Under these circumstances, the presence of two copies of Tyndale's work in this supposedly old-fashioned and conservative North Country household at Plumpton provides an impressive testimony to its compelling attraction.

Plumpton's other letter[4] proves even more revealing; its quality and its source cannot be conveyed except by verbatim quotation. It would appear that Isabel Plumpton had let fall a hint as to the danger of heresy involved in her son's ardours: not unnaturally at this date, if he were handling copies of Tyndale's New Testament. To him such strictures had become an irrelevance. Set beside the clear light of divine revelation

---

[1] *Plumpton Correspondence*, pp. 231–3.

[2] Several more editions appeared in 1535–6.

[3] A convenient reprint, ed. N. H. Wallis, was published (1938) by the Cambridge University Press. These passages occur on pp. 10–12.

[4] *Plumpton Correspondence*, pp. 233–4. This letter may well have been written *before* the one quoted above. It will be noted below that the writer urges his mother to use his father's New Testament, as if he had not yet sent her the copy mentioned above.

in this new and glorious age of discovery, what else could matter? Of his inestimable goodness, God has given him some understanding of the Scriptures. This being so, he is bound to instruct his brethren 'in the loving of the Gospell', especially the mother who has shown him 'so muche kindenes, besides all motherly kindenes'.

Wherefore I desire you, moste deare mother, that ye will take heede to the teachinge of the Gospell, for it is the thinge that all wee muste live by; for Christe lefte it that we shoulde altogether rule our livinge thereby, or els we cannot be in favour with God. Wherefore, I woulde desire you for the love of God, that you woulde reade the Newe Testament, which is the trewe Gospell of God, spoken by the Holy Ghoste. Wherefore, doubte not of it, dearly beloved mother in the Lorde, I write not this to bringe you into anie heresies, but to teache you the cleare light of Goddes doctrine. Wherefore, I will never write nothinge to you, nor saye nothinge to you, concerninge the Scriptures, but will dye in the quarrell. Mother, you have muche to thanke God that it woulde please him to geve you licence to live untill this time, for the gospell of Christe was never so trewly preached as it is nowe. Wherefore, I praye to God that he will geve you grace to have knowledge of his Scriptures.

The concluding passage, now unfortunately truncated, falls somewhat from this emotional level, but it expresses admirably, if at second hand, one of the more attractive emphases of the New Learning.

Ye shall heare perceive what the profession of our Baptisme is, which profession we muste have written in our hartes. Which profession standeth in twoe thinges; the one is the knowledge of the lawe of God, understandinge it spiritually as Christe expoundeth it, Math. v. vi and vii chapters;[1] so that the roote and life of all lawes is this, Love thy Lorde God with all thy harte, all thy soule, all thy mighte and all thy power, and thy neighboure as thy selfe for Christes sake.[2] And love onely is the fullfillinge of the lawe, as saithe S. Paule,[3] and that whatsoever we doe and not of that love, that same fulfilleth not the lawe in the sighte of God. And what the lawe doth meane ye shall finde in the prologue to the Rom[ans] in my fathers booke, called the Newe Testament. I write unto you because that I knowe you have a fervent [? love of God] and his lawes. . . .

The remainder of this remarkable letter is wanting. These concluding

---

[1] i.e. the Sermon on the Mount.
[2] Luke x. 27. Tyndale's version, presumably quoted a little inaccurately from memory. Tyndale (1534) has 'Love thy Lorde God, with all thy hert and with all thy soule, and with all thy strengthe, and with all thy mynde: and thy neighbour as thy sylfe.' We must, of course, allow for the possibility of mistranscription by Sir Edward Plumpton, who as a Roman Catholic would not be familiar with this English version.   [3] Rom. xiii. 10.

ROBERT AND ISABEL PLUMPTON 135

passages derive almost entirely from Tyndale, who has in his preface: 'The ryght waye: ye and the onlye waye to understonde the scripture unto our salvation, is, that we ernestlye and above all thinge, serche for the profession of oure baptyme or covenauntes made betwene God and us.' He then goes on to cite Matthew v. 6 and enlarges upon the ten commandments, which 'are comprehended in these two: love God and thy neyboure'. The phrase 'Love is the fulfillinge of the lawe' appears as a marginal note to the text.[1] Turning in accordance with Robert Plumpton's hint to Tyndale's prologue to Romans, we observe the lesson which the young man most wanted his mother to learn:

Lawe maye not be understonde here ofter the commune maner. . . . God iudgeth the grounde of the herte, ye and the thoughtes and the secret movynges of the mynde, and therefore his lawe requireth the grounde of the hert and love from the botome there of, and is not content with the oute ward worke only: but rebuketh those workes most of all which springe not of love from the ground and lowe botome of the herte, though they appere outward never so honest and good.[2]

One fact emerges very clearly from our reference to Plumpton's acknowledged sources. He was no mere craver after the unadorned Biblical text, but an ardent advocate of one of Tyndale's most constructive emphases. Here is an issue over which Catholics and Protestants are unlikely to approach agreement, yet I find it hard to resist the view that, in condemning the constructive along with the destructive aspects of the Protestant approach, both the Papacy and the king were also condemning the last slender chance of a truly English version of the Counter-Reformation. With all his faults, Tyndale had something positive to say which thoughtful men of all conditions were prepared to hear: if he were to be answered merely by indiscriminate abuse or by legalist repression, then Catholic ascendancy over the English mind was inevitably doomed. On this provincial level we may best appreciate the inwardness of the great European tragedy. Englishmen had, together with some other north Europeans, developed spiritual needs widely different from those of the Mediterranean peoples. They had already found their special affinity with the linked ideas of conversion and the vernacular Bible; neither Church nor State had mechanisms strong enough to hold the combining elements apart.

As for Robert Plumpton, we know nothing of his subsequent religious

[1] p. 8. [2] pp. 293-4.

life and we must recognize as mere conjecture the supposition of the editor of the *Plumpton Correspondence* that his marriage into the Norton family reconverted him to orthodoxy. There are two letters in the collection addressed to him, and both are business letters indicating little about his intellectual pursuits. One from his father bids him use his influence and efforts in London regarding certain lawsuits in the Court of Augmentations affecting the Plumptons and their neighbours.[1] The other, signed 'George Johnson, clerk', concerns rents, the price of beans at Gainsborough and Hull, together with other familiar topics of the chaplain turned estate agent.[2] Neither letter could possibly have been addressed to a mere head-in-air idealist. Despite the transparent sincerity and fervour of his beliefs, he looks like a shrewd and business-like young man who would not go out of his way to invite trouble as the Henrician persecution developed. Moreover, he may be taken as a moderate, who stopped short of the attack upon Transubstantiation, a far more dangerous pastime than the advocacy of Tyndale's Bible. For the social historian of the provinces, Robert Plumpton forms the perfect example of that fairly numerous and extremely influential group of young men who went up to the Inns of Court and brought back to their provinces—then showing so marked a tendency to stagnate—fresh currents of thought and conviction.

As for Isabel Plumpton, she survived both her husband and her eldest son Robert. Having made a will[3] of exceptional interest, she died in the summer of 1552, a safer time for those of the new beliefs. Discarding the traditional phraseology of her husband,[4] she used a testamentary form of her own. 'I comende my sowle into the most mercyfull handes of my Saveior and Redeemer, Jhesus Christe, throwghe whos paynfull passyon I undowtedly beleve to be eternally savid. My will is that my synfull body shalbe bewryed in the nexte [i.e. nearest] parishe churche wher it shall please my Lorde God to take me to his mercy.' These phrases undoubtedly indicate a warm personal conviction and, as she wrote or dictated them, her mind was certainly with the son who had introduced her to this conviction. 'And wher in consideracion of the tender love I bore to Roberte Plompton, my naturall son, [I grant out] severall patentes to Anne, Mary and Isabell Plompton his doughteres. . .'. In more senses than

---

[1] *Plumpton Correspondence*, pp. 234–5.
[2] Ibid., pp. 236–7.
[3] Printed in *Test. Ebor.* vi. 260–2. It was begun on 10 June 1551 and sealed 6 Jan. 1552. She died 30 June 1552.
[4] Ibid., p. 258. He died 11 July 1547.

one, Robert and his mother were led to the new outlook by love; their brief spiritual record is refreshingly free from any expression of hatred. They display only the evangelical affirmation which too many Protestants were to lose in the waste lands of controversy and which a more truly Catholic Church might still have made its own.

V

THE CLERICAL LEADERSHIP

1. *The Protestant Regular Clergy*

THAT the heretical movements of the thirties appealed to few of the northern parish clergy requires little explanation, for neither their virtues nor their limitations were likely to lead them in this direction. So far as one may generalize concerning a large and most heterogeneous group, these men united simple faith with low incomes, inelastic minds, and limited educational opportunities. Few were university men or trained in philosophy and theology. Their literary culture, though in certain cases far from contemptible, had in general a *démodé* and unadventurous character. They still read the *Legenda Aurea*, the *Vita Christi* of Landulphus, the commentaries of Denis the Carthusian, the devotional treatises of Richard Rolle, the chronicles of medieval England, and the tedious poetry of Lydgate. With the culture of Humanist Italy few were on nodding terms, while the *devotio moderna* had reached them in its least revolutionary guise. To such intellectual or anti-intellectual reactions were added the obvious dictates of class-interest. All heresy had become tarred with the brush of anti-clericalism: the mass of the clergy had every inducement to suspect a movement which always tended to diminish clerical privilege and which in its extremer forms denied ecclesiastical jurisdiction, denounced tithes, saw no need for an order of priesthood and above all refused to acknowledge the miracle of Transubstantiation conducted daily through the hands of the humblest or most sinful priest. In short, during the thirties and beyond, clerical distaste for religious change must be presumed widespread, even though there is good reason to suppose that reactionaries violent in thought or deed never became very numerous.[1]

The chief exceptions to this slow-moving conservatism naturally arose amongst university-trained theologians able to distinguish between the varieties of heresy, unafraid to follow their reasoning to logical ends and sufficiently free from rigid mental patterns to envisage some sweeping changes of approach to Christianity and ecclesiastical organization. Thanks to their university houses of studies, which were

[1] Cf. *infra*, p 166.

well attended almost to the Dissolution,[1] not a few monks and friars entered this intellectual category and returned to their dull provincial habitats as changed men. Many of them happened also to be men with less to lose in a revolution than their former university colleagues who had accepted high office in Church or State. A few, indeed, found something to gain. Despite modern popular notions, the religious orders cannot be claimed as bulwarks of conservative belief; on the contrary, many of their members, particularly friars, achieved notoriety as advocates of new doctrines. Amongst the active minority of educated religious men, it would seem probable enough that most were either open-minded or actually favourable to the cause of Reform. The present writer recently studied authorship among the last generation of English monks and found a dozen of them who actually wrote books about the issues of the Reformation. Of this dozen, all save one or two showed themselves uncompromising adherents of the Protestant cause. Again, an American scholar recently tabulated lists of twenty-two conservative and twenty-four Reforming bishops of the mid-century. Amongst the conservatives only one was a regular clergyman by origin, yet amongst the Reformers there were no less than sixteen ex-monks and friars.[2] Of the Reforming bishops, Holgate, Salcot, Hilsey, Hooper, Holbeach, and Ferrar are characteristic examples of university monks who specialized in theology and soon embraced the Reformation cause.

It seems less than reasonable to dismiss these men as a tiny group of freaks or individualists. On neither side of the struggle did the activist groups of monks and friars prove numerous: on the conservative side it did not extend far beyond the ranks of the small and select Carthusian order, which maintained its devotional traditions to the end, and which supplied from the London Charterhouse a noble group of martyrs. Between these lively Reforming and Catholic minorities there lay the unleavened lump of custom-ridden monasticism, showing all too rarely signs of spiritual or intellectual ferment, and ready enough, when the hour sounded, to take its pension and depart in silence. Writers of all creeds have united to abuse the Protestant monks and friars as renegades, creatures of Cromwell, Judas-like betrayers of their profession. Such critics have resolutely refused to envisage an explanation which to the present writer seems almost self-evident: that when these

[1] The Oxford registers contain, for example, the names of 357 members of religious orders during the period 1505–38 (A. G. Little, *The Greyfriars of Oxford* (Oxford Historical Soc. xx), p. 54).
[2] L. B. Smith, *Tudor Prelates and Politics* (Princeton, 1953), pp. 306–7.

religious broke their vows they mostly believed in what they were doing. To one touched by Lutheranism, who now thought belief in works was mere 'despair and carnality', there could be nothing valid about the professions made in ignorant and unregenerate youth.[1] These people also produced their martyrs, and it would be palpably absurd to suppose that sincerity was limited to their martyrs alone. For many educated men, the early sixteenth century proved a period of intense mental crises and revisions, a period of exposure to ideas as remorseless as those which later accompanied the French Revolution. At Oxford or Cambridge in particular, membership of a religious order did not shield a man from these ideas: indeed the stresses and the admitted imperfections of the religious life must often have magnified their impact.

In the diocese of York, some share in the dissemination of Protestant teachings was apparently taken during the early thirties by no less a person than John Bale, who later achieved such fame and notoriety as playwright, literary historian, audacious Reformer, and Bishop of Ossory.[2] About 1530 he came to the Carmelite convent at Doncaster, where he occupied the office of prior.

In 1535 a certain William Broman made lengthy testimony concerning heretical activities in the kingdom.[3] Amongst these occurs a statement to the effect that one Bale, a Whitefriar sometime prior of Doncaster, taught Broman about four years ago that Christ would dwell in no church made of lime and stone by man's hands, but only in heaven above. He adds this to an account of the anti-Transubstantiation teachings of Bale's friend and fellow Carmelite Dr. Barret, but he says neither that Bale had instructed him in Doncaster nor that he himself had ever visited the place.[4] The dates clearly indicate, however, that this propaganda occurred about 1531 during Bale's membership of the Yorkshire house.

A hitherto unnoticed document in Archbishop Lee's register[5] shows

---

[1] In Yorkshire this view of the monastic profession was most forcibly put by the layman Wilfrid Holme. Cf. *supra*, p. 120.

[2] See the valuable life by Jesse W. Harris, *John Bale, a Study in the Minor Literature of the Reformation* (Urbana, 1940).

[3] *L. & P.* ix. 230.

[4] Broman's other references are to events in Kent and elsewhere in the south.

[5] Reg. Lee, fo. 91. Dr. Harris apparently did not see this document. He and others have been accustomed to cite *Proceedings of the Suffolk Institute of Archaeology*, x. 199, for the statement that Bale became prior of the Ipswich Carmelites in 1533. As Bale was still prior of Doncaster in Aug. 1534, this unreferenced statement hence needs reinvestigation.

THE PROTESTANT REGULAR CLERGY

that Bale was already in trouble with the diocesan authorities the year before the compilation of Broman's testimony. It is a commission dated at Bishopthorpe 1 August 1534 and directed to the priors of Monk Bretton and Blyth, to William Ferrar, LL.D., and William Nevill, provost of the College of Rotherham. Whereas the archbishop has granted faculties to John Bayle, S.T.P., prior of the Doncaster Carmelites, and to Thomas Kirkby, S.T.P., warden of the Friars Minor of that town, to preach the gospel for the instruction of the common people, the two are now using opprobrious and undecent words against each other publicly from the pulpit.[1] Desiring to allay this grave scandal and to discover who is to blame, the archbishop charges the commissioners or any two of them to make a full inquiry, calling all the necessary witnesses and drawing up a written report. Nothing appears here as to the subject-matter of these disputes, or the precise reactions of local opinion: it seems evident, however, that Bale was openly preaching the new doctrines at Doncaster in 1534 and had consequently become involved in violent personal abuse with the conservative Franciscan. In Kirkby the redoubtable Reformer found an adversary of almost equal ability and conviction. A former Oxford Greyfriar, he had been admitted B.D. in 1523, after twelve years' study, and D.D. in July 1527, his composition being reduced to four pounds because of his poverty. In the November of the same year he was dispensed from the greater part of his Oxford regency as warden of the Greyfriars at Doncaster, and he continued to hold this office to the Dissolution. Before his quarrel with Bale he had already signalized himself as a zealous opponent of the king's divorce, though in later years he may have transferred his allegiance to the Protestant party.[2]

Probably as a result of this commission and in the same year, Bale underwent an examination before Archbishop Lee and in the presence of Geoffrey Downes, then prebendary of Holme Archiepiscopi in the church of York. Of this transaction the arch-Protestant himself wrote an account so characteristically boisterous that it would be spoiled by any *oratio obliqua*, though several of its allusions will call for investigation. It occurs in a work published in 1543, *Yet a course at the Romyshe foxe*, and in a passage bludgeoning the views of Bishop Bonner upon the invocation of saints. It purports to show that even the elderly Arch-

[1] 'Unus in alterum verba obpropriosa et indecentia palam in suggesto sive pulpito infert.'
[2] A. G. Little, op. cit., pp. 282–3. He is called both Kirkby and Kirkham. In 1539 he was admitted to the rectory of Colchester and in 1548 to that of St. Martin, Outwich, in the city of London. He resigned the latter in 1553 or 1554.

bishop Lee refused to countenance Bonner's heathenish extremism, a thing only paralleled by the chaplains of Bel the old god of Babylon, who ate up all the sacrifices:

The author examyned upon sayntes worshyppynge.

An olde dottynge doctor dodypoll. The answer of my lorde archebysshopp of Yorke.

What I schuld write of thys I can not tell, yt ys so folyshe. Savynge that I remembre viij years a go I was afore Edwarde Lee the archebysshopp of Yorke, where as I was examyned upon the artycle of honourynge and prayenge to the sayntes, devyded into xvij artycles. In the tyme of that examynacyon was there an olde doctour whych greatlye lamented (as my lorde [Bonner] dothe here) that he myght no longar make invocacyon to sayntes, and thought hym selfe halfe lost for yt, good doctour Downes standyne by and smylynge at hys folyshnesse. Unto whom the archebysshop sayd these wordes. Speake not (sayth he) of invocacyon concernynge sayntes. For that respecteth a peculyar worshypp onlye due unto God. And with that the man was pacyfyed, and argued no farder. So that I can se non agre with my lorde here in thys opynyon, unlesse they be blynde dastardes and asseheades, as thys olde doatynge fole was.[1]

Bale notes elsewhere that this examination took place at York and that he was later before Stokesley, Bishop of London, but always the *pius Cromvuelus*, on account of his comedies, had him liberated.[2] As for the 'olde dottynge doctor dodypoll',[3] whose difficulties Bale so uncharitably ridicules, this may well have been his Doncaster adversary Dr. Kirkby, summoned likewise before the archbishop. The position with regard to the smiling prebendary is more intriguing, since Geoffrey Downes had been Bale's own tutor at Jesus College, Cambridge. There can also be little doubt that the favourable attitude of this ecclesiastic, so long an important figure at York, sprang from something more than personal friendship. A man whom the violent Bale regarded in later years as his own 'olim in re theologica dignissimum patrem'[4] cannot have been a true neutral in the great debate. Downes and Cranmer proceeded M.A. and became fellows of Jesus at the same time (1515–16) and they were not the only senior members of that college to feel the force of Lutheran

---

[1] *Yet a course*, fos. 86a–86b.

[2] J. Bale, *Scriptorum Illustrium maioris Brytannie . . . Catalogus* (1557), p. 702.

[3] On this common term for a blockhead see *New Eng. Dict.*, s.v. doddypoll. It is used by Latimer in his *Third Sermon before King Edward*.

[4] Cf. Cooper, *Athenae Cantabrigienses*, i. 210.

doctrines.[1] Yet unlike his colleague and his pupil, Downes remained content to move with the times: he not only became (1537) Chancellor of York but adroitly contrived to retain that office under the successive régimes until his death in 1561.[2] We should do well to picture him on the present occasion, standing alongside Archbishop Lee, holding his peace and watching the quarrelsome friars with an enigmatic smile.

The report of the contest between Bale and Kirkby does not exhaust our knowledge of early Protestant preaching at Doncaster and elsewhere. In June 1534 the government had issued an order prohibiting preachers from contending with each other in the pulpit; they are moreover commanded to avoid altogether certain dangerous topics:

Item also to forfende that no preachers for a yere shall preache neyther with nor ayenst purgatory, honouring of saynctes, that priestes may have wyves, that faith onelie justifieth, to go on pilgremages, to forge myracles, considering these thinges have caused dissension amongst the subiectes of this realme alredy, whiche thanked be God is now well pacyfied.

Item that from hensfourth all preachers shall purelie, syncerelie and iustlie preache the scripture and woorde of Criste, and not myxe them with mannes institucions, nor make men beleve that the force of Goddes law and mannes law is like, nor that any man is able or hathe power to dispence with Goddes law.[3]

Lee's commission upon Bale and Kirkby was part of his campaign waged in accordance with this optimistic directive; others of his actions can be traced in his correspondence in the state papers. Over a year later, on 29 October 1535, Lee asked Cromwell for further information on the king's pleasure concerning preachers. The prohibition, he writes, has now expired; preaching against Purgatory has recommenced, 'wherwith the people grutche', though otherwise they diligently obey the royal command for the setting forth of the Royal Supremacy and the 'abolition of the primatie of Rome'. To avoid controversy, Lee has discharged a friar from preaching, since he preached at York in favour of Purgatory.[4] On 2 November, however, the archbishop reported a contrary episode. Cromwell had desired that John Best, a monk of Selby, should be licensed to preach, but Lee now replied that when the

[1] Cf. Harris, op. cit., p. 16.
[2] Most of the printed facts and references on Downes are in Cooper, loc. cit., but the York diocesan archives naturally contain innumerable references to his official activities over this long period.
[3] B.M. Cotton Cleop. E. v, fo. 294ᵛ. Cf. Burnet, *Hist. of the Reformation*, ed. Pocock, vi. 86–87; *L. & P.* viii. 869.
[4] Ibid. ix. 704.

Earl of Westmorland was at Selby, the said John had 'rayled and jested', saying it was hypocrisy to fast. Lee had therefore revoked a licence already given to Best till he 'were waxed sadder'.[1] Meanwhile the preaching friars found it impossible to keep out of trouble by avoiding the forbidden topics. Lee graphically reported his dealings with them in a letter which he merely dates '24 January', and which may almost certainly be ascribed to the year 1536.[2] Despite its paucity of names and dates, the central portion of this letter provides valuable insight into the relation between Reforming friars and northern public opinion. Lee acknowledges the order to suppress supporters of Papal authority and claims,

I knowe no man heere that in any maner goethe aboute to avaunce the said autoritie. . . . Contrarietie in preachinge I have not suffred ne have herde of anie, savinge that oone fryer in Yorke preched of purgatorie, whome (bicause he did it the Kynges pleasor not knowne) I furthwith discharged of preachinge, wherof I wrote to you by my brodre threasorer of Yorke; and oone oodre contention betwene the vycare of Doncastre and a light fryer there, wheropon I charged the saide vycare, that he in no wiese sholde preache of anie article mentioned in thordre taken by the Kynges highnes, and bicause I was crediblie enfourmed that the saide fryer preached some of the saide articles, and that aftre suche sorte that the people were mutche offended, I commaunded the vycare, that he sholde not suffre hym to preche, and forsomutche as the saide vycare and oodre[3] laied certayne articles against the saide fryer, wiche he had preched, I sent for hym first by a gentle lettre, but he wolde not come, but answerde me playnlie, he wolde aske cownsell, and so went to London. Aftreward at his retorne I cawsed hym to bee cyted, but he wolde not appeere, and nowe I have given commission downe to examyn tharticles, and forbicause he hathe preached mutche slawnderouslie, to thoffence of the people, I shall discharge hym of preachinge. There is also

---

[1] L. & P. ix. 742.
[2] This dating is clearly important. Strype placed this letter in 1538, not unnaturally assuming it to be an answer to some letters of the king and Cromwell on this topic, which may probably be dated 7 Jan. 1538, since the extant copies seem directed to Holgate as Bishop of Llandaff, rather than to his predecessor Athequa (cf. L. & P. xiii (1), 40, and compare ibid. x. 45, 46). But Lee's letter of 24 Jan. is apparently, despite its opening, not a reply to these, and should be placed in 1536 on several grounds:
   (1) Its mention of the recent visit of Lancelot Collins, treasurer of York, to Cromwell. Cf. L. & P. x. 163.
   (2) Its reference to Dr. Browne, Provincial of the Augustinian Friars, who would have been referred to as Archbishop of Dublin had the letter been written after 1536.
   (3) These activities of friars seem unlikely to have continued into 1537.
[3] i.e. other people.

a noodre frier of the gray sorte, of whome I ame nowe enfourmed, whom I shall also discharge, for he preachethe newe thinges, and that verie slaunderouslie, to the offense of the people, and whidre he have commission of me or not I doo not yet knowe. I admytted some at the request of doctour Browne,[1] pretendinge to me, that theye were discreete and well lerned, and sholde doo the Kinge good service. Odre preachers of novelties heere bee none, that I heere of, ne hathe been, savinge ii or iii that pretended to have the Kynges autoritie; with oone of them I spake, of whome aftrewarde I herde no great complaynte, and he shortelie aftre departed. The toodre hathe preched syns at Polles Crosse as wee heare, and there declared his lernenge, wiche is lieke his lief, bothe nowght, as the commen clamor of this contree is. All the Kinges maters the people heere reverentlie and obedientlie, but at suche novelties, speciallie handled withought charitie or discretion, the people grutche mutche, wheof heertofore I have advertised you by my letters. I trust there shalbee no defaulte fownde in me, but that I shall see the Kinges commawndement fulfilled to thuttremost of my power. And if herafter any shall come with the Kinges licence or yours, I trust you wolbee content, that I shall put them to silence as well as oodre, if they preache anye suche novelties.[2]

This letter comes, of course, from a markedly conservative prelate only too glad of the opportunity to suppress the new doctrines on grounds of public order, yet at the same time anxious to explain his actions to a minister with distinct Protestant sympathies. His analysis of public opinion is doubtless correct in its suggestion that the laity were under the predominant influence of conservative secular priests like the vicar of Doncaster, yet we shall soon encounter another analysis showing more 'progressive' forces at work.

Amongst the Henrician and subsequently Protestant friars of Yorkshire was Simon Clerkson, a Carmelite when in January 1535 he took his B.D. at Oxford.[3] Not long afterwards he became prior of the Whitefriars at York; he was holding this office in 1537–8 and on 27 November in the latter year he signed the deed of surrender.[4] In the previous July, Clerkson and his fellow prior of the London house assisted Bishop Longland at Wycombe in the examination of the heretic William Cowbridge. The bishop subsequently defended himself to Cromwell against

[1] George Browne, D.D., Provincial of the Augustinian Friars; made in 1536 archbishop of Dublin and the leading Henrician agent in Ireland; deposed for marriage by Mary (D.N.B.).
[2] B.M. Cotton Cleop. E. v, fos. 301–301ᵛ. For a synopsis of the whole letter see L. & P. x. 172.
[3] Register of the Univ. of Oxford, ed. Boase (Oxford Hist. Soc. i), p. 173. He is there wrongly given as a minorite. Cf. A. G. Little, op. cit., p. 54, n. 3.
[4] D.K. Rep. viii, app. ii, p. 51.

charges of over-severity toward this man and related that the two priors 'showed their learning to the party what error he [Cowbridge] was in'.[1] The task can have occasioned these learned men little difficulty, since the unfortunate defendant maintained various individual, not to say crazed views: for example, that priests were betraying God by breaking the host at mass, and that 'Christ' as distinct from 'Jesus' was the betrayer of the world. He also interpreted the words 'Accipite et manducate, hoc est Corpus meum quod pro vobis et multis tradetur' as 'Take ye and eat, this is the body wherein the people shall be deceived.'[2] Foxe claims that Cowbridge had been driven mad by starvation in the episcopal prison, but a letter probably written by him as early as 1536 seems incoherent to the point of madness.[3] That Prior Clerkson should have assisted in the prosecution of such opinions does not prove him a conservative, for scarcely one of Cowbridge's heresies would have been approved by the Lutherans themselves. It says little for the common-sense, let alone the humanity, of Longland and contemporary official-dom that no means were found to save this poor unbalanced creature from the stake. As for Simon Clerkson, the transition to a non-monastic world proceeded very painlessly. On 17 July 1539 Francis, Earl of Shrewsbury, presented him to the vicarage of Rotherham, which he held for fifteen years. His enthusiasm for the Henrician changes is adequately attested by a special licence which Henry VIII accorded him on 3 October 1541 during the course of the royal visit to Hull: it was issued formally on 27 October under the privy seal. Understanding that Clerkson is a bachelor in theology and excels in sacred learning (*sacrarum literarum cognitione pollet*), the king licenses him for the sake of preaching the Word of God to absent himself from the vicarage of Rotherham for the next ten years. During this period of non-residence, he may draw the profits of the vicarage, provided that funeral services are held, that the cure of souls is not neglected, and that he preaches at Rotherham once a quarter.[4] The present writer as yet knows nothing concerning the movements of Clerkson as an official preacher, but cannot doubt that, like so many of the friars, he moved on from the

[1] *L. & P.* xiii (1), 1434.

[2] Reg. Longland, fo. 284[v]. For other points see G. E. Wharhirst in *Lincs. Architect. and Archaeol. Soc. Rep.*, i, pt. ii, pp. 35–36.

[3] *L. & P.* x. 1253. I am not clear as to why the editor gave 1536, but it was presumably written before Cowbridge's imprisonment by the bishop and kept as proof of his guilt, or insanity.

[4] Rymer prints the text, from the patent roll, in *Foedera* (edn. 1712), xiv. 736; it is translated by J. Guest in *Hist. Notices of Rotherham*, pp. 73–74. Cf. also *L. & P.* xvi. 1308 (38).

Henrician position to views more advanced. In addition, his subsequent
career looks not altogether unworldly, since, while continuing to hold
Rotherham, he was presented in 1548 to the benefice of Stainby in
south Lincolnshire[1] and three years later exhibited a plurality-licence
at the Lincoln episcopal visitation.[2] By the end of the reign of Edward VI
he had apparently also identified himself with the new order by marrying, and so formed one of the more obvious targets for Catholic attack
by the outset of the Marian Reaction. Summoned to appear at York
on 16 April and again on 29 October 1554, Clerkson proved completely
contumacious and on the latter date suffered deprivation of the vicarage
of Rotherham. On this occasion letters testimonial under seal of the
archdeacon of Lincoln were produced in court; these probably reported
that he had already been deprived of Stainby. We know from the
Lincoln Register that this was now in fact the case, since on 5 October
another cleric had been admitted to Stainby, which lay vacant by
deprivation.[3] Though in the York act book Clerkson is not, like most
of the married clergy, specifically marked *conjugatus*, he is denoted as
regularis,[4] a distinction which could scarcely have held significance in
a summons other than one involving matrimony. His case appears
amongst those of the matrimonial offenders, though like other married
but defiant clergy he technically lost his benefice for contumacy.
Whether he had emigrated, the present writer remains unaware.[5]

Of the friars in York, Simon Clerkson was not the one who attained
greatest prominence in the post-Reformation Church. At the dissolution of the York Greyfriars in November 1538 one of its members was
Gilbert Barclay or Bartley;[6] he was then still young, having been
ordained deacon at Lincoln and priest at Northampton in 1535. The
London diarist Wriothesley relates that when in 1538 the king ordered
monks and friars to relinquish their habits, 'Doctor Barkley of the order
of Grey Fryers . . . was very loath to leave his ipochrytes coate till he
was compelled for feare of punishment.'[7] Foxe adds that the order proceeded from no less a person than Thomas Cromwell, who happened
to meet the unlucky Barclay near St. Paul's. 'Yea', said Cromwell,
'will not that cowl of yours be off yet? And if I hear by one o'clock that
this apparel be not changed, thou shalt be hanged immediately, for

[1] Lincoln Diocesan Records, P.D. 1548/16. This is certainly the same man, noted
as S.T.B.
[2] Ibid., Vj. 13, fo. 65.   [3] Ibid., Reg. 28, fo. 110.
[4] R. VII. A. 34, fo. 93.   [5] On the parallel cases, see *infra*, p. 200.
[6] D. K. Rep. viii, app. ii, p. 51.
[7] Wriothesley, op. cit., p. 82.

example to all others.'[1] Barclay seems to have accepted the spirit as well as the letter of this advice. Though his career in the forties remains obscure, he apparently came to accept the Henrician and Edwardian settlements with alacrity. In 1547 he obtained the rectory of Attleborough in Norfolk and at some later date married a wife who came to be notorious for her masterful character. After deprivation by the Marians in 1556 as a former regular, he joined the Protestant exiles at Frankfurt. Restored to his benefice under Elizabeth, Barclay was preferred to the bishopric of Bath and Wells; as a rather tired and ineffective prelate, he had to deal not merely with Mrs. Barclay but with the ultra-Protestant vagaries of his dean, the famous naturalist William Turner, whose career will subsequently engage our attentions.[2]

The cleric who next demands notice at this stage of the inquiry was not in fact a friar, but a member of an order deeply involved in parochial ministration and in many instances as much 'in the world' as the friars themselves—that of the Augustinian canons.

Robert Ferrar ultimately rose to the bishopric of St. David's and in 1555 showed a fortitude rare even amongst the martyrs of the Marian persecution when he was burned for heresy at Carmarthen. In his long history as a Reformer, some of the early phases belong to the diocese of York and here the pertinent evidence has been both misinterpreted and incompletely known. Ferrar was a native Yorkshireman, born some time in the reign of Henry VII at Ewood in Midgley, in the parish of Halifax, where gentry of his name flourished in the time of Elizabeth.[3] After or during a period of study at Cambridge he entered the Augustinian order and became a member of St. Mary's at Oxford. Here, like several others of the young men, he came under the spell of Thomas Gerard or Garret, the early Lutheran who has bulked so large in our study of Sir Francis Bigod. Ferrar was consequently among the group of Oxonians compelled in 1528 to recant and to carry the penitential faggot.[4] He nevertheless remained at the university, proceeding to his B.D. in 1533. Subsequently he became associated with a distinguished member of his own order, William Barlow, whom in 1535 he accompanied on an embassy to Scotland. That a known Reformer like Barlow[5] should have asked Cromwell to grant Ferrar a general licence

---

[1] Foxe, v. 396.
[2] The *D.N.B.* is very inadequate on Barclay; see also Baskerville in *E.H.R.* xlviii. 56, 201, and C. H. Garrett, *The Marian Exiles, 1553–1559*, p. 87.
[3] References in *D.N.B.*, s.v. Ferrar, Robert.   [4] Foxe, v. 428.
[5] On the complicated problems surrounding the early life of Barlow and his namesakes see Rupp, *Studies in the Making of the English Protestant Tradition*, ch. iv.

to preach[1] indicates that the latter had by no means abandoned his earlier opinions. At the beginning of June 1538 there occurred the death of the prior of St. Oswald's, Nostell,[2] and not long afterwards[3] Ferrar was appointed head of that house, one of the most important in Yorkshire. As he often acknowledges in his letters, he owed the position to the direct influence of Thomas Cromwell,[4] and since, like almost every other man in such an office, he sent Cromwell presents and finally accepted a fat pension,[5] he has been generally accepted as a pliant and self-seeking agent of the all-powerful minister. An attempt has indeed been made to group him with those who were pestering Cromwell for Yorkshire monastic lands.[6] This simple estimate, in itself consorting oddly with a subsequent heroic martyrdom, will not in fact survive a scrutiny of Ferrar's correspondence with Cromwell. The letter allegedly asking for the Nostell lands is actually a plea for the conversion of the priory into an educational and evangelistic institution. Acknowledging his personal debt to Cromwell, Ferrar beseeches him to be intercessor to the king

for the howse of Sainct Oswalde, whereunto by the goodnes of Godde it hath pleased his highnes at your mediation to preserve me, that it might be establesshed a colledge for the norishement of yowth in vertue and learnynge to thincrease and advauncement of the lyvelie worde of Godde, diligentlie, sincerelie and trewlie to be preached to Godde's people and the Kinge's in thees partes, whiche thankes be to the Lorde are right diligent, and with gladde hartes desirous to heare and learne the same.[7]

This letter was written from St. Oswald's on 5 September 1538. In the subsequent month Ferrar again gave Cromwell evidence of his missionary zeal. There were, he urged, almost none in these parts who sincerely, plainly and diligently preached the Gospel, though the people were hungrily desirous to hear and learn. 'Rodderham, Doncaster, Pontfrette, Wakefeylde, Leydys, Bradforde, Halyfaxe, Manchester and many others' had not one faithful preacher. Newcastle and the surrounding country were destitute of good pastors. Ferrar thought of going there after Christmas, 'to prove if it may please the Lord to give

[1] L. & P. x. 227.
[2] Yorks. Monasteries Suppression Papers (Y.A.S. Rec. Ser. xlviii), p. 61.
[3] Certainly before 5 Sept. 1538 (ibid., p. 62). [4] Ibid., pp. 62, 64, 67.
[5] Sometimes given as £100, sometimes as £80; its size was partly due to the fact that his office also carried with it the Bramham prebend in York Minster. Cf. Le Neve, op. cit. iii. 178.
[6] Yorks. Monasteries Suppression Papers, p. 58.
[7] Ibid., p. 62. Cf. L. & P. xiii (2), 285.

them any light through my poor service in His Word'.[1] Ferrar's view of the town-populations of the West Riding may be coloured by his own enthusiasm, but the towns regarded by him as receptive can mostly be proved so from record-sources.[2] It was Aske who spoke of the northern people as 'rude of conditions and not well taught the law of God';[3] their later history agrees entirely with the notion that many of them both needed and instinctively desired plainer, directer, more personal and more pedagogic forms of Christian teaching than those which the medieval Church supplied.

When in November 1539 the commissioners arrived to dissolve St. Oswald's, Ferrar 'uttered his conscience' to them before bowing to the inevitable, and recorded the fact in another letter to Cromwell.[4] He does not give the substance of this conscientious protest, but quite probably it related to his cherished scheme to convert St. Oswald's into a missionary college, now doomed to disappointment. Ferrar in this letter also begs Cromwell 'to be good and favorable to my poore feloose, servauntes and other poor people whyche hadde releyffe and socowre offe me theare'. Altogether, few heads of houses conducted themselves with as much dignity, consideration for their inferiors, and such constructive zeal as did Robert Ferrar. More to the present purpose, his phraseology places him unmistakably amongst that more disinterested group of the Reformers who saw in the Dissolution a great waste of opportunity for the endowment of education and preaching. His continued identification with the new doctrines and his failure to continue representing them during the last years of Henry VIII may now be explained by a reference in a recently explored act book of the York Court of Audience. Here it is baldly stated that on 10 September 1540 Robert Ferrar, late prior of Nostell, was summoned to reply to certain articles touching the safety of his soul and heretical pravity. He failed to appear and was thereupon excommunicated.[5] The present writer has discovered no sequel to these transactions: indeed, scarcely anything further is known concerning Ferrar's career until the days of Protector Somerset, when he suddenly emerged as a figure of national importance in the Reforming movement. One suspects that, having at first continued to live in the diocese after the dissolution of his house, he had been marked down by Archbishop Lee and attacked as a heretic

[1] *L. & P.* xiii (2), 953.   [2] Cf. *infra*, p. 247.
[3] *L. & P.* xii (1), 901, p. 405.
[4] *Yorks. Monasteries Suppression Papers*, pp. 72–73; cf. *L. & P.* xiv (2), 558.
[5] R. VII A.B. 2, fos. 128ᵛ–129.

immediately upon the fall of Cromwell. It would be of interest to learn whether the secular arm was at any stage invoked against him, and by what means he avoided further serious consequences. No doubt by September 1540 he had at least prudently withdrawn from Lee's jurisdiction.

Not far apart from Ferrar in point of background and outlook stood Robert Holgate, Master of Sempringham and prior of Watton.[1] Nevertheless, by superior caution and foresight, this other classic example of the Reforming, university-trained monk managed to avoid a frontal clash with Archbishop Lee and other conservative ecclesiastics; moreover, he proceeded to secure a bishopric and render himself so useful as a civil servant that he survived the fall of his patron Cromwell and became, as Lord President and Archbishop of York, the chief figure of both church and state in northern England. Like Ferrar he came of a small West Riding gentry family. He was born at Hemsworth about 1481, his being the fifth of the recorded generations of Holgates, each of which married into Yorkshire families of similar standing. At some date unknown he became a canon of the order of St. Gilbert of Sempringham and like many others used his membership as a stepping-stone to a long and distinguished career at Cambridge. Here he must have been in residence—probably at the Gilbertine house of studies near Peterhouse—for many years before he proceeded B.D. in 1523-4.[2] Here, too, he doubtless became familiar with many contemporaries destined to share his eminence and notoriety in the cause of Reformation. The early martyrs Barnes, Lambert, and Bilney were then active in Cambridge; so were their successors at the stake, Cranmer, Latimer, and Ridley. Holgate's future Reforming colleagues on the episcopal bench, Salcot, Hilsey, Hooper, and Holbeach, were not only fellow students but fellow monks. Whereas nearly all these future Protestants underwent a theological training, the future conservatives, like Gardiner, Bonner, and Sampson, were then students of canon and civil law. It has hence been rightly observed that in the education of the Henrician bishops may usually be found the essential clue to the positions which they ultimately adopted in the great conflict.[3] Robert Holgate nevertheless proved something of a hybrid. Monk, theologian, and Reformer as he was, he also showed some characteristics of the opposing legalist group. By temperament he was administrative rather than revolutionary,

---

[1] Detailed references for the succeeding paragraphs on Holgate will be found in the present writer's *Robert Holgate* (St. Anthony's Hall Publications, no. 8).
[2] And D.D. in 1536-7; cf. ibid., p. 4.   [3] Cf. L. B. Smith, op. cit., *passim*.

a Henrician who believed in achieving order by strong conciliar government, and who did not shrink from using the secular arm against sacramentarian extremists.[1]

In or before 1534 Holgate became Master of Sempringham and by 1536 prior of Watton in East Yorkshire, a place with which he was to retain intimate contact throughout his career, and where today the great prior's house stands substantially as he left it, one of our least-known yet most attractive monastic survivals. Undoubtedly he owed this sudden eminence to the favour of Thomas Cromwell: amongst his enemies the story circulated that he was 'Lord Cromwell's chaplain and admitted by him, having only been elected by three or four of his religion'.[2] He had moreover developed close links with the near-Lutheran group of divines circulating about the all-powerful minister. The chief evidence for this belief is Holgate's association with John Hilsey, formerly Provincial of the Dominicans and from 1535 Bishop of Rochester. Hilsey rapidly achieved notoriety amongst conservatives as the exposer of the Blood of Hailes, the Rood of Boxley, and other venerable frauds; he was one of the 'heretic bishops' whose punishment both the Lincolnshire and the Yorkshire Pilgrims of Grace so vociferously demanded.[3] There can be no doubt that Hilsey assiduously pushed Holgate into high office. In July 1536 he asked Cromwell to allow Holgate to enjoy his various offices *in commendam*, 'doubting not that he would do the king a good service'.[4] On 19 August Hilsey wrote more pointedly, urging Cromwell to promote Holgate to the vacant see of Llandaff.[5] His plea succeeded, and on 25 March 1537 he actually had the congenial duty of consecrating Holgate in the lady chapel of the London Blackfriars church. In view of these facts, Holgate's religious affiliations, even at this early date, cannot be mistaken. He nevertheless took care to avoid the sort of partisan prominence which Hilsey had attained. During the Pilgrimage of Grace, which had meanwhile occurred before his consecration, evidence certainly arose to show his unpopularity in the eyes of northern conservatives, yet it sprang less from specific attributions of heresy than from his notorious friendship with that *bête noir* of the Pilgrims, Thomas Cromwell. His priory of Watton, from which he had prudently withdrawn, became a storm-centre of the revolt, though the number of malcontents amongst the canons themselves proved extremely small. Locally, the movement

[1] Cf. *supra*, p. 32.   [2] *L. & P.* xii (1), 201, p. 92.
[3] Dodds, op. cit. i. 98, 353.
[4] *L. & P.* xi. 188.   [5] Ibid. xi. 260.

against Holgate sprang from the machinations of Bigod's associate, the yeoman John Hallam, who, according to the sub-prior, was 'greatly incensed against the Prior for putting him beside a farmhold'.[1] As soon as the rising collapsed and Holgate became a member of the Council in the North, his caution in the matters of theology stood him in good stead, since during his first year he had to serve under the loyalist but theologically conservative Bishop Tunstall. With such tact and industry did he behave that by November 1537 Tunstall was writing of him to Cromwell: 'Surely he is a man veray mete to serve the Kinge in these partes, of whose company I do take great comfort, seinge I have so wise a man to aske advise of, and so hole and intier to the Kinge as he is.'[2] By the following June Holgate replaced Tunstall in the presidency of the Council in the North and proceeded to hold it for eleven years. Whatever his religious predilections, he had come to appreciate the hard fact that under Henry VIII little was to be gained for a career, for the Reformation or for any secular ideal, save by becoming a Henrician. That during the thirties the same notion was successfully grasped by the other senior clergy of the diocese of York will become apparent in the chapter which follows.

2. The Convocation of York

In a study of clerical opinion, we may scarcely neglect the attitude adopted by the official representatives of the clergy in the Convocation of the Province of York. Only to a limited extent did this assembly represent the great body of parish priests. Though it included two proctors elected by the clergy of each archdeaconry, the bishops, deans, archdeacons, representatives of peculiars, heads of religious houses, and other *ex-officio* members outnumbered these ordinary members. Even after the dissolution of the monasteries, this preponderance continued. In the York Convocation of 1545, for example, about 60 persons actually attended, of whom only 21 represented the clergy of the archdeaconries. Both before and after the dissolution, the representatives of the diocese of York outnumbered those of the rest of the Province: in 1545 it sent 36 of the 60 members present.[3] How did these

[1] Cf. the present writer's *Robert Holgate*, pp. 7–9, for full references; also *supra*, p. 95.
[2] *State Papers of Henry VIII*, v. 122.
[3] *Records of the Northern Convocation* (Surtees Soc. cxiii), pp. 246–50. Apart from the superior size and institutional complexity of the diocese of York, its members naturally included fewer absentees than those from remoter dioceses.

people respond to the march of events during the first crisis of the Reformation?

The opinion of Froude on the subject has met with a degree of approval vouchsafed to few of his generalizations.

The Convocation of York [he wrote (*sub anno* 1536)] composed of rougher materials than the representatives of the Southern counties, had acquiesced but tardily in the measures of the late years. Abuses of all kinds instinctively sympathize, and the clergy of the North, who were the most ignorant in England, and the laity whose social irregularities were the greatest, united resolutely in their attachment to the Pope, were most alarmed at the progress of heresy, and were most anxious for a reaction.[1]

This passage is cited with approval by Dean Kitchin in his *Records of the Northern Convocation*.[2] Canon Dixon, while avoiding a story of continuous resistance to the king, gives the impression of bold and successful defiance in the earlier stages of the dispute.[3] Another writer speaks of the 'sudden collapse of the Northern Convocation in June, 1534', as if a stubborn resistance had been made until that date.[4]

These views call for close examination. We may pass over, as a matter of wider scope, Froude's grotesque attempt to establish a negative bond of union between the Renaissance Papacy and the allegedly barbarous Tudor north. Yet what of the Northern Convocation itself? Did Henry VIII really encounter bold or prolonged resistance from the official leaders of that conservative class, the northern clergy? Was the York Convocation notably more defiant than that of Canterbury? A brief survey along chronological lines should indicate the answers to these questions.

Our attention is first drawn by the events of the year 1531, when the king made his first great frontal attack on the clerical position. The threat of Praemunire for exercising independent jurisdiction in the ecclesiastical courts,[5] the peace-offering of an enormous subsidy by the Southern Convocation, the king's demand that an acknowledgement of his Supremacy be expressed in its grant, its subsequent consent with the cautious addition *quantum per Christi leges licet*, these are matters common to the authorities.[6] The southern grant was made on 4 March. The York Convocation followed suit on 4 May, when it granted

---

[1] *History of England*, ii. 508.   [2] *Surtees Soc.* cxiii, p. lxxi.
[3] *History of the Church of England*, i. 66–68.   [4] *V.C.H. Durham*, ii. 30.
[5] Not, as formerly supposed, for recognizing Wolsey's legatine authority (cf. J. Scarisbrick in *Cambridge Hist. Journal*, xii (i), 22 seqq.).
[6] Cf. Dixon, op. cit. i. 52–65; and, of the original authorities, especially Wilkins, *Concilia*, iii. 742–4.

£18,840[1] and made the required admission in the words '. . . ecclesiae
et cleri Anglicani, cujus singularem protectorem unicum et supremum
dominum, et quantum per Christi legem licet etiam supremum Caput,
ipsius majestatem recognoscimus'.[2] How long the matter of the
Supremacy was debated at York we do not know,[3] but it seems clear
that the uneasiness evident in the debates of the Southern Convocation
was fully shared at York, where, in addition, the government was not
strongly represented. Archdeacon Magnus,[4] the king's local agent,
wrote later:

For at the laste convocacion where as was graunted unto the Kinges
Highnes the great some of money to be paide in five years, with the recog-
nising his Grace to be *supremum caput*, &c., I had verey litle helpe but myself,
albe it the Kinges Highnes said that he wolde have sent other fookes after
me whiche came not, soe that therfor the Kinges causes were the longer
in treating and reasounyng or [ere] thay came to good effecte and conclusion.[5]

On 22 May the imperial ambassador Chapuys wrote to his master that
four days previously the clergy of York and Durham, as well as those of
the Canterbury Province, had sent the king a strong protest regarding
the supremacy which he claimed to have over them.[6]
    One of these protests, made individually[7] by Cuthbert Tunstall,
Bishop of Durham, is preserved. Its argument is of importance to our
subject. While Tunstall thinks the words *cujus singularem*, &c., will
not give offence to most people, he fears their misuse by those heretics

[1] Wilkins, op. cit. iii. 744. The amount, relatively to the wealth and numbers of
the northern clergy, was probably quite as great as the £100,000 granted by the
southern province.
[2] Quoted in Tunstall's protest, which is discussed below. Cf. Wilkins, op. cit.
iii. 745, and *Surtees Soc.* cxiii. 218-20.
[3] Atterbury (*Rights, Powers and Privileges of an English Convocation* (1701), p. 85)
notes that 'after frequent Debates and Adjournments, this Convocation came not to
a Resolution in the Point, till May 4, 1531; as appears by a Manuscript Diary of
what pass'd at the Meeting'. I have not encountered further mention of this diary.
[4] For various particulars regarding Magnus, 'a pluralist of uncommon distinction',
see *T.A.J.* xiv. 410; xxiv. 243 (n. 4). He was archdeacon of the East Riding from
1504 until his death in 1550. Already in this letter he complains that his 'oolde body
is nowe soe ofte clogged with infirmitie and unweildenes'.
[5] B.M. Cotton MS. Cleop. E. vi, fo. 257. The passages printed here and below are
taken from the original; for a version of the whole letter see G. Burnet, *History of
the Reformation*, ed. Pocock, vi. 52.
[6] *L. & P.* v. 251; cf. also ibid. xii (i), 786 (ii) 2.
[7] Such individual action was in consonance with the traditional independence of
the bishops of Durham, an attitude maintained by Tunstall; cf. *Surtees Soc.* cxiii.
16, 217.

who strive to diminish the authority of the bishops. The meaning of the words should be more fully explained. If it is meant that the king is Supreme Head 'in terrenis et temporalibus', this should be clearly stated and all will be well. If on the other hand the king claims supremacy 'tam in spiritualibus quam in terrenis et temporalibus', Tunstall himself must dissent, since this is repugnant to the opinion of the Catholic Church. The words 'Supremum Caput Ecclesiae' may have several senses, 'et ad propositionem multiplicem non sit danda simplex responsio'. At the same time, Tunstall places great emphasis on the honour, humility and obedience owed by priests to a Christian prince, debts which he himself will be the first to pay.[1] No other protests, whether collective or individual, have survived.

A famous and elaborate reply by Henry VIII defending and defining his supremacy remains amongst the Cotton manuscripts in the British Museum.[2] The date and the recipient of this royal counterblast are both matters of much significance for the history of the Northern Convocation. It was first printed in the *Cabala* and there arbitrarily headed 'King Henry the Eighth, to the Clergy of the Province of York, Anno 1533.'[3] Wilkins,[4] and more surprisingly the editor of the *Records of the Northern Convocation*,[5] accepted this heading, thus giving the impression that the northern clergy continued to wage the Supremacy controversy against the King for another two years. Strype,[6] followed by others,[7] compromised by placing Henry's reply in 1532. Francis Atterbury,[8] followed by the editor of the *Letters and Papers*,[9] placed it, though without giving reasons, in the year 1531, and considered it moreover a reply to Tunstall and not to the northern clergy collectively. In our opinion the date 1531 is a certainty and the claim that Tunstall was the recipient virtually so. The evidence is of course internal.

The king begins his reply, 'Right reverend Father in God, right trusty and well-beloved'. This might possibly apply to a bishop alone, especially if he were, like Tunstall, a prominent servant of the state. It might on the other hand apply to a bishop and one or two others collectively. The king states at the outset that he is replying to a

---

[1] Wilkins, op. cit. iii. 745; *Surtees Soc.* cxiii. 218–20.
[2] B.M. Cotton MS. Cleop. E. vi, fos. 220–5ᵛ.
[3] *Cabala, sive scrinia sacra: Mysteries of State and Government* (1663), pp. 244–8.
[4] Op. cit. iii. 762.   [5] *Surtees Soc.* cxiii. 221.
[6] *Eccles. Memorials* (edn. 1822), vol. i, pt. i, pp. 204–5.
[7] e.g. *V.C.H. Lancs.* ii. 42.
[8] Op. cit. ii. 85–88.
[9] *L. & P.* v, app. 9. Gairdner again adopts the view in his *English Church in the Sixteenth Century*, p. 109.

letter of 6 May written from York and containing a long discourse of
words used by the southern clergy in making their grant, 'the like
whereof should not pass'[1] in the northern province. The reference is
clearly to the Supremacy as expressed in the grant of 1531. The see of
York being vacant,[2] and no opposition being recorded of the Bishop of
Carlisle,[3] a strong prima facie case for Tunstall is at once established.
Tunstall, having made his formal protest against the terms of the grant
of 4 May, would naturally enough write to Henry a couple of days later
explaining his difficulties. It was typical of the frank relationship
between them and by no means their only correspondence of this controversial kind.[4] Moreover Henry's reply deals with exactly the same
difficulties and general attitude which Tunstall expresses in the extant
official protest we have just summarized.[5] A glance at the king's subject-matter will illustrate this fact.

'Ye interlace', he writes, 'such words of submission of your judgement
and discharge of your duty towards us, with humble fashion and behaviour.' This Tunstall had done too in his protest. Long passages
counter Tunstall's plea that the words 'quantum per Christi legem
licet etiam supremum Caput' lent themselves to perversion by the
weak or malignant. Surely the simplest proposition, says the king, is
liable to such perversion. Even if a man claimed to own land, he might
by such a perversion be reproved by the psalm Domini est terra. 'We
ought to apply and draw words to the truth, and so to understand
them, as they may signifie truth, and not so to wrest them, as they
should maintain a lie.' In this particular case, it would obviously be
absurd to call the king 'Caput Ecclesiae representans Corpus Christi
mysticum'; the addition of the words et cleri anglicani restrained the
meaning of ecclesiae 'and is as much to say the church, that is to say the
clergy of England'. The king then disposes of Tunstall's distinction

[1] The grant had actually been made on 4 May, but the king would not yet, if the
common practice were followed, have received official notice of it.
[2] From Wolsey's death on 29 Nov. 1530 until the bull of 30 Oct. 1531, promoting
Edward Lee.
[3] John Kite, 1521–37. Cf. D.N.B. for some particulars regarding his submissive
but moderate attitude.
[4] Burnet (op. cit., ed. Pocock, iv. 400–7) prints from Cotton MS. Cleop. E. v,
fos. 131–2, 134–7 (new reference) a controversy of 1539 between Henry and Tunstall
regarding the divine institution of auricular confession. The letter summarized in
L. & P. v. 820 is perhaps a continuation of the supremacy dispute between them.
[5] It is clearly a reply to something more than Tunstall's protest itself, a fact which
probably prevented Canon Dixon (op. cit. i. 67, n.) from believing it was a reply to
Tunstall at all. Surely, however, Tunstall would send the king a letter more elaborate
and reasoned than this dry and brief official protest.

between temporal and spiritual headship. Christ may indeed have given temporal power to princes and spiritual to the clergy, yet, by the very texts cited, the clergy are as much bound as any other men to obey princes. Christ and St. Paul were very far from exempting themselves from the jurisdiction of the temporal power. Hence the king has a spiritual headship, not indeed over such spiritual functions as the sacraments, which can have no earthly head, but over spiritual men and all their acts. After dwelling on the present reality and necessity of his control over the English Church, Henry returns to the main point of Tunstall's protest. Provided *ecclesia* were properly defined, there was reason neither for 'the doubt and difficulty you make to give a single answer' (Tunstall's *non sit danda simplex responsio*), nor for the distinction between headship *in temporalibus* and *in spiritualibus*.[1]

Hence the argument of this royal manifesto strengthens the already strong probability that it was directed, not against the Northern Convocation in 1532 or 1533, but against Tunstall alone, or Tunstall heading a very small group of dissentients, in May 1531. We have insisted at some length on this view, because it establishes a vital fact in the history of the Northern Convocation, namely, that its dispute with the king over the Royal Supremacy was very largely conducted by Tunstall and did not extend beyond the year 1531. In that year, moreover, the northern clergy, while doubtless delaying and showing reluctance, did not adopt an attitude noticeably more defiant than that of their southern colleagues. Tunstall indeed dared to argue against the king's view of his supremacy, but so, for that matter, did Archbishop Warham.[2] Even Tunstall's efforts proved tentative; they constituted a general plea for clerical privilege which in no way developed into positive support of the Papal Supremacy. The events of the subsequent years must now be surveyed somewhat more rapidly.

The Canterbury Convocation of 1532 saw the prolonged negotiations resulting in what is generally known as 'the Submission of the Clergy'. Little or nothing is known of the proceedings in the parallel northern session which began on 7 February,[3] and we can only presume that its assent was given with little or no opposition.

The meetings of 1533 had as their principal concern the Divorce, for the completion of which the explicit support of both convocations

---

[1] Actually the words *in terra* were finally prefixed to *Supremum Caput*, &c., in the king's official style (Close Roll, 26 Hen. VIII, m. 14d, printed in Rymer, *Foedera*, xiv. 549).

[2] Wilkins, op. cit. iii. 746; Burnet, op. cit., ed. Pocock, vi. 54–55.

[3] *L. & P.* v. 772.

seemed highly desirable. The Canterbury Province debated the king's questions between 2 and 5 April; it finally answered them, though with a number of dissentients, in his favour.[1] On the subsequent negotiations in the York Province we have much interesting evidence. The condition of affairs amongst the northern clergy and the preparations made to ensure the safe passage of the king's 'great matter' through their hands are illustrated by three items of the voluminous correspondence of Thomas Cromwell. On 21 April Archdeacon Magnus wrote the letter already cited, rejoicing that this time Dr. Rowland Lee[2] was coming to help at York.

The prelates and clergie there [he continued] woll not in anywise give firme credence to reaporte of any actes that be paste here, oonles the same be shewed unto thaym autentically, aither under seale or otherwise, or the Kinges mooste honourably [sic] lettres addressed accordingly. These twoe thinges in myn oppynnyon muste booth be doon, for withoute the same the prelates and clergie of the north parties, being farre frome knowledge of the Kinges mooste high pleasur, woll not for any credence be haistie to procede to any straunge actes, but woll esteme thaire reasons and lernyng to be as effectuall as other be.[3]

The Dean of York[4] on 2 May acknowledged a letter from Cromwell sent by Dr. Lee and assured Cromwell that he would do his best to get passed at York the same measures already passed by the Southern Convocation.[5] Five days later Lee himself wrote Cromwell a letter,[6] which depicts admirably the attitudes of the leading personalities—especially that of Tunstall—as well as the method of lobbying by which Tudor governments could further their will in Convocation.

Aftre most hartly [sic] recommendacions, it shalbe to advertisse you that accordyng to the Kynges plesure and hye commandment I have ben with my Lorde of Durram too tymes. At the fyrst tyme I declaryde to hym the Kynges plesure, accordyng to the credens yewyn to me, with also suche order as is taken in the Province of Canterbury and the instrumentes materiall for the accomplissement thayreof.[7] After long tract hys Lordshipe axyd me whether I whold command hym in the Kynges behalffe to be at Yorke at the

[1] Wilkins, op. cit. iii. 756–7. Cf. Dixon, op. cit. i. 150–4.
[2] Cf. D.N.B. He was at this time archdeacon of Cornwall, king's chaplain, Master in Chancery and Bishop-elect of Chester. He held for a short time prebends at York (L. & P. vi. 735) and Ripon (ibid. 1226).
[3] B.M. Cotton MS. Cleop. E. vi, fo. 257.
[4] Brian Higden, dean from 1516 to 1539 (Le Neve, Fasti, ed. Hardy, iii. 126).
[5] L. & P. vi. 431.
[6] P.R.O., S.P. I/76, fos. 27–27ᵛ. A brief summary is given in L. & P. vi. 451.
[7] The documents embodying the decision of the Canterbury Convocation.

convocacon, affirmyng that the Kyng hade yewyn hym in commandment to be in redynesse for the Scottes with hys counsell thayre. If I whold command hym to the contrary and to goo to York, hee whold. I answeryd hym and sayd that I hade sayd my message and the Kynges expectacon whas to have hys assistens in hys cause and fortherans, wherby hee myght know the Kynges plesure, and other commandment I hade not to yeve.

Than hee sayd it where better for hym to be awaye thane to doo noo good, prayng me to returne frome Durram by hym agane. And at my returne efsonys[1] in communicacion of the mater, I demandyd hys opinion and that hee whold subscribe the conclusion.[2] He mayd me answere that as yeytt hee whas not resolweyd and forasmiche as hee whas of the Lady Katren counsell at the begynnyng,[3] he whold not open hys mynd, but send it to the Kyng by hys owne serwand acordyng to hys consciens, and that by hys chanceler hee whold, after he where more effectually resolwyd in hys oppinion, send me his ferther mynd, *et sic finis*, but in noo wysse he whold subscribe.

I am sory to see soo littill stay towardes the Princes owr masteres honor by suche. It is noo merwell whane strangeres shall strangely sentire[4] whane wee owr selffes soo doo by hym by whome whee be supportyd, specially the thyng now doyne. Thus I wrytte you secretly. Whold Godd wee where of on mynd, but the diversites of myndes in owr selffes shall hurte hus. . . .[5]

I resaveyd after the former parte of thys wrytyng your moste lowyng letter to my singular comfurthe, and fere yee of noo good wyll in me, nether of labores nor peanes but to apply my diligens and industrie to the best of my simple wytt, and yeyt more to spend body and goodes duryng my lyve to serve my naturall lorde. Yester nyght late I cam to Yorke and have thys mornyng consultyd with Mr. Doctor Marshall[6] and junyd hym and Mr. Leghton[7] with the other to gether. Hee is, and soo affirmeys to be, tractabile if by thayre lernyng and ferther debaytement of the cause hee may discharge hys consciens. The Abbot of Fowntains,[8] I trust, wylbe good. Now I am[9]

---

[1] Eftsoons.

[2] The conclusion arrived at a month earlier by the Canterbury Convocation seems to be intended.

[3] On 1 Nov. 1528 the Bishop of Bayonne writes that of the counsel at Catherine's disposal only Tunstall, then Bishop of London, and two others are of her opinion (*L. & P.* iv (2), 4899).

[4] Probably a form of censure, in its common meaning 'to form an opinion'.

[5] A brief passage on other matters follows. Cf. *L. & P.* vi. 451.

[6] Cuthbert Marshall, S.T.P., prebendary of York 1526–50; archdeacon of Nottingham 1528–50 (Le Neve, op. cit. iii. 151, 195).

[7] Edward Leghton, D.D., an Oxford scholar introduced to convince Marshall. Cf. below for his letter reporting the success of the king's cause. On his appointments and livings cf. J. Foster, *Alumni Oxonienses*, s.v. Leighton, Edward.

[8] William Thirsk, later hanged for complicity in the Pilgrimage of Grace. For some important references cf. *V.C.H. Yorks.* iii. 137.

[9] This word in the original is a mere stroke, possibly intended for 'cum'.

towardes Byland, Newbrugh and Rywax.[1] The Abbot of Welbeke[2] wylnot fayle to doo the best hee can. The Abbot of Saint Maries[3] alsoo, but hee is not lernyd. Thayre shalbe as myche doyne as I may.[4]

The Divorce procedure in this convocation closely followed that of its southern counterpart. As in the latter the clergy had to answer two questions. The first was the business of the theologians:[5] 'An ducere uxorem cognitam a fratre decedente sine prole sit prohibitio juris divini indispensabilis a papa?' Twenty-seven theologians personally present and having letters of proxy from absent clergy to the number of twenty-four replied, as the king desired, 'Casum hujusmodi de jure divino esse indispensabilem per papam'. Two only disagreed. The second question belonged to the canonists: 'An carnalis copula inter illustrissimum principem Arthurum et serenissimam dominam Catharinam reginam ex propositis, exhibitis, deductis et allegatis sit sufficienter probata?' The forty-four canonists present, certain of them also representing five or six absentees, answered that it was sufficiently proved. Two of them, as with the theologians, dissented.[6] Who formed the courageous minority in each class, we are not told, but Tunstall certainly stood again at the head of the opposition. On 16 June we find Chapuys writing to the emperor that the Bishop of Durham had manfully opposed the Bishop of London[7] in the Northern Convocation over the Divorce, and, were it not that the king could not find a man more competent to govern the borders, he would have been imprisoned like Bishop Fisher.[8] Whatever the accuracy of this prejudiced reporter, opposition from the convocation as a whole had certainly been much feebler than that evidenced in the parallel Convocation of Canterbury.[9] Edward Leghton was able to relate on 15 May that the king's questions had been determined and answered in the York Convocation 'with as much towardness as ever I saw in my life, thanks to the labors of Dr. Lee'.[10]

---

[1] Rievaulx, a spelling frequent in the sixteenth century.

[2] John Maxey; cf. the references in *V.C.H. Notts.* ii. 136–7.

[3] William Thornton; cf. *V.C.H. Yorks.* iii. 110. For the charges brought against him by Archbishop Lee in 1535 see *Y.A.J.* xvi. 446–7, and for his defence, of which writers seem curiously unaware, *L. & P.* ix. 58.

[4] The letter concludes with references to private affairs in Convocation; cf. ibid. vi. 451.

[5] On this method of dividing the body cf. Dixon, op. cit. i. 152.

[6] Rymer, op. cit. xiv. 474–5; Wilkins, op. cit. iii. 767.

[7] Stokesley does not appear to have been personally present at York; he had, of course, been prominent in urging the king's cause in the Southern Convocation (Wilkins, op. cit. iii. 756).

[8] *L. & P.* vi. 653.

[9] Cf. the numbers and references in ibid. 311, 317.   [10] Ibid. vi. 491.

In the following year the king made the convocations and the universities his accomplices in throwing off the last vestiges of Roman jurisdiction. The York Convocation begun on 5 May 1534, obediently concluded, without a single dissentient, 'quod episcopus Romanus in sacris scripturis non habet aliquam majorem jurisdictionem quam quivis alius externus episcopus'.[1] Here again there were more signs of opposition in the Southern Convocation, where thirty-four members voted against the papal claims, one was doubtful and four remained favourable.[2] Again, with what little suitability this decision of 1534 may be called a 'sudden collapse' on the part of the Northern Convocation may be seen from our examination of the years 1531–3. Like the Supremacy Statute of the following November, this denial of Roman jurisdiction was little more than an 'ornamental coping-stone' to the building already erected by king and Parliament. There can, too, be little reasonable doubt that the northern bishops, chapters, religious houses, and collegiate churches made their individual renunciations of the Papal Supremacy during the same year. The original deeds, unlike many of those from the Southern Province,[3] have, however, perished, though Henry Wharton claimed to know their whereabouts in 1694.[4]

Throughout the subsequent years the Northern Convocation continued submissive. In January 1536 Archbishop Lee told Cromwell that he knew of no one thereabouts who advanced the Pope's authority,[5] an assertion which would seem to cover at least the leading clergy. In 1537 the three northern bishops gave their authority to the Bishops' Book,[6]

---

[1] The Record Office copy of the attestation, dated 1 June, is printed in Rymer, op. cit. xiv. 492–3. Another copy, omitting a few words and dated 2 June, is in Lee's Register, fo. 88, and printed in Wilkins, op. cit. iii. 782–3, and in *Surtees Soc.* cxiii. 232–3.

[2] Wilkins, op. cit. iii. 769.

[3] Cf. Rymer, op. cit. xiv. 487–527; *L. & P.* vii. 427, 665, 769 (2), 865, 891, 921, 1024–5, 1121, 1216, 1347, 1594, &c.

[4] Cf. *V.C.H. Lancs.* ii. 42. The reference here to Wharton's *De Episcopis et Decanis Londiniensibus*, p. 286, is surely incorrect, though remarks vaguely on this line occur on p. 242. Reference should rather be made to Wharton's *Observations* appended to the 1694 edition of Strype's *Cranmer*, p. 254. There Wharton says that he saw the original instruments from thirteen dioceses and that 'the Subscriptions of those of the other Nine Dioceses are to my certain knowledge yet remaining in another place, but I have not yet gained Copies of them'. The *V.C.H.*, loc. cit., assigns these renunciations to July and Aug., but they continued in large numbers from May until at least Jan. 1535 (cf. *L. & P.* vii. 665; viii. 31). Again, Wharton is wrongly accused of error for saying that some renunciations are on Close Roll, 25 Hen. VIII: cf. *L. & P.* vii. 665.

[5] Ibid. x. 172.

[6] Cf. *Surtees Soc.* cxiii. 241.

while three years later the two Convocations united to declare void
the Cleves match, a conclusion fully attested by the northern divines.[1]

The only moment of anything resembling defiance by a number of
the higher clergy in the north came at the height of the Pilgrimage of
Grace. While the lay council of the pilgrims was producing the well-
known Pontefract Articles, about fifteen northern divines, five of them
regulars,[2] held meetings in a parlour of the abbey at Pontefract.[3] The
story of these meetings has already been told[4] and a few observations
only are necessary to our purpose.

On 4 December 1536 the divines produced, as a result of the day's
discussion, a series of ten resolutions, being replies to certain questions
put to them.[5] These resolutions, extant in two manuscripts,[6] call for
reversion to a conservative religious policy. Purgatory, worship of
saints, the old rescinded holidays, pilgrimage, benefit of clergy, sanctuary, and images are all defended, though not all had as yet been
officially discarded. Payment of tenths and firstfruits to the king is
declared illegal, while 'landis gyven to God, the churche or relygyouse
men ma not be taken away and put to prophane uses by the lawes of
God'. Most important are the second resolution, that 'by the lawes of
the churche, generall counselles, interpreta[tion]ys of approved doctors
and consente of Crysten people the Poope of Rome hath ben taken for
the hedd of the churche and vycare of Cryste and so oughte to be taken',
and the ninth, that 'the Kinges highnes ne any temporall man may not
be Supreme Hedd of the churche by the lawes of God to have or exercise any jurysdiccons of poer spirituall in the same, and all actes of
parliamente made to the contrary to be revoked'. On the following day
these fifteen clergy met again, sanctioned those articles produced by

[1] *State Papers of Henry VIII*, i, pt. ii, p. 629; see for Lee and Tunstall p. 633, and for
other northern clergy p. 635.
[2] See the list in Dodds, op. cit. i. 382, and cf. *L. & P.* xii (i), 786 (p. 341); 1021
(p. 462).
[3] Ibid. 786 (p. 341).
[4] Dodds, op. cit. i. 382-6. The authorities are Aske's accounts (*L. & P.* xii (i),
698 (3); 945 (1)), Dr. Dakyn's statements (ibid. 786-9), a deposition of unknown
authorship, mutilated and almost valueless (ibid. 1011, pp. 454-5), and Dr. Pickering's statement (ibid. 1021).
[5] When examined, Aske could not remember any direct replies to articles he himself had put to them and thought the divines 'made their boke uppon other poyntes,
other inncerted by theymselfes or exhibited by some other unto theym' (*E.H.R.*
v. 573).
[6] P.R.O., S.P. 1/122, fos. 140-1; B.M. Cotton MS. Cleop. E. v, fos. 413 seqq.
The latter has been printed by Strype, Wilkins, and Kitchin, but the only trust-
worthy version is in Dodds, op. cit. i. 383-5.

the laity which reflected on the king's ecclesiastical policy and also added a few further resolutions of their own, requiring the continued study of the canon law, pardon for religious refugees, and other conservative measures.[1]

All this would seem to constitute a bold stand against the king. This impression is nevertheless much modified by further information as to the nature and events of the meeting. In the first place it must be remembered that the latter was in no sense a convocation and made no claim to be such.[2] It was a small revolutionary assembly, summoned by Archbishop Lee under pressure, and forming the clerical counterpart of the simultaneous council of laymen which produced the main articles of the rebels. This is indeed obvious from all the records, but needs to be mentioned since the ten resolutions have been, astonishingly enough, called a reply by the Northern Convocation to the king's well-known Ten Articles.[3] Such an assembly could not claim to be representative, even of the higher clergy. It clearly consisted only of those bolder spirits who were glad to identify themselves with the rising, and of such prominent clergy as the rebels happened to be able to coerce.[4] It met under fear of mob violence[5] and under pressure from laymen. Though Robert Aske denied using threats or compulsion,[6] he certainly interposed in the clerical meeting, insisting that the Papal Supremacy must be upheld and that he himself would fight to the death in this cause.[7] Even so, there was divergence on this crucial point. Dr. Marshall, archdeacon of Nottingham, spoke most for the papal claims,[8] while Dr. Sherwood, chancellor of Beverley, took the king's side. Some produced from their purses copies of the protestations made in 1531, complaining that the saving clause *quantum per Christi legem licet* was now omitted. Dr. Dakyn, rector of Kirkby Ravensworth,[9] who acted

---

[1] Cf. Dodds, op. cit. i. 385.

[2] It actually referred its determinations to the next convocation 'for lacke of tyme and instruccyon in thies artycles and wante of bookys' (ibid., loc. cit.).

[3] *Surtees Soc.* cxiii. 235.

[4] Tunstall, in whom the civil servant triumphed over the religious conservative, had avoided being forced to join the rebels by fleeing to Norham (Dodds, op. cit. i. 203–4).

[5] *L. & P.* xii (1), 786, p. 341; 789, p. 346.

[6] Ibid. 698, p. 312.

[7] Compare Pickering's account (ibid. 1021, p. 462) with that of Dakyn (ibid. 786, p. 341).

[8] Dakyn's phraseology suggests that Pickering, Brandsby, and Waldby supported Marshall. This seems almost certain of Pickering.

[9] Dakyn's statements (*L. & P.* xii (1), 786–9) naturally tend to tone down the remarks made against the king. But his confessions were open and naïve (cf. Dodds,

as secretary to the meeting, later claimed to have thought that this matter of the supremacy should be referred to a General Council. When on the afternoon of 5 December this committee of clergy took their articles to Archbishop Lee, he demurred at the article favouring the Papal Supremacy. Dr. Marshall and Dr. Pickering, the friar preacher, then insisted on the necessity of this article, which Lee finally allowed to remain as expressing 'the consent of Christian people'.[1] Three or four enthusiasts backed by the pressure of the lay rebels had overborne the lukewarm and undecided majority; unanimous opposition to the king was not forthcoming even from this unrepresentative and irregular body, meeting as it did amid the enthusiasm and fears of armed, and as yet successful rebellion.

The answers to the questions asked at the outset of this inquiry seem hence clear enough. They are not those given in the past. The resistance of the York Convocation to Henry VIII was practically limited to the year 1531 and even then it centred closely around Tunstall. Two years later the king's agents, doubtless realizing how widespread were conservative sympathies amongst both clergy and laity in the north, still thought the Northern Convocation needed very careful handling. Yet the easy outcome of the Divorce procedure somewhat belied this notion and made the preparations seem over-elaborate. After 1531 the Northern Convocation proved even more submissive than that of the Southern Province. Tunstall alone of the northern prelates maintained a policy not so much of opposition as of reluctant conformity. In 1535 he had abandoned even this and was obediently preaching the Royal Supremacy,[2] while in the following year he vigorously defended the king's cause against Reginald Pole[3] and by precipitate flight avoided implication in the Pilgrimage of Grace.

A study of the York Convocation, whatever points of intrinsic interest it may discover, yields no dramatic evidence concerning either Reformation or Reaction. The Convocation placed no brake whatever upon the changes of the day, yet it displayed little sympathy with any aspect of the Reforming movements. Like almost all the bishops whether conservative or innovating by personal outlook, it proved

op. cit. i. 386), and he was anxious to have his very precise and circumstantial account checked by reference to others (*L. & P.* xii (1), 788). He claimed that his experience in the Court of Arches had convinced him that appeals to Rome occasioned much contention and delay (ibid. 786, p. 343).

[1] Ibid. p. 341.
[2] Ibid. x. 1082; cf. Wriothesley, *Chronicle* (Camden Soc. new ser. xi), i. 34-35.
[3] Cf. Dixon, op. cit. i. 443-4.

solidly Henrician in practical action. Its records leave the broader questions of the social historian almost unanswered. How far, for example, did this co-operative body truly represent the attitude of the clergy? The present writer used to think in terms of a deep rift between the respectable and obedient senior clergy in Convocation and the mass of ultra-reactionary northern parish priests. He now feels uncertain whether this ultra-reactionary mass really existed. It would not be difficult to build up a plausible picture of clerical reaction by means of a judicious selection of anecdotes. From the voluminous records of the Pilgrimage of Grace one could produce the cases of several activist priests, secular and regular, who certainly regarded heresy, the Divorce and the Royal Supremacy with the same uncompromising hostility as Robert Aske himself. In the years which followed the Pilgrimage, a few parish clergy continued to become involved in charges of sedition.[1] Again, we shall soon encounter at least one clear example of a Yorkshire priest who held his cure throughout all the changes from the forties to the seventies, who obeyed all the orders from above, and yet recorded in detail his abhorrence of doctrinal and liturgical innovation.[2] Nevertheless, intellectual honesty would compel us to admit that our lists of both proved reactionaries and proved Protestants together embrace a tiny percentage of the thousand or more priests[3] in the diocese of York. Between the two stood that vast majority which will be forever inarticulate or silent. Thinking of their educational background and the books they owned, we may not doubt the existence of a general conservatism, a widespread distaste for the Cromwellian changes. Beyond this point the evidence will not carry us. If the parish clergy had good reason to fear heresy, they had small inducement to join, in heart or in act, the seditious opposition to Henry VIII. The average parish priest had nothing to gain from the triumph of northern feudal reaction; he did not share in any large measure those economic and legal grievances which in 1536 stirred so many laymen to revolt; his professional habits were not as yet threatened by any catastrophic doctrinal or liturgical changes. It remains difficult to see why any historian save a romantic papalist or a romantic Protestant should want to place him among the chief malcontents of the period. The reign of Henry VIII was not in general an age of romantics, and it would require a fervid imagination to transform its northern clergy into a body of romantic papalists. It requires effort to detach our minds from the

[1] Cf. the present writer in *Y.A.J.* xxxiv. 379 seqq.
[2] The case of Robert Parkyn, *infra*, p. 181.   [3] Cf. *infra*, p. 188, n. 1.

simple patterns imposed by the partisans and the dramatizers who until recently dominated our Reformation-history. Yet have not these historians overestimated the degree of doctrinal conviction and precision achieved by the average mid-Tudor priest? Have they not also taken for granted the solid blessings which the first two Tudors won for English society? Have they not thereby underestimated the force exerted by Henrician royalism upon clergy and laity alike? Here was a force virtually unsupported by professional soldiers and police. Compounded in part of fear and self-interest, it nevertheless contained much else besides. With a compelling if circumscribed logic, it bound even the priesthood, half willing accomplices in the subjugation of their order, to the conservative Erastianism of Henry VIII.

VI

PROTESTANTISM AND HERESY UNDER
EDWARD VI AND MARY

1. *The Prologue*

FROM our present viewpoint, the sources for the Edwardian Reformation are unduly dominated by dissolution and confiscation, the material detail of which is at most peripheral to the story of Protestantism. Nevertheless, the psychological effects of the dissolutions upon Protestantism remain important and appear almost entirely adverse to the cause. The chantries, colleges, and religious gilds were destroyed by politicians who, sincerely and otherwise, called themselves Reformers, while the benefits which they disgorged from the proceeds seemed meagre and grudging to all religious and public-spirited men, Reforming and traditionalist alike. The final confiscation, that of 'surplus' church plate, lacked even the decent hypocrisy of a doctrinal argument. All in all, only follies as monumental as those of Mary could have obliterated the opprobrium brought upon the Reformers by their political backers. Everything connected with these Edwardian governmental enterprises, even their psychological results, finds interesting illustration in the diocese of York. On the other hand, the more important part of our task, the discovery of positive evidence concerning the extension and development of Protestant belief, now becomes more difficult. Here lies no real paradox. Most of our knowledge of early Protestantism in society depends upon the records of its persecution, and in 1547 the persecution of all save a handful of extremist fanatics came to an end. On 4 May 1547 the Privy Council ordered Archbishop Holgate, President of the Council in the North, to liberate persons detained at York and elsewhere in the north for offences against the Statute of the Six Articles, since these offences had been pardoned at the coronation.[1] In the subsequent November Parliament swept away most of the earlier legislation against heresy, thus inhibiting in effect the action of ecclesiastical as well as lay courts and hence depriving modern historians of the chief indices to the advance of the

---

[1] Bodleian Tanner MS. 90, fo. 144, printed in *E.H.R.* ix. 543. It is tempting to suppose these heretics were Burdon and Grove (cf. *supra*, p. 34), yet there may have been others omitted from our sketchy records.

new doctrines. From this stage one may trace in fair detail the development of official policy in the diocese of York, yet its results upon regional society are less readily assessed.

During the later years of Henry VIII, and more especially during the reign of his son, the official programme cannot be regarded as homogeneous throughout England. Statutes, Privy Council orders, royal visitors, and royal injunctions admittedly provided the *leit-motif*, but the bishops superimposed their not always very harmonious orchestrations. Neither the conservative but obedient Edward Lee nor the Reformer and civil servant Robert Holgate wished to provoke needless trouble with the conservative forces of regional society, and under these circumstances the pace set from York might be expected, if anything, to drag behind that prescribed in some other dioceses. The surviving diocesan injunctions do not, however, support this notion. Whatever its effectiveness in remote places, diocesan policy did not lack confidence. Both archbishops might denounce the poverty and ignorance of their parish clergy or the backwardness of their laity, but after the collapse of the Pilgrimage of Grace both must have beome well aware of the weakness of the opposition. The popular view that Yorkshire was a hotbed of Catholic sedition throughout the Tudor period cannot be substantiated. The Wakefield plot of 1541 and the Seamer rising of 1549 were both, like the Pilgrimage itself, far from purely religious agitations. Moreover, neither of them attained much greater than parochial dimensions.[1] Seditious and activist conservatism remained after 1537 a localized phenomenon and, apart from Richmondshire, Ripon, and Wetherby in 1569, it never brought to arms any considerable area of either Yorkshire or Nottinghamshire.

The earlier parts of this chapter deal with officially recognized Protestantism, which has a recognizable prologue in the reign of Henry VIII. A convenient point of departure in the York diocese is formed by a set of injunctions given by Archbishop Lee, but preserved only by Burnet.[2] They can be dated in their present form 1538;[3] most of them are mere echoes of the Royal Injunctions of that year and of those issued in 1536. They represent above all a landmark in the history of Bible-study within the diocese. Priests must henceforth in no wise discourage any man from reading the English Bible and must ensure that their

[1] On these two movements see the present writer in *Y.A.J.* xxxiv. 151 seqq. and 379 seqq.
[2] Reprinted by W. H. Frere in *Alcuin Club Collections*, xv. 44–52.
[3] Parts may date from lost injunctions of 1537: on this problem cf. J. F. Mozley, *Coverdale and his Bibles*, pp. 169–70.

parishioners install a chained copy of a Bible of the largest volume in some open place of their churches. With what speed this order was obeyed, the few surviving documents do not enable us to be certain. The parson being obliged to bear half the cost, the provision of a Bible did not strain the resources even of a small parish. The churchwardens of Sheriff Hutton in 1538–9 had only to collect 3s. 2d.,[1] which was presumably half the price of a Coverdale Bible, the cheapest edition then available. In 1541, however, the churchwardens of Ecclesfield collected over 14s. for a Bible,[2] an amount representing the whole cost of the Great Bible of 1539.[3] These accounts incidentally show that some parishes owned small libraries of books, liturgical and otherwise. At Ecclesfield about 1540 the vicar, Edward Hatfield, M.A., presented several volumes of the Fathers and of medieval commentators to be perpetually chained in the church.[4] The fact that the inventories of church goods made in 1552 mention only about a dozen Bibles in Yorkshire, Durham, and Northumberland has been taken to indicate widespread disobedience,[5] yet this evidence lends no colour whatsoever to a notion so intrinsically improbable. The church goods commissioners were not ordered to list Bibles or other books and seldom did so.[6] On the argument from silence, one might also maintain that in 1552 there were only four copies of the Book of Common Prayer in these counties, and that only in Dewsbury was a parish register being maintained![7] The subsequent years have left few clues as to the extent of popular Bible-reading, though it is occasionally indicated in wills of the Protestant type.[8] I have sought in vain a local parallel to Robert Williams, the shepherd 'on Seynbury hill' in Gloucestershire, who wrote so bitterly in 1546, when, in his own words, 'the testament was obberagatyd [abrogated], that shepe herdys myght not red hit. I prey God amende that blyndnes'.[9] Whatever clothiers and yeomen-farmers may have done, it seems unlikely that, in the reign of Henry VIII, shepherds were perambulating the Yorkshire dales, Bible in hand. So far as concerns the Bibles kept in churches, they survived at least until the Marian Reaction, but in 1559 many Nottinghamshire and Yorkshire parishes testified that their copies had been seized and burned by Mary's

---

[1] Cf. J. S. Purvis in *Y.A.J.* xxxvi. 180–1.
[2] *The Registers of Ecclesfield*, ed. A. S. Gatty, p. 159.
[3] On the Bibles available and their prices, cf. J. F. Mozley, op. cit., p. 173.
[4] J. Eastwood, *Hist. of Ecclesfield*, p. 175.
[5] *Surtees Soc.* xcvii. 169.   [6] Ibid., pp. 1–7.
[7] Ibid., p. 169.   [8] Cf. that of Edward Hoppay, *infra*, p. 216.
[9] J. F. Mozley, op. cit., p. 284.

orders. Not improbably, however, some were smuggled away by devout or thrifty parishioners and survived to do service under Elizabeth.[1]

Lee's injunctions also order the clergy to read the daily Gospel and Epistle out of the English Bible, plainly and distinctly, an important liturgical development usually associated with the Royal Injunctions of 1547, but which nine years earlier was certainly ordered here and in some other dioceses, including that of Salisbury.[2] Dare we deduce that Archbishop Lee had mellowed since the day when he had condemned Tyndale's Bible even before he knew what was in it? On the other hand, Lee merely follows the Royal Injunctions of 1538 in forbidding the worship of images, 'lowting or bowing down' to them, and making them offerings. Images are henceforth to be suffered 'only as books, by which our hearts may be kindled to follow the examples of the saints'. Though God the Father is represented as an old man, the people must believe, not that he has any body or age, 'but that he is a nature and substance above all measure passing the capacity and understanding either of man's wit or angel's'. All images to which pilgrimages and offerings are made must be deposed and sequestered from the sight of man. The Lollards of Worksop and York thus saw officialdom move some distance toward one of their own chief positions not long after they had suffered persecution.

That a widespread shift of public opinion along these general lines was occurring during the forties is suggested by a study of the phraseology of Yorkshire and Nottinghamshire wills. During the early and middle years of Henry VIII, the accepted testamentary form involved bequeathing one's soul not only to Christ or to Almighty God, but also to the Blessed Virgin and the glorious company of the saints. There are naturally many minor verbal variations, and some wills include an actual plea for the intercession of the Virgin and the saints. Even before the advent of Reformation principles, all these elements were sometimes discarded by testators, and the mere omission of the Virgin and saints cannot at any stage be presumed necessarily to reflect active Protestantism; neither omission nor inclusion is bound to reflect the normal and personal convictions of a given testator, who may have been sick, repentant, or negligent and who in any case may have drawn

[1] For details, cf. ibid., pp. 299 seqq.
[2] Cf. Frere in *Alcuin Club Collections*, xv. 46–47. On Salisbury, cf. ibid., p. 54. In Feb. 1542 Convocation ordered curates to read to the people a chapter of the New Testament in English every Sunday and holy day (Wilkins, *Concilia*, iii. 860).

his will under the influence of a priest or legal adviser. Nevertheless, when all these cautionary factors are admitted, anything like a mass movement to omit all mention of the Virgin and of the glorious company of heaven must presumably echo some decline in the place occupied by their cults in the public mind. And such a movement does in fact occur. About 440 wills made in the period 1538–46 have been examined,[1] mainly those of the middle classes and gentry. For the years 1538–40 I have listed 76 'traditional' wills, and only 9 omitting the Virgin and the saints; in 1541–4, 82 of the former, but no less than 33 of the latter; in 1545–6, 99 traditional and 32 non-traditional. In a parish like Halifax, later a noted centre of Protestant opinion, somewhat more marked signs of the new outlook may be observed in the phraseology of Henrician testators. In 1538 William Holmes and Robert Thomson both rejected the intercession of the saints, commending their souls 'unto Christ Jesu, my maker and redeemer, in whom, and by the merits of whose blessed passion, is all my whole trust of clean remission of all my sins'. Again, whereas before 1537 Halifax testators leave their bodies to be buried in the church or churchyard of St. John the Baptist, from that year they usually say, 'in the church or churchyard dedicated unto God in the memory of the holy prophet St. John Baptist'. Such changes do not, however, represent Zwinglian or Lollard extremism: even Robert Thomson leaves a bequest to 'Our Lady service' in Halifax church.[2] Needless to add, a vastly larger collection of contemporary wills remains to be studied in manuscript at the York Probate Registry; even when this is done, the results should not be presented in any spirit of statistical pedantry. At the same time, there emerges already a very well-marked trend which cannot be accidental and which, it will shortly be noted, continues more markedly through the reign of Edward VI. A parallel decay of belief in the importance of masses for the dead is also indicated by the behaviour of many of the gentry and townsmen. The private dissolution, resumption, and embezzlement of chantry properties by patrons and others will shortly be discussed in another context. At this stage we shall merely note that the process did not begin in 1546, when Henry VIII threatened these institutions;

---

[1] Chiefly those printed in *Test. Ebor.* vi, *Richmondshire Wills* (Surtees Soc. xxvi), and *Testamenta Leodiensia* (Thoresby Soc. xix). The last cover a wide area of the West Riding. In transcribing wills, some editors have omitted the supposedly 'formal' clauses and so made their collections useless for our purpose.

[2] On these points cf. J. Lister in *Papers of the Halifax Antiquarian Soc.* (1907), pp. 76–77. E. W. Crossley's two volumes of *Halifax Wills* omit nearly all these religious phrases.

it was in full operation throughout the whole of the preceding decade, especially after the private Act of Parliament secured by the city of York in 1536 to dissolve nine chantries and other foundations.[1]

In general, it would seem unwise to assume that the harsh repression of heresy during the last six years of Henry VIII meant a static public opinion. The concept of this monarch as the Catholic and the arch-traditionalist has been of late too often exaggerated, especially by Anglican writers. Whatever his personal views on doctrine, whatever the reversal he staged in 1539, however effectively he limited the spread of extremism, his policy opened the door quite widely enough to allow Protestantism to insert a foot; neither his nor any subsequent government came near to closing that door, or to preventing the slow and inexorable entrance of the rest of the Protestant anatomy. Henry's famous last speech to Parliament formed at once an admission and a *cri de cœur*.

2. *The Official Programme: Clergy and Churches*

Amongst the later actions of Henry VIII, the appointment of Robert Holgate as Archbishop of York does not lack significance in the history of northern Protestantism. On the death of Lee in September 1544, the Earl of Shrewsbury, Bishop Tunstall, and others suggested that the president should be raised to the archiepiscopal see, since the king would thereby promote an honest and painstaking man, while also saving the president's salary.[2] The king, then in an economical mood, complied: in January 1545 Holgate was confirmed as archbishop and simultaneously lost £700 of his presidential salary of £1,000.[3] Though necessarily subservient to the Privy Council, he thence became the dominant regional figure during nearly five crucial years, retaining the presidency until displaced by Dudley's intrigues late in 1549[4] and the archbishopric until his deposition by Mary in March 1554.[5] The prosaic common sense which made Holgate so successful a judge and administrator extended itself to his theology. In 1548, when under Somerset's liberal régime opinion was relatively free and fluid, a number of bishops and doctors were examined upon the offices of the Church and in particular upon the eucharist. To questions on the central doctrine of the latter, Holgate's replies proved distinctly more conservative

---

[1] Cf. *infra*, p. 206. [2] *L. & P.* xix (2), 239.
[3] *State Papers of Henry VIII*, v. 405.
[4] A. G. Dickens, *Robert Holgate*, pp. 16–17, gives references.
[5] Cf. ibid., p. 27.

than Cranmer's. The oblation and sacrifice of Christ in the mass, he wrote, 'is the presenting of the very body and blood of Christ to the heavenly Father, under form of bread and wine consecrated in remembrance of his passion with prayer and thanksgiving for the universal church'. On the other hand, he urged that 'the gospel should be taught at the time of the mass' and that consequently the mass should be in English.[1] His further evangelical, scriptural, and educational emphases will soon engage our attention, but even these brief replies indicate the character of his leadership as president and archbishop. He showed himself a notable forerunner of the Anglican compromise at its most comprehensive: he demonstrated that broad churchmanship which appeals so commonly to politicians, administrators, and laymen generally. Despite the long years he devoted to academic theology at Cambridge, his practical experience of men and affairs must have helped to influence his theological judgement; as a statesman he perceived that in some measure Englishmen could 'have it both ways' by agreeing on a judicious blend of old and new, wherein each man could, within limits, select the emphases which appealed to him. Of texts, dogmas, and distinctions there was no end, but an imperilled nation could not await the advent of revealed truth. The practical problems of church, state, and society called out for speedy solutions and with truly English pragmatism such men as Holgate accepted careers from the Crown on the level of conciliar administration and justice, where solutions of a sort could be achieved. They were prepared to give Caesar rather more than what most churchmen thought his due, if Caesar could supply harmony, order, and a framework of social discipline within which Reformation and education might transform mankind. The complicated feuds, affinities, and disorders of Tudor Yorkshire afforded no small support to this Baconian, almost Hobbesian, philosophy; its strength in terms of human happiness will best be appreciated by those who know in detail the horrors of the French Wars of Religion or of the Thirty Years War in Germany.

To conservative opinion a daring and even outrageous innovator, Robert Holgate also displayed some characteristics of the medieval ecclesiastical statesman. Like Wolsey, he furnishes a late example of the founder-prelate, and left some imposing memorials of his concern for charity and education in his native county and diocese. Amongst his early actions as archbishop was the foundation by letters patent (1546–7) of his three schools at York, at Hemsworth, his birthplace, and at

[1] Burnet, op. cit. v. 197 seqq.

Old Malton;[1] their three foundation-deeds[2] constitute no less than an educational manifesto of the New Learning. The masters may be laymen or priests; each must have understanding in the Hebrew, Greek, and Latin tongues and teach them to such as he judges apt. These seem the first English school statutes to prescribe Hebrew and thereby to set a fashion often followed down to the Restoration.[3] The masters' chief task naturally remained the teaching of Latin, and the complete restriction of these schools to the Tudor equivalent of secondary education becomes quite explicit. Both masters and their ushers are expressly ordered to teach written Latin and exonerated from instructing any scholar not already able to read. The long school days with their breaks, mealtimes, daily psalms, and collects, are meticulously prescribed; so are the details of the financial management, which is regarded both from the schools' viewpoint and from that of their tenants, whose rents and gressoms are not to be enhanced. Most exacting of all are the duties of the masters and ushers, who are bound to continued presence in school. On Sundays they must sit in church with their charges and cause the 'said Scholars (except such as shall sing in the choir) two and two of them devoutly to say their matins together and seven psalms, or to be reading of Scriptures, and that done, to be reciting over such things as they have learned and to be other ways well occupied during the time of service in the said church'. On this point, the founder may seem severe, yet he stands curiously in advance of later Protestant practice, with its inhuman subjection of the young to sermonizing.

In an apology addressed from his imprisonment to the Marian government,[4] Holgate claims to have been instrumental in setting up two further schools in the diocese of York. One of these was East Retford; a copy of its foundation charter actually occurs in Holgate's episcopal register.[5] Again, in September 1544 St. John's College, Cambridge, was appealing for Holgate's help in connexion with the threatened endowments of its protégé Sedbergh.[6] Once again, he and St. John's also became associated in the management of the refounded Pocklington School.[7] Though the new school and hospital at Kirkby

---

[1] L. & P. xxi (2), p. 332 (72).
[2] Cf. N. Carlisle, *A Concise Description of the Endowed Grammar Schools* (1818), ii. 817, 858, 919. The York deed is printed in full in *Archbishop Holgate Soc. Record Series*, no. 1.
[3] Foster Watson, *The English Grammar Schools to 1660*, ch. xxxii.
[4] Edited by the present writer in *E.H.R.* lvi. 450 seqq.
[5] Fos. 53–57ᵛ.   [6] *T.A.S. Rec. Ser.* xxxiii. 337–8.
[7] P. C. Sands and C. M. Haworth, *Hist. of Pocklington School*, pp. 20–21.

Ravensworth were chiefly a product of Marian Catholic zeal, especially that of Dr. John Dakyn, Holgate also occurs on the roll of its benefactors.[1] In his apology, the fallen archbishop also called to witness that he has spent great sums on alms, in gifts to both universities, to the Inns of Court, and to 'fyndinge poore men's children meate, drinke, cloith, lodginge, lernynge'.[2] After his release he made a will (27 April 1555) devoting his personal lands to the endowment of a hospital at Hemsworth for a master and twenty aged brethren and sisters.[3] He was careful on this occasion to lavish *douceurs* on a Master of Requests and the Solicitor-General to ensure the execution of his scheme by Queen Mary's favour. The hospital, like the York and Hemsworth schools, flourishes to this day. All in all, it seems surprising that Holgate was until recently seldom mentioned save as an avaricious prelate who despoiled the see of York to his own advantage. The unsubstantial character of this last charge has been elsewhere demonstrated by the present writer.[4] It is true that on his elevation to the see, Henry VIII had forced him to surrender its franchises and over sixty of its manors, but Holgate had no choice in the matter; similar transactions were forced on other new bishops. Moreover, the Archbishops of York acquired in exchange very substantial grants of ecclesiastical patronages: their 'impoverishment' was highly relative and their ecclesiastical powers enhanced. The new archbishop had in fact already laid the foundation of his personal fortune by service to the State.

We should pass beyond the due bounds of our subject if we allowed our study of Holgate's educational ideals to develop into a general essay upon the Reformation and the schools of the diocese of York. Not many years ago, the writer would merely have made reference to the voluminous books and articles of the late A. F. Leach, whose valuable pioneering work included many aspects of the history of grammar schools in this diocese of York. Of late two points have become increasingly clear: that Leach seriously exaggerated the untoward effects of Reformation developments upon the finances of these schools,[5] and that, in limiting his purview to endowed grammar-schools, he ignored a large if somewhat obscure sector of English education, that of the unendowed schools of various types. The whole subject being now in flux, historians of education must beware the

---

[1] T. D. Whitaker, *Hist. of Richmondshire*, i. 120–1.   [2] *E.H.R.* lvi. 455.
[3] *Surtees Soc.* cxvi. 232–5.   [4] *Robert Holgate*, pp. 18–19.
[5] For an extended critique on Leach's work cf. Joan Simon, 'A. F. Leach on the Reformation', in *British Journal of Educational Studies*, iii, no. 2, pp. 128 seqq. and iv, no. 1, pp. 32 seqq.

dangers of an exaggerated reaction against the pioneer. In the diocese of York, as elsewhere, the substitution of a fixed stipend for a landed endowment must have damaged the interests of many schools, yet the small number destroyed, and the vast number of Elizabethan foundations and re-endowments has already attracted our notice.[1] The mid-Tudor age, one of inflation, dissolution, and a sense of economic insecurity, cannot for a moment be classed with its Elizabethan and Jacobean successors as an age of creative endowment, since it was far too heavily preoccupied with the defence of existing schools against unimaginative statesmen and steel-hearted officialdom. If in England the more interesting educational theorists of the mid-century were inevitably men of the New Learning such as Thomas Becon, the history of the schools seems unlikely to provide heavy weapons for modern sectarian gladiators of any persuasion. In the diocese of York, as elsewhere, enlightened Catholics and enlightened Reformers were united at least in their anxiety to mitigate the untoward effects of contemporary changes upon education, as well as to use the schools for propagating their respective creeds. While Holgate made his school-statutes a treatise on the ideals of the New Learning, Dr. John Dakyn drafted the statutes of Kirkby Ravensworth to exclude all suspicion of heretical teaching, and the Marian chapter of York stated that it had refounded St. Peter's School to educate pastors able 'to ward off and put to flight the ravening wolves, the devilish men with ill understanding of the catholic faith, from the sheepfolds committed to them'.[2]

Thanks in part to one of the scrappiest and least complete episcopal registers in the magnificent series at York, relatively little is yet known concerning Holgate's diocesan administration. In normal medieval practice, the cumbrous machine of officialdom was expected to grind along with little personal intervention on the part of the bishop; Tudor civil service prelates, both conservative and Reforming, had been amply provided by their predecessors with suffragans, vicars-general, receivers-general, official principals, registrars, proctors, notaries, apparitors, whose labours, judicial, administrative, and financial, set bishops free to do the work of the nation. When we turn to this mechanism after a re-reading of the Gospels, it may seem repellent to the point of fantasy. Contemporary Lollards, Bible-readers, and Protestants experienced similar emotions, while in far wider circles ecclesiastical materialism and jurisdiction became ever more unpopular. Despite this *malaise*, only a small minority of powerless extremists seriously

[1] Cf. *supra*, p. 5. [2] *T.A.S. Rec. Ser.* xxvii. 50.

demanded total revolution, so deeply was the system grounded in the social organization and socio-religious concepts of the day. The Protestant bishops, even those who had been among its more serious critics in earlier years, found themselves in no posture to conduct a basic simplification of the machinery. Amongst the most radical and apostolic was John Hooper of Gloucester, yet during his short episcopate (1551–3) he sat continually in his own consistory court and ruled his diocese, it has been rightly said, 'with a severity and authority immeasurably greater than that of any other sixteenth-century bishop of Gloucester'.[1] From very radical experiments, whether revolutionary or authoritarian, Robert Holgate was debarred both by a cautious temperament and, during the greater part of his episcopate, by his multifarious secular duties as President of the King's Council in the North. Not unnaturally, royal injunctions bulk very large in the diocese during the early years of Edward VI. Upon the metropolitan church the royal visitors imposed three sets of injunctions during 1547: the general cathedral injunctions,[2] a rule regulating the use of copes,[3] and a special set concerning many important aspects of cathedral services and administration.[4] The Nine Lessons are abolished, a shorter mattins and one daily High Mass provided. Evensong and compline are somewhat simplified; hours, prime, dirges, and commendations must no longer be sung but said privately; anthems become limited to six, their texts being prescribed. All services and lectures in divinity must no longer be held in Latin, but in English. The royal commissioners then pass outside the Minster to attempt some diocesan reforms of the type which appealed broadly to laymen. All suits in the ecclesiastical courts must be finished within four sessions after the 'response' has been made; all persons holding ecclesiastical jurisdiction must by themselves or by lawful substitute visit the places subject to them and take order against offences; otherwise their rights are forfeit. This shaft the visitors doubtless aimed chiefly at the dean and chapter, together with other holders of peculiars. Appended to these injunctions is a further one given on 1 November 1547 to the dean and chapter by Sir John Hercie, Roger Tonge, D.D., William Moreton, and Edmund Farley, commissioners of King Edward VI 'for the visitation throughout the diocese and province of York'. This injunction attacks the inefficient keeping of testamentary records in the peculiar courts. Copies and extracts of probates and

---

[1] F. D. Price in *Church Quarterly Review*, April–June 1939, p. 95.
[2] *Alcuin Club Collections*, xv. 135–9.
[3] Ibid., p. 153.   [4] Ibid., pp. 153 seqq.

administrations needed by poor suitors could not be found, and the chapter are henceforth forbidden to conduct such business except in the presence of a registrar. Non-radical though it be, all this makes excellent sense to a modern observer acquainted with the bad habits of contemporary diocesan administration. Along with many similar royal and diocesan injunctions, it should serve to remind a now forgetful generation that there was a genuine element of reform in the official Reformation; that even Edwardian Protestantism was linked with some long-needed cleansing of Augean stables, as well as with secular and hypocritical rapacity.

The transmission of the initial Edwardian programme to the out-lying portions of the diocese finds its best illustration in a series of undated injunctions given by six royal commissioners to the clergy and laity of the deanery of Doncaster.[1] Three of these commissioners, Tonge, Moreton, and Farley, are those who attempted to reform the testamentary jurisdiction of the dean and chapter, a fact which, placed alongside internal evidence, seems to place these injunctions early in the year 1548. They follow the familiar lines of the general royal articles and injunctions of the previous year. From the viewpoint of early Protestantism, an interesting clause is the one which orders all priests to study daily two chapters of the New Testament and one of the Old, 'forasmuch as heretofore you have not, by any means, diligence or study, advanced yourselves unto knowledge in God's word, and his scriptures, condignly, as appertaineth to priests and dispensators of God's testament'.[2] Parishioners must be taught that fasting in Lent and other days merely represents man's law, alterable by the magistrates and dispensable in case of sickness or other necessity: here is a change doubtless popular with the local gentry, who had been not infrequently plagued on this score by the ecclesiastical courts.[3] A more *recherché* feature of the Doncaster injunctions is a series of fifteenth-century English formulae to be spoken at the sprinkling of holy water, the distribution of holy bread and the ceremony of the pax. They explain the precise symbolism of these ceremonies:

> Of Christ's body this is a token;
> Which on the Cross for our sins was broken;
> Wherefore of his death if you will be partakers,
> Of vice and sin you must be forsakers.

[1] This document was preserved by Burnet; reprinted in ibid. 171–5.
[2] Ibid., p. 174.
[3] Cf. the case of Anne Bulmer (1543), who had to produce the testimony of two London physicians (R. VII. A.B. 2, fo. 339).

This pleasant but shortlived antiquarianism—the ceremonies themselves were soon to be abrogated—seems also to have been practised by Latimer in his diocese of Worcester.[1] The injunctions also order the churchwardens to make collections for the parish alms-chest, the parish clerk to cease perambulating the parish with holy water, but instead to accompany the churchwardens, listing the names and sums of charitable subscribers so that the poor might pray for the right people. Some part of the alms should be lent to young married couples or—a foretaste of the Elizabethan Poor Law—be used to acquire stocks of material upon which the poor might be set to work, and so, through the sale of their products, to replenish the alms-chest. And whereas drunkenness, idleness, and brawls resulted from the assembly of revellers at wakes, or on Plough Monday, these festivities are now forbidden on pain of a forty-shilling fine for each offence. If Edwardian Reform has its prologue under Henry VIII, it certainly foreshadows Elizabethan official religion in its social motivation, desire for practical efficiency, literary emphases, and half-pragmatic, half-puritan discouragement of excess. That many other resemblances must be added to this list will become clear when we examine the reforms of Archbishop Holgate.

During the year 1548 a succession of Privy Council orders abolished numerous 'superstitious' ceremonies, together with images in the churches. The subsequent year saw the First Prayer Book and November 1550 the final order to replace altars by communion-tables. Such commands from above are easy to list, but it is of more significance to find what actually happened in the parishes. How swiftly were these orders executed in a huge and generally conservative diocese like that of York? Here diocesan records provide as yet no information comparable with that of the Elizabethan visitation books. The parish chests divulge only fragmentary information: churchwardens' accounts for these years are few in number; they seldom give precise dates and have no occasion to record many of the changes involved. Nevertheless, those few known to the writer suggest a ready obedience in the parishes. Excellent example is afforded by the accounts of Sheriff Hutton, which, in spelling luxuriant even by Tudor rural standards, show the vicar and churchwardens of this quiet country parish extremely active and incurring considerable expenses in order to carry out the Reformation changes.[2] Some of their acquisitions must have had the charm of novelty: 'Item, pd more than we resavyd for byyng off the

[1] Cf. *Alcuin Club Collections*, xv. 172, n. 2.
[2] Extracts and commentary by J. S. Purvis in *Y.A.J.* xxxvi. 178 seqq.

coloke of Herassimus. viijd.' In 1547 seven parishioners visit Northallerton to see the royal visitors; locks are obtained for the alms-chest,
copies of the injunctions bought, church goods inventoried, a communion table constructed, and numerous official journeys made to York.
Then the process duly goes into reverse on the accession of Mary. The
parish had good reason, financial and otherwise, to acknowledge the
reality of both Reformation and Reaction. The same impression of
lively compliance and appreciable expense also emerges from the
Rotherham accounts, which show written copies of the Edwardian
service-books being compiled for temporary use until printed copies
arrived.[1] At St. Michael's Spurriergate in York, where there are also
contemporary accounts,[2] the images were promptly removed in 1547
and seem to have created something of a pother: 'Item to a laborar for
beryng moke owt of the churche and the churche yerd, what tyme the
seyntts was takyn down, ijd.'

The earliest known edition of the First Prayer Book is dated 7 March
1549; its general use was enforced throughout the country, including
the York diocese, from Whitsunday, 9 June.[3] Some local parishes were,
however, using it as early as those of London. Vicar Haldesworth of
Halifax was no Protestant zealot, but his parish register specifically
notes 'the first children that were christened in English, being Pask
Day', i.e. 21 April.[4] Fortunately we boast also in the diocese a local
chronicler to pull together those stray hints; he is in many respects
unique amongst provincial writers of the period and, as a conservative
priest, highly interested in the process of liturgical change, wherein he
himself acted as an unwilling collaborator. Appropriately for our
present purpose, he has a habit of giving more or less exact dates.
Robert Parkyn, curate of Adwick-le-Street near Doncaster, was a
transcriber and author of wide literary tastes, which ranged from
Rolle and Lydgate to Fisher and More; his life and writings have
already been the subject of numerous published articles[5] and they
belong in themselves not to the theme of Protestantism, but to that of
Reaction. His narrative of the Reformation[6] was written during the

---

[1] J. Guest, *Historic Notices of Rotherham*, p. 178, prints extracts.
[2] Extracts of various periods are printed in J. Croft, *Excerpta Antiqua*, pp. 12 seqq.
[3] *E.H.R.* lxii. 69–70.
[4] J. Lister in *Papers of the Halifax Antiq. Soc.*, 1908, p. 53.
[5] By the present writer in *E.H.R.* lxii. 58; *Notes and Queries*, 19 Feb. 1949, p. 73;
Bodleian Library Record, iii, no. 29, p. 34, and iv, no. 2, p. 67; *Trans. of the Hunter
Archaeological Soc.* vi, no. 6, p. 278; *Cambridge Antiquarian Soc.* xliii. 21; *Archiv für
Reformationsgeschichte*, Jahrgang 43 (1952), p. 54.
[6] Printed in *E.H.R.* lxii. 58 seqq.

reign of Mary and he thus had no motive to exaggerate his obedience and that of his brother clergy to the Edwardian changes; on the contrary, he would have been tempted to point with pride to any observable resistance-movement. It seems clear enough that, to the best of Parkyn's knowledge, no such movement ever developed. A reader who troubles to compare the dates of the governmental orders[1] abolishing candles, ashes, images, palms, creeping before the cross, and so forth, with the dates given by Parkyn for the introduction of these changes into the churches, will observe that in each case compliance within the deanery of Doncaster must have been immediate. I note only one exception in this series. The discontinuance of holy bread and holy water early in 1548 he describes as enforced 'in many places of this realme, butt specially in the sowth parttes, as Suffolke, Norffolke, Kentt & Waylles, &c'.[2] Here apparently comes an isolated case of delay, probably on account of the attempted local purification of these particular rites by the royal commission, which has just been noticed. The immediate assumption of both Prayer Books in the north is clearly implied by Parkyn, who again remarks that 'in the monethe of Decembre (1550) all allters of stoyne was taken away also furthe of the churches & chappels from Trentt northewardes and a table of woode sett in the qweare'.[3] While it is true that in some places altars had been removed at earlier dates, the relevant orders to the bishops had in fact only gone out from the Privy Council in November 1550.[4] In some of these matters, Parkyn's personal knowledge may not have extended beyond his own deanery, and it would be ridiculous to claim on this evidence that in every remote parish obsolete practices and objects were instantly eradicated. The Sheriff Hutton churchwardens' accounts show that some at least of the church furniture and books condemned by the Edwardian changes were not destroyed but concealed, only to be restored to use after the accession of Mary.[5] The image of Our Lady of Pity at Bainton may have been duly removed, but it survived, was re-erected and ultimately reported to the royal commissioners of 1559 as an object of pilgrimage.[6] Three fine alabaster effigies now in Nottingham Castle were discovered carefully buried beneath the site of the high altar in Flawford church, while an alabaster reredos in good condition has recently come to light on the site of the house of Holy

---

[1] These will be found in the notes to the text, pp. 66–67.
[2] E.H.R. lxii. 68. [3] Ibid., p. 72.
[4] E. Cardwell, *Documentary Annals*, i. 89.
[5] J. S. Purvis in *Y.A.J.* xxxvi. 188.
[6] S. L. Ollard, *Notes on the Hist. of Bainton Church and Parish*, p. 22.

Priests near Hungate, York. Many of the numerous superstitious objects reported in early Elizabethan visitations[1] were probably pre-Edwardian in origin. Even in 'progressive' Hull there is said to have been a conservative group which murmured when the images in Holy Trinity church were destroyed.[2] Despite these and other surreptitious retentions, the extant evidence nevertheless points remorselessly to a pattern of compliance. Parkyn's own case constitutes one of the clearest pointers; it indicates that even the most traditionally minded priests were in a cowed and obedient frame of mind. They would make no move except under governmental order; they hesitated even to accept that of local lay notables. A significant illustration of this cautious mentality occurs in the passage where the chronicler describes Mary's triumphant entry into London on 3 August 1553, followed by the execution on 22 August of Dudley's followers.

In the meane tyme in many places of the realme preastes was commandyde by lordes and knyghttes catholique to say masse in Lattin withe consecration & elevation of the bodie and bloode of Christ under forme of breade and wyne with a decentt ordre as haithe ben uside beforne tyme, butt suche as was of hereticall opinions myght nott away therwithe, butt spayke evill theroff, for as then ther was no actt, statutte, proclamation or commandementt sett furthe for the sayme; therfor many one durst nott be bolde to celebratte in Latten, thowghe ther hertts was wholly enclynede thatt way.[3]

On 18 August Mary sanctioned, though she did not compel, the introduction of the Latin mass. Parkyn continues that this service had been put down from Pentecost 1549 until the beginning of August 1553,

butt then in many places of Yorke shire preastes unmariede was veray glade to celebratt & say masse in Lattin withe mattings & evin songe therto, accordynge for veray ferventt zealle and luffe that thai had unto God & his lawes. And so in the begynninge of Septembre ther was veray few parishe churches in Yorke shire but masse was songe or saide in Lattin on the fyrst Sonday of the said monethe or att furthest on the feast day of the Nativitie of our Blisside Ladie,[4]

that is by 8 September.

Throughout the successive vicissitudes of the mid-Tudor period,

---

[1] Cf. A. G. Dickens, 'The First Stages of Romanist Recusancy in Yorkshire', in *T.A.J.* xxxv. 161 seqq.

[2] Hadley, *Hist. of Kingston-upon-Hull*, pp. 88–89. This account is circumstantial, but I am unaware as to the nature or location of the original. Signs of religious division occur in Hull during the reign of Mary. Cf. *infra*, p. 219.

[3] *E.H.R.* lxii. 79.

[4] Ibid., p. 80.

almost every parish priest in the diocese placed conformity to the government before religious conservatism, strong as the latter instinct must have been with the majority. Some of them might shudder to think of souls in Purgatory without masses—we knew from their correspondence that this is true of Parkyn and his colleague William Watson of High Melton[1]—and they might reverently bury the beautiful alabaster reredoses fashioned by the craftsmen of Nottingham and York. None, however, was inspired to revert to the conduct of those parish priests who had joined the Pilgrimage of Grace or become involved in the Wakefield Plot of 1541. Unlike many of their fellow clergy of the West Country and Oxfordshire in 1549, none of the local priests joined the Seamer Rising of that same year: it was led by a yeoman and a parish clerk. Ten years later, even the ultra-conservative Parkyn was settling down to the Elizabethan Prayer Book at Adwick-le-Street, where he swallowed his prejudices and retained the curacy until his death in 1569.

What of the less conservative and the Protestant elements among the priesthood, with whom our present interests chiefly lie? Parkyn has also something to say of them, yet so affronted and preoccupied is he by the scandal of clerical marriage, that the quality of his guidance must fall under grave suspicion. This ugly subject the good man approaches from a somewhat oblique angle. In 1548, he tells us, the pixes hanging over the altars, wherein lay Christ's body in form of bread, were despitefully cast away as things abominable, and heretics did not pass the blessed hosts contained in them without villainously despising them, 'utterynge such wordes therby as it dyd abhorre trew christian eares for to heare'. But for Christ's mercy, it was marvel that the earth did not open and swallow such villainous persons, as it did Dathan and Abiram. Such persons denied the mass, stiffly affirmed that Messias was not yet born, and so finally denied all sacraments except matrimony, because it was first instituted 'in paradise terrestrie': they affirmed also that it was lawful for priests to marry women, using them as their wives, which was very pleasant to many, for they were married in very deed, both bishops and inferiors,

beynge so blyndide with carnall concupiscens thatt thay prechide and tawghtt the people oppenly, that it was lawfull so to do by God's law, and enactyde the sayme. Wich preastes so mariede when thai dyd celebraitt wolde mayke no elevation at masse after consecration, butt all other honest preastes dyd according to tholde laudable faction [fashion], in remembrance how our

---

[1] Cf. their letters in *Trans. of the Hunter Archaeological Soc.* vi, pt. 6, pp. 278 seqq.

Saveyor Christ Jesus was elevaitte uppon a crosse of tree for mankynde redemption.[1]

This curious attempt to equate not merely apparent disbelievers in Transubstantiation, but holders of the more fantastic sacramentarian and anabaptist beliefs with those who advocated and perpetrated clerical marriage cannot be taken seriously: Parkyn starts to be useful on this topic of marriage when he comes forward with information about actual people. Soon afterwards he relates how Archbishop Holgate himself proceeded to give 'lewde example' by marrying one of Parkyn's own parishioners: Barbara, daughter of Roger Wentworth Esq. of Hamthwaite near Adwick-le-Street.[2] In Christmas week 1549 the banns were asked both at Adwick—probably by the scandalized chronicler himself—and at Bishopthorpe, where the marriage actually took place on 15 January 1550. Actually, divulges Parkyn in a loud aside, they had been secretly married earlier, 'as the heretyk Doctor Tonge reporttyde in the Kyngs Majestie his cowrtt, yea, & that he dyd solemnizaitt the sacramentt of matrimony unto tham his selffe'.[3] This obliging cleric was presumably Dr. Roger Tonge, the royal visitor whom we have seen in the deanery of Doncaster and at York in 1547-8. He was a royal chaplain and a conspicuous preacher in favour of the Edwardian settlement; in March 1549 he received the deanery of Winchester, though he apparently died before his installation, being actually buried on 2 September.[4] The story of the secret marriage is not one which Parkyn would have invented, and though the present writer does not know of any relevant case in the King's courts before the time of Tonge's death, no disproof is thereby provided. In his subsequent apology to the Marians, Holgate ungallantly gives political pressure as his excuse for entering into matrimony: 'that he being of the aige of threscoore and eight yeares maried a gentilwoman called Barbara Wenteworth by the councell of Edwarde then Duke of Somersett and for feare of the laite Duke of Northumberlande using to call him papiste, and he thought verelye then that he myght have done soo by Godes lawes and the Kinges'.[5] This story may also be substantially true, since it is certain that Dudley procured Holgate's ejection from the presidency and subjected him to prolonged bullying in order to force him into surrendering the Watton lands in return for a fee-farm.

[1] E.H.R. lxii. 68.
[2] For references to the family see the present writer in E.H.R. lii. 430.
[3] E.H.R. lxii. 71-72.
[4] References in E.H.R. lii. 431.
[5] E.H.R. lvi. 452.

Holgate's known moderation in matters of religion would certainly give Dudley sufficient grounds for the taunt of papistry.

Whatever his reasons for marrying at this advanced age, the archbishop failed to exercise his customary caution and foresight in choosing a spouse. Already in May 1549 Barbara Wentworth had brought a nullity suit in one of the ecclesiastical courts at York against Anthony Norman, a young gentleman with whom she had transacted a child-marriage eighteen years earlier, when she had been five and he seven years of age. The evidence of her numerous witnesses[1] indicates the weakness of Norman's position in canon law; since attaining the age of discretion, twelve years, she had consistently refused to accept him, saying she would never do so, 'because she coulde not fynde in her harte to love hym'.[2] No evidence of consummation appeared to these witnesses, for Norman had lived at Arksey and Barbara with her parents. She had only been seen to kiss him 'whan that he had bene fourth of the towne'. On the other hand, the 'lowe pepill theraboutes' considered them man and wife, since 'they were maried in the face of the churche'. These records include no judgement, but Holgate's public marriage in January 1550 shows that Barbara must have won her suit against Norman. Nevertheless, the archbishop's domestic felicity was again troubled in November 1551 when the pertinacious Norman took his case up to the Privy Council. The latter began by issuing a peremptory summons to Holgate and his wife, but speedily cancelled this and remitted the case to the judgement of Holgate's former colleagues of the Council in the North. Their verdict must also have proved favourable, since early in 1553 the Privy Council smiled on the marriage by authorizing the grant of Scrooby and other extensive lands to Holgate and Barbara in survivorship.[3] As for Anthony Norman, he was the son of an important alderman of York[4] and may almost certainly be identified with the Anthony Norman who occurs frequently in the Doncaster court rolls and who was at this time deeply in debt.[5] It is impossible to believe that his chief objective was to reclaim the unresponsive Barbara. In the July before his appeal to the

---

[1] R. VII. G. 404; cf. *Robert Holgate*, pp. 24–25.

[2] Canon law covering this point is clearly set out in E. Gibson, *Codex Juris Ecclesiastici Anglicani* (1761), p. 415.

[3] References in *Robert Holgate*, p. 26 and *E.H.R.* lii. 434–5.

[4] *Test. Ebor.* v. 213–15; a point hitherto overlooked by the present writer. Numerous references to the father occur in *York Civic Records* (Y.A.S. Rec. Ser. cvi), iii, and a pedigree in *Glover's Visitation of Yorks.*, ed. J. Foster, p. 558.

[5] *Calendar to the Records of the Borough of Doncaster*, ii. 104, 120, 124, 128, 133; Cf. *E.H.R.* lii. 435–6.

Privy Council he must certainly have heard how John Ponet, Bishop of Winchester, an even more distinguished Edwardian prelate than Holgate, had been divorced 'with shame enogh' from the wife of a butcher of Nottingham, and had to pay 'a sartyne mony a yere dureynge hys lyffe' to her rightful spouse.[1] But Holgate was much richer than Ponet, and the financially embarrassed Anthony Norman must have seen in his mind's eye a beautiful fantasy taking shape!

However we may dismiss these unlucky complications, the whole episode probably damaged Holgate's authority and the credit of Protestantism in the diocese. Murmurs were heard not only in the privacy of the curate's study at Adwick-le-Street, but also amongst the more conservative denizens of the Minster, where a young deacon named John Houseman supported the anti-marriage party and, according to his later claim, was deprived of his stipend by the archbishop.[2] Amongst the laity of the diocese, the popular taboo against clerical marriage lingered into the Elizabethan period. As late as 1586 Anne Grecyan of Seamer was charged at the diocesan visitation: 'she callethe the curate's children preistes' calves and sayth it was never good worlde sence mynisters must have wyves'.[3] Nevertheless, undeterred by such local opinion or by the not very dignified adventures of their archbishop, many Edwardian parish clergy swiftly plunged into matrimony. The evidence for this fact, recently investigated and printed by the present writer,[4] completely alters the picture of early clerical marriage in the diocese drawn by Dr. Frere;[5] it is located mainly in two act books of the York Court of Audience covering the period March 1554 to November 1555,[6] the period when the Marians were at work compelling the secular clergy to separate from their wives and divorcing the ex-regulars. From these and other sources, the records of seventy-seven certainly married clergy and another ten in the 'highly probable' category have been extracted. Still other cases remain doubtful, while

---

[1] Machyn, *Diary*, p. 8; *Greyfriars' Chronicle*, p. 70. Ponet had published a defence of clerical marriage in 1549 and soon after this first débâcle showed conviction by marrying again.

[2] Cf. A. G. Dickens, 'Two Marian Petitions', in *Y.A.J.* xxxvii. 376 seqq. Though Holgate had little trouble with his clergy, he did refuse to accept the presentation of William Brogden to Womersley, on the grounds that this priest was seditious and a 'sower of noghty doctrine'. Brogden brought a case against him (R. VII. G. 431) and was duly instituted by the Marians.

[3] R. VI. A. 9, fo. 105ᵛ.

[4] *M.R.D.Y.*, pt. i, includes a census of all the married clergy of the diocese known to the writer.

[5] Cf. ibid., pp. 3–5.   [6] R. VII. A. 33, 34.

these somewhat scrappy records of the Court of Audience seem in any event unlikely to include every such case which came before the York courts. In addition, since several priests avoided the attentions of the latter for years, it becomes probable that others, especially among the numerous unbeneficed, may have escaped all proceedings throughout the short reign of Mary. A few others married, yet died before the onset of the persecution in 1554. Altogether, the total number of those who married within about four years must have exceeded, perhaps very substantially, the figure of 100: in terms of loose probability, they constituted about a tenth of those in priest's orders throughout the diocese.[1] This fraction, though less than half that observed by Miss Grieve in Essex,[2] seems somewhat higher than might have been anticipated in a much more conservative area, where a fairly high proportion of the clergy consisted of middle-aged former monks. It may well prove to be nearer the national average than the figure for Essex.

From our present viewpoint, the important problem remains to be answered. How far should clerical marriage in 1549–53 be regarded as a function of Protestant belief? Discounting, as we must, the lurid simplifications of Robert Parkyn, we should nevertheless concede that Protestant doctrine had for many years shown itself increasingly insistent upon the right of the clergy to marry; again, that a priest who took advantage of Edwardian statute-law to marry was clearly exhibiting an emancipation from important Catholic canons backed by centuries of usage throughout western Europe. In Essex, then one of the most markedly Protestant counties of England, clerical marriage proved very common. Finally, the Marian government took marriage almost exclusively as the criterion for deprivation. All the same, when full allowance has been made for these various links, the assumption that a married priest must necessarily have held a consistent and extensive range of Protestant opinions would carry us well beyond the evidence and beyond common sense itself. It will soon be shown that the Marian courts at York were prosecuting numerous laymen for heresy at the same period as they were separating and divorcing the clergy from their wives; had these clergy also signalized themselves at any stage as

---

[1] The number of parishes and chapelries probably approached 900, and, although pluralism was very widespread, pluralists commonly maintained curates in parishes they could not serve personally. Allowing for the recent dismissal of about 300 chantry priests, the total may have approached 1,200.

[2] H. Grieve, 'The Deprived Married Clergy in Essex', in *Trans. Royal Hist. Soc.*, 4th ser. xxii. 141 seqq. shows that of 319 priests certainly beneficed in Essex, about 88 were deprived for marriage.

overt Protestant partisans, they would also have been charged with heresy. Only in one or two cases[1] is any such suspicion breathed against a married priest. Few of the rank-and-file parish clergy who married also became notable at any stage of their lives for devotion to Reformation principles; again, they are not conspicuously drawn from those areas or towns of the diocese most likely to have been subject to external Protestant influences.[2] While one may stoutly maintain that the clergy were the most literate and refined element in Tudor society, one cannot feel that clerical marriage and celibacy are matters for discussion primarily along doctrinal lines. The history of the medieval clergy indicates that many would certainly have chosen the married state had the laws of the Church permitted. It might not be unduly materialistic to remind ourselves that hitherto many a country parson had been that social and economic anomaly: a farmer without a farmer's wife, and without a couple of husky sons to till the glebe in his advancing years. If the increasing material prosperity of the Elizabethan clergy be any guide, it certainly suggests that, whatever the struggles of the unlucky and the over-prolific, a wife and a family did in general prove an asset in a *kulak*-economy.[3] There is no evidence that the clergy were exposed to pressure or persuasion to marry by the archbishop or other diocesan officials; this could scarcely occur, since the archdeacons and other senior clergy in contact with the rank and file were themselves mostly unmarried and inclined toward traditionalism. As our knowledge of the mid-Tudor clergy advances, we shall no doubt continue to find them a most heterogeneous group of personalities, concerning whose motives free generalization will prove reckless. Precisely because we already know so much of them, we can think of them as extremely human beings living in an age when men readily rationalized their earthly human impulses into theological principles. And one may justifiably doubt whether all those who married even troubled to undergo this easy process! The thick-booted glebe-farmer of yeoman family background, with his wains, horses, and sacks of malt, his couple of books and grammar school latinity, his useful intimacy with his parishioners: here is a type far from universal, yet one we often en-

---

[1] Cf., e.g., the case of William Utley, curate of Hull, *infra*, p. 225.

[2] Of 81 whose residences are certain, 23 are from Notts., 22 from the West Riding, 16 from the East Riding, 13 from the half of the North Riding then in the diocese, and 7 from York.

[3] Cf. the comparisons made by F. W. Brooks on the basis of the Lincoln inventories for probate in *Journal of the British Archaeological Association*, 3rd ser. x. 23–37.

counter, or think we encounter, in letters, wills, and inventories. He is unlikely to have experienced profound spiritual struggles or textual searches when the king's law at last allowed him to take a wife. But in later Anglican England he has somehow ended by being well-nigh refined out of existence; to see his closer equivalents we must visit the more bucolic corners of Catholic lands. When at home we attempt to trace the metamorphosis of the medieval parish priest into the Anglican reverend gentleman, the adage *cherchez la femme* may prove to have a variety of applications!

Meanwhile the course of clerical matrimony did not at first run smoothly. When the testing-time came under Mary, those many married priests who appeared in the York Court of Audience proved in all save a very few cases contrite and submissive. If some had married as a gesture of Protestant belief, they now showed themselves poor soldiers of the Reformation. Having admitted to marriage while within orders, each offending cleric was deprived of his benefice—a severer penalty than that commonly imposed for adultery—and agreed to live chastely and separately from his 'pretensed' wife. Not infrequently the wife also appeared in court and gave a parallel undertaking; a public penance of the type associated with common sexual offences was followed by apology to the congregation for the evil example given. On certification that this had been performed, absolution and restoration to sacerdotal functions enabled the cleric to seek another living, provided it were not in the same place where he had sinned.[1] In the cases of former regular clergy an actual sentence of divorce was read; the Marians took the view that ex-religious were still fully bound by their vows; on occasion they might even compel a divorced ex-nun to provide herself with a monastic habit![2] With the detailed experiences of these people, attractive reading as they make, we are not now concerned. The attitude which underlay their submission we should find more relevant, could it be ascertained. Certainly the social position of the married clergy slumped dismally on Mary's accession. Parkyn tells us that they were now openly mocked by the populace, 'for the common people wolde pontt tham withe fyngers in places when thay saw tham';[3] he himself vociferously rejoices at their discomfiture: 'Hoo, it was ioye to here and see how thes carnall preastes (whiche had ledde ther lyffes in fornication

---

[1] Numerous actual examples and complications are given by the present writer in *M.R.D.T.*, pt. i.
[2] Cf. ibid., pt. ii, p. 16.
[3] *E.H.R.* lxii. 79.

with ther whores & harlotts) dyd lowre and looke downe, when thay were commandyde to leave and forsayke the concubyns and harlotts and to do oppen penance accordynge to the Canon Law, whiche then toyke effectt.'[1] With many, one may well conjecture that submission represented the easy way out of a difficult position and the quickest return-route to the familiar clerical way of life, with its privileges and its comforts. Again, John Foxe sardonically suggests that some of the clergy had already had their fill of the blessings of matrimony: having embarked without due circumspection, they were afterwards contented of their own inconstant accord to be separated from their wives.[2] On the other hand there remain factors in the psychology of our Tudor ancestors less vulgar and less obvious to modern eyes. In an age when many martyrs suffered for religion, the man of ordinary stature was nevertheless easily persuaded of his own error by worldly misfortune and by public disapprobation, for in these things he readily saw the divine wrath. This age of abject apologies, of inward self-abasement not only before principalities and powers but also before natural misfortunes, this age had learned little from the Book of Job or from that neglected saying of a more august Authority: 'Think ye that these Galilaeans were sinners above all the Galilaeans, because they have suffered these things? . . . Or those eighteen upon whom the tower in Siloam fell, and killed them, think ye that they were offenders above all the men that dwell in Jerusalem?'[3] Robert Parkyn himself is quick to detect, not only in the sweating sickness but even in the currency-inflation, the vengeance of God against national apostasy.[4] More to our point, Robert Holgate's apology, though by Tudor standards not a specially cringing document, shows him utterly convinced of the wrongfulness of his marriage. It remains fair to add that Anthony Blake, vicar of Doncaster, was subsequently suspected of renewing contact with his repudiated wife and had to produce compurgators to prove that his visits had been of an innocent nature.[5] Several of the separated clerics are known to have taken back their wives immediately upon the establishment of the Elizabethan régime. One hardy vicar choral of Beverley, Robert Thwenge, even told the Marian judges 'that he hade rather continew with his wyf and lyve lyke a laman yf yt mighte so stand with the law',

[1] Ibid., p. 82.   [2] Foxe, vi. 439.
[3] Luke xiii. 2, 4.
[4] E.H.R. lii. 73. The present writer failed there to explain the true meaning of 'dearth without need': i.e. dearness without shortage of commodities, or, in modern terms, inflation.
[5] Cf. for details, M.R.D.Y., pt. i, pp. 12–13, 22.

and being asked whether he wished to be restored to sacerdotal ministration, *respondebat quod non*.[1] Such uxorious enthusiasm was rarely displayed in the diocese of York and there seems no special reason in this
case to connect it with religious convictions.

On the fringe of this extremely human if rather unromantic spectacle,
there stand the few obvious Protestants: at these in turn we propose to
glance, with a view to detecting, if possible, their common factors. At
least five of them were men of such distinction as to gain places in the
Dictionary of National Biography. Thomas Cottesforde had in 1541 been
committed to the Fleet by the Privy Council for publishing an epistle
of Melancthon in violation of the Six Articles; his theological background was again shown by a translation of Zwingli.[2] The diocese saw
him but briefly, since he was not appointed to the prebend of Apesthorpe
at York until July 1553, and was deprived for marriage sometime before
19 May 1554. By that time he had fled abroad—he may have gone as
early as the previous September—and died *venerabilis senex* at Frankfurt
in December 1555. Credited with some sixteen works, he was a devotional writer rather than a controversialist, though, as if to demonstrate
the falsity of Robert Parkyn's simplifications, he wrote two tracts
against Anabaptism.[3] By far the most distinguished of the Edwardian
prebendaries of York was William Turner, the father of English botany.
A Northumbrian by birth, he was taught Greek at Cambridge by
Nicholas Ridley, his companion in archery, tennis and theological
opinions. He was also one of the famous early Protestant circle which
met at the White Horse. Relinquishing his fellowship at Pembroke
Hall in 1540, he became a travelling preacher, and suffered imprisonment about 1542 for preaching without a licence. His books were pro-
scribed[4] and he was banished in 1546; travelling in Holland, Germany,
and Italy, he became intimate with the great naturalist Conrad Gesner
at Zürich. Soon after the accession of Edward VI he returned to England and was rapidly installed as chaplain and physician to Protector
Somerset. The latter does not appear, however, to have furthered his
material interests, since in September 1548 Turner wrote to William
Cecil, then Somerset's secretary, describing himself as 'in mediis meis

---

[1] *M.R.D.Y.*, pt. i, pp. 11–12, 27. Thwenge appears on a pension list of 1553 as a
vicar with a pension of £5 per annum (G. Oliver, *Hist. Beverley*, p. 188).
[2] *The Confession of the Faith of Huldrik Zwinglius*, published in English at Geneva,
1555.
[3] *M.R.D.Y.*, pt. i, pp. 17, 23; *D.N.B.*; Cooper, *Athenae Cantabrigienses*, i. 140; C. H.
Garrett, *The Marian Exiles, 1554–1559*, p. 129.
[4] Cf. *supra*, p. 12.

cruciatibus et humana omni consolatione destitutum', but thanking Cecil for the promise of preferment and hoping it would be distant from the court.[1] Poverty, ill health, and a large family had made him very querulous and Archbishop Holgate, in seeking to attract him to the north, may unduly have been influenced by the memory of Turner's earlier missionary years. Concerning this friendship we learn something from a letter of 11 June 1549: 'Master Cicell, I thank yow for your paynes tayken about the obteyning of my lycence, which if I had, sealed, I wold shortly occupi in York shyre, for the Archbishop of York hathe written unto me to cum to hym with all the spede that may be, whiche thynge I wold gladly do, if I had theyrto my Lordis Gracis consent.' Turner goes on to explain that he cannot go to Winchester, as suggested by the Protector, without receiving a prebend there. 'My chylder have bene fed so long with hope that they ar very lene; I wold fayne have them fatter if it were possible.'[2] The prebend of Botevant in York was at last given to him on 12 February 1550, yet he held it for little more than two years; if the archbishop entertained any sanguine hopes concerning his impact upon the north, they must have been disappointed. From the first he seems to have been unwell and restive at York, promising that if he were allowed to retain his 'poor prebend' while going abroad on a health cure, he would correct the English Bible and complete his great *Herbal*. In the following year he gained promotion to the deanery of Wells, resigned the York prebend in 1552, and, having spent the Marian period in exile, returned to Wells under Elizabeth.[3] His sojourn at York is unlikely to have contributed much to the furtherance of Protestantism there; in any case, his views were too advanced to allow him many points of contact with the rest of the chapter and with the local clergy; his acceptance illustrates the broadmindedness of Archbishop Holgate, since Turner detested most forms of ceremonial and successfully trained his dog to snatch off the square cap of a bishop dining with him.[4] His significance in the history of the diocese lies less in his Protestantism than in his position as the first of the scientist-physician-clergymen in the north, of the succession which

---

[1] W. Turner, *Libellus de re herbaria novus*, ed. B. D. Jackson (1877), p. iii.

[2] Ibid., loc. cit.

[3] Holgate had at least one other eminent scientific friend: Edward Wotton, President of the Royal College of Physicians and author of *De Differentiis Animalium*, whom he appoints one of his executors (*Robert Holgate*, p. 24).

[4] On William Turner see C. E. Raven, *English Naturalists from Neckham to Ray*; *Libellus de re herbaria Novus*, ed. B. D. Jackson; *D.N.B.*; C. H. Garrett, op. cit., pp. 314–15.

included John Dee,[1] John Jones,[2] and Timothy Bright.[3] To the present writer these remarkable men, along with the proto-copernican John Field, seem altogether worthy to be regarded as the first moderns in our regional history; they serve to remind one that the period of the Reformation saw the birth of a movement destined to prove in the long run even more important to the nation, to Western culture, and to mankind. The third quarter of the century saw meeting in this region the Rolle–Lydgate 'medieval' world of Parkyn, and the world of William Turner, which was substantially that of Harvey and Evelyn.

Certain other notable figures amongst the Protestant clergy had a less exiguous connexion with the diocese. John Plough, a native of Nottingham, proceeded B.C.L. at Oxford in 1543–4. In 1538–9 he had succeeded his uncle in the rectory of St. Peter's, Nottingham, which he resigned in 1550 to become vicar of Sarratt in Hertfordshire. Notorious for his Protestant opinions by the accession of Mary, Plough wisely fled the country, resided at Basle, and engaged in various controversies both with Catholics and with other Reformers. His works are now lost, but their general tenor appears from three known titles: *An Apology for the Protestants*; *A Treatise against the Mitred Men in the Popish Kingdom*; *The Sound of the Doleful Trumpet*. The first of these is known to have been a counterblast to *The Displaying of the Protestants* by that indefatigable Catholic Miles Hoggarde, whom Bale so uncharitably latinized as *insanus porcarius*. John Plough returned to England in 1559 and accepted the benefice of East Ham from his fellow exile Grindal; I have seen no evidence that he married, or of proceedings brought against him in the diocesan courts.[4]

The connexions of Robert Wisdom with the diocese of York are not known to have begun until 1550, but he had twice been in serious trouble for Protestant heresies during the preceding decade. A bachelor of divinity in one or other of the universities, he fell foul of Bonner on 17 July 1541 on account of a sermon, but was released on his submission the following day. In a Lenten sermon of 1543 at St. Mary Aldermary, Wisdom commended Thomas Becon and, on the information of Miles Hoggarde, was committed by the Privy Council to the Lollards' Tower, where he wrote a *Vindication of himself against certain articles charged upon*

[1] On Dee and his work at Manchester see (in addition to the items in C. Read, *Bibliog. of Brit. Hist., Tudor Period*) *Chetham Soc.* xxiv and new ser. vi. 101 seqq.; F. R. Johnson, *Astronomical Thought in Renaissance England*, pp. 135 seqq.
[2] Cf. the present writer in *Archiv. für Reformationsgeschichte*, Jahrgang 43 (1952), pp. 64–65; W. T. Freemantle, *Bibliog. of Sheffield*, pp. 128–32.
[3] Cf. W. J. Carlton, *Timothe Bright*; *Thoresby Soc.* xv. 30–37.
[4] *D.N.B.*, s.v. Plough and Huggarde; C. H. Garrett, op. cit., p. 252.

him.[1] On the following 8 July he formally recanted at Paul's Cross. During this phase he was acting as curate in various London and Essex parishes, but after the second clash with authority he retired with Thomas Becon into Staffordshire and continued to preach the Reformed doctrines. In May 1546 two Yeomen of the Chamber were sent by the Privy Council to arrest him—with what result does not appear—but the accession of Edward VI both removed the immediate peril and put him in the running for promotion. According to the York register, it was not until 1550 that he obtained the rectory of Settrington, the former Bigod living now fallen into the patronage of two London gentlemen, Francis Stanley and John Gervis. Two years later Cranmer suggested Wisdom for the archbishopric of Armagh, and but for the advent of Mary his advancement might have been rapid.[2] Wisdom had meanwhile given clear testimony concerning his doctrinal affinities. In 1550 he had published *A Postill . . . or collection of moste godly doctrine upon every gospell through the year*, translated from a work of the eminent Lutheran commentator Antonius Corvinus.[3] It was not his only translation from Lutheran sources,[4] but, unfortunately for his literary reputation, he obtained more notice through a handful of verses than by these more solid achievements. Having in 1551 contributed an item to the collection of poems on the death of the Duke of Suffolk, he soon afterwards wrote lines prefixed to the second edition of Bale's *Scriptores*. Falling thence under the now mysterious spell of Sternhold and Hopkins, he composed a metrical translation of Psalm cxxv:

> . . . And as about Ierusalem,
> The mighty hyls doo it compasse,
> So that no enmies comes to them
> To hurt their towne in any case:
> So God in deede in every neede
> His faythfull people doth defend,
> Standing them by assuredly,
> From this time forth world without end . . .[5]

---

[1] Printed in Strype, *Eccles. Memorials* (1822), vol. i, pt. ii, pp. 463–79.
[2] Biographical references are in *D.N.B.*; Cooper, *Athenae Cantabrigienses*, i. 259–61; *M.R.D.T.*, pt. i, p. 29; and C. H. Garrett, op. cit., pp. 339–40. The first two are totally inaccurate on the events of 1541–3, for which see S. Bailey in *Journal of Eccles. Hist.* ii. 180–9.
[3] *Short-Title Catalogue*, no. 5806; on Corvinus see *Allgemeine deutsche Biographie*, s.v.
[4] He also translated two sermons by Tilemann Hesshusen, the distinguished Lutheran theologian and controversialist, who befriended him on the Continent. This work does not appear to have survived. On Hesshusen see ibid., s.v.
[5] Cf. *The Whole Booke of Psalmes* (J. Crespin, Geneva, 1568), p. 62. In the editions

and so forth, through five laboured and rhythmically insensitive stanzas. At the end of the standard editions of the metrical psalms appears another child of his muse, the metrical prayer beginning,

> Preserve us lord by thy dere word,
> From Turk and Pope defend us Lord,
> Which both would thrust out of his throne
> Our Lord Jesus Christ thy deare sonne.[1]

It is disturbing to realize that our Elizabethan and Stuart ancestors more or less willingly mouthed these and such other lines Sunday by Sunday until almost the end of the seventeenth century. The early Protestant poets were admittedly unfortunate in their literary birthplace; at this grim moment in the history of English verse, Catholic beliefs themselves gave no firmer guarantee against bathos, a fact which may be verified in the metrical *Life of Christ*, written by our Yorkshire chronicler Robert Parkyn.[2] As for Wisdom, he did not fail to attract ridicule from Denham, Butler, and other denizens of a more polished age, which unduly despised the literary struggles imposed upon these humble founders of modern English verse. It was too easy for Bishop Corbet to apostrophize Wisdom:

> Thou once a body, now but air,
> Arch-botcher of a psalm or prayer
> From Carfax come. . . .

The modern reader must merely regret that he perpetrated nothing so colourful as the rendering of the fifty-eighth Psalm by his colleague John Hopkins:

> O God, break thou theyr teeth at once,
> Within theyr mouth throughout;
> The tuskes that in their great chawbones,
> Like Lions' whelpes hang out.

And whatever his poetic talents, Robert Wisdom was unquestionably a zealous and sincere Protestant, deeply remorseful over his own lack of courage to embrace martyrdom. Amongst his minor writings occurs

A revocation of that shameful byll that Winchester [i.e. Gardiner] devised and Wisdome redde at Paules Cross in London on the Relique Sunday,

---

attached to Barker's Bible of 1615 and 1617, Wisdom's version appears in the body of the psalter after that by W. K.

[1] This is the last of the group of versified prayers at the end of all these editions of the Psalms.

[2] Cf. the present writer in *Bodleian Library Record*, iv, no. 2, pp. 67–76.

July 14 MDXLIII, wherein the said Wisdom meekely confesseth his fraylty and fearful weakness, wherby he for fear of deth fell to this impiety and sheweth himself earnestly repentant and sorry of that gret slander and occasion of evil that he then committed against the congregation of God, and also desireth all faithfull Christians to forgive him that offence and to receive him again reconciled to the true Church of Christ.

This he had written before the end of 1543 while in Staffordshire.[1] As a twice-relapsed heretic, he can have entertained no doubts about the danger represented by the advent of Mary, though the precise date of his flight overseas is not known. The story that he opposed Knox and Whittingham in the quarrels at Frankfurt has now been questioned[2] and his first certain appearance there is in November 1555. Meanwhile his Yorkshire interests had been duly liquidated. The York Audience act books show him as summoned, yet contumacious, on 9 and 13 April 1554, while on the subsequent 30 September Richard Thorneton was instituted to Settrington, vacant by the deprivation of Robert Wisdom *clerici uxorati*. Returning with the other exiles, he successfully appealed to Elizabeth's Royal Visitors for the restitution of his benefice, which he held until his death in 1568. Throughout this last decade he was also archdeacon of Ely and now probably spent little time in Yorkshire, since the registers at Wilburton near Ely record the death of his wife Margaret in 1567 and show entries concerning four of his children.

Amongst the important Edwardian clergy of Yorkshire must be numbered a man who, though curiously unnoticed by local historians, achieved the unique distinction of being both a Marian exile and also a martyr to the Marian persecution. John Rough[3] was born a Scotsman and brought up a blackfriar of Stirling. As with a more august Reformer, his movement toward the new doctrines was accelerated by visits to Rome. Having received a dispensation to serve the Earl of Arran as a secular chaplain, he then managed to extract a yearly pension of £20 from Henry VIII, for 'promoting his reputation and interest in those parts'. To put the matter less tactfully than Foxe, the ex-dominican had become an English agent, yet his later career suggests that his religious motives may have outweighed his financial acumen; like many contemporary Protestant Scots he doubtless saw Henry VIII as agent of the Gospel rather than as a foreign oppressor. Being in danger from his enemies, he crossed the border to Carlisle soon after the

[1] Cf. S. Bailey, op. cit., pp. 186 seqq.
[2] C. H. Garrett, op. cit., p. 340.
[3] His story is mainly told by Foxe, viii. 443–9; cf. also *D.N.B.* and Garrett, op. cit., p. 274.

battle of Musselburgh.[1] A timely visit to the Protector then secured
a renewal of his government pension, and Rough was sent back by
Somerset to preach at Carlisle, Berwick, and Newcastle. Here he not
only married a Scotswoman, but also encountered Archbishop Holgate,
who called him 'unto a benefice nigh, in the town of Hull, where he
continued until the death of that blessed and good king Edward the
sixth'.[2] Feeling his own weakness to endure the forthcoming persecution, he then fled along the natural route from Hull into Friesland, 'and
dwelt there at a place called Norden, labouring truly for his living,
knitting of caps, hose and such like things'. There he must have met
many fellow refugees. Norden lies not far from Emden, then a major
centre for English exiles and the chief base of the pamphlet-warfare
against Mary.[3] That the diocesan archives contain no mention of
Rough's ministry under Edward VI need not be regarded as throwing
any doubt upon the circumstantial story by Foxe, who had no motive
for inventing these details. We possess in fact nothing like a complete
list of the curates of the two Hull churches during the mid-Tudor
years; their records are all the thinner since they were legally mere
chapelries of Hessle parish. While holding a curacy at Hull, it is possible
that Rough went out to preach the settlement elsewhere in Yorkshire.
Foxe reports, for example, a conversation between him and 'one Master
Farrar, a merchant of Halifax whom he happened to meet in London'
after returning from exile.[4] That his work proved more effective than
that of most northern Reforming clergy, appears from the terms in
which Dr. Watson, later Bishop of Lincoln, accused him before Bonner.
Though, alleges Foxe, Rough had earlier saved Watson's life,[5] Watson
'detected him there to be a pernicious heretic, who did more hurt in the
north parts than a hundred besides of his opinion'. It is more than
possible that the growing Protestant tradition in Hull bore a substantial
debt to this resourceful minister: one of his nation who could practise
evangelism with success in northern England, where it was held insult-
ing to call a man a Scot, must indeed have boasted a considerable
personality. The rest of John Rough's story falls outside the present
theme, except in so far as it demonstrates his strength and sincerity.
Lacking yarn and other materials for his work, he decided to visit
England, arrived in London during November 1557, heard of a secret

[1] i.e. Pinkie, 10 Sept. 1547.   [2] Foxe, viii. 444.
[3] Garrett, op. cit., p. 49.   [4] Foxe, viii. 448.
[5] Here I suspect Foxe of exaggeration. Watson was imprisoned and in severe
trouble with the Privy Council in 1550–1, but I know of no evidence that his life was
in imminent peril. Cf. D.N.B., s.v. Watson, Thomas.

society of Protestants, joined them and was accepted as their minister. Within a short time an informer betrayed him to Bonner, before whom he signified his continued adherence to the Edwardian doctrines and confessed to mixing with English refugees and London heretics. His journey thence to the stake was equally expeditious.

The group of York prebendaries appointed under Edward VI shows, as would be anticipated, more definite signs of Protestantism than do the rest of the married clergy. William Clayborough became prebendary of Ampleforth in September 1549; in the same year he was also master of Bawtry Hospital and in 1550 vicar of Kinoulton. Deprived for marriage in May and June 1554, he first submitted to an office of reconciliation, but later became contumacious and suffered excommunication in May 1555.[1] Thomas Wilson, an ex-monk of Monk Bretton and vicar of Silkstone from 1546, received in 1550 the prebend of Bilton, the rectory of Badsworth, and the mastership of St. John's Hospital, Ripon. Having married a woman named Moreton, he proved repeatedly contumacious when summoned by the Marians in April 1554; later that month he appeared in court and was divorced. In June he again absented himself and was excommunicated; in September letters were actually sent to the Crown to procure his arrest.[2] William Pierpoint, LL.D., was a pluralist of aristocratic Nottinghamshire background. Prebendary of Husthwaite from 1551, he had held the rectories of Holmepierpoint and Widmerpool since 1527. On 29 May 1554 he refused to answer the charges brought against him 'et hoc propter conscienciam ut dixit'. He was deprived and sentenced to penance, public apology, and a profession of chastity in the presence of his wife. These obligations he ultimately performed and so was restored to sacerdotal functions.[3] There can be little doubt that his initial scruples were of a Protestant order. One of his relatives, Edward Pierpoint, was a Protestant exile in Frankfurt in 1557;[4] another, Edmond, married into the Yorkshire family of FitzWilliam, which included at least two more exiles.[5] Another Edwardian appointee to the chapter who may belong to this group was Miles Wilson, S.T.B.; he occurs as prebendary of Ulleskelf from 1551 and was deprived for marriage in 1554.[6] Outside Minster circles a few other married clergy seemingly defied the Marian jurisdiction; most

[1] References in *M.R.D.Y.*, pt. i, p. 23.

[2] Ibid., p. 28.

[3] His case is very prolix: for fuller particulars, see ibid., pp. 13, 26. He received the benefices of Cosgrave and Torlaston in 1557-8.

[4] C. H. Garrett, op. cit., p. 249.

[5] Ibid., p. 154.

[6] *M.R.D.Y.*, pt. i, p. 29.

were in all likelihood Protestants. John Hoode, S.T.B., rector of Stokesley, also held the benefices of Dallinghoo and Welby Ash in the diocese of Norwich. Summoned to York under the Marian Reaction, he proved steadily contumacious, was deprived of Stokesley in August 1554, and doubtless saved himself further trouble by dying in the following year.[1] John Howsyer, rector of Handsworth, also refused to appear at York in April 1554 and, still contumacious, suffered deprivation of his benefice in the subsequent August. On this occasion letters were displayed to the effect that he had already been deprived of Culmington in Hereford diocese.[2] John Gamble, a former monk and vicar of Sheriff Hutton, was divorced in April 1554 from his wife Margaret Dykson and thereafter became contumacious.[3] So was William Latymer, rector of Kirkby in Cleveland, who failed to attend, was deprived and ultimately in 1559 restored to his living by the Elizabethan royal commissioners.[4] The case of Simon Clerkson, the former prior of the York Carmelites, has already been examined.[5] A B.D. of Oxford, specially licensed by Henry VIII to preach throughout the kingdom and described as excelling in sacred learning, he obviously moved forward with the Edwardian Reformers. Summoned by the Marian authorities, he persistently failed to appear and was deprived of the vicarage of Rotherham in October 1554.[6] Edward Maude, M.A., had been appointed vicar of Darfield in 1551; deprived for marriage in April 1554,[7] he may possibly be identical with the cleric of those names who occurs as rector of Blithe in 1558 and who died in 1570.[8] A strong atmosphere of Protestantism and later of Puritanism clings about this genealogically complex West Riding family. A Richard Maude *jadis ministre* occurs among the exiles at Geneva in November 1557; Bale gives a John Maude in his list of exiles,[9] while a younger Edward Maude was 'preacher of the word' at Northowram from 1582 to 1588; he died in 1598 as vicar of Wakefield and first master of Wakefield Grammar School.[10]

These names do not necessarily exhaust the proved or probable

[1] *M.R.D.Y.*, pt. i, p. 24.   [2] Ibid., p. 25.   [3] Ibid., p. 23.

[4] Ibid., pp. 25, 29.   [5] *Supra*, pp. 145-7.

[6] *M.R.D.Y.*, pt. i, p. 23.

[7] Ibid., p. 26.

[8] *Consistory Wills* (Y.A.S. Rec. Ser. xciii), p. 50. I am not certain that, as Lister supposed, he was the nephew and 'servant' of Dr. Haldesworth, vicar of Halifax. The parish had several branches of the family and several Edwards. Cf., e.g., *Halifax Wills*, ed. E. W. Crossley, ii. 155, 171.

[9] References in C. H. Garett, op. cit., p. 226.

[10] J. W. Walker, *Wakefield, its Hist. and People* (edn. 1934), p. 246.

adherents of Reforming views among the diocesan clergy;[1] as our bio-graphical knowledge of the latter advances, we should be able some-what to extend the list. Even as it stands it shows a number of common characteristics quite apart from clerical marriage. Scarcely any member of it may be placed among the humbler rank-and-file of the parish priests. Nearly all these men had attended one or other of the universities and thus belonged to a small *élite* amongst the diocesan clergy. Some of them were intellectuals, Lutherans, and publicists. Even the exceptions were mostly pluralists with unusual means and connexions outside the diocese of York. Few can be shown to have had long residence within the latter, and few evinced any special voca-tion or aptitude for disseminating Protestant teaching throughout the diocese. If they show some resemblances to the men who introduced Puritanism some thirty years later, they lacked time to gather congrega-tions about them and, with one or two exceptions, are not known to have operated in the chief centres where early Protestantism or late Lollardy continued to show vitality. Altogether, while Archbishop Holgate succeeded in gathering together an 'advanced' group within the chapter of York, he failed to enlist a numerous phalanx of preachers and enthusiasts in the parishes.

There are signs that, within the cathedral itself, his efforts became most vigorous and effective in the last year or two of his episcopate; they find admirable illustration in his Minster injunctions of 15 August 1552, one of the most original and comprehensive early codes for a cathedral church in a Protestant nation.[2] These injunctions fall between the passing of the Second Act of Uniformity and the date when the Second Edwardian Prayer Book became operative. They begin with the routine charge to obey the various royal injunctions, but proceed almost immediately to the dominant theme of education. One learned man shall be speedily provided by the dean and residentiaries to read the divinity lecture at such times as the chancellor is not bound to read it. When the chancellor is lecturing personally, the learned man shall be occupied in preaching the Word of God in the parish churches pertaining to the cathedral. Vicars choral, deacons, and other inferior ministers must attend daily and give diligent ear to the divinity lecture,

---

[1] I have not included a few clerics of Yorks. and Notts. background who figure in Miss Garrett's census of Marian exiles. Robert Hutton, William Turner's associate, was ordained deacon in York Minster in July 1553 and had earlier translated *The Summ of Divinity* (1548) (C. H. Garrett, op. cit., p. 195). Note also Henry Cockcroft, John Pulleyn, John Staunton, in ibid., pp. 121, 262, 297.

[2] Reg. Holgate, fos. 57 seqq., printed in *Alcuin Club Collections*, xv. 310-21.

so that it may appear how much they profit when examined by any of the prebendaries or by the reader himself, who is charged to examine them at least once a month. A detailed schedule of forty-seven Sunday sermons assigns these throughout the year to the various prebendaries; on the remaining five Sundays, the dean, the Bishop of Hull, Drs. Rokeby, Downes, and Babthorpe will preach. A fine of 20s. and other censures will follow upon every default. The residentiaries must regularly attend chapter-meetings and duly reside, unless prevented by absence on the king's affairs, by matters of ecclesiastical jurisdiction or by the plague, which during the past two years had been rampant in York. Unmarried canons are not to invite women to their houses, except—and these exceptions seem wide—noblewomen, their kinswomen, and 'other strangers being women, and them not commonly, but for a meal'. Canons are also enjoined to communicate every Sunday and holy day and to officiate in their habits as prescribed by the king. There must be instituted as many vicars choral as the endowment of the Bedern College will bear, each man to have £10 and his room. There follows a system of fines for vicars arriving late for service. Vicars choral and deacons must commit to memory each week 'one chapter of S. Paul's epistles in Latin after the translation of Erasmus beginning at the first chapter of the Epistle to the Romans'. Each must have a New Testament in English and read a chapter daily after dinner.[1] Deacons failing to attend the grammar school daily and to apply themselves to study may, after three warnings from a residentiary, be expelled and others called to their places. Even the choristers must learn 'without book' every week, or at least every fortnight, a chapter of the Gospels or Acts in English and be examined upon them.

As might be anticipated from his moderate and reverent views on the eucharist, Holgate appears anxious that the significance of the communion service should not be diminished. 'Also we exhort *et obsecramus in visceribus Jesu Christi* the Prebendaries, the Vicars and others to prepare themselves affectuously to receive the Lord's Supper every Sunday or other days in the week as they shall be moved, after just trial of themselves by God's grace.'

In the Minster no other music than plainsong may be used, 'so that every syllable may be plainly and distinctly pronounced, and without any reports or repeatings which may induce any obscureness to the

---

[1] Those living in community in the Bedern were to have a common reading: married vicars who kept their own table must also read aloud, so that their wives and servants might hear.

hearers'. The lessons must be read distinctly and loudly, so that all 'which shall be sung and read may be well heard and understood of the lay and ignorant people'. Presumably for the same reason, organ-playing is utterly forbidden during mattins, evensong, and communion.[1] All this is intelligible enough as a consequence of the laudable determination of the Reformers that the simplest lay-people, even those unable to use primers, should truly understand the whole of the service. Another clause, however, says that organs 'ought and must be ceased and no more used within the Church of York', and orders the master of the choristers, who normally played, to come down and sing in the choir.[2] Despite the former partial prohibition, this one, literally interpreted, would prevent organ-playing even outside the services; if this is what Holgate meant to do, he was guilty, like many other Edwardians, of an excessive radicalism. Whatever be the case, there can be no doubt that organ-playing, at least during service-time and possibly at other times, was in 1552 forbidden not only in the Minster, but throughout the diocese.[3] On the other hand, the archbishop orders the full number of choristers to be maintained in the Minster, 'without covin or colour of such as be unable, either for that they have no knowledge in music or that their breasts be changed. And that none be admitted to be chorister but such as shortly after may be made able to serve in the quire and do other duty in the said Church.'[4]

The positive side of these reforms finds its clearest illustration in the articles referring to the Minster Library, which Holgate wanted to see something more than the fossil into which it degenerated in later times. Three of the vicars must have keys to it and one be constantly present while the library is in use by anyone save a canon or other dignitary.

Also, we will and command that the ancient doctors of the Church (those we call ancient that did write within 600 years after Christ's Ascension), Musculus' Commentaries upon Matthew, and John[5] Brentius upon Luke, Calvin and Bullinger upon the Epistles, Erasmus' Annotations on the New Testament be provided with all convenient speed so that they be placed in

---

[1] Article 24, *Alcuin Club Collections*, xv. 320. [2] Article 25.
[3] Cf. Parkyn in *E.H.R.* lii. 74. It is noticeable that the churchwardens of Sheriff Hutton repaired their organs on the accession of Mary. At Heptonstall the organ seems to have been dismantled and put in the charge of a parishioner. Cf. J. Lister in *Papers of the Halifax Antiq. Soc.*, 1908, p. 55. [4] Article 23.
[5] The christian name of Brentius and probably intended as such, not, as formerly supposed by the present writer, a reference to the commentary (1545) of Musculus on John.

the Library on this side of the feast of Pentecost next ensuing by the Dean and Residentiaries of the Church of York, to the end that such as be not of ability to provide them, or that by other occasion have them not in readiness, may resort to the Common Library and there peruse them accordingly.[1]

This interesting passage clears up any ambiguity as to the opinions and studies of Holgate and his party amongst the canons of York during the later stages of the Edwardian Reformation. These prescribed books, though few in number, extend widely across all the more advanced schools of the time; they include not only Calvin, but Bullinger, the successor of Zwingli at Zürich, and the two distinguished and recent Lutheran exegetes, Wolfgang Musculus[2] and Johann Brenz.[3] It is not easy to envisage conservative dignitaries like Dr. Dakyn, or even Dr. Rokeby, enjoying these studies, but the position remained fluid and we have no right to assume that such men remained ignorant of the continental Reformers: after all, even Robert Parkyn himself possessed a copy of Calvin at his death in 1570.[4]

Several others of Holgate's Minster Injunctions have a decidedly Protestant flavour. No minister of the Church must henceforth shave his crown; the monuments and tabernacles 'where images did stand' over the high altar must be taken down and replaced by sentences of Holy Scripture; all those holding dignities or prebends must subscribe to the Forty-Two Articles of Religion. The merely administrative articles are numerous and show Holgate's customary zeal to preserve the fabric and ensure the proper keeping of accounts. He had no intention of allowing the vast building to fall derelict; he attempted even to cope with the ancient problem of the pigeons, 'as well by the sparring of the doors as by any other means that can be devised'. His article on the clock-keeper has an irritated and personal ring: 'if he upon convenient warning do not amend his diligence in keeping of the said clock, the same keeper to be removed or else a more cunninger man to be assigned in his room, being paid for his pains forth of the fee of the said keeper of the said clock'.

Time lay indeed at the heart of his problem. If this programme was ever fully translated into actuality at York, the achievement must have proved highly ephemeral, since less than a year elapsed between its

---

[1] Article 18.
[2] This commentary had appeared in 1544 (*Allgemeine deutsche Biographie*, s.v. Musculus).
[3] This may refer to his homilies on the Acts, not to a work on St. Luke's Gospel (edns. 1535, 1541; cf. *B.M. Cat. of Printed Books*, s.v. Brentz).
[4] *E.H.R.* lxii. 62.

promulgation and the triumph of Queen Mary. For all its unattractive hostility toward organ-music, it illustrates the genuine idealism which still flourished alongside the machinations of Dudley, which its author had even more reason to detest than had the Catholics. It represents the late autumnal fruit of Edwardianism, but it clearly contains the seeds of Elizabethan Anglicanism, even those of the puritan component which was to rend the national Church asunder. The Edwardian cathedral has a good claim to be considered the birthplace of the new national Church, and no cathedral may claim the title more justly than that of York, for the programme of 1552 helps to place Archbishop Holgate amongst the most authentic forerunners of Anglicanism. He displays the whole range of its genius: its literary, scriptural, sermonizing, and pedagogical zeal, its frank reliance upon the secular arm, its sense of an ordered society embracing all men from archbishops to clock-keepers, its often heartfelt, yet cool and unmystical devotions, its sound business methods and institutional piety, its desire to seize the best of all the continental worlds, to fuse them into an alleged unity, its gaze of bland incomprehension upon the quirks of foreign logicians, its curiously English genius for creating organizations able to breathe and grow in strange atmospheres and stranger times.

3. *The Laity: Materialism and Disillusion*

The Tudor layman cannot for a moment be envisaged as inhabiting an ethereal world where rival doctrinal systems, untrammelled by mundane and workaday forces, contended for his soul. Modern observers with a selective religious theme always run into danger of exaggerating the role of religious convictions and divisions in the daily life of the people. On the one hand, we must eschew both economic totalitarianism and the habit of equating Tudor parishioners with the theologically desensitized members of modern industrial communities. On the other hand, it would be equally unrealistic to forget that the material exigencies of life were then extremely hard and demanding: working hours were of excessive length, material amenities few, disease rampant, pain unassuaged, personal violence common, debt and financial anxiety almost universal. Our mid-Tudor period also saw Englishmen exposed to politico-social and economic pressures of exceptional strength. Amongst the former must be numbered the fear and caution engendered by the collapse of earlier rebellions, the catastrophic decline of the Percy interest in Yorkshire, the vigilance and the growing equitable jurisdiction of the Council in the North, the decline of feudal franchises and sanctuaries, the positive rewards offered to the gentry by careers under the Crown. So far as economic forces and adjustments are concerned, the dislocating factor of inflation was but the dominant feature of a widely disturbed prospect. The tendency of recent research, like that of knowledgeable Tudor opinion, has been to attribute a relatively modest causal role to the dissolutions and to allied aspects of the Crown's ecclesiastical policy. If, for example, we turn to the mid-century records of the city of York, we find it deeply preoccupied by a complex material struggle; by the process of industrial decline operative for at least a century, but now patent enough to disturb this most complacent and xenophobic of communities; by the shaping of procedures to cope with the deserving and the undeserving poor; by the expenses of the Scottish Wars, by the virulent plague of 1550 and the equally destructive sweating sickness of 1551. In consequence of the Chantries Act, it is true, the municipality had also to assume and continue the functions of the hospitals and to compete with outside speculators for desirable guild-properties, but these were amongst its more simple and soluble problems; they cannot have bulked nearly so large to most contemporaries as they do to historians of local institutions and of Reformation-economics. So far as mere doctrinal disputes are concerned, we should, in the case of so well-documented a community, hear a good deal of them had they been a dominant feature of its daily life. In later years the Romanist recusants constituted but a small proportion of York's population, yet their affairs bulk very large both in civic and in national archives. In short, if one thinks of Edwardian and Marian York as primarily occupied by disputes and material problems born of the Reformation, one is thrusting aside an immense mass of evidence in favour of an imaginative abstraction. In the efforts of York to salvage what could be salvaged from the ecclesiastical wreckage, there was nothing new. If in 1549 its main concern was to secure the magnificent hall and lands of the guilds of St. Christopher and St. George,[1] it had already in 1536 obtained by private Act of Parliament the dissolution of nine chantries and other religious endowments in order to relieve the municipal finances.[2] No religious motives are alleged in support of this transaction.

The present writer would not be thought cynical, yet he must frankly confess himself unable to think of Yorkshire gentry, aldermen, yeomen, or clothiers as nearly related in temperament, views, and

---

[1] *York Civic Records* (Y.A.S. Rec. Ser. cx), v, index, s.v. Guild.
[2] Cf. the present writer in *Y.A.J.* xxxvi. 164 seqq.

behaviour either to a Robert Aske or to a Margaret Clitheroe. If the mass-evidence counts for anything, the great majority partook amply of that mundane utilitarianism which marked mid-Tudor Englishmen of all classes and counties. We need not produce the big-scale profiteers like Richard Whalley of Welbeck, Crown Receiver for Yorkshire, who in 1552 was deprived for malversation,[1] or like John Bellow, Crown Surveyor in the East Riding, whose dubious enterprises exposed him to elaborate inquiries in the reign of Mary.[2] When the late William Page edited the Yorkshire Chantry Surveys, he easily assembled from those documents and one or two others a considerable list of 'patrons' and other laymen who had 'resumed' or simply appropriated the possessions of chantries, almshouses, and religious guilds. At Conisborough, Thomas Boswell or Bosvile of Stainton about 1537 entered upon a messuage and lands of the chantry;[3] at Wathe, Thomas Markenfield about 1542 seized land of St. John's chantry;[4] at Halifax three years earlier, Sir Edmund Ackroyd took possession of the lands of the Frith chantry;[5] at Northallerton, Lord Dacre and Sir Charles Brandon —we shall soon note the latter's pious Protestant will—in 1544 converted to their own use the lands of the almshouse founded by Sir James Strangeways, and this without finding a priest or paying anything to the thirteen paupers;[6] at Burnsall, about the same time, Geoffrey Proctor, cousin and heir of the founder, sold the lands of the chantry in Rilstone chapel to the Earl of Cumberland;[7] at Metham, the patron Sir Thomas Metham attempted to do similarly and was resisted by the priest;[8] at Holy Trinity, Goodramgate, York, Robert Holme of Elvington, claiming to be patron, abstracted a valuable chalice about 1539.[9] Meanwhile the corrupt administration of the conjoined guilds of St. Christopher and St. George, the most famous and wealthy in York, had in the thirties provoked violent quarrels between the notables of the city and occasioned a spectacular dispute in the Star Chamber[10] during which much dirty linen was washed and the reputation of an

---

[1] D.N.B., s.v.

[2] For the accusations made against him in 1556–7 by Sir John Constable, see *Acts of the Privy Council 1554–6*, pp. 271, 276; ibid. *1556–8*, pp. 49, 62, 65, 106, 166. The East Riding County Record Office has an interesting MS. book showing an elaborate local inquiry into Bellow's activities.

[3] *Yorks. Chantry Surveys* (Surtees Soc. xci, xcii), p. 170. Cf. on Bosvile, *infra*, p. 208.

[4] Ibid., p. 101.   [5] Ibid., p. 296.   [6] Ibid., p. 123.

[7] Ibid., p. 255.

[8] Ibid., p. xi, citing Star Chamber Proc., Hen. VIII, Bundle 19, no. 264.

[9] Ibid., p. 52.

[10] *Yorks. Star Chamber Proceedings* (Y.A.S. Rec. Ser. xlv), ii. 13–36.

alderman's wife severely impugned. Further research might enormously extend this list of cases, taken from one or two easily available printed sources.[1]

The secularization of ecclesiastical properties proved a highly infectious notion; the diocese happens to afford one of the best contemporary illustrations of the reasoning which accompanied it. Michael Sherbrook, rector of Wickersley near Rotherham, compiled at various times in the reign of Elizabeth a tract defending the monasteries.[2] He recalls that his father, along with partners, had bought some of the timber of the church of Roche Abbey, including all that of the steeple, together with the bell-frame. Thirty years afterwards, Sherbrook asked his father whether he thought well of the monks, and of religion (i.e. monasticism) then used. 'And he told me, Yea: for, said he, I did see no cause to the contrary. Well, said I, then how came it to pass you was so ready to destroy and spoil the thing that you thought well of? What should I do? said he. Might I not, as well as others, have some profit of the spoil of the Abbey? For I did see all would away; and therefore I did as others did.'[3] Turning to the Edwardian dissolutions, Sherbrook testifies that he saw churchwardens selling off articles for a penny which had cost twelvepence, 'as I myself can witness that bought part of the church goods'. Many others of easy conscience 'took many things away without commissions, seeing all things were put to the spoil'. They plucked up the brass of tombs and gravestones in the church, or stole bells from the steeple. Thomas Bosvile living at Tickhill Castle[4] 'a very shyfter, I will not say a theif & sithence made a minister, stole the great bell forth of the steeple in St. Johnes [i.e. at Laughton-en-le-Morthen] & carried it away in the night'.[5] Thomas Bosvile[6] was in fact a Duchy of Lancaster official with a possibly legitimate role in the dis-

---

[1] Before the dissolution the guild priests of the popular fraternity of Corpus Christi at York sold its goods and bestowed the money 'at there owne discretions' (*Surtees Soc.* xcvii. 113). This type of action presumably does not represent personal corruption, but a disposition to outwit the spoilers.

[2] B.M. Add. MS. 5813, fos. 5–29, is an eighteenth-century transcript, which the present writer has prepared for publication in Y.A.S. Rec. Ser. He has already discussed it at length in *Church Quarterly Review*, July–Sept. 1940, pp. 236 seqq.

[3] fos. 20ᵛ–21.

[4] Sherbrook merely says 'one gentleman, whose name was Boseville, dwelling then at Tyckell-Castle'. But cf. J. Hunter, *South Torks.* ii. 345, and *Ducatus Lancastriae Cal. to Pleadings*, i. 262, which shows him as deputy steward of Tickhill honor bringing a case against others for the detention of church plate.

[5] fo. 27.

[6] Thomas Bosvile was ordained priest in 1564, instituted to the vicarage of Penistone in 1570, and died 1574.

solution, but even so, Sherbrook was probably not wronging him, since this future vicar of Penistone seems identical with the Thomas Boswell of Stainton, whose activities at Conisborough have just been noted. Just or unjust, such remarks illustrate the inevitable scandals and the lowering of public morality which both preceded and succeeded the Edwardian Chantries Act. To this atmosphere we have witness more strictly contemporary than that of Sherbrook.

John Hamerton of Monkrode and Purston Jaglin, Sub-controller of the Household to Henry VIII and Mary, admittedly belonged to a family notable for its conservatism.[1] On behalf of the neighbouring town of Pontefract he petitioned Cardinal Pole about 1557 for the repair of the church of the Trinity Hospital there.[2] In this petition he does not claim that the Reformation had involved the town in economic ruin. He does argue that Pontefract once had an abbey, two colleges, a friary, an ancress, a hermit, four chantry priests, and one guild priest, yet now by all these it is 'nether releveyd bodely nor gostly'. The unlearned vicar hires two priests to serve the cure, the tithe-farmers batten upon the benefice, 'and every one catchyth apece, but the pore nedy members of Chryst catchyt none at all'. The town has, in short, fallen into misery 'both bodely and gostely, sence the godly fundacyons afore sayd hath bene so amysse orderyd, and mysse usyd, and the holy sanctures of God so petefully defilyd and spoulyd'. Here was an ultra-conservative's view of an exceptionally unfortunate town at the worst moment of the changes,[3] yet the first impact of these changes also dismayed people who did not share Hamerton's religious views. The town of Beverley obtained considerable restitutions from the Edwardian government after making a strongly-worded complaint that the Crown had seized lands given to the maintenance of the Minster, and that a town of over 5,000 people lacked an endowed grammar school.[4] According to its somewhat unreliable early historians,[5] Hull petitioned the Crown to the effect that the clergy were beggared, learning despised, the people like to grow barbarous, atheistical, and rude, that ignorance and Popery would again soon overrun the nation if the

[1] Cf. J. J. Cartwright, *Chapters in Yorkshire History*, p. 71, and for details of the branches my note in *T.A.J.* xxxvii. 378.

[2] The text is fully printed with commentary by the present writer in *T.A.J.* xxxvii. 376 seqq.

[3] Cf. ibid., pp. 379–81.

[4] The text is printed in *Surtees Soc.* xcii. 542–3. On the grant cf. G. Oliver, *Hist. Beverley*, p. 189. On the obscurities which surround the grammar school between 1456 and 1562, see Leach in *T.A.S. Rec. Ser.* xxvii, pp. l–liii.

[5] Cf. *supra*, p. 28.

maintenance of learned and pious ministers were to be threatened.[1] The original of this petition is no longer extant and unless further evidence emerges, the accuracy of the account certainly cannot be guaranteed. Yet the fact remains that at Hull the Edwardian government refounded the hospitals, secured the threatened churches, and subsidized the grammar school and the clergy from the revenues of chantry lands:[2] all this in addition to the very extensive grants made to the town by letters patent of 1551.[3] A third instance is that of Sheffield, which depended on its local magnate, the conservative Earl of Shrewsbury, and with his support made a successful petition for restitutions to the Marian government.[4] In the long run those towns which had powerful friends or special claims to favour suffered little material loss, but even they were at first alarmed and irritated by the apparently indiscriminate attitude of the Crown. One might thus reasonably suppose that the crisis of endowments damaged the reputation of Protestantism in minds as yet uncommitted, so inhibiting its development. The suggestion of hypocrisy which could be directed against the Reformers probably derived little from the monastic dissolutions, a non-doctrinal action against bodies regarded with highly mixed sentiments and involved for the most part with an inarticulate rural society. On the other hand, the Edwardian dissolutions chiefly affected articulate and turbulent townsmen; they threatened ecclesiastical, charitable, and educational endowments, they demanded troublesome defensive action, they seriously modified parish life and intolerantly attacked the intercessory beliefs of a still considerable part of the nation. The Elizabethan cleric Michael Sherbrook was pitifully ignorant concerning the monasteries of his childhood, but he knew everything about the local failure of the Edwardians to preserve the writing and song schools at Jesus College, Rotherham. 'So it appeareth, whether the foundation touched superstition or sincere Religion, all was one: for all was fish which came into the net.' He proceeds accordingly to ridicule as whited sepulchres the ecclesiastical statutes of Henry VIII and Edward VI: 'thou shalt well perceive the fair speeches there set

---

[1] J. Tickell, *Hist. of Kingston-upon-Hull*, p. 207, cites 'Town's Records'. This, unfortunately, provides no guarantee that he saw the petition.

[2] Details in ibid., p. 208.

[3] A full translation of the letters patent is in J. R. Boyle, *Charters and Letters Patent granted to Kingston-upon-Hull*, pp. 69–80. Cf. *Cal. Pat., Edward VI, 1550–1553*, p. 334.

[4] Text of petition and other details in J. Hunter, *Hallamshire*, ed. A. Gatty, pp. 239 seqq.

down to be spoken to bring foul acts to pass. *Fistula dulce canit, volucrem dum decipit auceps.*[1]

Sherbrook was an antiquarian and rather cranky clergyman, but his view must represent one facet of public opinion; had there been no counterbalancing factors in the rapidly developing situation, it would have taken Protestantism longer to live down these embarrassing associations and to make headway in provincial society. If, however, the Edwardian politicians had jeopardized the credit of the Reformation, the Marian politicians proceeded utterly to ruin that of the Counter-Reformation. The history of Mary's reputation in the diocese of York cannot, however, be presumed exactly to have coincided with its counterpart in south-eastern England. Everywhere her accession was accompanied by spontaneous rejoicing. Parkyn relates how the news was received on 21 July 1553 at York and on the following day at Pontefract, Doncaster, Rotherham, and many other market towns, 'wheratt tholle comonalltie in all places in the northe parttes grettlie reiocide, makynge grett fyers, drynkinge wyne and aylle, prayssing God'. He then excepts the heretics and those libidinous reprobates, the married clergy, whose plight has already been described.[2] This account cannot be dismissed as mere partisan enthusiasm: a princess placed on the throne by the spontaneous action of the East Anglian gentry and people can scarcely have been less popular in more conservative areas, where her early trials had aroused such heartfelt sympathy during the Pilgrimage of Grace. What may be sensed in the subsequent years is not the growth of a general hostility. The un-English persecution was made to look even less English by the Spanish Match and the Spanish advisers. We have no adequate evidence as to its influence on public opinion in the diocese of York; while no shred of evidence suggests that it was popular, yet the relatively unsensational proceedings against local heretics, about to be described, cannot have provoked the disgust so apparent in London and the neighbouring counties. If Mary failed to build upon an excellent foundation in the remoter provinces, it was probably because she took their loyalty for granted, because she failed to show personal interest in their welfare, failed to make adequate restitutions or sales to communities whose charitable and religious activities were still impaired as a result of the Edwardian changes. As the writer has tried elsewhere to show in detail, first the Edwardians, with their second thoughts, and then the Marians, handed out a few small favours and made a few small restorations, a little here and a very

[1] B.M. Add. MS. 5813, fo. 17ᵛ.　　　　[2] *E.H.R.* lxii. 78–79.

little there,[1] but by 1558 hard-headed provincials cannot have seen enough to be impressed by either. The further charge that Mary failed to introduce England to the creative spirituality of the Catholic Counter-Reformation is also true, yet it is a hard saying. During those five years of her reign, what materials suitable for use in England were available? Certainly something more exciting than Reginald Pole and his bundle of Roman documents was needed. By 1554 it was nearly forty years since Papal jurisdiction had been effective in England and twenty years since its legal abolition. Except for well-read and thoughtful conservatives, the Papacy must have receded rather deeply into the mists; for the moment, it can have represented not a positive governmental asset, but one more unfamiliar concept to be instilled into the people by a propaganda-organization as sketchy and unreliable as that which had served the Protestant cause under Edward VI.

In the diocese of York we are bound to take a cleric, Robert Parkyn, as our well-read conservative, but we might well accept the city council of York as exemplifying the uninspired, uncommitted middle class. At the beginning of his chronicle Parkyn cursorily mentions the abolition of papal power by Henry VIII: at its end he devotes a few enthusiastic phrases to the restoration of papal authority, which had just occurred. Elsewhere throughout his numerous and lengthy writings I cannot recall seeing any reference to the Pope or the problems surrounding papal authority throughout Christendom, except it be at second-hand in a transcript which he made during his last years from a translation by the Catholic exile Thomas Stapleton.[2] These facts adequately represent the experience of a traditionalist cleric of his generation: of his thirty-five years or so as a priest, only four were spent under the Roman jurisdiction; at the end, well into Elizabeth's reign, there came a genuine, though literary, contact with the Catholic *émigrés* and the Counter-Reformation. Otherwise a lifetime of religious conservatism was expressed by a love of the old laudable ceremonies, by a devotion to the doctrine of Transubstantiation, by the study of fourteenth-century mysticism, by an admiration for Fisher and More, by hatred of both Seymour and Dudley, by an abhorrence of clerical marriage. It seems quite unlikely that contemporary Yorkshire laymen were more papalist than this zealous cleric. Though by no means lost in admiration for Renaissance Rome, Catholics of the previous generation like More and Aske had a far livelier sense for the unity of Christendom

---

[1] Cf. *M.R.D.T.*, pt. ii, pp. 23 seqq.
[2] Cf. *Notes and Queries*, vol. 194, no. 4 (19 Feb. 1949), p. 74.

and for the historic contribution of Rome toward that unity. If so intellectual and imaginative a concept had inevitably grown rather dim in a Marian priest like Parkyn, it seems to have vanished amongst the prosaic, insular, unliterary, and non-theorizing aldermen of York. When Pole came to reconcile the realm with Rome, these latter received and copied, as they did all governmental missives, Mary's long and enthusiastic order to light bonfires: 'soo beyng desyrous that all our subjectes of every degree myght so exercise theym selffes in prayer, fastyng and works of charytie as they may showe theym selfs trewe children of the holy Catholik Church wher unto they be now reconsyled'. Following this ardent paean from above, the city council merely entered the brief minute: 'After whiche lettre openly redde, it was agreed that warnyng shall be gyven for bonefiers to be made within this Citie on Sonday at night next accordyngly with rejoysyng and thanksgyvinge to God *for his mercyfullnesses nowe and alle tymes*.'[1] The dominant characteristic of the York oligarchy was a suspicion of new and external ideas. At this curious moment of their history, Rome had also entered into this category; one finds it difficult to call them either Protestants or Catholics.

Apart from Parkyn, who wrote in 1555 with Marianism at its zenith, there is singularly little to indicate that the people of the York diocese followed Mary in her ardours. It seems more probable that, like the previous régime, she ended by creating apathy and disillusion.[2] On the other hand, it would be equally difficult to prove that the fires of Smithfield lit candles of Protestantism in our diocese, or that the threat of Spanish overlordship provoked a local wave of disloyalty. Had these occurred, the gentry and people of coastal Yorkshire received at least one chance to demonstrate their sentiments. In April 1557 Thomas Stafford and his foolhardy little band invaded the realm, calling upon Englishmen to rise and overthrow 'an unrightful and most unworthy queen' who had 'forfeited the crown; because she, being naturally born half Spanish and half English, sheweth herself a whole Spaniard in loving Spaniards and hating English, enriching Spaniards and robbing English'. Through the extreme incompetence of the Privy Council[3] and of the Earl of Shrewsbury, an unworthy successor to Holgate in

[1] *York Civic Records* (Y.A.S. Rec. Ser. cx), v. 112–13. Italics mine.
[2] Late Marian records have cases of absenteeism from church so leniently treated as to make it clear that heresy was not suspected. Cf. the large group at Wakefield in R. VII. A.B. 39, under 2 Sept. 1557.
[3] Cf. the prior warnings given it by the ambassador in France, who actually pointed to Scarborough, in *Foreign Calendar, 1553–8*, pp. 293–8.

the presidency of the Northern Council, they easily took possession of Scarborough Castle. Though a few men with local connexions had joined Stafford's party, it included no names of weight[1] and failed to interest the local population. Within a few days the castle had fallen to the Earl of Westmorland and Sir Thomas Percy; the rebels were on their way to London and execution.[2] The whole affair proves little about Protestantism in the north, yet had a militantly anti-Marian party existed there, the list of Stafford's accomplices would have become somewhat more impressive.

In this account of the laity, we have so far been making oblique approaches and trying to set Edwardian Protestantism in its proper psychological setting. The time has come to seek more direct and definite information on the progress made by Protestantism and heresy. Thanks to our advancing knowledge of the York diocesan records, the subject can now be somewhat more fully illuminated than was possible a few years ago.

4. The Laity: Protestantism and Heresy

The various sets of Edwardian injunctions show their framers by no means unmindful of the laity, though it was in the main through a more disciplined, educated, and convinced clergy that these official Reformers hoped to effect religious and social change. Even at this stage, few can have anticipated the preponderant importance of books as opposed to pulpits. The explosive qualities of the vernacular Bible, though already feared by authoritarians, had not yet fully manifested themselves, while the Book of Common Prayer had scarcely begun its subtle yet slow penetration of the English mind. As for the curious third member of this disparate trio, the martyrology of Foxe, it had not yet been written, or even presented with its chief theme by that midwife of English Protestantism, Queen Mary.

The immediate impact of official Edwardian Protestantism upon

---

[1] William Stowell, gent., of Bagborough, Somerset, and Scarborough, John Sherlles, gent., of Scarborough (alias John Grasset of Rouen), John Proctor alias Williamson, yeoman of Hackness, together with Richard Saunders, gent., of Wymersley.

[2] A good many useful references for the Stafford affair are given by A. Rowntree, *Hist. of Scarborough*, pp. 214 seqq. On Stafford's companions see also C. H. Garrett, op. cit., pp. 96, 262, 271, 294; Strype, *Eccles. Memorials* (1822), vol. iii, pt. ii, pp. 513–19; *Cal. Pat. Philip and Mary 1557–8*, p. 106 (Richard Saunders). The arrests in Yorkshire in July and September were not certainly concerned with sedition (*Acts of the Privy Council, 1556–8*, pp. 123, 169).

the laity cannot accurately be gauged in any diocese. At York the recently discovered heresy cases under Mary throw most valuable light upon the development of anti-Catholic opinion around the mid-century, yet much of this material we shall find little connected with the official Edwardian programme. Before examining it, we may reasonably glance at some clues nearer the beaten track and mostly arising in the reign of Edward VI itself.

Still acknowledging their limitations, the present writer has tabulated a further 323 wills, made from 1547 to early 1553 inclusive. The omission of the Virgin and the saints, a custom frequently noticeable since 1540,[1] now shows a more marked rise. During the first two years of the new reign, 'traditional' wills retain a numerical superiority: in 1547 they number 24 against 15 others; in 1548, 24 against 19. In 1549 they are for the first time outnumbered: 23 'traditional' to 24 'new style' wills. In 1550 the former number only 18, while the latter rise to 31; in 1551 the respective figures are 21 and 35; in 1552 and the first half of 1553, the two again draw level with 29 each. Throughout the whole reign, this batch of wills yields 139 'traditional', 153 'new style', and 31 'neutral': a very great advance for the second fashion, as compared with the position during the later years of Henry VIII. So far as the cult of the Virgin is concerned, it ostensibly declined more markedly than these figures indicate, since a number of wills counted here as traditional do in fact omit mention of the Virgin, while retaining that of the company of heaven. An interesting parallel is here afforded by the order given by the York corporation in April 1549, that the Corpus Christi play be given complete, 'excepte the assumpcon of our Lady, coronacon of our Lady and dieng of our Lady'.[2] A few of these 323 people, perhaps 14 or 15, not only make these omissions, but, like the Halifax testators of 1538,[3] go out of their way to express their reliance for salvation upon the merits of Christ alone, or upon God's mercy, unaided by other merits and intercessions. The Wakefield clothier Thomas Cockhill says in 1549: 'I bequeath my saull to Almightie God my creator and redeemer, in whos mercy I *onlie* trust to have my saull saved.'[4] His fellow townsman William Watts describes himself as a smith, but was a fairly substantial man with copyhold lands and livestock. He writes in 1552: 'Fyrste I bequeath and comende my sowle to the abundante mercy of Almighty God my creator, trustinge through

[1] Cf. *supra*, p. 172.   [2] *York Civic Records* (Y.A.S. Rec. Ser. cx), v. 15.
[3] *Supra*, p. 172.
[4] *Testamenta Leodiensia* (Thoresby Soc. xix), p. 241.

our *only* saveyor Jesus Christes passion and deathe to have remission of all my sinnes and to come to everlastinge salvacion.'[1] George Hall, a comfortably placed yeoman of Allerton Grange, Leeds, has in the following year: 'First and pryncipallie I bequeath my soull to Almightie God my maker and Redeemer, trustinge by the *onelie* merytes of Christes passion in his bloude to be saved, and after this liff to have the fruytion of his deitie, worlde without ende.'[2] Sir Charles Brandon, some of whose Yorkshire manors came from his wife Elizabeth Pigot of Ripon, writes in 1551, 'I confesse that there ys no other salvacon for me but by the sheddinge of Christes most pretious bloode, into whose handes I comyt my soule.'[3] Elizabeth Place of Halnaby in Richmondshire was a daughter of Christopher Lord Conyers of Hornby, and hence a niece of Sir Francis Bigod's wife.[4] She ventured in 1553 a miniature treatise on good works and redemption: 'I begwhett and wyll my soul to God, desyering hym, for the bloyd of his sone Jesu Cryst, to accept it in to his kingdom, for by his deith and passyon I do clame it, and not by no gude warks, and yet all the gud warks that I can do is no less than my dewtye.'[5] Nearby at Jolby in Croft parish Christopher Dodsworth, apparently of the minor gentry, specially adjures his executors in 1551 to use no rites at his funeral repugnant to the king's laws and injunctions; he bequeathes his soul to Almighty God, 'who I trust, of his infynite marcey, for the death of his sonne, my saveyour, will accepte and receyve the same in the kyngdome of heaven, apon the dissolution of this my mortall bodie, and there to rest with Christ and all other the blessed and elect companye of heaven, untill the last daye, when I assuredlie beleve that this my mortall bodie shall rise, then joyned to the sowle, and then for ever to rest in the joyes of heaven'.[6] This constitutes a clear denial of the doctrine of Purgatory, long a chief target of the Reformers and soon to receive summary condemnation in article 23 of the Forty-Two Articles. At Kirkby in Kendal Thomas Wilson makes a will just after Mary's accession consisting almost entirely of pious sentiments and trusting the testator will be saved by the merits of Christ 'and by no other means'.[7] Much the most elaborate and interesting testamentary essay I have encountered is that by Edward Hoppay, a yeoman of Wakefield family, but living in Skircoat, Halifax, at the time he composed it on 10 May 1548. Its value as a social docu-

[1] Ibid., p. 331.   [2] Ibid., p. 349.
[3] *North Country Wills* (Surtees Soc. cxvi), p. 216.
[4] *Glover's Visitation of Yorks.*, ed. J. Foster, pp. 71–72.
[5] *Richmondshire Wills* (Surtees Soc. xxvi), p. 74.
[6] Ibid., p. 72.   [7] Ibid., p. 77.

THE LAITY: PROTESTANTISM AND HERESY 217

ment is all the greater as it shows no evidence of composition by a priest;[1] it seems indeed faithfully to reflect the results of Protestant teaching and Bible-reading upon a middle-aged or elderly yeoman of modest means. The testator first commits himself to God's mercy, by which and by the merits of Christ he has, and shall have, remission of sins and resurrection of body and soul. He continues,

I beleve that my Redemer lyveth, and that at the last daye I shall arise out of the erthe and in my fleshe shall se my Saviour.[2] This my hoope is laid up in my bosome unto the last daye, that I and all other faithfull shall appere bifore the maiestie seatte of God ... and towchyng the welthe of my saull, the faith that I have takyn and reherced is sufficient, as I beleve, without any other man's worke or workes. My beleve is that theire is but one God and one mediator betwixt God and man, whiche is Jesus Christe, so that I accepte non in hevyn, neither in erthe, to be my mediatour betwixt God and me, but he onlie ... and towchyng the distribution of my goodes, my purpose is to bestowe them that they may be accepted as the fructes of faithe, so that I do not suppose that my merite be by bestowyng of them, but my merite is faithe in Jesus Christe only, by which faithe suche workes ar good accordyng to Christe wordes, Matthew 25, *I was hungre and thou did gyve me meate*, etc. And it folowithe, *that ye have done to the lest of my brether, you have done it to me*.[3] A good warke maketh not a good man, but a good man makith good workes. For a righteouse man lyveth by faithe. And thus I rest in consciencie concernyng my faithe.[4]

Here is a wide range of 'official' Protestant teachings, well assimilated and keenly felt by a literate but relatively uneducated man of the people, who had probably begun these contacts long before the accession of Edward VI.

It would be absurd to assume that all lay people necessarily saw the worship of the Edwardian Prayer Books as violently repugnant to time-honoured notions and phrases. In 1550 William Kaye of Wakefield bequeaths his soul to God and to all the holy company of heaven, but he arranges to 'have the blissed communion celebrate the day of my buriall withe all other godly prayers conteyned in the common book of service'.[5] I have not yet encountered a testator desiring to combine

---

[1] None appears among the beneficiaries or executors. One of the latter is the testator's son, also Edward, but not identical with Edward Hoppay, priest of the Brigges chantry at Halifax (*Surtees Soc.* xcii. 295). This latter priest, though no doubt related to the testator, wrote a strongly conservative will in 1556 (*Halifax Wills*, ed. E. W. Crossley, ii. 139–40).
[2] Based, very freely, on Job xix. 25, 26.
[3] Matt. xxv. 35, 40.   [4] *Halifax Wills*, ii. 39–40.
[5] *Testamenta Leodiensia* (Thoresby Soc. xix), p. 256.

the cult of the Virgin or actual intercession of the saints with Prayer Book practice, but isolated examples of such a phenomenon would occasion little astonishment. In this period of flux and uncertainty, long before the continentally trained seminary priests and the penal laws had started to clarify people's allegiances, it may be that some parishioners of basically traditional views experienced the attractive force of the vernacular services.

The wills, like some of the court cases about to be discussed, suggest the continuance of a sharp division of opinion in many parishes, yet under Edward VI there appears here little or no evidence for a persecution either of sacramentarians or of traditionalists. Students of the record sources should perhaps here be warned that a striking apparent exception springs merely from a reckless conjecture by the editor of the *Acts of the Privy Council.* An entry in the Council Register for January 1548 gives particulars of recognizances for the appearance of John Lister and Arthur Mawde of Halifax, clothiers, and of Elizabeth Mitton, woman-servant, to answer to charges made by Dr. Haldesworth, vicar of Halifax.[1] The editor headed this entry 'Recognizance upon a charge of heresy', whereas it was quite certainly one of theft, concerning which Haldesworth's petition and other documents happen to have survived elsewhere.[2] In a very few cases, however, notorious resisters of change may have incurred injury at the hands of powerful Protestant opponents. An example is forthcoming in the case of the York physician Thomas Vavasour, who became so prominent a sufferer for Roman Catholicism in Elizabethan times. According to the seventeenth-century martyrologist Father Grene, Vavasour 'was forced to fly, and was banished his country in King Edward's days, through the malice of heretics, who suborned one Mr. Cheek, schoolmaster to King Edward, to procure his banishment, which Cheek, after his return in Queen Mary's time, did ask him mercy, confessing his fault'.[3] This story admittedly represents a late tradition, but its circumstances have a ring of veracity. Sir John Cheke, who 'taught Cambridge and King Edward Greek', was secretary to Queen Jane and underwent imprisonment in 1553–4 for complicity with Dudley; he subsequently played an important part on the Continent in the pamphlet-war against Mary. If he had been instrumental in banishing Vavasour under Edward VI,

---

[1] *Acts of the Privy Council, 1547–1550,* pp. 162–3.
[2] Cf. J. Lister in *Papers of the Halifax Antiquarian Soc.* (1908), pp. 46–53.
[3] H. Foley, *Records of the English Province S. J.,* iii. 237, from Grene's MS. 'F' at the English College, Rome.

he had further good reason for placating the York doctor, since he was kidnapped near Brussels in 1556, brought back to England, and forced to abjure Protestantism.[1] It would be more to our purpose to know the identity of Vavasour's enemies in York. Holgate and some of his Reforming canons must have known Cheke very well and would have had ample inducement to banish so pertinacious an opponent as Vavasour. Their part cannot, however, be proved. The phrase 'banished his country' should in Tudor parlance mean merely banished from the York area.[2] The Vavasour case must have been quite exceptional; a story more probably characteristic of local division is that of the Hull merchant Walter Flynton, apparently a leader of the local traditionalist opposition-group. After Mary's accession he spoke opprobrious words to the Mayor and 'sclaunderyd dyvers of the towne that they were berers of suche as neyther favored the Kynge or Quene's procedynges, with dyvers other thynges'.[3] This conduct obviously had its dangers in a town only too vulnerable to charges of Protestant sympathy; the more so since Flynton had taken his case to the Marian Council in the North. The civic authorities totally disfranchised him and only restored him on payment of a fine and on the intercession of the Earl of Shrewsbury. On such an occasion, self-protection demanded that the minutes of the corporation should be tactful and reticent, yet one cannot help suspecting that passions ran high.[4]

At this stage we may turn to discuss the considerable body of evidence concerning the advance of Protestantism which emerges from Marian records. Amongst the carriers of anti-Catholic opinions in the years around the mid-century must be numbered some of the little theatrical companies. The propagandist plays of John Bale form only one of the many known links between the nascent national drama and the Reformation,[5] but it is naturally during the reign of Mary that measures to suppress such players become most frequent and noticeable.[6] Though many companies were active in the diocese, I have only encountered one charge of Protestantism levelled against them. On 30 April 1556 the Privy Council informed the President of the Council

---

[1] On Cheke cf. *D.N.B.*, and Garrett, op. cit., pp. 114–17.

[2] Cf. Sir Francis Bigod's use of 'my country', *supra*, p. 65.

[3] Hull Corporation Bench Book iv, fos. 2ᵛ–4.

[4] Another example of this sensitivity appears in the vigorous denials made in 1556 by Henry Gray, vicar of Lund, that he had ever been suspected of heresy concerning the sacrament of the altar (R. VII. G. 600).

[5] E. K. Chambers, *The Medieval Stage*, ii. 216 seqq.

[6] Many examples occur in *Acts of the Privy Council*, *1554–6* and *1556–8*.

in the North that certain lewd persons to the number of six or seven in a company, wearing the livery of Sir Francis Leke, had wandered about the north parts and represented certain plays and interludes. These contained very naughty and seditious matter touching the king's and queen's majesties and the state of the realm, and to the slander of Christ's true Catholic Church. The Council in the North must instruct justices of the peace to repress such performances; also contact Sir Francis Leke, ordering him to seek out the players and send them up for inquiry and punishment.[1] We do not know the outcome, but had the registers of the Northern Council survived, we might have learned more of this case and its like. The life of John Bale, Reformer, friar, and dramatist, does at least symbolize this small facet of Reformation history. To the wandering friars had succeeded the wandering players: they were the last of that varied fraternity of the road which for over two centuries had been so busily dissolving the structure of medieval society.

Under the Marian persecution, the phraseology of wills can no longer be expected to register fairly the overall balance of public opinion. It does not, however, lack a certain interest and relevance. An examination of 330 Yorkshire wills made in the Marian years shows over eighty, or about a quarter, as non-traditionalist, and so out of harmony with the régime. Of these, only about eighteen positively enunciate Protestant doctrine, but in all likelihood the great majority of the eighty may be taken as convinced Protestants. Those who resist pressure and continue to reject the 'safe' Catholic usages must surely now include a very large element of the convinced, as distinct from the mere followers. On the other side, amongst the traditionalist majority, a small group likewise pass beyond time-honoured forms to display positive enthusiasm for Catholic dogma on the intercession of the Virgin and the saints. Yet another small group adopts a series of individual forms attempting to comprehend both Catholic and Protestant beliefs. William Barker, a farmer of Newton Kyme, begins as a Protestant: 'First I bequeath my soull to Almightie God my maker and to his onelie sonne Jesu Christ my Redemer and Saviour, in whome I put my hooll hope and trust of salvacione through the merites of his blessed passion.' Then, however, he alters course by adding: 'to his blessed mother and virgyne sancte Marie, and to all the holie company of heaven, to pray for me, havinge great nede thereof'.[2] Such broad churchmen, it must be

---

[1] Letter printed in Strype, *Eccles. Memorials* (1822), vol. iii, pt. ii, pp. 413–14.
[2] *Testamenta Leodiensia, 1553–1561* in *Thoresby Soc.* xxvii. 48.

stressed, seem few in number; only about half a dozen occur in this large group of wills. Another interesting feature of the group is the fact that until the year 1555 Catholic and non-Catholic forms appear in roughly equal numbers. Thereafter the former become heavily preponderant; how far through mere timidity in the face of rising persecution, how far from persuasion or pressure by local clergy, how far from genuine reconversion to Catholic beliefs we shall never know. Taken as a whole, these wills certainly suggest that a solid Protestant minority had been created and that it persisted throughout the reign of Mary. It looks, indeed, rather more impressive in numbers than might have been anticipated, but as the great majority of the wills so far examined come from the West Riding, they may somewhat exaggerate its strength. One must at all costs avoid statistical pedantry when attempting to derive doctrinal and social impressions from testamentary records. I am nevertheless encouraged to suppose that the paragraphs tentatively devoted to this field may not be thought excessive, since the resultant picture broadly conforms with that deducible from quite different types of sources. For example, the Halifax district, notable then and later for Protestant radicalism, does not fail to supply during the Marian years an exceptionally high proportion of non-traditionalist and Protestant wills.[1] Fortunately, we no longer depend upon all these narrow and tantalizing glimpses of Protestant development in the lay mind, for we can now produce from the York diocesan records a number of heresy cases against laymen, which, though dating from the Marian persecution, obviously illuminate also the preceding years. These cases derive largely from the same act books of the Court of Audience which contain the proceedings against the married clergy;[2] from the spring of 1554 to the autumn of 1555 they were conducted alongside the latter and for the most part before Dr. John Rokeby, the vicar-general, and Dr. John Dakyn, archdeacon of the East Riding. The former of these dignitaries was a distinguished canonist and also, as befitted a Vice-President of the Council in the North, a prudent politician: over a long period he served a most heterogeneous succession of archbishops, ending with the Puritan Grindal himself.[3] Dakyn, already familiar to us in a number of situations, had now decisively thrown in his lot with the

---

[1] For some examples, see the summaries in J. Horsfall Turner, *Hist. of Brighouse, Rastrick and Hipperholme*, pp. 219–20. The two volumes of *Halifax Wills* again provide little help here.
[2] Chiefly from R. VII. A. 33, 34, and A.B. 39.
[3] For references to Rokeby and Dakyn, see *M.R.D.Y.*, pt. i, pp. 6–8.

Marians, and, thanks to Foxe,[1] went down to history as the judge of Yorkshire's sole Marian martyr. The brothers Richard and John Snell came from Bedale in Richmondshire, by this date in the diocese of Chester, and Dakyn proceeded against them under a commission granted by the bishop of that diocese. After a spell of imprisonment, John Snell recanted, but then in a fit of remorse drowned himself in the Swale. Richard, who stood firm, was condemned by Dakyn and burned at Richmond in September 1558, immediately after which event Dakyn returned home and, says Foxe melodramatically, 'never joyed after, but died'. The burning, its date, and the part played by Dakyn are confirmed by the Richmond parish register and by the report of the royal commissioners of 1559.[2] Dakyn did indeed die in the subsequent November, a fact as likely to reflect his own sensitivity as the judgement of God. The case is otherwise not of special interest, since Foxe obviously knew nothing about the doctrines or influences involved. His picturesque account suggests that the people of Richmond showed a certain rough sympathy with the unfortunate brothers. When John Snell submitted, they organized a money-subscription for his benefit, while at the execution Richard's agonized cry, 'Christ help me', was answered by one Robert Atkinson, 'Hold fast there, and we will all pray for thee.'

Of the Smithfield martyrs, few can be in any sense claimed for the diocese of York and of these the most eminent, Bishop Ferrar, had maintained of late years little connexion with his former sphere of activity.[3] A case somewhat more pertinent is that of John Leaf, a native of Kirkby Moorside in the Vale of Pickering, who went up to London, became apprenticed to a tallow-chandler, and fell in with Tyndale's one-time assistant John Rogers, destined to be the earliest of all the Marian martyrs. Leaf, still aged only nineteen, was soon afterwards suspected and imprisoned by his ward-alderman. Examined by Bonner, he staunchly denounced both Transubstantiation and auricular confession. Frankly acknowledging himself a 'scholar' of Rogers, he professed to believe in the same doctrines as Bishop Hooper, John Cardmaker, and other recent martyrs. On 1 July 1555, scarcely five months after his teacher, he ended his life at the stake. His companion in martyrdom was the distinguished former prebendary of St. Paul's, John Bradford, who spoke to Leaf his famous valediction: 'Be of good comfort, brother, for we shall have a merry supper with the Lord this

---

[1] Op. cit. viii. 739, reprinted in *M.R.D.T.*, pt. ii, pp. 15–16.
[2] P.R.O., S.P. 12/10, p. 283. [3] Cf. *supra*, p. 148.

THE LAITY: PROTESTANTISM AND HERESY 223

night.'¹ The case of this youth illustrates some features already familiar: working-class mobility and the 'democratic' character of the London Protestant circles which a provincial sojourner could so readily enter. One seeks in vain to learn whether Leaf had caught any of the Lollard-Protestant notions current in the North Riding, and had thus gone to London already predisposed to receive instruction. Foxe, our sole informant, knew little or nothing about his earlier life or the length of his stay in the capital. Unless the martyrologist's account of Leaf's examinations is grossly idealized, he seems to have been a lucid and determined young man, by this time well grounded in the new opinions. Yet perhaps the most interesting feature of the record is the statement that he could still neither read nor write. After his examination two bills were brought into his prison and read to him: one a list of his confessions, the other a recantation. He chose to sign the former, and being unable to use a pen, took a pin, pricked his hand, and sent the document back to Bonner signed in his blood.

Not without a sense of anticlimax, we must now leave this atmosphere of high tragedy in order to view the repertoire of tragi-comedies, sometimes tinged with farce, enacted in the York Court of Audience. In examining these cases, we speedily become aware that when Robert Parkyn described villainous attacks upon the sacrament of the altar, he was not merely repeating lurid rumours from the south. At all events, many people were denying the Real Presence in his own diocese: it is the commonest heretical offence in these Marian act books. Robert Bigott, 'kepinge an alehouse in Beverley', was charged on 19 April 1554 that he 'dothe not only hym self rayle agaynst tholly and blessyd sacrament of thalter, but also haith many and sondry other evill disposyd persons resortinge to his howse that in lyke maner rale agaynst the same most holly sacrament'. He denied the charge and was ordered to purge himself by the oath of eight of his neighbours.² The same offence, 'unreverent speaking of the sacrament', and similar sentences are recorded immediately afterwards in connexion with seven other Beverley men.³ The trouble in Beverley simmered on, however, throughout the reign. Three years later, on 10 June 1557, the judges accused Gawin Brakenrige of Beverley 'that when the priest came to hyme, havinge the sacrament of the altare to ministre unto hyme, he said the priest brought the devell'. Brakenrige confessed and submitted himself

¹ Foxe, vii. 192–4.   ² R. VII. A. 33, fo. 37ᵛ.
³ Ibid., fos. 38–38ᵛ; Edward Smethley, Thomas Bothe, Nicholas Willimat, Thomas Settrington, John Jennison, Erkewald Shepperde.

to the correction of the law. The judge, Dr. Dakyn, thereupon enjoined him 'that upon Setterday next he shall go thorowe the markett of Beverley and ther to knell downe in the market and say that he was sorie that he had spoken such develishe wordes and desire God of forgivenes, and Sir Thomas Mitchell[1] to declare the said wordes to be the cause of his penance, and such penance to do at Catwike the Sonday after and at Olrome the Sonday next after'.[2] Beverley proved in fact a notable centre of unrest; we shall shortly observe other cases there of a somewhat different type.

Several Leeds people also attracted attention early in the reign. Christopher Jackson of that town was accused on 10 May 1554 'that he is one of the new sorte, for that he rayled agaynst the sacramentes and burnyd the image of Our Lady'. He confessed to the latter action, saying he had been sworn thereto by the commissioners appointed in that behalf. Along with him appeared thirteen other Leeds men described as 'bussy fellowes of the new sorte'.[3] The curate of Leeds reported that they had 'usyd themselfes well & godly' since Michaelmas last and, on their humble submission, they escaped with a warning, which included the proviso 'that they do handle the church wardens of Ledes gently and other the inhabitantes that dyd present them, and that they gyve them no fowle wordes otherways than becomethe them from hensfourth'.[4] It would thus appear that the churchwardens and others of Leeds went so far as to present people whose main offences had in fact taken place before the accession of Mary. Unfortunately, the book gives no more precise account of the obviously animated relations which ensued between the rival groups. As for Christopher Jackson and two other serious offenders, William Taylor and Henry Ambler, they were admitted to purgation.[5] A few days later, William Stable of Leeds was also ordered to produce compurgators.[6]

On 12 May 1554 George Gower, gentleman, was questioned 'quid sentit et credit de Sacramento altaris post verba consecracionis prolata?' He hastened to reply 'that he belevith yt to be the very body and

---

[1] This Thomas Mitchell's will, with its details of his own books, is printed in *Halifax Wills*, ed. E. W. Crossley, ii. 167–9. It was proved 20 Oct. 1558.

[2] A.B. 39, 10 June 1557. Certification is demanded as usual.

[3] Robert Wilson, Richard Gledell,—Strickland, Robert Jackeson, Henry Ambler, Thomas Ambler, William Lyndall, John Kinge, William Taylor, Henry Fyshe, Alexander Richardson, Nicholas Jackson, Anthony Harrison.

[4] R. VII. A. 34, fo. 2.   [5] Ibid., fo. 1ᵛ.

[6] Ibid., fo. 23; 25 May 1554.

blode of Christe and for the transubstanciation, he belevith as the universall churche teachith and haith taughte'.[1] The answer presumably cleared him, since no sentence or any other sequel is recorded. This man was probably George Gower of Stittenham and thus a cousin of Thomas Gower, one of the few Yorkshire gentry in exile under Mary, having been suspected of complicity with Dudley. Thomas nevertheless turned informer against his confederates, gained permission to return, and was made Master of the Ordnance in the North, which office he continued to hold under Elizabeth.[2] The Gower family thus struck no very resonant blow for the Protestant cause. Meanwhile many other anti-Transubstantiationists were active in Yorkshire. George Walker of Oswaldkirk, detected along with William and Elizabeth Walker, denied on 16 June 1554 the charge that he had failed over a long period to do reverence to the sacrament 'in the tyme of the levacion thereof'.[3]

Later in the same year a more serious offence took place at Hull. Of William Utley, late curate of Hull, it was alleged on 3 October 'that he the said Utley was consentinge and present to, and at the takinge awaye of the blissed sacrament forth of [*blank*] in Hull apon Tuysday or Weddynsday in Witson weke last, betwixte six and tenne of the cloke before none the said day'. He denied the offence and was purged by six compurgators from Hull. Utley and his wife subsequently agreed to separate, and he was ordered penance in St. Mary's, this doubtless being the church from which the 'sacrament' had been abstracted.[4] The actual offenders seem to have avoided detection.

On the previous 30 July certain similar cases of sacrilege at Halifax had been brought to trial. To Richard Best the judges objected 'that the same night that the sacrament was taken fourthe of the churche of Hallifax, there came to his house aboute midnight the same nighte, and callyd of hym, twoo persons, and that he rose upp and went to the feldes, and that they three beinge in the feldes to gether, thone of the said persons saide to the other, "I must goo you know whither," and so departed'. Best corrected the alleged time of this mysterious behaviour to 2 a.m., but otherwise admitted that the conversation had taken

[1] Ibid., fo. 8.
[2] *Glover's Visitation of Yorks.*, ed. Foster, p. 226; C. H. Garrett, op. cit. p. 165; D.N.B., s.v. Gower, Thomas.
[3] Ibid., fo. 50ᵛ. Compare John Ingle of Blunham, Beds., who in 1519 failed to communicate at Easter, and at the elevation 'deponit caput suum inclinatum et ridet stulte' (Lincoln Record Soc. xxxiii. 113).
[4] A. 34, fos. 84ᵛ, 87.

place. He was ordered to reappear the following Thursday. Meanwhile William Dene of Halifax faced the accusation 'that he is suspectid within the parishe of Hallifax to be one of them that pullyd downe the crucifyx and took away the sacrament furthe of the churche there'. He denied this completely, and was also told to return on Thursday. When the day came, Best and Dene were both absent and pronounced contumacious, *pena reservata*. At this stage it would seem that the original charge collapsed, since on the Saturday, 4 August, both the accused were caught on other charges. Best admitted receiving the sacrament last Easter without first making confession; besides a similar admission, Dene abjectly called himself 'a grete swerer'. The penances awarded these two men were different: only in Best's case was attention clearly drawn to the suspicion of doctrinal unorthodoxy. Standing before the pulpit in Halifax church he had to 'affyrme the contentes of a schedule which the curate shall then rede to be true, and that he belevith them from the bothom of his harte'. Penance completed, if his conscience permitted, he was to receive the sacrament. In the case of William Dene, on the other hand, the priest had merely to declare 'that he dothe the same penance for common drunkennes and sweringe'. At the same time, Dene was compelled to repeat the performance in the church of Wakefield on the following Sunday—an exceptional elaboration if he were, in fact, no more than a foul-mouthed drunkard. It could be, though the evidence remains far from conclusive, that he accepted these discrediting personal charges in order to avoid further and more dangerous investigations into heretical behaviour. Alongside these two men, Edward Ridinge of Ovenden Wood in Halifax parish received penance in the same forms as William Dene; the priest 'to declare in the pulpit that he dothe the same for lokinge downe at the tyme of the elevacion of the sacrament in tyme of masse and for refusinge of hallywater'.[1] The offences against the sacrament both at Halifax and at Hull should be viewed alongside these stories and in the light of the Elizabethan reputation of the two places as centres of militant Protestantism.

One interesting and comparable case comes from Wakefield. On the afternoon of 28 June 1555 an office was held against John Nodder and his wife Isabella, evidence being given on oath by one Henry Watkinson of that town. The nature of Nodder's main offence may be gathered from the fact that the judges interrogated him 'whether he do beleve whether after the wordes of consecracion spoken by the preste over [it] the brede be by the virtue of the said wordes of Christe turned into

---

[1] The Halifax cases are in A. 34, fos. 77–77ᵛ, 78; 78ᵛ, 79, 79ᵛ.

the verie bodie of Christe and no brede remanynge there after the wordes of consecration so spoken'. Immediately hereafter the notary has written the words 'yea or naye': though he then struck them out of the official record, they no doubt represent the verbal actuality of the question in court. Nodder's immediate reply is omitted. The judges then, however, questioned him concerning the other articles delivered to him in writing. To each article Nodder exhibited a written reply. So far as may be judged, these replies took the form of a submissive confession of orthodoxy, since we are told that he read them publicly and confessed spontaneously to their contents. Mrs. Nodder then underwent interrogation on the same articles and replied that she believed all and singular of them. The judges licensed them to renew mutual contact and ordered them to return at a subsequent date. Whether in fact they had been imprisoned does not appear. Nodder next attended on 28 August, when he was enjoined 'that upon Wednisday the next he come into the church of Wakefeld and to bringe his wif with hyme and there to be confessed of the curat . . . and . . . upon Sonday next after, at the offertorie tyme of high messe . . . he and his wif to declare ther faith, accordinge to the articles maid in that behalf, godelie before the holl parishoners, and after the messe be done to receyve the blissed sacrament of thaultare'. When, however, on 3 September the pair were duly summoned to certify performance, they failed to appear, were pronounced contumacious, and excommunicated. Exceptionally, the actual form of the excommunication pronounced by Dr. George Palmes is given on a subsequent page. Possibly because the act book (R. VII. A. 34) ends shortly after this date, the Nodders then vanish and the present writer has so far failed to recover their trail. Sacramentarian heresy presumably headed their offences; we may also from the above particulars deduce with certainty that they had been charged with denying Confession.[1]

A far more attractively documented affair began on 20 April 1556, when John Bonsaye of Beverley—a pensioned choirman of the Minster there[2]—confessed to the charge of speaking openly and publicly against Transubstantiation, saying that the Body of Christ was *spiritually* present in the Sacrament, 'et ibi adest verbum et evangelium Dei'. The judges asked him whether, after the words of consecration, any other substance remained besides that of Christ's Body. In reply Bonsaye said 'that he beleveth after the wordes of consecration spoken by the prest

---

[1] For the Nodder case, see A. 34, fos. 127ᵛ, 128, 133ᵛ, 134, 135ᵛ.

[2] G. Oliver, *Hist. Beverley*, p. 188. He was apparently in deacon's orders.

there remayneth the trewe substance of the bodie and blode of Christ and none other substance of brede or wyne'. They next asked him 'whether he beleveth that if a man beinge in dedlie syne receyveth the verie trewe bodie and blode of Christe in the sacrament', to which Bonsaye replied 'that he thinkes the man beinge in dedlie synne receyveth it not'. This answer implied disbelief in Transubstantiation and, as we shall see, entailed further consequences. To the question, 'What is a sacrament?' the accused cautiously answered 'that he cannot tell'. Here Dr. Dakyn showed him a certain book beginning 'The voice of the people', and asked him whether it were his book or not. Bonsaye confessed 'that it is his book and that he keped the same a longe tyme, and after delyvered the same to John Pesegrave'. To the query, 'What he beleveth of the Pope's holienes?' he answered 'that he beleveth the Pope's holienes is Christe's vicare in erth and hath auctoritie to remite syne and to governe Christe church in erthe'. The unsatisfied judges warned Bonsaye to return, 'et hinc', records the notary Thomas Cowper, '*Mr. Johannes Dakyn deliveravit michi librum predictum et duos alios libros, unus incipiens*, The Ymage of God, or laye mans booke, *alter incipiens*, The Governance of vertue, *et postea dicti tres libri deliberati fuerunt domino Thome Mitchell comburendi apud Beverley*'. In striking corroboration, the Beverley governors' accounts for this year actually contain an item of 4d. paid for faggots for burning books in the Saturday market.[1]

The three titles themselves throw interesting light upon the Protestant literature then circulating among 'advanced' literates of the diocese. *Vox Populi or the people's Complaint* (1549) was by the well-known poet and dramatist Nicholas Grimald, chaplain to Ridley, a prisoner of the Marians in 1555, but finally one of those who recanted.[2] *The Governance of Vertue*, also first published in 1549, came from the pen of that famous Protestant divine, Thomas Becon; it was a strongly controversial but able work, understandably obnoxious to Catholic opinion and destined to remain popular throughout the Elizabethan age and beyond.[3] *The Image of God or laie man's booke*, appearing first in 1550, was

---

[1] G. Poulson, *Beverlac*, p. 311.

[2] It is not recorded in the *Short-Title Catalogue*, and I am not aware that any copies have survived. Wood suggests that it was mainly directed against pluralism, but may not have known much about it (*D.N.B.*, s.v. Grimald, Nicholas). On Grimald's work as a Protestant dramatist cf. E. K. Chambers, *The Medieval Stage*, index, s.v.

[3] Further editions, 1560, 1566, 1578, 1607 (*S.T.C.*, nos. 1725–9); reprinted in Parker Soc. (1843), *Early Works of Thomas Becon*, pp. 393 seqq.

also to gain a wide circulation in more favourable times.[1] It constitutes
a penetrating attack, not only upon Transubstantiation and other
Catholic beliefs, but also upon Anabaptist and Arian heresies. Its
author was Roger Hutchinson, fellow of Eton, deprived for marriage
under Mary and dying about May 1555.[2] Altogether one can feel no
surprise that a man who confessed to owning and circulating such books
should have been subjected to a most rigorous inquisition.

It is clear that, after the proceedings on 20 April, Bonsaye was given
some pointed instruction on Transubstantiation. Upon his reappearance in court on the morning of 22 April he was asked whether 'he
beleveth that a man beinge in syne receyveth the blessed sacrament
to his dampnation or no'. Significantly enough, he replied 'that he nowe
being better instructe doth so beleve, and submittes hyme self to the
catholike church and the judges of the same and to ther correction'.
His case being then postponed until one o'clock in the afternoon, his
friend John Peesgrave came forward to answer the charge 'that he hath
hade in his custodie thre bokes written aganste the catholike faith of
Christe'. Peesgrave admitted he had them 'this half yere last', and was
immediately assigned the following penance:

that upon Satterday come a sevenet he shulbe readie bare-foted, bare-leged,
in his jackett with ij grete papers, the one apon his brest, the other apon his
bake, conteinying the cause of his penance doinge, at Beverley in the markett
tyme, and so to go aboute the marketes;[3] that done, he to stande after the
same sorte at the markett crose and ther Sir Thomas Mitchell, or els Sir
Robert Robynson, the schole-maister ther, to declare the cause of his said
penance doinge, and to cast the said iij bookes in the fier and see theme
godelie burned accordinglie. The contentes of the wordes to be written in
the said papers followeth: 'This man hath kept hereticall and sediciouse
bookes contrarie to the lawes.'

A corporal oath was then imposed upon Peesgrave, binding him to
execute the penance.

This subsidiary offender having been sentenced, John Bonsaye
returned for the afternoon session and read a certain paper schedule
of abjuration covering all and singular charges made against him and
confessed by him. He also took an oath on the gospels in accordance
with the provisions of this schedule. The latter, originally kept with
the act book, seems like so many important loose papers to have

[1] Further editions, 1560, 1573, 1580 (ibid., nos. 14019–22); reprinted in Parker
Soc. (1842), *The Works of Roger Hutchinson*, pp. 1 seqq.
[2] *D.N.B.*, s.v. Hutchinson, Roger.
[3] i.e. the two market-places of Beverley, still extant.

vanished, leaving us cheated of further details. The inevitable penance then follows:

that to morrowe he shalbe redie in his gowne, bare hedded with a faggot on his lefte shulder and a taper of wax in his right hande, in the Cathedrall Churche of Yorke before the begynnynge of highe masse, and ther to knell all masse tyme, and when the ministers of the quier prepareth to go with procession and ther knelinge before the highe altare in godlie meditacions and prayer unto the procession go forth, and then to go before the said procession as it shall go to the chapiter doore and no forther.[1]

In these Beverley cases we admittedly encounter neither martyrs nor trained theologians, yet we are now definitely in contact with 'informed' and literate Protestantism, maintained into the later years of the reign. On the basis of our present information, we have no right to suppose that activities of this type had become very common in the diocese, even in its larger centres of population. These latter, the reader will have observed, produced the vast majority of all types of anti-Catholics recorded in our Marian books.

With the Beverley men and their little Protestant library we may sense an atmosphere more characteristic of East Anglia than of the diocese of York. In this connexion, some significance attaches to the case of Thomas Miles of Thorpe, Suffolk, who, while visiting Scarborough, spoke against the sacrament. On 11 April 1554 he found himself before the court at York and rewarded with a humiliating penance.[2] Heresy reached Yorkshire by sea as well as by land, just as it had originally reached the south-eastern counties by sea from the Low Countries; again as the Counter-Reformation in the form of its seminary priests was to enter Yorkshire through the fishing villages around Whitby, and Hampshire through the coastal villages of the Solent.

After meeting these readers of up-to-date Protestant literature, we re-encounter the older traditions of radicalism. On 2 November 1555 Christopher Kelke, *armiger*, of the city of York, had to reply to certain articles touching the safety of his soul *ac crimen Lollardie*. Two days later the court ordered proclamations to be affixed to the church doors of Holy Trinity, Goodramgate, summoning Elizabeth Goodricke, Agnes Slater, and all other persons able to testify to the truth of this charge of Lollardy. On this day also, Kelke appointed his proctors for the case. On 12 November a letter from William Garnett, rector of Holy Trinity, certified that the summons had been duly made; Elizabeth Goodricke, along with Agnes Halliday and Elizabeth Toller, was

[1] A.B. 39, 20 and 22 Apr. 1556.   [2] A. 33, fo. 21ᵛ.

sworn and examined. The details of the charge are nevertheless irritatingly omitted, though the proceedings seem to have occupied both the morning and the afternoon. Four days later, Kelke produced as witnesses Mr. Stephen Tubley, Doctor of Medicine,[1] and John Clayby, priest: the case proceeded, but still uninformatively recorded, on 19 and 20 November.[2] The judges on this last day read out a final decree *in scriptis prout apparet per schedulam*, yet thus far the present writer has failed to discover its purport, or, for that matter, any precise account of the offence imputed to Christopher Kelke. Under these circumstances it would clearly seem imprudent to dogmatize concerning the degree of significance attributable to the term Lollardy. Nevertheless, though it had often been popularly used as a general synonym for heresy, it seems unlikely that the most learned canonists in northern England would suddenly and pointlessly revive the term *crimen Lollardie* for repeated use in this one particular case, if his offences had not closely corresponded with the Lollardy more distinctly prevalent in their younger days. Probably enough the Lollard sacramental heresy figured amongst them. The defendant belonged to the well-known family of Barnetby in Lincolnshire and Great Kelk in the East Riding. Two Christophers, father and son, were living in 1555, but as the father would not have been described as 'of York', this alleged Lollard must have been the son, then a very young man.[3] Whatever his links with the Lollard heresy, it should not be assumed that he lacked contact with modern Reforming circles. His cousin was Roger Kelke, fellow of St. John's, Cambridge, a Marian exile, an associate of Grindal, and later a notoriously puritanical master of Magdalene College.[4]

The medieval doctrine of the Eucharist was not the sole target of radical attack, for gestures of ridicule and contempt were directed at other Catholic rites and at the clergy who practised them. After a long break, some Yorkshiremen seem to have regarded the revival of 'pretty' ceremonies with emotions not dissimilar from those with which the less respectable of their Victorian descendants might have observed

---

[1] Tubley's will was proved 10 June 1558 (*Wills in the York Registry, 1554-1568*, Y.A.S. Rec. Ser. xiv. 167). After showing insolence to other citizens, he and his family were bound over to good behaviour in 1555 (York House Book xxi, fos. 88ᵛ-89).

[2] For the Kelke case see A. 34, fos. 139, 139ᵛ, 140, 140ᵛ, 141.

[3] Cf. *Harleian Soc.* li. 556. The son was over 21 in 1557, and his mother's age was given as only 38 in 1556-7; he died some time after 1581.

[4] Garrett, op. cit., pp. 202-3.

Anglo-Catholic ritualism. On Whit Sunday 1554, Gabriel Walker of Rothwell, during the 'casting of sence at *Veni Creator*', was alleged to have given evil example by saying ' "What is yon? A Christinmas play in faythe. Yonder is a gay Yole layke!¹ I wold my Jenne saw yonde; she wolde laugh at yt", and with laughinge he often tymes repetyd the said wordes.' On 22 May 1554 Walker tried hard to explain away this incident with a somewhat schoolboyish story. According to his own account, he saw

a prest there in a cope and twoo boyes upon ether hand of hym, with twoo baskettes, and whan that the prest cast sence, the boyes cast flowers agaynst the sencers and that he, musinge what they ment thereby, demandyd of one William Taylor his neighbore what it signifyed, and he answeryd hym that it signifyed the comynge of tholly Gost; and he answeryd him agayne that it was a praty pastyme and that he wished lytill Jen[ne] his doughter were theyr to see yt.

Unimpressed, the judges adjourned the case and committed Walker 'to the archiepiscopal prison designated for heretics'. Back in court again on 25 May, doubtless thinking the 'lark' not worth the candle, Walker was assigned penance in the church of Rothwell, the curate to declare that he did it 'for disturbing of his neighbours at the tyme of the insensinge of thalter'.²

The use of holy water provided another butt for 'busy fellows of the new sort'. On 7 July 1554 Leonard Worlesworth of Penistone received penance, the curate there to explain the reason:

for that he did misuse hyme self in the same pulpite, and also that he did misuse hyme selfe otherwise in castinge water in the church after the priest casting holie water, contrarie to the laudable use of the church; and then he, the said Leonarde, to saye openlie to the people, 'It is trewe that the curate speaketh, and I shall desire youe all, for as much as I have offended in mis-usinge my self, as is afore, contrarie to the order of the church, to forgive me, desiringe youe all and most especially the youth to take example at me and so not to enterprise any such like hereafter, for I am verie sorie for my mis-doing herin, never by Godes grace intending to attempte the like.'³

As in earlier years, refusal of auricular confession was another offence which occasionally brought people into conflict with the ecclesiastical courts. In the case (13 December 1554) of Agnes Sampson of Aber-

¹ Sport, play; northern form from O.N. *leikr* (*New Eng. Dict.*, s.v. Lake). Compare the western rebels of 1549, who compared the Edwardian service with 'a Christmas game' (A. L. Rowse, *Tudor Cornwall*, p. 271).
² For the Walker case, see A. 34, fos. 15ᵛ, 23.
³ A. 34, fo. 66ᵛ. He had then to do similar penance in Burton church and to certify.

ford, the York judge adopted a somewhat unusual procedure. The accusation was to the effect that 'she sayd that she wold never be confessyd of a prest'. She appeared, but what defence she made we are not told. The judge merely committed his powers to the vicar of Sherburn to inquire into the truth of the charge, and should the vicar find it true, 'then he to put hir to penance and to certifye the same *veneris post Pauli prox.*, and that she shall come to the parishe churche upon Sonday next come a seven [night], and there openlie to confesse her self unto the preist'.[1] Some other cases of failure to confess may represent either doctrinal objection or mere slackness. On 21 June 1555, for example, William Byns and John Burkynshay of Bingley admitted to receiving the Eucharist the previous Easter without confessing, and were immediately ordered to go on two Sundays in procession 'with either of theme a candle of a penny pece in ther hand and a booke or a paire of bedes in the other hand, before the crosse'.[2]

The crucifix itself seems to have provoked some parishioners into crude expressions of scorn. Marmaduke Walker and John Wilson of Knapton in Wintringham parish appeared together on 6 May 1555. It was said that 'upon Easter daye last past at Evensong, when the prest came furth of the quere to the funte, havinge the crucifix of Christe in his armes, he [Walker] asked the said John Wilson and spake these wordes to the same. "Whether will he goo with that in his armes to christen it," the said John Wilson annsweringe and said to the said Marmaduke, "No, he will drowne it." ' Walker admitted the words attributed to him, but Wilson maintained 'that when the said Marmaduke did saye to hyme the wordes aforsaid, he badde hym hold his peax, he wist not what he said'. The judges do not appear to have appreciated working-class humour and assigned the same penance to both men, namely,

that upon Sonday the next they both present in the parishe churche of Wyntryngham, bare-foted, bare-leged, bare-heded, havinge a candle of the price of ij^d in either of ther handes, at such tyme as the prest prepareth hyme self to go in procession, and so to go before the crose abowte the church, and at the comyng into the church with procession to kneell in the channcell before the altare unto thoffitorie tyme, and then to offer ther candles and to come downe with the prest to the pulpit, and ther the prest to declare that the said [Marma]duke [doth] the penance aforesaid for spekynge the wordes aforsaid, and that the said John did the said penance assigned before to hyme bie reason the said wordes now proved by hyme, and after the declaracion

[1] A. 34, fo. 100.   [2] A. 34, fo. 126^v.

of the prest they shall confesse openlie as is afore, and desier forgivenes of God and of the con[gregation].[1]

That such anti-clerical and anti-ritualistic scorn was in no sense limited to radical Yorkshiremen may be evidenced from the *comperta* of Pole's metropolitical visitation of the diocese of Lincoln. Here in 1556 the offences and atmosphere of the York act books are somewhat closely reproduced. Sometimes, it is true, the popular attacks seem more or less dignified, as when Thomas Troughton said, 'The belles of the church be the Devill's trumpets . . . the ivel Churche did ever persecute the goode Churche, as they do now', this last, we are told, being spoken *de hereticis combustis apud London*. The authentic proletarian touch appears rather in the case of the Bedford man, who, to ridicule the clergy, shaved the crown of a child under two years of age. But a much lighter sense of humour was displayed by Laurence Burnebie of Brampton, who, seeing the vicar ceremonially opening the church-doors with the staff of the cross, exclaimed, 'What a sport have we towards! Will our vicar ronne at the quintine [i.e. tilt at a target] with God Almightie?'[2]

Cases of this type should instil caution. They indicate that not everybody who got into trouble with the Marian authorities was a studious and informed Protestant, let alone a potential martyr. Our Tudor ancestors tended to be coarse, unrestrained, and indiscreet in both speech and deed. In addition, these legal records are usually cryptic and apt to leave unexplained the most vital motives and intentions. Under such circumstances we distinguish with difficulty between thoughtful rejection of tradition and mere crude irreverence. All the difference in the world lay between devout bibliolatry and, on the other hand, the scorn of the free-thinking layman which Lollardy or some more 'orthodox' Protestantism had doubtless helped to trigger off, but had not always diverted into pious courses. Certain of these laymen seem to represent third-hand derivatives of the old heresies, sometimes amounting to materialist rationalism. It would be presumptuous to connect their ideas too closely with those recent attacks made upon the sacrament of the altar by Thomas Becon and other learned Protestant controversialists.[3] True, our records are likely to exhibit uneducated defendants in their worst light, yet the martyrology of Foxe can scarcely have avoided the converse idealization. It has

[1] A. 34, fos. 120ᵛ–121.
[2] Printed in Strype, *Eccles. Memorials* (1822), vol. iii, pt. ii, pp. 390–2.
[3] For examples of anti-sacramentalism among the Edwardian Protestant scholars, see J. H. Blunt, *The Reformation of the Church of England*, ii. 394 seqq.

drawn a simplified pattern of apostolic and Biblical piety with which these popular adversaries of Marian clericalism signally fail to conform. The social historian of the Reformation deals with complex phenomena, too frequently hidden, not merely from the sectarian gladiators, but also from more sober scholars who begin their thinking with doctrines and ideologies rather than with records concerning the behaviour of actual human beings.

The Marian heretics resemble the predominantly Lollard heretics of the thirties not merely in their opinions, but also in their temper and their response to persecution. They are unheroic and submissive: like their predecessors they belong not to a Book of Martyrs but to the world of ordinary men, who, whatever their aspirations and rejections, lacked that iron assurance which led to a voluntary and painful death. Beneath the forest trees lay a broad, tangled, thorny, and yet resilient undergrowth. The Marian persecution may temporarily have restrained the spread of this undergrowth, but the great trees which it also felled soon proved themselves to have sown countless saplings. The forest of Protestantism was spreading relentlessly across the landscape of the nation.

VII

CONCLUSION

DURING the three reigns preceding the accession of Elizabeth, the religious characteristics of society in the diocese of York present features of great complexity. They seem little amenable to the customary period-divisons or to simple labels such as Catholic and Protestant; their development is geared somewhat remotely to that of the Westminster–Greenwich history so commonly accepted as the history of mid-Tudor England. The picture which has emerged corresponds equally little with 'the reactionary and barbarous Tudor north', the concept based upon a tendentious simplification of the Pilgrimage of Grace, and upon the notion that England north of Trent can roughly be equated with the Borders or at least with conservative backwaters like Richmondshire.

The 'official' Reformation admittedly manifests itself in the diocese at every stage. At its outset appears the would-be Man of Destiny, Sir Francis Bigod, a consistent and enthusiastic adherent of the new doctrines, at once patron and pupil of Thomas Garret, in his turn among the most influential of the earliest group of English Lutherans. Alongside his aspiration to bring the light of the Gospel to the north, Bigod had many relevant advantages: a humanistic education in Wolsey's household and at Oxford; great estates in Yorkshire, and a quasi-noble prestige which transcended in some measure the unpopularity of his advanced views. Again, he enjoyed a close personal association with Thomas Cromwell, and felt a burning sense of mission which caused him not only to maintain chaplains to preach the Reformation in the north, but even to seek a dispensation to become a married priest, or to preach as a layman. In the strange story of his downfall, we have seen the first tendrils of the Lutheran Reformation withering temporarily in the north: withering not merely against the wall of popular and clerical conservatism, but amongst the weeds and briars of neo-feudal affinities, of lawlessness and localism. Disillusioned by the cares of debt and expecting overmuch from the Crown, Bigod himself was finally beguiled from the cause of centralization and the cult of the State. In addition, he was seduced by a genuinely intellectual development: a desire to achieve primacy for a restored and purified clerical estate, a plan to install a race of godly preachers in control of the

Church, an ideal, in short, which carried him far beyond the Henrician Erastianism of his *Treatise against Impropriations*. By 1536 it had made him a man of the future as well as a man of the past. Unfortunately a successful Henrician needed above all to be a man of the moment. Under prevalent conditions, a presbyterian, neo-feudal magnate scarcely provided a feasible solution for the political, social, and religious problems of Yorkshire. No longer did the king and Thomas Cromwell need such regional satraps; even had they done so, they would doubtless have avoided choosing a young intellectual of highly independent views. Bigod's final inability either to win over the conservative leaders of the Pilgrimage of Grace or to stay aloof from the course of rebellion destroyed him long before he had approached his goal. The regional administration of the north fell into the hands of another protégé of Cromwell, the obedient and dutiful ex-monk Robert Holgate, who not only attained the Presidency of the Council in the North, but survived his patron to become the first Protestant Archbishop of York.

The story of early Protestantism among the gentry of the diocese of York is necessarily obscure, since we lack almost all their day-to-day correspondence. The few well-documented exceptions spring from 'accidental' occurrences: the preservation of the Plumpton letters, or the survival of Wilfrid Holme's poetical manuscript until it found an Elizabethan publisher. The gentry had a fair chance of meeting the new doctrines: in youth especially they formed a mobile group and many who lacked Bigod's opportunities did at least spend a period at the Inns of Court. There it was that Robert Plumpton, John Lascells, and, in all likelihood, Wilfrid Holme, became Protestants. The missionary role of such gentlemen in the provinces was apparently limited by the tendency of younger sons like Lascells to make careers in London or at court, and by the caution instilled into heirs like Plumpton, whose proselytizing seems to have been limited to his own family circle. Their emphases might take several forms: Plumpton was a literary convert of Tyndale, one of those smitten with the desire to reinterpret early Christianity and to recapture the atmosphere and the 'message' of the New Testament. On the other hand Wilfrid Holme, writing a political poem in deceptively medieval verse-forms, displayed not merely a Lutheran Erastianism and a hero-worship of Henry VIII, but also a range of Renaissance-Humanist ideas closely akin to those of the *Epistolae Obscurorum Virorum*. To such a man, the fig-tree was green, the new age at hand, when the cobwebs of philosophy, the hair-splitting of the scholastics, the superstitious mumbo-jumbo of saints, relics, and pilgrimages, the fusty world of ignorant, immoral monks and nuns should be swept away; when the industrious family layman, ruled by an enlightened monarch and guided by modern scholarship, would march forward by the light of the Gospel into a new and glorious future. Behind his forbidding and un-Erasmian façade, we meet in Wilfrid Holme a figure straight from the pages of the textbook, however startling his geographical and social position as head of an ancient Yorkshire rural family.

From about 1540, or rather earlier, wills and other records from the diocese of York illustrate the rising tide of disbelief in Purgatory, masses for the dead, chantries, the cult of the Virgin and of the saints. Most of these wills naturally derive from the gentry and middle classes; their waning piety also appears in numerous resumptions or embezzlements of chantry endowments. Such actions became fairly frequent from the late thirties, but as early as 1536 the corporation of York did not scruple to lighten its financial burdens by dissolving, through private Act of Parliament, nine chantries and some other foundations. Amongst the gentry and the town oligarchies it is not always easy to distinguish between the two motivating forces: the rejection of 'superstitious' institutions and the prevalent mood of utilitarianism, enhanced by economic insecurity and monetary inflation. Only a few of the secularizing gentry are known Protestants, while in the case of the well-documented dissolutions at York, no religious motives are alleged and none need be presumed.

Throughout the whole period, the conservatism of all the social classes bears the stamp of tradition and immobility, not that of the activist Counter-Reformation. To the clergy this generalization seems especially applicable. A number of them took active parts in the Pilgrimage of Grace, while a few chantry priests somehow became implicated as minor figures in the Wakefield Plot of 1541; apart from such few exceptions, the clerical record remains one of extreme caution and subservience. This feature, one of great social and political importance, owes something to the leadership of the senior clergy, whose behaviour in the Northern Convocation proves on close inquiry very different from that described by Froude and other dramatizers. The idea that this Convocation resisted the Royal Supremacy is based upon a misunderstanding of the documents; indeed, throughout the whole Reformation-crisis it responded as obediently to the claims and orders of the Crown as did the Convocation of Canterbury. At the height of the Pilgrimage of Grace a few conservative upper clergy met under busy pressure from Aske, but even then they differed substantially on the merits of papal jurisdiction. As for the parish clergy, a few are known from their writings to have held most conservative views, yet even they unquestionably obeyed the royal and episcopal injunctions. The evidence shows that this group deplored the cessation of time-honoured ceremonies, the insults offered to the doctrine of Transubstantiation, and the prohibition of masses for the dead; it shows little evidence of concern over the cessation of papal jurisdiction. The popular notion that monks and friars were staunch upholders of tradition proves as untrue in the diocese of York as in many others. Among the small group of Protestant clergy in the reign of Henry VIII, ex-religious like John Bale, Robert Ferrar, and Robert Holgate are prominent, while others of like origins appear as Edwardian Reformers. The formerly accepted view that very few northern clerics availed themselves of Edward VI's permission to marry is now disproved by reference to the Marian proceedings against the married clergy. From 1549 to 1553 probably about one-tenth of those in priest's orders embarked upon matrimony, but despite the emphasis laid upon this offence by the Marian government and ecclesiastical courts, it remains clear that marriage in itself does not prove organized Protestant convictions. Of the eighty or more married priests prosecuted under Mary, the great majority submitted to separation—or in the case of ex-regulars, to divorce—from their wives; they thereupon suffered deprivation, did public penance, were restored to sacerdotal functions, and could then re-enter the competition for benefices.

These matrimonial processes of 1554–5 constituted the only mass-purge of the clergy throughout the Tudor period. Amid the married priests may, however, be detected a small core of determined and genuine Protestants. Their biographies and publications show in this category at least six of the York prebendaries appointed under Edward VI; so do those of some dozen of the parish clergy, and further research may add more names to the list. Most of the radicals belonged to the minority of intellectuals and university-trained priests; those who did not were pluralists, whose means and contacts likewise raised them from the rank and file. The mass of the diocesan parish priests may possibly represent one of the less mobile elements of the population: many seem to have attended grammar schools near their birthplaces or to have been attracted into a nearby monastery during their teens. Some had served for a while as the neighbouring squire's or pluralist's chaplain, or else in a chantry, before obtaining a local benefice; many were certainly active farmers of their glebes and tied down to a life not unlike that of a yeoman. To the new opinions their vested interests were even less conducive than their way of life; almost every brand of Protestantism involved a determined attack upon Transubstantiation, so tending to diminish clerical power and prestige. And social historians content with mundane analyses usually end by wronging a good many of the Tudor clergy. In the circle of Robert Parkyn, curate of Adwick-le-Street, we find a conservatism based upon disinterested piety, upon mystical studies in the Rolle tradition, and upon a deep anxiety over the welfare of souls deprived of satisfactory masses. The known facts and the probabilities roughly agree upon a tripartite division of the clergy: a cautious, slow-moving, and unintellectual majority: some small knots of pious ultra-conservatives well-versed in late-medieval and traditional books of devotion, and conforming involuntarily to the Reformation-changes: another minor group of convinced Protestants, consisting of seculars or ex-monks trained in the universities, of prebendaries and preachers imported by Archbishop Holgate, of well-connected pluralists, some with a background outside the diocese and all with opportunities to detach themselves from the narrowness of life in the home parish.

The most interesting and novel part of our inquiry has concerned heresy and Protestantism amongst the common people and middle classes. We have tried to show that historians need not adopt a defeatist attitude when questioned as to what the early Reformation meant in the minds of obscure working-class and middle-class people. From the York diocesan records and from some other sources we have extracted and summarized details of proceedings against some thirty-two named heretics in the time of Henry VIII and against about forty-five others during the reign of Mary. The numerical significance of such extant cases depends on our estimate of certain underlying problems. In the first place we may well ask whether they represent all or almost all of the actual heresy-trials conducted during these reigns, or whether there are likely to have been many more, the records of which have perished. So far as the Council in the North and the Six Articles persecution are concerned, we can speak with little precision. The entry-books of the Council have perished, and its surviving reports are in some years very infrequent. We have no reason, however, to suppose that it was constantly dealing with heretics. Foxe and the York civic records in fact also provide information concerning all the cases mentioned in the Council's official reports. The problem regarding the coverage afforded by the diocesan records is more important and more complex. What gaps occur in the extant records of each court likely to have tried heretics? The lesser courts, such as those of the archdeacons and of the peculiars, have left extremely few traces within this period, yet this probably matters little, since one may scarcely suppose that serious cases of heresy ran their courses in these petty courts without reference to higher authority. Visitations apart, two diocesan courts normally took cognizance of such cases: the Court of Audience or Chancery, the act books of which have provided the bulk of our material, and the Consistory Court. The books of the former do not effectively begin until 1534,[1] before which date many cases relevant to our theme and period might have been tried. Otherwise, though in places carelessly and incompletely compiled, this series probably misses but few cases and yields a most informative picture.[2] At first glance the act books of the Consistory Court seem equally impressive, since, except for one important gap between the years 1551 and 1554, they stretch across the period in unbroken sequence.[3] Our suspicions are at first aroused by the fact that this enormous mass of Consistory material refers almost purely to instance-cases, that is to cases of party against party, as opposed to office-cases, where offenders were prosecuted by the court. The writer has perused several of these large volumes from cover to cover without finding a single office-case.[4] Can it then be assumed that during these years the Consistory Court had relinquished all office jurisdiction, and with it cognizance of presentations for heresy? Quite apart from such an intrinsic improbability, there exist more precise reasons for rejecting this hypothesis. Though some complexities are involved, and though certainty in these matters must await more detailed research into the York court-procedure and record-keeping, it seems highly probable that the cases of the heretics Robynson, Vanbellaer, Browne, Sparrow, and the Johnsons took place in the Consistory Court.[5] Their details, it will be recalled, come

---

[1] R. VII. A. 35 is an Audience Book purporting to cover 1525–9, but it lacks office-cases and hence fails to cover heresy. The problem of these 'specialized' act books is discussed immediately *infra*. I observe no Audience Book of any sort for the years 1529–34.

[2] Cf. R. VII. A. 35, A.B. 2, A.B. 21, A.B. 37, A.B. 33–34, A.B. 39.

[3] R. VII. A. 26–29, A.B. 1, A. 30, A.B. 26, A. 31–32, A.B. 44, A.B. 20, A.B. 28, A.B. 31.

[4] See A.B. 1 under 25 Oct. and 22 Nov. for a possible office-case: the records in these books are brief and cryptic; I am not clear that it is a genuine one.

[5] Those of Gibert Johnson and Robynson are said to have been tried *in loco consistoriali alme curie Ebor.*, that of Denise Johnson *in loco consistoriali curie Ebor.*, and that

entirely from the Archbishops' Registers. In the extant act books of the Consistory Court no mention occurs of these cases; here on their dates no transactions, either instance or office, appear. It seems thus difficult to avoid the conclusion that office-cases, including some for heresy, were in fact transacted during the long gaps in the Consistory act books and that they were recorded in act books now lost. The phenomenon of separate books, for instance- and office-cases respectively, occurs else-where, notably at Lincoln.[1] It certainly cannot be claimed that the Archiepiscopal Registers fill this gap: they contain a selection of rele-vant and interesting documents, yet, as already shown, very numerous heresy cases, some of them important, occurred without leaving a trace in the register. Altogether, though few dioceses can boast at this period so remarkable a coverage as that at York, we must reckon with the likelihood of a number of lost cases of heresy. The present writer nevertheless finds it difficult to suppose these so numerous or so significant as to disturb the main lines of the picture already presented.

Against the generally conservative background of the thirties, forties, and fifties, Lollard and continental Protestant notions were more widely disseminated in the diocese of York than it has hitherto been customary, or indeed possible, to suppose. The case for this view does not, of course, depend upon arguments indicating the incomplete-ness of our documentation of prosecutions for heresy. Even if some un-foreseen discoveries enabled us to double the number of such recorded prosecutions, the real extent and nature of heresy and sub-heresy would not become much more apparent. Likewise no one would claim that the recorded Elizabethan prosecutions for Romanist recusancy revealed the whole extent of Catholic and traditionalist beliefs in the population. In both these fields the surviving records resemble the visible portions of an iceberg, but with this difference, that no constant factor enables the observer to calculate the dimensions of the part submerged. With our Lollards and early Protestants, this task presents

---

of Vanbellaer *in loco consistoriali*. This 'consistorial place' was a section of the Minster, probably in the north transept; courts other than the Consistory sometimes met in it (C. I. A. Ritchie, *The Ecclesiastical Courts of York*, p. 15 and *supra*, p. 43). *Alme curie* was the normal title of the Consistory, but the present writer is in no position to assert that it was never used of any other court. The only alternative for these cases is the Court of Audience, the act books of which are missing during these periods—except during that of Denise Johnson, which does not occur in the Audience act book. On the whole, it thus seems unlikely that any of the above cases was tried in the Audience Court and probable that the Consistory Court is really meant.

[1] Cf. *Lincs. Archives Committee, Archivist's Report, 1950–51*, pp. 26 seqq.

unknowns even greater than those surrounding Romanism under Elizabeth, since recusancy and non-communicancy at least involved public acts and became subject to elaborate reports and censuses. In the case of mid-Tudor heresy, no element of potential treason brought into play the full resources of the state-machine; with reasonable caution, friendly neighbours, and an unobservant parish priest, many a man may have entertained heterodox views without grave risk of prosecution. We have seen how laymen tended to conceal other laymen attacked by priests. At Hull and Halifax gross offences against the sacrament escaped unpunished, though their perpetrators must have been widely known. Tudor neighbourliness might not indeed extend far. It apparently did not extend to offences by aliens or by strangers from other parts of England, who form, at least in the thirties, a suspiciously large section of the defendants in court.

A far more important consideration lies, however, in the very nature of mid-Tudor heresy. It was so often fragmentary, fleeting, and elusive: it involved a climate of opinion rather than a number of specific heretics, each with an integrated theology and under the guidance of educated leaders. When in 1542 the parish clerk of Topcliffe refused Confession because 'there was a saying in the country that a man might lift up his heart and confess himself to God Almighty and need not to be confessed at a priest', he proceeded to swear, perhaps quite honestly, that he could not recall the names of those who said this. He was reporting a phenomenon which could not effectively be tracked down by authority or one which we may now turn into statistical surveys. Heretical ideas floated freely about the country and were held—with most varying degrees of conviction and piety—by people who did not for a moment claim to be theologians and had no intention of going to the stake. From the viewpoint of orthodoxy, herein lay the formidable character of the movement; it was a hydra which survived attack by the normal repressive weapons. On the opposite front, Henry VIII found papalism a relatively simple animal; it could be checked by a strictly limited number of decapitations.

These interesting qualities the rise of non-Catholic beliefs must have owed in large part to its Lollard basis. Scholars who seek an historical understanding of the English Reformation would be wise to think a little less about Bucer, Bullinger, and even Cranmer, and somewhat more in terms of a diffused but inveterate Lollardy revivified by contact with continental Protestantism. This hypothesis finds powerful support in the records of the diocese of York. Here, it may reasonably be suggested, we witness the later repercussions of that Lollard revival which had manifested itself in southern England during the first three decades of the century. Several well-documented heresy cases of the late twenties and thirties prove indistinguishable from those of the early years, when Luther and Zwingli had not yet even begun to formulate their doctrines. In substance and in name, Lollardy continued into the reign of Mary, increasingly merging with the newer Protestant doctrines, yet continuing throughout the diocese to colour the popular heresy with its unmistakable tints. Wherever we search at these levels of society, we detect the late-medieval English heresy. Some of the Henrician offenders, for example, were 'Dutchmen' by origin, yet every one of their numerous and carefully recorded beliefs has its Lollard precedents, while not one of them can claim exclusively Lutheran, Anabaptist, or other continental antecedents. Under Henry VIII the demonstrable infiltration of foreign Protestantism to form a mixed heresy on this popular level occurs only in the cases of a tiny handful of semi-educated offenders. Lollardy had on the whole survived through its resilience; it had its heroes, but the great majority of its adherents were not superhuman figures drawn from the pages of Foxe. Its growing amalgamation with Protestantism did not alter this feature. The martyrologist provides indeed the narrative of Valentine Freez, burned at York in 1540 along with his wife, and that of Richard Snell of Bedale, who suffered at Richmond in 1558. Yet the average neo-Lollard or Lollard Protestant behaves quite otherwise when we meet him in the Court of Audience at York. He is a man of ordinary courage; he trembles at his danger, makes excuses, displays penitence, submits to instruction, does penance, and is thenceforth careful to keep his convictions to himself. Late Lollardy and early Protestantism occurred much more extensively than one would gather from Foxe, who knew very little about the minor figures in the remoter provinces. On the other hand, they remained by that same fact much less heroic and godly, much less Elizabethan in atmosphere.

The character of this native medieval tributary to the English Reformation finds excellent illustration in the records at York. The popular heresy is directed against the supposed *ministerium mechanicum* of hierarchic Christianity. Its nature compares closely with the summary attempted by Foxe.[1] It takes three chief courses. It assiduously attacks saint-worship, images, relics, holy-bread, holy-water, and the attribution of a sacred character to buildings, places, and things. Again,

[1] *Supra*, p. 9.

it denounces Confession to priests. Why, asked one young artisan with brutal frankness, why should I confess an affair with a pretty woman to my knavish confessor, who, given the chance, would use her similarly? If, he continued, I believe steadfastly in God, calling to Him with a sorry heart for my offences, God will forgive me.[1] Yet the most vital element in the popular heresy was its denial of the corporal presence of Christ's Body in the eucharist. This was the offence which brought more offenders into serious trouble than any other: if today we still venture to take notice of conscious motivation, we might well urge that the early Reformation-struggle in England was primarily waged not over the royal divorce, the sovereignty of the State, or the possession of the monastic lands, but over the sacrament of the altar. Throughout the heresy cases in the York courts, sacramentarian offences seem to play an increasing part as time passes. Under Henry VIII they occupy the predominant role in rather less than half the cases: under Mary, in considerably more than a half. In both groups the same three denials dominate the popular heresy, while a fourth element, the desire for direct and personal study of the Bible and of its modern commentators, is indeed represented, but only in three or four cases. In the diocese of York we are not ostensibly dealing, even around 1530, with Lollard communities whose life still centred around illicit Bible-reading. So far as this evidence goes, the Lollard tradition had become diffused and sometimes even manifested itself in scepticism rather than in affirmation by the time it began to meet with Tyndale. Its historical importance may lie in the fact that it united with the more worldly types of anti-clericalism to form an extensive platform of critical dissent upon which the various newer movements could build. The discovery that even the society of a northern and conservative shire was to some extent still permeated by a diluted Lollardy seems to provide an important missing link in the history of the English Reformation. It helps to show that the latter did not originate as a mere foreign doctrine imported by a handful of intellectuals and mysteriously imposed by the monarchy against the almost unanimous wishes of a Catholic nation. The foreign seed fell upon a ground prepared for its reception, and prepared by something more than anti-clericalism or royal propaganda. Nevertheless, on the basis of our regional examples it might well be questioned whether Lollardy could much longer have retained a recognizable profile had new forces not ranged themselves behind some of its principles and gradually assumed intellectual leadership. Perhaps its emphasis

[1] *Supra*, p. 48.

had come to bear too purely upon negations; its clichés, now widely disseminated in society, had too often got into the wrong mouths. At all events, they seem to have harmonized remarkably well with the devastatingly outspoken dissent which has always formed one pole of the Yorkshire temperament, just as an emotional religiosity formed the other.

Regarding the mechanics of the dissemination of Lollardy and the allied Protestant doctrines, our evidence points along lines which might readily be anticipated. We have encountered a good many examples drawn from the mobile elements in the lower and middle reaches of society. A cloth-worker goes to ply his craft in East Anglia and returns to spread heresy; two York tailors working in London join a Protestant circle and flee back to York after the execution of their leader; a coasting vessel brings a heretical merchant from Suffolk into Scarborough; a Northumbrian is taken up for ridiculing saints' days beneath a York parson's window; the Protestant music-master of Rotherham College hastens off to London to win Cromwell's favour; an illiterate youth from Kirkby Moorside apprentices himself to a London tallow-chandler, finds distinguished Protestant teachers, and achieves martyrdom; a company of players wander through the north, attacking Mary and her Catholic beliefs; a York painter, having escaped from a monastic novitiate, settles and marries in Colchester, where he betrays his heretical opinions; his brother travels to the capital, smuggles a file into the bishop's private prison, rescues another Protestant victim, is himself imprisoned by the Bishop of Lichfield, returns to York and is burned on the Knavesmire. In short, though these stories obviously possess exceptional features, they forbid us to think in terms of a static and stodgy population. The remote vales where men lived like vegetables from the cradle to the grave, the moors and fells with their pockets of humanity isolated from the south behind broad rivers and bare hills: these milieux existed, yet they have never embraced the majority of northern men. The circulation of people and the flow of ideas were little impeded by geographical barriers or by poor roads, least of all by poverty, which in fact so often becomes not a clog but a spur to movement and readaptation.

Under these circumstances, we should be pedantic to attempt maps purporting to show the distribution of Protestantism and heresy throughout the diocese. Reference to the foregoing pages suggests, however, that these beliefs were broadly disseminated in all the Ridings of Yorkshire. Taking from our text 106 of the more obvious Protestants and heretics with given names and residences, I note that 48 come from the West Riding, 19 from the East Riding, 16 from the North Riding, 16 from York, and only 7 from Nottinghamshire. Of these 106 names, for what they are worth in this context, 41 come from three places: York, mainly under Henry VIII; Leeds and Beverley, almost wholly under Mary. Other centres of heretical and Protestant opinion, and much under-represented by these scrappy statistics, were Halifax, Hull, Wakefield, and Rotherham. The clothiers of Halifax and the merchants and mariners of Hull were both in their different ways closely knit communities; both avoided giving away much detailed evidence to contemporary persecutors and modern historians. The recorded adventures of Hull seamen amongst the Lutherans of Bremen and Friesland lend little support to the notion that such men contracted continental heresies by direct precept from Dutchmen and Germans. The story does not fail, however, to add another example of the ingress of Tyndale's New Testament from the Continent. English books printed abroad, and coastal contacts with south-eastern English ports: these may provide the right keys to the role of the ports and traders in the development of Protestantism.

Considering its relatively large population and the fact that its people lived beneath the recording eye of authority, York makes no very dramatic or sustained contribution to the story. During the last decade of our period it became spiritually and culturally somewhat inert, a place oppressed by disease, slump, taxation, and dissolution; also perhaps by the loss of its local printing-presses. Altogether, during the forties and fifties it seems tempting to imagine that something less than a half of the more convinced Protestants in the diocese may have lived in or near six or seven towns, while the rest were very widely scattered. At most, however, such an estimate may claim to represent little more than intelligent guess-work, owing to the nature of the phenomenon itself and to the extreme incompleteness of its surviving records.

The communities which displayed the most marked Lollard-Protestant tendencies before 1558 proceeded in each case to develop puritan tendencies in Elizabethan and Jacobean times. The fact cannot be purely coincidental; at the very least, the social atmosphere and connexions of the Yorkshire ports and weaving towns showed themselves equally hospitable to both ideologies. It might be rash to call the Lollard wing of the movement the ancestor of Independency, yet the two appealed to the same sorts of people for similar reasons. That

future research may even trace certain Protestant family-continuities—
as, for example, with the Maudes of Halifax[1]—looks probable enough.
In general, however, I suspect that such direct and precise links with
Elizabethan Protestant activism may prove hard to demonstrate in
detail or in very many cases. And only myopic regionalists will fail to
stress the role of fresh, extraneous influences and externally trained
clergy upon the rise of puritanism in the diocese of York. However
many-sided and complex its forms, puritanism in the last resort owed
most of its characteristics to Calvinism, a system which had exerted
little influence within this region before 1558. Again, its transmission
to the north cannot be dissociated from a number of parsons with a
common background in the 'advanced' University of Cambridge.
Viewed locally, the causal connexions between the first waves of the
Reformation and those which arrived late in the century may remain
somewhat indeterminate and conjectural. Yet local traditions and
climates of opinion have a subtle and persistent strength; inadequate
documentation does not entitle us to deny their reality or their historical
significance. To be concrete, Halifax under Edward VI is recognizably
en route toward the Halifax which, in the days of the Anglo-Puritan
Vicar Favour, so loudly boasted its ultra-Protestant loyalties and its
freedom from Romanists.

Some attempt has been made to put into due context the spell of
'official' Reformation which followed the capture of the state machine
by Reformers and quasi-Reforming politicians in 1547. In the York
diocese under Archbishop Holgate, the imposition of Edwardianism
was not marked by hesitancy or excessive caution: its chief opponents
had been cowed by disaster and by strong conciliar government.
Reasons have been given for believing that both royal and episcopal
injunctions were promptly and readily obeyed by the diocesan clergy
and churchwardens, even by those of known reactionary views. In
Holgate, who had held the presidency of the Northern Council for
seven years before his accession to the archbishopric, the Edwardian
cause found a local leader whose statesmanlike (or *politique*) compromise
between Catholic and Lutheran beliefs denotes him as among the most
prophetically Anglican of the Edwardian bishops. Apart, however,
from its fatal lack of time, the success of official Edwardianism in the
diocese seems to have been limited by two adverse factors. It failed to
achieve what Sir Francis Bigod had earlier attempted: it failed to
organize evangelical missions. Despite the conspicuous example of the

[1] Cf. *supra*, p. 200.

martyr John Rough, there were among the Edwardians but few precursors of the seminary priests, or of those travelling preachers like Gilpin and Bunny, who brought Elizabethan puritanism to the north. In very large measure a province had to give birth to its own evangelists, whether Protestant or Romanist; yet when opportunities were great elsewhere, so many northerners of 'progressive' temperament, who had to go southward for education and patronage, did not return to their own country. Again, we have observed that the Edwardian Reformers suffered grave handicaps through their involvement with the shortsighted and unscrupulous politicians who thought to solve a misunderstood inflation by continuing to expropriate the Church. Exaggerated emphasis has hitherto been accorded to the idea that secularization helped the Reformers by creating a 'vested interest' in Protestantism. If it did so, why did this vested interest make no significant move to check the Marian persecution? Surely, the vested interest remained little more than secular in character. A large group of the recipients of church lands, from the Duke of Norfolk downwards, were convinced conservatives in religion. So long as the Marian government avoided the restoration of these lands to the Church, the vested interest did not render, and had no reason to render, practical services to the Reforming cause. On the contrary, secularization gravely injured that cause. When the pseudo-Protestant politicians turned from the relatively safe hunting-ground of the monastic lands to make raids in the dangerous field of parochial endowments, they could still appeal to the greed of many laymen, yet in the last resort they were bound to repel more than they attracted. This dichotomy between profit and repulsion can be admirably exemplified from the social records of the diocese of York. In such an atmosphere of disillusion and selfhood, the area had little chance of becoming profoundly Anglicanized during the five or six effective years of official Edwardian Reformation. Nevertheless, the evidence of wills and similar documents suggests that the temporary withdrawal of persecution gave the various anti-Catholic groups a much-needed breathing-space. During the years 1547–52 the rejection of intercessory beliefs and saint-cults was advancing more rapidly than during the last years of Henry VIII. At the same time, this rejection can clearly be shown to have begun before 1540; it cannot be ascribed merely, or even chiefly, to Cranmer's Prayer Book. Despite the liabilities entailed by the inglorious political leadership of Dudley, the new doctrines were by 1553 better fitted to profit from persecution than they had been in 1547. The intervention of Mary proved in the

highest degree creative for her opponents, for it came at the precise
moment when Protestantism needed spiritual prestige and had become
solid enough to thrive on challenge. From this point, however, the
mental responses of northern society may in some measure diverge
from those of the dominant counties of the south-east.

Alongside the married clergy, numerous lay heretics appeared in the
church courts at York before the Marian judges, while at Halifax and
Hull, heretical confederacies forcibly removed the reserved hosts
from the churches. On the other hand, no ferocious persecution occurred, and there is no evidence for any northern parallel to the wave
of disgust engendered in the south-east by the fires of Smithfield.
Though we lack extensive information concerning regional opinion on
the actions of Mary, there is again little or no evidence of ardent
Marianism, except early in the reign and amongst the small ultra-
conservative clerical group. On the side of the laity there is some
evidence of indifference, as well as of actual heresy. This apparent
absence of popular enthusiasm must owe something to the political
caution of the new government, which did not very seriously attempt
a policy of restitution and re-endowment, and which took the loyalty
of the remoter and more conservative provinces for granted. If the
slow-moving majority was not violently antagonized, it may well have
become bored and disappointed. Once again, the fresher disclosures
of the period concern popular lay heresy. The Marian courts were not
in general punishing Edwardian Anglicans: these heretics of 1554-8
ostensibly belonged to the same species as their predecessors under
Henry VIII. Two or three of them might be reading Becon or Hutchinson or Grimald, just as previously a few had read Tyndale and Frith,
yet the great majority remained to all appearances neo-Lollards or
semi-Lollards rather than recognizable Lutherans or Anglicans. They
show the old doctrinal emphases; they remain evasive, unheroic,
unliterary, and sceptical; scarcely any would have seemed in a single
detail out of place in the church courts twenty or thirty years earlier.
In this corner of society, time seems almost to have stood still. The
world of popular heresy had survived, much of it oddly oblivious to
royal and episcopal propaganda, Protestant, Catholic, and Erastian. A
major revelation of our story is this failure of both Church and State
to establish anything approaching spiritual uniformity or to bind the
laity, as they had bound the clergy, to their chariots. At no stage, not
even under Elizabeth, did English authority accomplish this feat,
though it was left to our egregious second Stuart king to make the

national Church so uncomprehensive as to lose a respectable minimum of control over a turbulent scene.

The foregoing inquiries have enabled us to detect more clearly this heavy ground-swell within English society; they have pushed back the beginnings of regional dissent and of religious heterogeneity far behind the Elizabethan age. The Edwardians and the Marians alike failed, it would seem, to hustle the slow blend of new and old forces in the English mind. The spectacular events of 1534–58 still play a large part in the historical textbook, but historians of the English people may increasingly find them superficial, since the origins of religious change occurred much earlier and the really epoch-making developments somewhat later. While, on the one hand, the survival of a diffused Lollardy helps to explain so many features of the mid-Tudor scene, on the other hand the popularization of the newer religions surely cannot be made to precede the middle decades of Elizabeth. Whatever its theological continuities, the vitality of Roman Catholicism had to be re-created in its limited sector of English society by the seminarist invasion of the seventies and eighties. Similarly, Anglicanism cannot claim to date, as a spiritual force amongst the people, from the Prayer Book of 1549 or from the Act of Uniformity ten years later; only the age of Hooker saw it develop an appeal upon a national scale, an ethos extending outside a small cultured circle. At this same period, both inside and outside the national Church, Calvinist puritanism still fought for a following. If all three developed at last into established and unshakeable phenomena amongst Englishmen and Americans, none may claim to be other than a late-comer upon the Tudor scene. The present writer has hitherto conducted detailed religious and literary investigation mainly within the diocese of York: if compelled to establish major landmarks in both these fields of mental history, he would prefer to place the end of the Middle Ages and the rise of modern movements around the eighth decade of the sixteenth century. And he feels no doubt that the thesis might be maintained for other large regions of England. Yet dissent, in the looser sense of the word, had been present long beforehand: it had arisen *pari passu* with the slow breakdown of the medieval synthesis and it broadened into the very *Zeitgeist* of the Tudor age. The pious Nonconformists who hailed Wyclif as the morning star of the Reformation were saying something with profounder implications than they realized.

We have already compared the religious history of the mid-Tudor period with the growth of a forest: if the reader will tolerate one more crude parable, we might also compare it with a lake. It had both muddy shallows and capricious eddies, yet it was fed by rivers and in turn gave birth to other rivers. Of the feeders, the broad stream of medieval orthodoxy and the spectacular but less voluminous cataracts of continental Protestantism have tended to monopolize our vision. The Lollard river, deep, murky, and quiet, has inevitably suffered neglect, since it ran underground and seldom emerged before reaching the lake. As for the effluent rivers, Anglican, Catholic, and puritan, these have now become familiar in outline, though still imperfectly charted around the points where they leave the lake's Elizabethan shores. Yet the foregoing work seeks at least to indicate that we have still much to learn concerning the lake itself, that even now we may gain new knowledge of its actual waters, as distinct from those sedimentary deposits which have become the main preoccupation of twentieth-century map-makers. Beyond that oft-encountered earthiness and disillusion, even mid-Tudor society had its spiritual turmoil and tension, its vast potentialities, and its epoch-making decisions. It forms more than a period of survivals and prehistories; it has a quality of its own which we can best recover by switching to new lines of inquiry and new sources of factual information. It looks after all integral enough to the story of a small but intensely vital nation; a nation which above all others was destined during the subsequent two centuries to revolutionize the prospects of Western Man.

LIST OF MANUSCRIPT SOURCES

PUBLIC RECORD OFFICE

1. *Documents concerning Sir Francis Bigod, cited* supra, *pp. 62–104* passim.
   S.P. 1/86, fos. 126–8.
   S.P. 1/89, p. 110.
   S.P. 1/92, p. 193.
   S.P. 1/93, pp. 50–51.
   S.P. 1/94, pp. 24–25, 42, 115, 116.
   S.P. 1/101, pp. 38–39.
   S.P. 1/103, p. 86.
   S.P. 1/105, p. 9.
   S.P. 1/106, p. 220.
   S.P. 1/114, pp. 198–202.
   S.P. 1/116, fos. 88, 163–4.
   S.P. 1/118, fos. 123–123^v.

2. *Miscellaneous documents*
   S.P. 1/76, fos. 27–27^v (*supra*, p. 159).
   S.P. 1/122, fos. 140–1 (*supra*, p. 163).
   S.P. 2/6, fos. 133–6 (Holgate's Apology; *supra*, p. 175).
   S.P. 12/10, p. 283 (*supra*, p. 222).
   S.P. 15/7, no. 8 (Hamerton's petition; *supra*, p. 209).
   C. 142/50, no. 72 (*supra*, p. 55).
   E. 36/119, p. 74 (*supra*, p. 29).
   E. 36/139, fo. 102 (*supra*, p. 32).
   E. 150/1227, no. 11 (*supra*, p. 55).
   E. 315/288, fos. 31 seqq. (*supra*, p. 55).

BRITISH MUSEUM

Cotton, Cleop. E. v, fos. 131–7 (*supra*, p. 157).
Ibid., fos. 301–301^v (*supra*, p. 145).
Ibid., fos. 413 *seqq.* (*supra*, p. 163).
Ibid., vi, fos. 220–5^v (*supra*, p. 156).
Ibid., fo. 257 (*supra*, p. 159).
Additional MS. 5813, fos. 5–29 (*supra*, pp. 208, 211).

BODLEIAN LIBRARY

MS. Eng. Poet. B. 1, fos. 4^v–15 (letters mentioned *supra*, p. 184, n. 1).
MS. Eng. Poet. e. 59 (Parkyn's *Life of Christ*; cf. *supra*, p. 196).
MS. Lat. Th. d. 15 (Parkyn's *Narrative of the Reformation*; cf. *supra*, p. 181).

A fuller account of these (and other MSS. upon which the account of Robert Parkyn is based) will be found in the articles cited p. 181, n. 5, especially in *Archiv für Reformationsgeschichte*, Jahrgang 43 (1952), pp. 55–57.

YORK DIOCESAN RECORDS AT THE
BORTHWICK INSTITUTE, YORK

R. I. 26 (Reg. Bainbridge; *supra*, p. 16).
R. I. 27 (Reg. Wolsey; *supra*, pp. 17–19, 24, 26).
R. I. 28 (Reg. Lee; *supra*, pp. 19–21, 24, 28, 140).
R. I. 29 (Reg. Holgate and Heath; *supra*, pp. 175, 201).
R. VII. A.B. 2 (*supra*, pp. 36 *seqq.*, 150, 179)
R. VII. A.B. 21 (*supra*, pp. 49 *seqq.*)
R. VII. A. 33, 34 (*supra*, pp. 147, 187 *seqq.*, 223 *seqq.*)
R. VII. A.B. 39 (*supra*, pp. 213, 230)
} Act Books of the Court of Audience or Chancery.

R. VII. G. 404 (*supra*, p. 186).
For other Act Books, including those of the Consistory Court, see *supra*, p. 241.

LINCOLN DIOCESAN RECORDS

Reg. 28, fo. 110 (*supra*, p. 147).
P.D. 1548/16 (*supra*, p. 147).

CORPORATION OF HULL

Bench Books 1, 2, 3, 3a, 4 (*supra*, pp. 28, 219).

CORPORATION OF YORK

Housebooks, xiii–xxii, *passim*. The greater part is printed in *York Civic Records* (Y.A.S. Rec. Ser.), iii–v.

INDEX TO PRINTED AUTHORITIES

In the notes to the text, the short title of each printed work normally occurs under the first reference, but thereafter the author's name is often merely followed by the words 'op. cit.'. The present index is thus needed to facilitate reference to titles. Used in conjunction with the notes, it will also serve as an informal bibliography.

Thoresby Society, 3, 172, 194, 215, 217, 220.
Thornley, I. D., 87.
Thoroton, R., 33.
Tickell, J., 28, 210.
Tonge's Visitation (Surtees Soc. xli), 61.
Topographer and Genealogist, 91.
Trollope, E., 33, 34.
Turner, J. H., 221.
Turner, W., 193.
Tyndale, W., 134.

Valor Ecclesiasticus, 37, 39, 40, 42, 78.
V.C.H., Durham, 154.
— *Lancs.*, 162.
— *Notts.*, 161.
— *Yorks.*, 3, 55, 62, 64, 79, 86, 115, 160, 161.

Walker, J. W., 200.
Wallis, N. H., 133.
Wallis, P. J., and Tate, W. E., 5, 76.
Walton, M., 3.
Ward, H. L. D., 127, 129.
Watson, F., 175.
Wharhirst, G. E., 10, 146.
Wharton, H., 162.
Whibley, C., 105.
Whitaker, T. D., 5, 6, 63, 176.
Wilkins, D., 154, 155, 156, 158, 159, 161, 162, 163, 171.

Wills in the York Registry (Y.A.S. Rec. Ser. xi), 115.
Wisdom, R., 194, 195, 196.
Withycombe, E. G., 23.
Wood, A., 58.
Wood, A. C., 39, 41.
Wriothesley, C. (Camden Soc., new ser. xi, xx), 11, 12, 147, 165.

Y.A.J., 2, 54, 55, 60, 84, 96, 106, 108, 114, 118, 155, 161, 166, 169, 170, 180, 182, 183, 187, 206, 209.
Y.A.S. Rec. Ser., 2, 4, 35, 36, 86, 88, 114, 115, 149, 150, 175, 177, 186, 200, 206, 207, 209, 213, 215.
York Civic Records (Y.A.S. Rec. Ser. cvi, cviii, cx, cxii), 2, 35, 186, 206, 213, 215.
— *Mercers and Merchant Adventurers* (Surtees Soc. cxxix), 3.
— *Wills, Consistory* (Y.A.S. Rec. Ser. xciii), 200.
Yorks. Chantry Surveys (Surtees Soc. xci, xcii), 40, 207, 209, 217.
— *Fines* (Y.A.S. Rec. Ser. ii), 114.
— *Monastic Suppression Papers* (ibid. xlviii), 149, 150.
— *Schools* (ibid. xxvii, xxxiii), 175, 177, 209.
— *Star Chamber Proceedings* (ibid. xli, **xlv**, lxx), 86, 88, 207.

Zeeveld, W. G., 13, 57, 58, 130.

GENERAL INDEX

Hessle, 198.
Hewet, Andrew, 31.
Hexham, John, abbot of Whitby, 67, 83–86.
Hexhamshire, 87.
Higden, Brian, Dean of York and vicar general, 18, 26, 159.
High Melton, 184.
Hilsey, John, Bp. of Rochester, 139, 151–2.
Hinderwell, 54–55.
Hobbes, Thomas, 112.
Hoggarde (Huggarde), Miles, 194.
Holbeach, Henry, Bp. of Lincoln, 139, 151.
Holbein, Hans, 78.
Holburn, 36.
Holden, *alias* Alexandere, Thomas, 39–40, 42.
Holderness, 1, 3.
Holdsworth, *see* Haldesworth.
Holgate, Barbara, *née* Wentworth, 185–6.
Holgate, Robert, master of Sempringham, prior of Watton, Bp. of Llandaff, president of the Council in the North, Abp. of York, 30, 32, 51, 139, 144 n., 168–9, 178, 180, 191, 193, 198, 201, 219, 237, 239–40, 248; family, education and monastic career, 151–2; flees from Pilgrimage of Grace, 95; becomes president, 152–3; and Abp., 173; his theology, 173–4; work for education, 174–6; marriage, 185–7; his Minster Injunctions, 201–5.
Holland, 25, 192; *see also* Netherlands.
Holme, Isabel, 114.
Holme, John, 114.
Holme, Robert, 207.
Holme, Seth, 115.
Holme, Thomas, 115.
Holme, Wilfrid, 102, 105, 114–31 *passim*, 237–8; family background, 114–15; literary knowledge, 116; summary of his book, 117–31; account of the Pilgrimage of Grace, 117–18; anti-monastic views, 119–21; erastianism, 121–2; attack on superstition, 122–5; the Galfridian prophecies, 126–30.
Holmepierpoint, 199.
Holmes, William, 172.
Holy Bread, Holy Water, rejection of, 18–20, 48, 179, 232, 244.
Hoode, John, 200.
Hooke, *see* Sparrow.
Hooker, Richard, 251.
Hooper, John, Bp. of Gloucester, 139, 151, 178, 222.
Hopkins, John, 196; *see also* Sternhold.
Hoppay, Edward, 170 n., 216–17.
Hoppay, Edward, priest, 217 n.

Horde, Dr., 82.
Hornby, 61; Castle, 63.
Hospitals, 79, 175–6, 209.
Housebooks, *see* York, city of.
Houseman, John, 187.
Howard, Queen Katherine, 34.
Howden, 45.
Howsyer, John, 200.
Huby, 115.
Hull, 3, 15, 24, 27–28, 57, 96–97, 99–101, 117, 136, 146, 183, 198, 209–10, 225–6, 243, 247, 250.
— aldermen of, 100, 118.
— Bench Books, 28 n., 219 n.
— Beverley Gate, 101.
— Bp. of, *see* Pursglove, Robert.
— Blockhouse, 81.
— clergy of, 189 n., 198, 225.
— heresy and Protestantism in, 24–27, 198, 225, 247.
— historians of, 28–29.
— Holy Trinity, 24, 28, 183.
— mayor and corporation, 219.
— merchants, sailors, &c., of, 3, 24–27, 219, 247.
— St. Mary's, 225.
Humber, River, 3, 25, 84.
Hunmanby, 56–57.
Huntington, 114, 115, 131.
Huntington Library, 114 n.
Huss, John, 11.
Hussey, John, Lord, 29, 75.
Hutchinson, Roger, 75, 229, 250.

Images, 46, 119, 163, 171, 182–3, 244; *see also* Saints, cult of.
Impropriations, 63, 69–74, 107.
Incense, 232.
Independency, 247.
Inflation, 191, 238.
Ingle, John, 225 n.
Ingram (Yngram), William, 40–42.
Injunctions, the Royal, 169, 171, 178–80, 201, 214.
— Episcopal, 171, 201–205.
Inns of Court, 14, 60, 132–3, 136, 237.
Ipswich, 48.
Ireland, 127, 145 n.
Italy, 138, 192.

Jackson, Christopher, 224.
Jackson, Nicholas, 224 n.
Jackson, Robert, 224 n.
Jackson, Thomas, 45.
James, St., Epistle of, 10 n.
Jenney, Serjeant Christopher, 81 n., 85, 89.
Jerome, William, 104, 106.
Jerusalem, 129, 191.

Jervaulx Abbey (Jarvys), 76, 79–82, 113; *see also* Lazenby, George; abbot of, *see* Sedbergh, Adam.

John, King of England, 54, 117, 127.

Johnson, Denise, 23, 24, 241, 242 n.

Johnson, George, 136.

Johnson, Gilbert, 17–19, 21, 23, 241.

Johnson, Sir Thomas, 45–46.

Jolby, 216.

Jones, John, 194.

Joye, Henry, 36–37.

Joye, George, 12.

Judges, ecclesiastical, 16, 18, 20, 22, 26, 43, 49, 221–34 *passim.*

Katherine of Aragon, Queen, 161; *see also* Divorce, the Royal.

Kaye, William, 217.

Kelk, Great, 231.

Kelke, Christopher, 230–1.

Kelke, Roger, 231.

Kellet, Dr., 24.

Kendal, 2, 4, 118.

Kendal, deanery of, 1.

Kendal, *alias* Sadler, Stephen, 24.

Kent, 60 n., 182; Lollardy in, 8, 22.

Kiddall, 45.

Kinge, John, 224 n.

King's Bench, 41.

Kingston-upon-Soar, 41.

Kinoulton, 199.

Kirkby in Cleveland, 200.

Kirkby in Kendal, 216.

Kirkby Malhamdale, 4.

Kirkby Moorside, 222, 246.

Kirkby Ravensworth, 164, 176.

Kirkby, Thomas, warden of Greyfriars, Doncaster, 141–3.

Kirkby Wiske, 6.

Kitchin, Dean, 154, 156.

Kite, John, Bp. of Carlisle, 157.

Knapton, 233.

Knaresborough, 81; Forest of, 4; Friary of St. Robert, 97, 100.

Knowles (Knolles), Alderman John, 100, 118.

Knox, John, 197.

Lackenby, Robert, 50.

Lambert, John, 106, 151.

Lancashire, 2, 94.

Lancaster, Duchy of, 208.

Landulphus, 138.

Langley, nunnery of, 79.

Langrige, Dr. Richard, 20, 24.

Lascells, John, 33–34, 237.

Latham, Ralph, 65.

Latimer, Hugh, Bp. of Worcester, 11, 39, 76–77, 105, 151, 180.

Latimer, John Nevill, third Baron, 61–65

passim, 68, 132; his daughter Margaret, 61; *see also* Nevill, William.

Latymer, William, 200.

Laughton-en-le-Morthen, 208.

Laxton, 42.

Layton, Richard, dean of York, 78, 82 n, 91, 119.

Lazenby, George, 'the monk of Jervaulx', 79–82, 113.

Leach, A. F., 176.

Leaf, John, 222–3.

Lee, Edward, Abp. of York, 16, 17, 23, 49, 51, 75–77, 82, 141–5, 150–1, 161–2, 164–5, 173; his injunctions, 169–71; his register, 19–21, 23, 24, 28, 140.

Lee, Rowland, Bp. of Coventry and Lichfield, president of the Council of Wales, 31–32, 159–61, 246.

Leeds, 149, 216, 224, 247; curate of, 224; Protestantism in, 224.

Legh, Dr. Thomas, 78, 82 n., 85, 91, 119.

Leghton, Dr. Edward, 63, 160 n., 161.

Leicestershire, 79.

Leke, Sir Francis, 220.

Liberties, 83–84, 87, 208 n.

Lichfield, Bp. of, *see* Lee, Rowland.

Lincoln, 147; archdeacon of, 147; Bps. of, *see* Smyth, Longland, Watson; chancellor of, 25; prebendary of, 25.

— diocese of, 1, 2 n.

—— heretics in, 8, 17, 25, 145–6.

—— records of, 25, 147, 189 n., 242.

—— visitations of, 147, 234.

Lincolnshire, 39, 54, 117, 147, 152.

Linley, 45 n.

Lisbon, 125.

Lister, John, 218.

Llandaff, Bp. of, *see* Holgate.

Lockington, 56.

Lodge, Mr., 66.

Lollards, Lollardy, 7–9, 13, 16, 21–22, 24, 26, 38, 48, 51–52, 75, 106, 171, 177, 201, 231, 234–5, 242–5, 250–2.

— connexions with Continental Protestantism, 10.

— influence and dissemination, 243–6.

— main beliefs of, 9, 244–5.

London, 4, 12, 14, 22, 27, 32, 43, 57, 74, 76–77, 102, 145, 183, 195, 198, 211.

— Bps. of, *see* Fitzjames; Stokesley; Tunstall; Bonner; Ridley.

— Carthusians of, 81, 139.

— Cheapside, 104.

— churches and religious houses in, 58, 105, 141 n., 147, 152, 194.

— Fleet Prison, 192.

— heretics in, 27, 33, 116, 222–3.

— Inner Temple, 132; *see also* Inns of Court.

London, Lambeth Palace, 70 n.

London, Lambeth Palace, Lollards'
  Tower, 31, 194.
— Newgate, 104.
— Paul's Cross, 104, 145, 196.
— St. Paul's, 75, 147.
— Smithfield, 8, 33, 43, 104, 213, 250.
— the Tower, 105.
London, diocese of, 8; heretics in, 8, 31.
London, Dr. John, Warden of New
  College, Oxford, 58 n., 59.
Longland, John, Bp. of Lincoln, 8, 10 n.,
  59, 145–6.
Lonsdale, deanery of, 1.
Lounde, William, 45.
Luddington, 132.
Lumley, George, 98–100, 104–5, 110.
Lumley, Lord, 98.
Lund, 219 n.
Luther, Martin, 11, 19, 21, 25, 34, 244.
Lutherans, Lutheranism, 8, 10, 13, 24–
  27, 51, 58, 106, 119, 121, 140, 142–3,
  148, 152, 195 n., 204, 236–7, 250.
Lydgate, John, 116, 138, 181, 194.
Lyndall, William, 224 n.

Macedon, Philip of, 122.
Magic, 16, 124.
Magnus, Thomas, archdeacon of the
  East Riding, 155, 159.
Malome, William, 50.
Malton, 56, 88, 95, 175; prior of, see
  Todd, William.
Manchester, 149, 194 n.
Mann, Thomas, 8.
Markenfield, Thomas, 207.
Markham, family of, 23 n.
Markham, Sir John, 39.
Marriage of clerics, 147–8, 184–92, 197–
  200, 211–12, 239; see also Divorce of
  clerics.
Marrick Nunnery, 120.
Marshall, Dr. Cuthbert, archdeacon of
  Nottingham, 43, 160, 164–5.
Marshall, William, 11.
Martyrs, Protestant, 6–7, 31–34, 149,
  151, 222–3, 244, 246; Catholic, 79–82.
Mary I, Queen, 168, 170, 173, 182–3,
  188, 190, 194–5, 197–8, 205, 211, 213–
  15, 218, 225, 239–40, 244–5, 247, 249–
  50; see also Reaction, the Marian.
Masham, 47.
Mass, the Latin, 183; see also Eucharist.
Masses for the Dead, 18, 45, 184, 239–40.
Matthew, Thomas, 43.
Maude (Mawde), family of, 248.
Maude, Arthur, 218.
Maude, Edward, vicar of Darfield, 200.
Maude, Edward, vicar of Wakefield, 200.
Maude, John, 200.
Maude, Richard, 200.

Mauleverer, Lady, 61.
Mauleverer, Sir Francis, 61 n.
Mauley, Constance de, 54.
Mauley, the eight Peters de, 54.
Mauley, lands of, 56.
Maunsel, William, 118.
Maxey, John, abbot of Welbeck, 161.
Meaux Abbey, 54.
Melancthon, Philip, 11.
Melton, see High Melton.
Melton, William, chancellor of York,
  16.
Merchants, 3, 14; see also Hull.
Merlin, 129; see also Prophecies, political.
Metham, 207.
Metham, Sir Thomas, 207.
Methley, Richard, 81 n.
Mettringham, Thomas, 44–46.
Middleham Castle, 80.
Middlewood, Serjeant, 102.
Midgley, 148.
Midlands, the East, 33.
Miles, Thomas, 230.
Milton, John, 113.
Mitchell, Thomas, 224, 228.
Mitton, Elizabeth, 218.
Mobility of Population, 14, 48, 223, 246.
Monasteries, see Religious Houses;
  Friars; Monks; Nuns.
Monk Bretton Priory, 141, 199.
Monks, Canons Regular, 30–31, 39, 71–
  74, 78–87 passim, 89, 91, 93–96, 104,
  113, 138–9, 143, 148–53; 160–1, 199–
  200, 208, 238–9; see also Religious
  Houses.
Monkrode, 209.
Monmouth, Geoffrey of, 126.
More, Sir Thomas, 14 n., 181, 212.
Moreton, William, 178–9.
Moreton, see Wilson, Thomas.
Morison, Sir Richard, 70, 130.
Morton, John, Abp. of Canterbury, 9.
Mouldwarp, prophecy of the, 126–9.
Mountgrace Priory, 79–82; see also
  Methley; Norton, John.
Mudde, Thomas, 81.
Mulgrave, 56, 94, 102, 105; Castle, 54,
  64, 83, 88, 90.
Municipalities, see Towns; York; Hull.
Musculus, Wolfgang, 203–4.
Music in churches, 202–3.
Musselburgh, 198.
Mycolow, Mr., 25.

Netherlands, 10, 22, 30, 230; see also
  Amsterdam; Antwerp; Dutchmen.
Nevile, Sir Edward, 60.
Nevill, John, baron Latimer, see Latimer.
Nevill, Robert, alias William, provost of
  Jesus College, Rotherham, 39, 42, 141.